Interdisciplinary Studies in Human Rights

Volume 11

Human rights are one of the normative cornerstones of contemporary international law and global governance. Due to the complexities of actual or potential violations of human rights and in light of current crises, new and interdisciplinary research is urgently needed. The series Interdisciplinary Studies in Human Rights recognizes the growing importance and necessity of interdisciplinary research in human rights. The series consists of monographs and collected volumes addressing human rights research from different disciplinary and interdisciplinary perspectives, including but not limited to philosophy, law, political science, education, and medical ethics. Its goal is to explore new and contested questions such as the extraterritorial application of human rights and their relevance for non-state actors, as well as the philosophical and theoretical foundations of human rights. The series also addresses policy questions of current interest including the human rights of migrants and refugees, LGBTI rights, and bioethics, as well as business and human rights.

The series editors are Members of the Centre for Human Rights Erlangen-Nürnberg (CHREN), an interdisciplinary research center at Friedrich-Alexander-University Erlangen-Nürnberg. The Advisory Board brings together human rights scholars from a wide range of academic disciplines and regional backgrounds. The series welcomes suggestions for publications of academic research falling into the series subject matter.

Max-Emanuel Geis • Adam Bosiacki •
Christoph Safferling
Editors

Dealing with Totalitarian Regimes and Human Rights

A Polish-German Dialogue

Springer

Editors
Max-Emanuel Geis
University of Erlangen-Nuremberg
Erlangen, Germany

Adam Bosiacki
University of Warsaw
Warsaw, Poland

Christoph Safferling
University of Erlangen-Nuremberg
Erlangen, Germany

ISSN 2509-2960 ISSN 2509-2979 (electronic)
Interdisciplinary Studies in Human Rights
ISBN 978-3-031-57337-8 ISBN 978-3-031-57338-5 (eBook)
https://doi.org/10.1007/978-3-031-57338-5

This Springer imprint is published by the registered company Springer Nature Switzerland AG
The registered company address is: Gewerbestrasse 11, 6330 Cham, Switzerland

Preface

Poland and Germany share the trauma of World War II despite having had tremendously different experiences and responsibilities during that period of European history. The subsequent period that saw a confrontation with communism is another common feature in the two neighbouring states' shared history and memory, which experienced rather reciprocal effects of their immediate past. The approaches and attitudes to fascism and the ideologically penetrated style of government taken by, and within, both Poland and Germany are therefore a highly relevant field of discussion that has been explored by several disciplines. It is this context that inspired the cooperation between Wydział Prala i Administracji Uniwersytet Warszawski and Friedrich-Alexander-Universität Erlangen-Nürnberg's Law School, which sought to open critical dialogue about the similarities and dissonances that defined the two nations' efforts to recover from war, dictatorship and massive human rights abuses and thereby dive into both countries' distinct paths of engaging with their shared history, particularly in the areas of law and legal policy. With the two initiators of the cooperation being scholars of different aspects of constitutional law, this attention quickly spread into questions of criminal law and civil law as outflows of state and legal theories. When the first "German-Polish Dialogue" on the topic of "policies of dealing with the past" took place in Erlangen, Germany, from October 28 to 31, 2018, the presentations covered a wide range of academic fields of interest, which were further looked into during the mirroring conference held in Warsaw, Poland, from October 21 to 24, 2019. These discussions carved out the future research focus on post-war politics of the past as influenced by constitutional and general legal traditions. Although the results of these two events were already precious to us at the time, we were not conscious of how dear the memories would be in the following 2 years, when similar meetings were not possible. The findings that emanated from these two conferences are now presented in this book.

The chapters are not presented in chronological order. They are rather grouped and rearranged according to the contours of the substantive content, beginning with the contributions of those that provide the historical backdrop for the constitutional, human rights and state protection issues of the second half of the twentieth century in the cooperating countries. *Christoph Safferling* outlines the evolution of direct forms of systematic legal processing of war crimes affecting Germany by linking the Treaty of Versailles with the Leipzig War Crime Trials and the Nuremberg Military Tribunals. With co-author *Philipp Graebke*, he intensifies the focus on defence in the Nuremberg Trials as a stress test for what proceeded to become a concept acknowledged as a universal human right. *Gurgen Petrossian* contrasts the development of reappraisal mechanisms with the examples of the Taleat Pasha Trial and the Istanbul Trial, examining how the legal system of the Ottoman Empire tried—and failed—to bring justice to the victims of World War I. *Adam Bosiacki* then reflects on the positive normative value of the Nuremberg principles and raises the question of why they have not been applied to the human rights abuses of the communist regimes in Poland and other Eastern European countries.

The second part of the publication is then devoted to the institutional emancipation of Poland and Germany from the regimes of injustice that shaped their history. First, *Christoph Safferling* reports from his vast research on the formative years of the Federal Ministry of Justice, investigating the extent to which the agency was burdened with personnel, techniques and work ethics from the Nazi era and how this affected its function as the nerve centre of the "new" legal entity, "Bundesrepublik Deutschland". *Jana Kuhlmann* portrays the Federal Public Prosecutor's Office as another big player in the legal policy landscape, which likewise affected the self-image of the redefined German democracy through its role as a "state protector", initially focussing intensely on communist agitation. *Kamil Slominski*, in comparison, discusses the combat of all three branches of power against communist ideology ,and propaganda in the legal order of the Second Republic of Poland and the modern Polish state. *Andrzej Piątkowski* ultimately lays out the legal framework for those bodies meant to defend the continuity of the state and the guarantees it provides, if necessary, by force—and how, if not closely monitored, they can unfold their inherent subversive potential, paving the way for a totalitarian regime.

The final block ties the previous narratives together, working out the meta-level that opened up for Poland and Germany when weaving their experiences into the fabric of their reconstituted states. *Max-Emanuel Geis* starts with the Weimarian Methodological Debate in the constitutional doctrine and continues to elaborate on the concept of "fortified democracy", which evolved from Germany's bitter realisation that the young Weimar democracy had not integrated mechanisms into its Constitution to prevent Hitler's seizure of power, which was not objectionable from a formal legal standpoint. *Hilde Farthofer* then gives an extensive overview of Germany's reappraisal of its National Socialist past from 1945 until today, and *Adam Bosiacki* adds the Polish perspective on the legal aspects of settlements with totalitarianism in Poland, particularly after 1989. *Dariusz Mańka* further substantiates these remarks through his analysis of Polish reprivatisation law in the context of transitional justice since 1988. The compilation concludes with *Jarosław Kostrubiec's* essay on the legal status of the unique facility that is the Polish Institute of National Remembrance and its role in the prosecution of war crimes against the Polish nation.

As the politics of dealing with the past formed the background for the implementation of modern concepts of human rights protection, elaborating on the perspectives of contemporary legal history can help analyse factors that favour or hinder functional capability and the integrity of transitional governments and their respective states. We sincerely hope to contribute to this global endeavour while continuing to deepen Polish-German friendship and academic cooperation.

This book would also not have been possible without the intensive work of so many colleagues. Research and student assistants, in particular at the Law School in Erlangen, took on the task of editing and formatting the individual chapters. These were Jana Kuhlmann, Anna Pacurar, Dr. Gurgen Petrossian, Luise Hohenstein, David Hecht, Melanie Rosa, Sabrina Roch, Maximilian Zech, Miriam Schäfer and Sara Kasapoğlu.

We would also like to thank Springer-Publishing House and its executive editor for law, Dr. Brigitte Reschke, for accepting our collection of papers for publication in the series, Interdisciplinary Studies in Human Rights, edited by the professors Markus Krajewski, Petra Bendel, Heiner Bielefeldt, Andreas Frewer and Manfred Pirner.

The book is dedicated to German-Polish friendship and the memory of the many victims of dictatorships in the twentieth century and in the hope of a flourishing future for the rule of law, human rights and peace for our countries and for Europe.

Erlangen, Germany — Max-Emanuel Geis
Warsaw, Poland — Adam Bosiacki
Erlangen, Germany — Christoph Safferling
December 2023

Contents

Editors and Contributors

About the Editors

Max-Emanuel Geis is a professor of German and Bavarian public and administrative law at the Friedrich-Alexander-University Erlangen-Nuremberg. Furthermore, he is a justice at the Bavarian Constitutional Court. He is also a member of the evaluation committee of the German Council of Science.

Adam Bosiacki is a professor of public law and legal history at the University of Warsaw. He is the director of the Institute of Sciences on State and Law and the head of the Department of the History of Political and Legal Thought. He has been a visiting scholar in a number of academic units, including the Max-Planck-Institute in Frankfurt, Harvard University and the Hoover Institute at Stanford University. He is also teaching at the Jagiellonian University in Krakow.

Christoph Safferling LL.M. (LSE), is a professor of criminal law, criminal procedure and international law at the Friedrich-Alexander-University Erlangen-Nuremberg and the director of the International Criminal Law Research Unit. He is the director of the International Nuremberg Principles Academy and the Whitney R. Harris Fellow of the Robert H. Jackson Center in Jamestown, New York, USA.

List of Contributors

Adam Bosiacki University of Warsaw, Warsaw, Poland

Hilde Farthofer Institute for Criminal Law and Criminal Justice at the University of Erlangen-Nuremberg, Erlangen, Germany
Federal University of Applied Administrative Science, Faculty of the Federal Police of Germany, Lübeck, Germany

Max-Emanuel Geis University of Erlangen-Nuremberg, Erlangen, Germany

Philipp Graebke Friedrich-Alexander-University Erlangen-Nuremberg, Erlangen, Germany

Jarosław Kostrubiec Faculty of Law and Administration of the Maria Curie-Sklodowska University, Lublin, Poland

Jana Kuhlmann Upper Regional Court in Hamburg, Hamburg, Germany
Friedrich-Alexander-University Erlangen-Nuremberg, Erlangen, Germany

Dariusz Mańka Department of History of Political and Legal Doctrines, Faculty of Law and Administration of the University of Warsaw, Warsaw, Poland

Gurgen Petrossian Friedrich-Alexander Erlangen-Nuremberg University, Erlangen, Germany

Andrzej F. Piątkowski University of Warsaw, Warsaw, Poland
Bureau of Research of the Chancellery of the Sejm, Warsaw, Poland

Christoph Safferling University of Erlangen-Nuremberg, Erlangen, Germany

Kamil Słomiński University of Warsaw, Warsaw, Poland

Part I
Treaties and Trials: Historical Backdrop

The Nuremberg Trial Against the Major German War Criminal Before the International Military Tribunal (1945–1946)

Christoph Safferling

Abstract The Nuremberg Trial is recognised as the basis of modern international criminal law. In less than one year, the four allied powers which had pursued a costly victory over Nazi Germany presented convincing evidence for the German aggression crimes before the International Military Tribunal. This chapter contains a brief outline of this revolutionary international criminal trial, its accused, the core crimes, and the procedure. It also takes up criticism that was formulated particularly by German defence lawyers, scholars and politicians even decades after the termination of the trials, like the non-retroactivity principle or the 'victors' justice'—denunciation. Ultimately, it puts the Nuremberg Trial into the perspective of a further reception of the Nazi past of Germany as well as the development of international criminal law in this respect.

1 Introduction

Between 1933 and 1945, Germany was ruled by the National Socialists led by the 'Führer' Adolf Hitler. The fascist ideology of the Aryan 'master race' resulted in an inhuman governmental system in which Jews, Sinti, Roma, homosexuals as well as political dissidents, religious people and other minorities were systematically persecuted. In order to unite Europe under the swastika flag, Hitler waged an unprecedented war of aggression and annihilation against all of Europe with the help of German armed forces (the Wehrmacht) and paramilitary units (such as the Sturmabteilung (SA) and Schutzstaffel (SS)). Only with enormous efforts of the Allied powers of the USA, the United Kingdom, France, and the Soviet Union, was it possible to put an end to Hitler's activities. With Germany's unconditional capitulation on 8 May 1945, the reign of terror, which was not only responsible for millions of war victims, abducted slave labourers, prisoners of war and refugees,

C. Safferling (✉)
University of Erlangen-Nuremberg, Erlangen, Germany
e-mail: christoph.safferling@fau.de

M.-E. Geis et al. (eds.), *Dealing with Totalitarian Regimes and Human Rights*, Interdisciplinary Studies in Human Rights 11,
https://doi.org/10.1007/978-3-031-57338-5_1

but also for the systematic extermination of six million Jews and other minorities in so-called concentration or extermination camps in Eastern Europe, came to an end.

After the end of the war, the victorious Allied powers established an International Military Tribunal (IMT) in order to sentence the politically and militarily responsible Nazis still alive. The charges were based on three international crimes as stipulated in Article 6 of the IMT Charter: (1) crimes against peace, (2) war crimes, and (3) crimes against humanity.

A total of 24 persons were charged: Hermann Göring, former Reich Minister, as the highest-ranking defendant; Rudolf Hess, Hitler's deputy in the Party; Joachim von Ribbentrop, former Reich Foreign Minister; Robert Ley, a leading member of the Party; Wilhelm Keitel, the Chief of Armed Forces High Command; Ernst Kaltenbrunner, Head of the Reich Security Main Office as well as the Security Service and Security Police; Alfred Rosenberg, a leading ideologist of the NSDAP; Hans Frank, Governor General in occupied Poland; Wilhelm Frick, Reich Minister of the Interior; Julius Streicher, founder and publisher of the anti-Semitic weekly 'Der Stürmer' and former Gauleiter of Franconia; Walter Funk, Reich Minister for Economic Affairs; Hjalmar Schacht, President of the German Reichsbank; Karl Dönitz, Supreme Commander of the Navy; Erich Raeder, Supreme Commander of the Navy (until 1943); Baldur von Schirach, Head of the Reich Youth organisation and District Leader of Vienna; Fritz Sauckel, Chief Representative of Forced Labourers; Alfred Jodl, Head of the Wehrmacht Operations Staff; Martin Bormann, Hitler's secretary; Franz von Papen, Vice-Chancellor in Hitler's 1st Cabinet (1933); Arthur Seyß-Inquart, Reich Minister of the Interior and Chancellor of Austria, later also Reich Minister; Albert Speer, Reich Minister for Armament and Ammunition, Hitler's Chief Architect; Constantin von Neurath, Reich Foreign Minister until 1938, Reich Protector of Bohemia and Moravia; Hans Fritzsche, Head of Reich Ministry of Public Enlightenment and Propaganda; Gustav Krupp von Bohlen und Halbach, President of the Reich Association of the German Industry.

At the same time, the following organisations were indicted: the Reich Government, the Corps of Political Leaders, the SS, the Security Service, the Secret State Police (Gestapo), the SA, the German General Staff and the High Command of the Wehrmacht.

The trial commenced on 18 October 1945 with the presentation of the indictment to the judges in the great hall of the Higher Court in Berlin. From 20 November 1945, 21 defendants were tried in Courtroom 600 of the Palace of Justice in Nuremberg.[1] The trial concluded on 1 October 1946 with the proclamation of sentence. Twelve defendants were sentenced to death by hanging,[2] seven were

[1] The defendant Ley was able to evade the trial by suicide; Croup was found to be too old; Bormann was missing; the proceedings against the latter were carried out in absentia.

[2] Göring, von Ribbentrop, Keitel, Kaltenbrunner, Rosenberg, Frank, Frick, Streicher, Sauckel, Jodl, Seyß-Inquart, Bormann.

sentenced to long prison terms[3] and three were acquitted.[4] The following organisations were declared criminal: Corps of Political Leaders, the Gestapo, the Security Service, and the SS. On 16 October 1946 the death sentences were carried out, only Göring succeeded in killing himself beforehand.

2 Substantive Legal Basis

The Nuremberg Trial of Germany's Major War Criminals was the first truly international criminal trial in human history.[5] Based on the London Agreement of 8 August 1945, which was passed by the victorious Allied powers after tough negotiations and signed by a further 18 states,[6] a special military tribunal was established with four main and four substitute judges.[7] All four victorious powers sent delegations of prosecution teams each with different areas of responsibility. The USA was clearly a 'heavyweight' from both the material and the personnel point of view. The entire process was strongly shaped by the US Chief Prosecutor, Supreme Court Justice Robert H. Jackson. Pre-eminently, he found in his rhetorically sophisticated opening speech the words that awarded the tribunal its overall moral legitimacy:

> The wrongs which we seek to condemn and punish have been so calculated, so malignant, and so devastating, that civilisation cannot tolerate their being ignored, because it cannot survive their being repeated. That four great nations, flushed with victory and stung with injury, stay the hand of vengeance and voluntarily submit their captive enemies to the judgement of the law is one of the most significant tributes that power has ever paid to reason.

This new phenomenon in legal history of course raised a number of legal problems, all of which cannot be discussed here. The importance of the Nuremberg Trial manifests itself particularly in the creation of a list of international 'core crimes' as well as in the breach of the international legal principle of state sovereignty and the principle of non-retroactivity based on the rule of law.

---

[3] Hess, Funk, Dönitz, Raeder, von Schirach, Speer, von Neurath.

[4] Fritzsche, Schacht, Von Papen.

[5] The legal construction is, however, controversial; it is partially believed that this is a purely a court of the occupying forces, the legitimacy of which is not based on the principle of universality; i.a. Klefisch (1947), pp. 45–49; Maser (1977); Kaleck (2012), pp. 17–19.

[6] These were: Greece, Denmark, Yugoslavia, the Netherlands, Czechoslovakia, Poland, Belgium, Ethiopia, Australia, Honduras, Norway, Panama, Luxembourg, Haiti, New Zealand, India, Venezuela, Uruguay and Paraguay.

[7] International Military Tribunal (1947), pp. 115, 118.

2.1 The Core Crimes

The IMT Statute contained three core crimes: (1) crimes against peace (Article 6 a of the IMT Statute); (2) war crimes (Article 6 b of the IMT Statute) and (3) crimes against humanity (Article 6 c of the IMT Statute). Additionally, there is the specific manifestation of the 'conspiracy for a crime against peace'[8] contained in Article 6 of the IMT Statute. This list of international crimes represents an absolute novelty in human history. Consequently, the legitimation of these crimes in the course of the Nuremberg Trial as well as its aftermath was highly controversial. This applies particularly to the aforementioned 'crimes against peace'.[9] It is true that the so-called Briand-Kellogg Pact of 1928 provided a contractual basis for outlawing war in international politics; however, this did not correspond with a prohibition in the field of criminal law. In comparison, the second offence, war crimes, was relatively undisputed.[10]

On the basis of various Geneva Conventions as well as the Hague Convention of 1907, there were indeed certain acts that were forbidden as a means and methods of warfare being put under penalty. The specific group of crimes against humanity, on the other hand, constitutes a completely new creation. They represent the attempt of forming the unprecedented cruelty and systematic extermination of humans into a precise term as well as into a criminal offence. The particular crimes hereunder, such as murder, torture, enslavement, extermination and the like, are quite unquestionably recognised as criminal acts in all civilised states.[11] What remains unclear, however, is how to accurately express that these 'simple crimes' occurred in a context representing an attack on humanity as a whole. The Nuremberg proceedings were relatively cautious in this category, and thus the offence was only used in connection with a warlike act. The unfortunate result of this restrictive implementation is that crimes against the German population were not an issue in the Nuremberg Trial of the major perpetrators of war crimes.[12] Nonetheless, with the formulation of crimes against humanity in the Nuremberg Statute, the conceptual as well as the legal basis for this new subsuming international offence was laid. In the Control Council Law No. 10, the offence was opened and the prerequisite of its connection to war was dropped.[13] The modern definition of the offence, such as in Article 7 of the Rome Statute of the International Criminal Court, deems the international character fulfilled, when an individual offence occurs in the context of an extensive or systematic attack on civil population, whereas the element of war or an armed conflict is no

---

[8] Cf. more precisely Safferling (2010), pp. 65–82.

[9] Cf. Kranzbühler (1949).

[10] Cf. Woeltzel (1962), pp. 172–174; Von Arnauld (2019), Rn. 1003.

[11] Cf. Jescheck (1952), pp. 298–300.

[12] In the opening speech by Robert H Jackson, which was very much oriented towards the 'conspiracy', the Reichspogromnacht was mentioned, but not in the judgement; see International Military Tribunal (1947), p. 120.

[13] Cf. in detail Kirsch (2008), pp. 269–288.

longer required. This list of criminal offences was confirmed by the United Nations as the 'Nuremberg Principles' in 1946.[14]

2.2 *The Holocaust*

It is striking that genocide is not included in the list of international crimes. The crime of genocide was legally non-existent in 1945. It was only three years later, on 8 December 1948, that a resolution by the General Assembly of the United Nations succeeded in adopting the Convention on the Prevention and Punishment of the Crime of Genocide.[15] This criminal offence is linked to crimes against humanity while emphasising the destruction of groups with a particular positive identity; nationally, ethnically, racially or religiously defined groups.[16] The existence of the Convention and thus the crime of genocide is owed to the tireless commitment of the Polish lawyer Raphael Lemkin. Lemkin himself managed to escape from the Third Reich via Scandinavia to the USA. Still, he lost nearly his entire family in the Holocaust.[17] After the end of the war, he advised Robert H. Jackson's US prosecutor's team and tried to materialise his idea of a genocide offence, but this novel approach of his did not succeed.[18] Only three years later, he achieved a breakthrough. Today, genocide occupies first place among the core international crimes in Article 6 of the Rome Statute of the International Criminal Court. Thus, the crime of genocide found its historical origin in the National Socialists' offences against the Jewish people and other minorities, but it did not come into effect during the criminal investigation in the immediate aftermath of the war.

2.3 *Main Indictments*

Another fact becomes clear here: in the Nuremberg Trial of the main perpetrators of war crimes, the major issue according to the US indictment doctrine was to punish the waging war of aggression.[19] Contrastingly, the Holocaust, the destruction of minorities and 'degraded beings', receded into the background. Although this does not meet our current perception, it follows from the legal framework as outlined above as well as the fact that the true extent of the extermination machinery in

[14] Affirmed by the General Assembly of the United Nations on December 11, 1946 as principles of international law under the heading 'Nuremberg Principles' (GA-Res. 95 [I]).

[15] Cf. Schabas (2010), pp. 19–34.

[16] Cf. Gil Gil (2000), pp. 381–397.

[17] For the little researched biography of Raphael Lemkin, see Cooper (2008).

[18] Cf. Barrett (2010), pp. 35–54.

[19] Cf. Safferling (2011a), § 4 Rn. 30.

Auschwitz and elsewhere only became clear in the course of the Trial or rather some years later with the finding of the so-called Wannsee Protocol in 1948.[20]

3 State Sovereignty and the Non-Retroactivity Principle

For the first time in the history of mankind, the principles of state sovereignty and immunity for heads of state and members of the government as well as the legal prohibition on retroactivity were deferred in support of punishing the leading statesmen.

3.1 State Sovereignty

Already after the First World War, the legal basis for the punishment of the German Emperor Wilhelm II, who had been identified as the aggressor, was provided for by the Versailles Treaty (Article 227 Versailles Treaty). However, such a trial never took place, the two main reasons being: (1) the British proposal-based offence of ‘crimes against the sanctity of treaties’ was rather vague and thus inapplicable; (2) the Netherlands granted the persecuted emperor political asylum after a lengthy dispute.[21] Carrying out trials against war criminals was ultimately entrusted to Germany, that is to say to the national judiciary, pursuant to the Versailles Treaty.[22] Ultimately, twelve persons of the list of approximately 890 suspected war criminals were indicted before the German Imperial Court of Justice in Leipzig in 1921/22. These proceedings went down in history as the so-called Leipzig Trials.[23] The limited number of those actually persecuted was accompanied by significant judicial leniency; ultimately, there were eight convictions.[24] One thing became clear in these proceedings: the national judiciary is not fully capable of prosecuting its own citizens as war criminals. The mild prison sentences, combined with early releases and reprieves, exemplify the failure on a broad front when it comes to applying the overall deterrent effect of criminal trials as a standard for the Leipzig Trials.[25]

---

[20] Cf. Kastner (2001), p. 268.

[21] Cf. Bassiouni (2002), pp. 244–291, 271–275 and 283–285.

[22] Pursuant to Article 228 of the Versailles Treaty, the Allied compiled a list of names with alleged German war criminals. It was initially planned to extradite these people, which the German government was able to avert by prosecuting war crimes through its own courts.

[23] Cf. Gerd Hankel (2003); Wiggenhorn (2005).

[24] Only four of which were actually prosecuted under international criminal law; cf. Hassel (2009), p. 55.

[25] This connection is clearly stated by Robert H. Jackson, the US chief prosecutor, in his opening speech in Nuremberg, cf. International Military Court (1947), p. 100; see also Jung (1992), pp. 96–106.

With the Moscow Declaration of 1943, the Allies therefore committed themselves to prosecuting the worst Nazi criminals after the victory over Nazi Germany. Law enforcement was now meant to take place at different levels and, especially where there was no explicit territorial reference, a coordinated international criminal prosecution should be established. After the unconditional surrender on 8 May 1945, work began on the international prosecution of the main war criminals in addition to the administrative organisation of the occupied territories. Although the most important figures and representatives of the Nazi regime, namely Hitler and Goebbels, had already evaded criminal prosecution by committing suicide, there were still some major representatives still left such as Göring, Hess as Hitler's deputy, Dönitz as Hitler's successor, several Wehrmacht generals such as Keitel and Jodl, various Reich ministers, such as von Ribbentrop and Albert Speer, as well as other representatives of the terror regime. With these indictments on the level of political leadership in Nazi Germany, it became clear that the principle of immunity for crimes committed in a public function no longer applied to serious crimes against humanity.[26] The indictment of the military leadership made it impossible to invoke 'acting on command' in as a ground for exclusion from individual responsibility.[27]

3.2 Non-Retroactivity

Since then, core crimes have been punishable even in cases where respective national law is designed in such a way that the offences concerned do not constitute its violation. Even though, according to general constitutional principles (which were also valid at the material time), the retroactive application of criminal law is not permitted, this rule cannot apply where the very foundations of civilised society themselves have been compromised by the accused. This thesis, despite initially contradicting the strictly positivistic legal dogmatics, is not only based on a profound moral conviction, but also on a universal understanding of justice, as well as on the fundamental attitude of the global community, not to allow its foundations to be concussed.[28] Shortly after the conclusion of the prosecution of Nazi crimes in Nuremberg, the European states adopted a human rights constitution with the enactment of the European Convention on Human Rights and the establishment of the Council of Europe, which reflects precisely these values.[29] The principle of the prohibition of retroactivity was recognised in Article 7 of the European Convention on Human Rights, but at the same time it was stated in Paragraph 2 that this

[26] Cf. Article 7 of the IMT Statute.

[27] Both reasons for exclusion are described by Robert H. Jackson in his opening speech as outdated and contrary to the principle of individual responsibility, cf. International Military Court (1947), p. 149.

[28] Cf. Harris (2008), p. 502.

[29] Cf. Safferling (2011a) § 13 Rn. 2.

prohibition of retroactivity can have no effect if the act is punishable according to general legal principles recognised by civilised nations. The Federal Republic of Germany initially made an obvious attempt to retrospectively justify the Nuremberg Trials (so-called Nuremberg Clause[30]) based on an exception to the *nullum crimen* principle by setting a proviso at the ratification, which was officially withdrawn in 2001.[31]

3.3 Selectivity and Legitimacy: Nuremberg Trials as an Example of Victor's Justice?

The legitimacy of criminal proceedings depends, inter alia, on their uniform application.[32] Arbitrary punishment contradicts the rule of law in a crucial way. After Nuremberg, international criminal law found itself in precisely this case. The Cold War made it politically impossible to carry out the attempts of the United Nations to establish a permanent international criminal court. Such efforts were officially discontinued already in the early 1950s.[33]

What had been achieved in Nuremberg continued to have an effect on other levels as well. In 1949, the Geneva Conventions were comprehensively redefined, with a number of specific criminal threats. The additional protocols made further progress in 1977. Similar developments could be observed at the level of human rights. Progress was made not only in relation to the Council of Europe and the European Convention on Human Rights—human rights also celebrated their breakthrough in 1966 with the adoption of the International Covenant on Civil and Political Rights. As mentioned above, with the passing of the Genocide Convention in 1948, a new criminal offence was specified. All of this happened in the aftermath of Nuremberg. However, international criminal prosecutions no longer took place, even though there was no lack of occasions for it. For almost 50 years, the legitimacy of 'Nuremberg' was tainted by the fact that the only ones persecuted were the defeated Germans, as a consequence of which there was a widespread opinion in Germany that the Nuremberg Trials were merely an act of 'victorious justice'.[34] Only shortly after the end of the Cold War, a breakthrough took place. As a brutal civil war unfolded on the territory of the former Yugoslavia, the United Nations reacted in

[30] Cf. Ambos (2018) § 10 Rn. 84.

[31] See the 6th report of the Federal Government on its human rights policy in foreign affairs and in other policy areas (Human Rights Report), 2000/02, 36. The withdrawal had also become necessary as, after the reunification of German, the question of non-retroactivity became relevant again. This was shown in particular by the case before the ECtHR, Streletz, Kessler, Krenz v. Germany, 22 March, 2001, Reports 2001-II; previously BVerfGE 95, 96; on this issue also Werle (2001), pp. 3001–3008; Peters (2003), p. 6.

[32] Cf. Steinke (2012), p. 12 ff.; as well as Stolle and Singelnstein (2007), p. 37.

[33] Cf. Conze (2012), p. 189.

[34] Cf. Eser (2006), pp. 53–59.

memory of the Nuremberg Trial by setting up an international criminal tribunal as a sub-organ of the United Nations Security Council. Despite this step being formally and politically so unusual, it indicated that the idea of international criminal prosecution, as practised in Nuremberg, was by no means forgotten. On the contrary: the Statute of the International Tribunal for Yugoslavia of 28 May 1993 was strongly reminiscent of the Charter of the International Military Tribunal of 8 August 1945.[35]

After that, everything came about very quickly. Just a year later, another tribunal was set up by the United Nations Security Council to prosecute the Rwandan genocide.[36] In 1998, an international conference finally approved the Rome Statute for the International Criminal Court, which came into force on 1 July 2002. The belief that a core set of human rights is also binding for every statesman, and that the principle of state sovereignty has to recede where the protection of these human rights is at stake, became a globally recognised principle.

4 Criminal Procedure Law

A major challenge to international criminal law is the law of criminal procedure.[37] In the run-up to the Nuremberg Trial of Major War Criminals, it was disputed among the victorious allied powers whether a constitutionally equipped criminal procedure should actually be applied, or whether a summary examination would be perfectly sufficient, since the guilt of the accused was assumed to be proven.[38] It is to the merit of the American Chief Prosecutor Robert H. Jackson in particular, that an attempt was finally made in Nuremberg to conduct criminal proceedings that would meet the rule of law. According to Robert H. Jackson, in his speech to the American Society of International Law on 14 April 1945, it must be assumed that the defendants are innocent, should the Allies decide in favour of criminal proceedings taking place. One who is not capable of acquitting the accused, if necessary, may not conduct criminal proceedings.[39] Despite all the individual criticism, it can be observed that this principle was taken seriously in the Nuremberg Trial of major war criminals, which can be affirmed by the fact that von Papen, Fritzsche and von Neurath were acquitted against the grim resistance of the Soviet judges. The Statute drew strongly on the adversarial model of the US procedural law, which the German defence

[35] Report of the Secretary-General Pursuant to Para. 2 of Security Council Resolution 808 (1993), 3 May 1993, S/25704, §§ 35, 47; UN Security Council resolution 827, 25 May 1993; Zimmermann (2006), pp. 266–276.

[36] UN Security Council Resolution 955, 8 November 1994.

[37] An overview of the individual difficulties can be found in Safferling (2012).

[38] Cf. Smith (1977), pp. 32–38; Weinke (2006), pp. 10–24.

[39] Cf. Robert H. Jackson, 13 April 1945, Washington D.C. American Society of International Law.

lawyers were not familiar with and thus found it difficult to cope with.[40] Even among the French and Soviet prosecution teams, there was a lack of clarity regarding the Anglo-American practice of criminal proceedings.[41]

Notwithstanding the fact that the criminal proceedings in Nuremberg left much to be desired in terms of fairness from today's perspective, it must be borne in mind that the defendants were appointed a defence attorney each, and that they were given sufficient time and opportunity to provide evidence to exonerate themselves. Moreover, sufficient comprehensibility was granted by an elaborate interpreting system—making it the world's first event with simultaneous interpretation.[42]

5 After Nuremberg

With the Nuremberg Trial of the main war criminals, criminal investigation of the Nazi crimes of violence was far from over. The Nuremberg Trial, however, has far-reaching significance to this day which goes beyond the specific case.

5.1 *Post-War Period*

As a result of 'Nuremberg', there were further Nazi criminals prosecuted and tried by national courts. The proceedings that have gone down in history as 'Subsequent Nuremberg Trials' were solely under US responsibility pursuant to the Control Council Act No 10.[43] Simultaneously, trials against war criminals were held in the French[44] and British[45] zones as well as in the Soviet-occupied zone,[46] but did not receive the same attention and importance as the twelve follow-up trials carried out in Nuremberg prior to 1949.[47] One of the reasons for this was that the United States' indictment strategy focused on different professional groups such as doctors,[48]

[40] Cf. Kranzbühler (1949). In summary on the role of defenders in Nuremberg cf. Safferling and Graebke in the volume. In great detail: Seliger (2016).

[41] Cf. Safferling (2012), pp. 52–58.

[42] Cf. Ramler (2010), p. 75.

[43] Further trials were conducted under US responsibility in Dachau. See Lessing (1993); Bryant (2007), pp. 111–122, and the anthology Eiber and Sigel (2007).

[44] Cf. Moisel (2004).

[45] On the proceedings under the Royal Warrant of 18 June 1945 see Hassel (2009).

[46] Cf. Rüping (2006), pp. 186–195; Weinke (2006), pp. 112–115.

[47] Cf. Kastner (2001), pp. 227–283; Harris (2008), pp. 532–550.

[48] This is the only entirely documented subsequent process so far, cf. Dörner et al. (1999).

lawyers,[49] members of task forces,[50] industrialists[51] and diplomats.[52] While the Trial of major war Criminals may serve as a model for international criminal justice, the Subsequent Nuremberg Trials do not represent an international enforcement of international criminal law. However, despite their national character, they remain significant for the development of substantive international criminal law as well as for the international moral claim for punishment. It was also a way for the Western Allies to lead Germany back into the community of civilised states.[53] Not only did the Nuremberg Trial of major war criminals trigger a whole range of national criminal trials in the immediate post-war period (i.e. well over 10,000 criminal cases worldwide), but they also launched a lasting effort to punish the worst crimes regardless of time and space. The spectacular trials that followed, such as the Ulm Einsatzgruppen Trial,[54] the so-called Auschwitz Trial in Germany,[55] the Eichmann Trial in Jerusalem,[56] the trials against Papon, Touvier or Barbie in France[57] and many more are an example thereof. These trials remain part of the commemorative culture in Europe.[58]

5.2 The Way to The Hague

Even though further development of the international criminal justice system was not possible during the Cold War, the memories of 'Nuremberg' were reinstated after its end. The statute of the Yugoslav tribunal of 28 May 1993 clearly bears traits of the IMT Statute of 8 August 1945.[59] Just one year later, the United Nations Security Council founded a further tribunal to prosecute the genocide in Rwanda. In 1998, an international conference in Rome finally passed the Statute of the International Criminal Court (ICC). Four years later, on 1 July 2002, the Statute came into force and the ICC commenced its work.[60] The belief that a core set of human rights is

[49] Safferling and Luber (2017) with further references.

[50] Cf. Earl (2013), p. 127.

[51] Especially on Case V, the trial of Flick et al.: Jung (1992); cf. also Jeßberger (2009), p. 924.

[52] Cf. Blasius (2000), p. 190; Kastner (2010), p. 499; cf. also Conze et al. (2010), p. 375.

[53] This is the argument brought forward by Priemel (2016).

[54] Cf. Krausnick and Wilhelm (1981).

[55] Cf. Werle and Wandres (1995); Balzer and Renz (2004); Pendas (2006); Düx (2010), p. 287.

[56] Cf. Arendt (1964).

[57] Cf. Fekl (2005), p. 39.

[58] Cf. Safferling (2011b), p. 147.

[59] The then General Secretary of the United Nations Boutros-Boutros Ghali made several express references to the International Military Tribunal in Nuremberg in his preparatory report on the establishment of the Yugoslavia Tribunal, cf. Report of the Secretary-General Pursuant to Para. 2 of Security Council Resolution 808 (1993), May 3, 1993, S / 25704, §§ 35, 47.

[60] For a comparison of the IMT Statute with the Rome Statute, cf. Zimmermann (2006), pp. 247–258.

also binding for every statesman and that the principle of state sovereignty has to recede where the protection of these human rights through criminal law is at stake, became a globally recognised principle.[61]

Documents

International Military Tribunal (1947) Trial of the Major War Criminals. Vol. II. Nuremberg

International Court of Justice, D.R. Congo vs. Belgium, judgement of 14 February 2002, Reports 2002, 121

Jackson R H (1945) Rule of law among nations. Address presented at American Society of International Law, Washington D.C., 13 April 1945

Report of the Secretary-General Pursuant to Para. 2 of Security Council Resolution 808 (1993), 3 May 1993, S/25704, §§ 35, 47;

UN Security Council resolution 827, 25 May 1993

UN Security Council Resolution 955, 8 November 1994.

References

Ambos K (2018) Internationales Strafrecht, 5th edn. C.H. Beck, Munich

Arendt H (1964) Eichmann in Jerusalem. Ein Bericht von der Banalität des Bösen. Piper, Munich

Balzer F-M, Renz W (2004) Das Urteil im Frankfurter Auschwitz-Prozess (1963-1965). Pahl-Rugenstein, Bonn

Barrett JQ (2010) Raphael Lemkin and 'Genocide' at Nuremberg. In: Safferling C, Conze E (eds) The Genocide Convention 60 years after its adoption. T.M.C. Asser Press, The Hague, pp 35–54

Bassiouni CM (2002) World War I: 'The War to End all Wars' and the birth of a handicapped international criminal justice system. Denver J Int Law Policy 30(3):244–291

Blasius R (2000) Der Wilhelmstraßen-Prozess gegen das Auswärtige Amt und andere Ministerien. In: Ueberschär GR (ed) Der Nationalsozialismus vor Gericht. Die alliierten Prozesse gegen Kriegsverbrecher und Soldaten 1943–1952. Fischer, Frankfurt a. M., pp 187–198

Bryant M (2007) Dachau Trials - Die rechtlichen und historischen Grundlagen der US-amerikanischen Kriegsverbrecherprozesse, 1942-1947. In: Radtke H, Rössner D, Schiller T, Form W (eds) Historische Dimensionen von Kriegsverbrecherprozessen nach dem Zweiten Weltkrieg. Nomos, Baden-Baden

Conze E (2012) Völkerstrafrecht und Völkerstrafrechtspolitik. In: Dülffer J, Loth W (eds) Dimensionen Internationaler Geschichte. Oldenbourg Wissenschaftsverlag, Munich

[61] At least before an international criminal tribunal, the principle of immunity for criminal offences committed by leaders in the performance of their public office by leaders no longer has the effect of hindering proceedings. This may be different before national judicial bodies, cf. IGH D.R. Congo vs. Belgium, judgement of 14 February 2002, Reports 2002, 121; s. also Kreß (2003), pp. 25–43.

Conze E, Frei N, Nayes P, Zimmermann M (2010) Das Amt und die Vergangenheit. Deutsche Diplomaten im Dritten Reich und in der Bundesrepublik. Pantheon, Munich

Cooper J (2008) Raphael Lemkin and the struggle for the Genocide Convention. Palgrave Macmillan, London

Dörner K, Ebbinghaus A, Roth KH, Weindling P (eds) (1999) Der Nürnberger Ärzteprozess 1946/47. Wortprotokolle, Anklage- und Verteidigungsmaterial, Quellen zum Umfeld. K.G. Saur, Munich

Düx H (2010) The Auschwitz-Trial at the Landgericht Frankfurt and its importance for the prohibition of genocide. In: Safferling C, Conze E (eds) The Genocide Convention sixty years after its adoption. T.M.C. Asser Press, The Hague, pp. 287-296

Earl H (2013) Beweis, Zeugen, Narrative: Der Einsatzgruppen-Prozess und die historische Forschung zur Genese der "Endlösung". In: Priemel K, Stiller A (eds) NMT. Die Nürnberger Militärtribunale zwischen Geschichte, Gerechtigkeit und Rechtschöpfung, Hamburger Edition, Hamburg

Eiber L, Sigel R (2007) Dachauer Prozesse: NS-Verbrechen vor amerikanischen Militärgerichten in Dachau 1945-48. Wallstein Verlag, Göttingen

Eser A (2006) Das Internationale Militärtribunal von Nürnberg aus deutscher Perspektive. In: Reginbogin H, Safferling C (eds) Die Nürnberger Prozesse: Völkerstrafrecht seit 1945. K. G. Saur Verlag, Munich, pp 53–60

Fekl W (2005) Affaires Barbie/Bousquet/Touvier/Papon. In: Doll J, Fekl W, Loewe S, Schmidt B, Taubert F (eds) Frankreich-Lexikon, 2nd edn. Schmidt, Berlin

Gil Gil A (2000) Die Tatbestände der Verbrechen gegen die Menschlichkeit und des Völkermordes im Römischen Statut des IStGH. Zeitschrift für die gesamte Strafrechtswissenschaft 112(2): 381–397

Hankel G (2003) Die Leipziger Prozesse. HIS Verlag, Hamburg

Harris W (2008) Tyrannen vor Gericht. Berliner Wissenschafts-Verlag, Berlin

Hassel K (2009) Kriegsverbrechen vor Gericht. Nomos, Baden-Baden

Jescheck H (1952) Die Verantwortlichkeit der Staatsorgane nach Völkerstrafrecht. Ludwig Röhrscheid Verlag, Bonn

Jeßberger F (2009) Die I.G. Farben vor Gericht – Von den Ursprüngen eines Wirtschaftsvölkerstrafrechts. Deutsche Juristenzeitung 64(19):924–932

Jung S (1992) Die Rechtsprobleme der Nürnberger Prozesse. Mohr Siebeck, Tübingen

Kaleck W (2012) Mit zweierlei Maß. Verlag Klaus Wagenbach, Berlin

Kastner K (2001) Von den Siegern zur Rechenschaft gezogen: Die Nürnberger Prozesse. Edelmann Verlag, Nuremberg

Kastner K (2010) Strafrechtliche Verantwortlichkeit für administratives Unrecht: der Wilhelmstraßen-Prozess (1948/49). In: Jahn M, Kudlich H, Streng F (eds) Strafrechtspraxis und Reform. Festschrift für Heinz Stöckel zum 70. Geburtstag. Duncker & Humblot, Berlin, pp 499–520

Kirsch S (2008) Zweierlei Unrecht – Zum Begehungszusammenhang der Verbrechen gegen die Menschlichkeit. In: Michalke R, Körberer W, Pauly J, Kirsch S (eds) Festschrift für Rainer Hamm. De Gruyter Recht, Berlin, pp 269–288

Klefisch T (1947) Gedanken über Inhalt und Wirkung des Nürnberger Urteils. Juristische Rundschau 23(2):45–49

Kranzbühler O (1949) Rückblick auf Nürnberg. Zeit-Verlag E. Schmidt o.J., Hamburg

Krausnick H, Wilhelm H-H (1981) Die Truppe des Weltanschauungskrieges. Die Einsatzgruppen der Sicherheitspolizei und des SD 1938-1942. Deutsche Verlags-Anstalt, Stuttgart

Kreß C (2003) Der Internationale Gerichtshof im Spannungsfeld zwischen Völkerstrafrecht und Immunitätenschutz. Goltdammer's Archiv für Strafrecht 150:25–43

Lessing H (1993) Der erste Dachauer Prozess (1945/46). Nomos, Baden-Baden

Maser W (1977) Nürnberg. Tribunal der Sieger. Econ Verlag, Düsseldorf

Moisel C (2004) Frankreich und die deutschen Kriegsverbrecher. Wallstein Verlag, Göttingen

Pendas OD (2006) The Frankfurt Auschwitz Trail, 1963-1965. Genocide, history, and the limits of the law. Cambridge University Press, Cambridge
Peters A (2003) Einführung in die Europäische Menschenrechtskonvention. C.H. Beck, Munich
Priemel K (2016) The Betrayal. The Nuremberg Trials and German Divergence. Oxford University Press, Oxford
Ramler S (2010) Die Nürnberger Prozesse. Peter Lang GmbH, Internationaler Verlag der Wissenschaften, Frankfurt a.M.
Rüping H (2006) Zwischen Recht und Politik: Die Ahndung von NS-Taten in beiden deutschen Staaten nach 1945. In: Reginbogin H, Safferling C (eds) Die Nürnberger Prozesse: Völkerstrafrecht seit 1945. K. G. Saur Verlag, Munich, pp 199–208
Safferling C (2010) Die Strafbarkeit wegen 'Conspiracy' in Nürnberg und ihre Bedeutung für die Gegenwart. Kritische Vierteljahresschrift für Gesetzgebung und Rechtswissenschaft 93(1): 65–82
Safferling C (2011a) Internationales Strafrecht. Springer, Berlin/Heidelberg
Safferling C (2011b) Gericht und Menschenrechte – Arenen der Erinnerung. In: Bubmann P, Deinzer R, Luibl HJ (eds) Erinnern, um Neues zu wagen. Europäische Gedächtniskulturen - evangelische Perspektiven (Reihe Bildung evangelisch in Europa). GPM, Erlangen, pp 147–156
Safferling C (2012) International criminal procedure. Oxford University Press, Oxford
Safferling C, Graebke P (2011) Strafverteidiger im Nürnberger Hauptkriegsverbrecherprozess: Strategien und Wirkung. ZStW 123(1):47–81
Safferling C, Luber M (2017) "Der Tempel der deutschen Justiz muss wieder eingeweiht werden" – Der Nürnberger Juristenprozess nach 70 Jahren, Juristische-Arbeitsblätter 2017, pp. 881–887
Schabas W (2010) Genocide in international law and international relations prior to 1948. In: Safferling C, Conze E (eds) The Genocide Convention 60 years after its adoption. T.M.C. Asser Press, The Hague, pp 19–34
Seliger H (2016) Politische Anwälte? Die Verteidiger der Nürnberger Prozesse. Nomos, Baden-Baden
Smith BF (1977) Der Jahrhundert-Prozeß. Fischer, Frankfurt a.M.
Steinke R (2012) The politics of international criminal justice. Hart Publishing, Oxford
Stolle P, Singelnstein T (2007) On the aims and actual consequences of international prosecution of human rights crimes. In: Kaleck W, Ratner M, Singelnstein T, Weiss P (eds) International prosecution of human rights crimes. Springer, Heidelberg/Berlin
Von Arnauld A (2019) Völkerrecht. C.F.Müller, Heidelberg
Weinke A (2006) Die Nürnberger Prozesse. Munich 2006
Werle G (2001) Rückwirkungsverbot und Staatskriminalität. Neue Juristische Wochenschau 54(41):3001–3008
Werle G, Wandres T (1995) Auschwitz vor Gericht: Völkermord und bundesdeutsche Strafjustiz. C.H. Beck, Munich
Wiggenhorn H (2005) Verliererjustiz. Die Leipziger Kriegsverbrecherprozesse nach dem Ersten Weltkrieg. Nomos, Baden-Baden
Woeltzel RK (1962) Nuremberg trials in international law. Stevens & Sons, London/New York
Zimmermann A (2006) Das juristische Erbe von Nürnberg – Das Statut des Nürnberger Internationalen Militärtribunals und der Internationale Strafgerichtshof. In: Reginbogin H, Safferling C (eds) Die Nürnberger Prozesse: Völkerstrafrecht seit 1945. K. G. Saur Verlag, Munich, pp 266–277

Christoph Safferling studied law in Munich and London. He received his doctoral degree at the University of Munich in 1999 and passed the bar exam in 2000. From 2006 to 2015 he was a professor at the Philipps-University of Marburg, and the Director of the International Research and Documentation Centre for War Crimes Trials. Since 2012 he is a member of the International Academic Commission at the Federal Ministry of Justice for Critical Study of the National Socialist Past. Since 2015 he holds the chair for criminal law, criminal procedure, and international law at the Friedrich-Alexander-University Erlangen-Nuremberg and the current president of the International Nuremberg Principles Academy (as of December 2023).

His main fields of research are: international criminal procedural law, the mental elements of the crime, and the history of international criminal law. He is co-editor of the German Law Journal. He is the author of 'International Criminal Procedure' (OUP 2012), and is the co-author of the studies 'Die Akte Rosenburg. Das Bundesministerium der Justiz und die NS-Zeit', Munich, C.H. Beck 2016, and 'Staatsschutz im kalten Krieg. Die Geschichte der Bundesanwaltschaft zwischen NS-Vergangenheit, Spiegel-Affäre und RAF', Munich: dtv 2021).

Failed Justice and the Victims of the Eastern Front of the First World War: Criminal Justice–Vigilante Justice–Political Justice

Gurgen Petrossian

Abstract This chapter examines justice for the victims of the First World War from three perspectives: First, it will consider the Istanbul trials and their outcome. Second, it will scrutinise the trial of the political assassin *Soghomon Tehliryan* and its outcome as well as its impact on the international community, and, third, it will observe the recognition and satisfaction of victims as political justice.

1 Introduction

In 2019, the US House of Representatives[1] and the US Senate[2] passed resolutions rendering the recognition of the Armenian Genocide a part of US policy. In 2021, US President Joe Biden also recognised the Armenian genocide.[3] In the US, seeking recognition was one of the central political and moral goals of the victims of the genocide, and only a century later the victims were able to receive some recognition of their suffering, however, not from the perpetrator. Turkey not only avoids recognition, but also denies genocide.[4] The political recognition[5] of the damage

[1] 116th Congress (2019–2020).

[2] Edmondson (2019); see also 116th Congress (12 December 2019).

[3] Deutsche Welle (2021) US President Joe Biden recognizes Armenian genocide. Deutsche Welle, 24 April 2021, https://www.dw.com/en/us-president-joe-biden-recognizes-armenian-genocide/a-57324601 (Last accessed 1 December 2023).

[4] Petrossian (2019a).

[5] See, e.g. France, Great Britain, and Russia Joint Declaration (1915) Department of State, Washington, 29 May 1915. https://www.facinghistory.org/resource-library/totally-unofficial-raphael-lemkin-and-genocide/france-great-britain-and-russia-joint-declaration-1915 (last accessed 1 December 2023) *calling* 'crimes of Turkey against humanity and civilization'; see also Paylan and Klonowiecka Milart (2015), pp. 558 et seq.

G. Petrossian (✉)
Friedrich-Alexander University of Erlangen-Nuremberg, Erlangen, Germany
e-mail: gurgen.petrossian@fau.de

M.-E. Geis et al. (eds.), *Dealing with Totalitarian Regimes and Human Rights*, Interdisciplinary Studies in Human Rights 11,
https://doi.org/10.1007/978-3-031-57338-5_2

and suffering of the Christian population of the Ottoman Empire was not the only instrument for justice for the victims.

In the first quarter of the 20th century, after the First World War, a special court was set up to punish the perpetrators of the massacres and the deportations of Christians in the Ottoman Empire during the First World War. However, these trials in Istanbul which were aimed at punishing the main perpetrators, were not successful and have historically been referred to as a 'farce'.[6] They would hardly have attracted attention if the trial of *Soghomon Tehliryan* in Berlin in 1921 had not caused such an international response. The trial of this avenger marked the first attempt at rethinking international law and victims' interests. This chapter discusses three instruments of justice—criminal, frontier and political justice for the victims by using the example of the genocide in the First World War.

2 Criminal Justice

After British troops had occupied Constantinople, international[7] pressure gave rise to the initiative to punish war criminals and those who committed the atrocities. In November 1918, the new government under the leadership of *Vizier Ahmet Izzet*, and later *Vizier Ahmet Tevfik*, initiated investigations against the members of the Committee of Union and Progress (CUP)[8] for the crimes committed against the Armenians. These were to be carried out regardless of the rank and status of the person.[9] The reports on the expulsion and extermination of the Armenians and on the entry into the War of the Ottoman Empire were prepared by the Ministry of the Interior in cooperation with the Ministry of War and the press. As a result, a large amount of evidence and testimony as well as numerous official and unofficial documents were collected at regional and governmental levels.[10] On 14 December 1918, the Sultan's special decree N233 established the special tribunal.[11] Before the establishment of this tribunal, Sultan Mehmet VI gave a speech in which he mentioned:

> Such misdeeds and the mutual slaughter of sons of the same fatherland have broken my heart. I ordered an inquiry as soon as I came to the throne so that the fomenters might be severely punished, but various factors prevented my orders from being promptly carried out.[12]

[6] Kevorkian (2011), p. 771; Rikhof (2014), p. 287.

[7] Cp. Kloian (1985), p. ix.

[8] See more in Kieser (2020), pp. 61 et seq.

[9] Cmp. Nuremberg principles I and III, UN General Assembly (1947), paragraph (a); see also Cassese (2009).

[10] Dadrian and Akçam (2011), pp. 59 et seq.

[11] Kevorkian (2011), p. 776; Akçam (2007), p. 284; Balint (2013), p. 86.

[12] Sondhaus (2011), p. 393.

After the first arrest of officials in January 1919, protests began among Ottoman civilians to free their 'national heroes'. As a result, detainees were not held in strict conditions and their relatives or other detainees were able to communicate and visit each other.[13] The intensity of the demonstrations, especially after the execution of one of the convicted persons,[14] forced the British authorities into not punishing a number of senior officials.

A total of 63 trials were held in the parliament building in Istanbul, with the files of merely 24 remaining until today.[15] The death penalty was imposed twenty times over the course of these 63 trials, however, only three of those sentenced to death were ultimately executed.[16] The court cases were documented using the procedural protocols published in the '*Takvim i Vekai*' newspaper.[17] Articles 226–230 of the Sevres Treaty of 1920 included the provision of the establishment of the Tribunal and the punishment of those charged with violating the laws and customs of war.

2.1 The Tribunal

The criminal and criminal procedural law of the Ottoman Empire of 1906 was similar to French law and, therefore, followed an inquisitorial system. During the trials, the defendants mostly raised the issue of the privileges of the officials. In response to that, the Tribunal stated that the indictment did not contain any political crimes, but was limited to the criminally relevant acts, and thus any objections based upon the ministerial privileges, i.e. their immunity, could not be accepted.[18] The Tribunal dealt with criminal offences such as the murder of Armenians, illegal individual usury, the entry of the Ottoman Empire into the War and the overthrowing of the government. The defendants were divided into three groups, namely the organisers, the immediate perpetrators and those who had been involved in 'economic crimes'.[19]

2.2 The Main Trial (Taleat et al.)

The main charges were brought against the cabinet of the Ottoman Empire and the leaders of the CUP. The proceedings were carried out in two phases; from 28 April to

[13] Kevorkian (2011), p. 771.

[14] Anumyan (2014).

[15] Dadrian and Akçam (2011), pp. 94–95.

[16] Petrossian (2019b), p. 60.

[17] Petrossian (2019b), pp. 70 et seq.

[18] Papazyan and Sahakyan (1989), p. 48.

[19] Balint (2013), p. 89.

17 May and from 3 June to 5 July 1919. As a consequence of the growing unrest, the British decided on 28 May 1919 to transfer over 100 suspects alleged of having been responsible for the massacres to Malta in order to try them before their own court.[20] They were, however, exchanged for British prisoners of war on 23 October 1921 without a trial, according to the agreement with Mustafa Kemal, President of the Grand National Assembly in Ankara.[21] Among the defendants, the main actors of the Ottoman Empire, *Mehmed Teleat (Talaat) Pasha*, Minister of the Interior and *de facto* leader of the Ottoman Empire, *Damad Ismayil Enver Pasha,* Defence Minister and *Ahmet Cemal Pasha*, Minister of the Navy, were also indicted *in absentia*.

The prosecutor of the Tribunal accused the members of the CUP of having already decided beforehand to enter the War in order to be able to implement their secret plans, in other words, to finally solve the '*Armenian question*'. In the indictment, the prosecutor clearly emphasised the assertion that those responsible externally claimed to be fighting for national interests, yet in reality, they wanted to make private and personal profit from the whole situation by destroying, robbing and torturing their own population under the impression of war.[22] According to the indictment and the judicial records, the Central Committee of the CUP consisted of two different organisations; a public one based on the party statutes and the other one based on secret orders and rules. The coordination of the crimes was left to carefully selected secretaries.[23]

The investigation showed that the coded correspondence between the officers contained, among other things, the note '*to be destroyed*', a clear indication that the expulsions according to the 'deportation law' were not the ultimate goal of the government, but merely served as a method to execute the killings of non-Muslims. In response to the indictment, the defendants justified the necessity of the deportations as measures of state defence and refused to admit that the crimes happened during the deportations.[24]

Based upon the evidence adduced, and according to the correspondence between the Central Committee and the special organisation '*Teşkilât-ı Mahsusa*', the Tribunal found that the massacres in Yozgat, Bayburt, Trabzon and other places had been organised by the CUP as part of its policy.[25] The Tribunal confirmed that, with the approval of the CUP, Kara Kemal, the Minister of Supply, had set up commissions that organised the seizures of the deportees' property and delegated the execution thereof to companies and individuals.[26]

The judgment of the Tribunal sentenced the members of the Ottoman Triumvirate to death and despite the procedural interruptions and strong political pressure from

[20] Crowe (2011), p. 18.

[21] See more in Akçam (2007), p. 362.

[22] Papazyan and Sahakyan (1989), p. 48.

[23] Dadrian (1989), pp. 299 et seq.

[24] Papazyan and Sahakyan (1989), pp. 36–52.

[25] Dadrian (1989), p. 305.

[26] Petrossian (2019b), pp. 70–71.

the public and in spite of the absence of the main defendants, other defendants received different sentences, however, the majority of them were transferred to Malta.[27]

2.3 The Follow-Up Trials

Compared to the Nuremberg follow-up trials, in which the prosecution focused on specific groups of people (legal trial, medical trial, industrial trial, etc.), the trials in Istanbul had a predominantly regional focus, e.g. the Yozgat trial, Trabzon or the Harput trials. In those proceedings, those responsible for the regional expulsions were brought to justice. In the Yozgat trial, the first Istanbul trial, the *Kaymakam* (governor) of the city of Yozgat was sentenced to death (and was subsequently executed) for organising the attacks on the deportees, killing and looting the Armenians. The same scenario attacks on the deportees was repeated in the Trabzon case, where the defendants were accused of having received the secret orders to deport and attack the Armenians. Those who remained in the city of Trabzon were temporarily placed in hospitals and hotels, and later embarked on a mission to cross the Black Sea. On the high seas, however, they were thrown into the water and drowned. In the Harput, Bayburt, Erzincan and other trials, the defendants were convicted of the organisation of mass murder and the deportation of the Armenians from the cities.[28]

2.4 Summary

The Istanbul trials lasted until the end of 1920, and already during the establishment of the Republic of Turkey, the outcome of the trials was declared null and void.[29] Moreover, the 1923 Treaty of Lausanne settled the question of individual responsibility for the crimes of the First World War. The agreement on borders and minority rights between the major powers and the Turkish Republic ruined the *criminal justice* for mass murders and war criminals. The struggle for independence and the establishment of the Turkish Republic led to the abolition of the Treaty of Sèvres,[30] the norms, orders and judgments issued during the occupation of Istanbul.

The Istanbul trials were, alongside the Leipzig trials, one of the first attempts to establish international criminal law, and the Nuremberg trials were also able to build upon them. Compared to the Leipzig trials, however, the Istanbul trials also

[27] See Kramer (2006), p. 444.

[28] See narrow in Yeghiayan (1990), p. 171; Petrossian (2019b), pp. 60–80.

[29] Balint (2013), p. 98.

[30] The Treaty of Sèvres (1920) was not even signed by the Ottoman Empire.

succeeded in bringing high-ranking personalities to court.[31] In the Istanbul trials, the evidence presented played an important role in establishing the CUP's intent to destroy a group as a whole, which is now referred to as genocidal intent. The decisions of the Tribunal show that the killings of the Armenians were planned and organised. Although the main objective of the trials was to politically manifest the Allied victory, they also resulted in the prosecution of those chiefly responsible at both local and governmental levels. The Tribunal punished those who were not present at the trial particularly severely. The crucial part of the outcome of the trials is that those who were predominantly responsible for the atrocities escaped the Tribunal's convictions. This led to further frustration within the victim community.

3 Vigilante Justice

The unsuccessful post-war trials in Istanbul in 1919 would hardly have attracted any attention, had the trial of *Soghomon Tehliryan* in Berlin in 1921 not generated such an international response. The cause of the proceedings is the deliberate killing of one of the key political figures of the Ottoman Empire: *Taleat Mehmet Pascha*, Minister of the Interior and last Grand Vizier of the Ottoman Empire during the First World War.

After the First World War, *Mehmet Taleat Pascha* lived under the false name of '*Ali Salih Bey*' as an insolvent trader in Berlin where he supported Turkish nationalism from afar. Despite his attempts to remain undetected, he was traced by an Armenian student named *Soghomon Tehliryan*, who shot him on 15 March 1921 and subsequently surrendered. About three months later, the assassin was free again and made his way to San Francisco where he died in 1960 without further trial. In the two-day trial from 1 June to 2 June 1921 at the Berlin Moabit Local Court, *Soghomon Tehliryan*'s innocence was established and he was acquitted. This acquittal provoked a rethinking of international law customs and theories which have become extremely topical today, e.g. the genocide convention, state sovereignty, humanitarian intervention and state responsibility.

Soghomon Tehliryan was born in Bagarich, western Armenia, in 1896, where he received his primary school education. He began his education at the Central University of Erzincan, from which he graduated in 1912, and moved to Serbia in 1913. Although he planned to study in Germany, he travelled to Armenia after the outbreak of the First World War to take part in the volunteer movement. The genocide had a profound effect on his life, especially when he visited his parents' home in his city after the Russian offensive in 1916 and lost consciousness.[32] In 1920, *Tehliryan* joined the Daschnaktutiun Party's '*operation Nemesis*', which aimed to expose and eliminate the 'architects' of the genocide. The list of people

[31] Cmp. Lattimer and Sands (2003), p. 123.

[32] Tehlirian (1993).

to be eliminated was drawn up on the basis of the Istanbul judgment. *Soghomon Tehlirian's* task was to kill and then to surrender to the German authorities.[33]

On 3 December 1920, *Tehliryan* arrived in Berlin as a mechanical engineering student and rented a room, attended German courses and began to track down his victim. On 15 March 1921, the victim was shot and the perpetrator surrendered.

From the beginning, the idea of 'Operation Nemesis' was to create a personal context and emotional connection between *Tehliryan* and *Taleat* in order to justify the killing. For this reason, a parallel biography of *Tehliryan* was created and was officially recognised until the 1950s.[34] He presented himself in the proceedings as an eyewitness to the expulsion and massacre of his family in Erzincan in 1915. He described in detail that in June 1915, the order came that the Armenians of Erzincan should be ready to leave the city. Three days later, the Armenians were brought out of the city early in the morning and, within a few hours, the deportees were attacked by the gendarmes who raped and killed *Tehliryan's* sister and cruelly murdered his mother and brother. However, only he survived the massacre. After he had learned that the Russian forces had captured the city Erzincan, he went back to the city to find the money hidden at his home, however, as soon as the pictures of the massacre came back to him, after he fainted.[35]

Later he went back to Tbilisi and lived with the money he obtained from Erzincan. He found out about those responsible for the event through the newspapers and, in 1921, when he came to Berlin to study, he heard that *Taleat* was in Berlin. He even suddenly met him once in the streets. Two weeks before the murder, he had a vision of his mother's corpse, which appeared and told him:

> You saw that Taleat is here and you are completely indifferent? You are no longer my son.[36]

From that point in time, he decided to kill *Taleat* as his mother had ordered him to do so. He often had visions like this from the massacre, and he often saw his mother, too. On 15 March 1921, when he suddenly noticed *Taleat* on the balcony of his room, he saw his mother's vision once again. When *Taleat* walked out of his apartment a few minutes later, he thought of his mother and ran after *Taleat* with the gun.[37]

This parallel story of *Tehliryan*, of course, played an important role in the criminal proceedings and in the acquittal, however, in a number of points, it was simply not true. In truth, he never actually experienced the massacre of his family; he was wounded in battle, not during the massacre. His mother's spirit, in turn, was a hallucination which he dreamed in Erzincan and which had influenced him greatly.[38]

---

[33] Bogosian (2015), p. 104.

[34] Until the publication of Tehlirians Memoirs.

[35] Der Prozess 'Talaat Pascha', Stenographischer Prozessbericht (1921), pp. 6–10.

[36] Der Prozess 'Talaat Pascha', Stenographischer Prozessbericht (1921), p. 14; see also Jacobs (2019), pp. 35–36.

[37] Der Prozess 'Talaat Pascha', Stenographischer Prozessbericht (1921), p. 19.

[38] Tehlirian (1993), pp. 90 et seq.

The seizures he had experienced in Erzincan had also plagued in Berlin. This was later used to question the defendant's psyche and to acquit him for being temporarily insane.[39]

3.1 The Indictment

The basis of the indictment was § 211 of the Criminal Code of the Empire (Reichsstrafgesetzbuch; RStGB) from 31 May 1871:

> A person who intentionally kills a human being, if he has carried out the killing with deliberation, shall be punished by death for the crime of murder.

The prosecution demanded the maximum possible penalty for the offence under § 211 RStGB; accordingly, Tehliryan was to be proven to have '*deliberated*' the murder. In order to establish this, the prosecution examined whether the act had been calmly, clearly and intelligently deliberated. This was the case when a perpetrator was able to become aware of the meaning of the act, his motives, the means required to execute it, the consequences of it, the moral inhibitions and the circumstances that militate against it. These had to have an effect on him in order to allow the individual points to be weighed against each other and based upon these purely rational considerations to make a decision to act.[40]

The prosecution did not doubt that the case was a political murder, in which the perpetrator acted out of political hatred and vindictiveness. In the course of the taking of evidence, however, it became necessary to examine whether *Taleat* had actually been the 'architect' of the Armenian massacres. To this end, the prosecution based its pleading on General von Sanders's testimonies[41] and made it clear that the Ottoman government had received reports that the Armenians had conspired with the Entente and were determined to strike the Ottoman Empire from behind in order to achieve their independence as soon as the warlike situation permitted it. As a result, the 'dislocation' of the Armenians was ordered to enforce the military necessity.

Even the documents presented, which were supposed to serve as evidence of *Taleat's* responsibility, had not convinced the prosecution, as the prosecution believed that the authenticity of such documents, signed by prominent personalities during the War, was rather questionable. At the same time, the prosecutor questioned the objectivity of the Tribunal in Istanbul, since the new government had come to power with the help of the Entente and the heads of the old system had been declared enemies. Although there was no evidence that *Taleat* was the author of the extermination, *Tehliryan* was firmly convinced of *Taleat's* guilt. As evidence of his act of

[39] See more in Petrossian (2020), pp. 95 et seq.

[40] Cmp. Liszt (2018), p. 311.

[41] Cmp. Der Prozess 'Talaat Pascha', Stenographischer Prozessbericht (1921), p. 86; von Sanders (1920).

revenge, the prosecution insisted that the defendant had purposefully travelled from Erzincan to Europe, had traced *Taleat* and had shot him with the pistol he had brought with him from the Ottoman Empire. Finally, the prosecution identified the missing elements of his insanity defence. Although the prosecution believed that the defendant had epileptic seizures, these had actually had no effect on the murder.

3.2 Defence

In return, the defence endeavoured to prove the existence of *Tehliryan's* epilepsy caused by his experience and its effect on his actions pursuant to § 51 RStGB and the associated temporary insanity.

In accordance with § 51 RStGB '*a criminal act [...] is not present if the perpetrator at the time of the commission of the act was in a state of unconsciousness or pathological disturbance of the mental activity, by which his free determination of the will was excluded*'.

The defence highlighted *Taleat's* special role in the organisation of the massacres. The main argument of the defence at that point in the proceedings was a single telegram from the witness, which was supposed to show what *Taleat* meant by '*how many of the Armenians are already dead and how many are still alive*'. The defence pointed out that without the well-coordinated management attributed to *Taleat*, systematic deportations and killings would not have been possible.

On the matter of excluding the deliberation, the defence pointed out that the 'deliberation' as such does not refer to the entire preparation of the murder, but only to the last decision. According to the German Empire Court, the time at which the act was perpetrated was decisive. Therefore, it was to be proven whether the act was committed out of a storm of passion, strong emotions, or out of cold, calculated deliberation. A planned, deliberated and prepared act, however, is never a murder if at the moment of its execution there was no 'deliberation'.[42]

Regarding the question of whether the perpetrator had actively made the decision to commit the murder or not, the defence indicated that the reports compiled by the medical experts should help the jurors to decide whether his mental illness had influenced the determination of his will at that moment.

The defence emphasised that when there is an overwhelming notion that completely dominates the person concerned, which is only capable of bringing about the crime and dwarfs everything else, no longer the whole ego, but rather a pathological part of the ego is committing the crime. The defence pointed out that the defendant had drunk cognac that day, not to give himself the courage to commit the crime, but as a result of a stomach ache. Only then, when he had already drunk a

[42] Der Prozess 'Talaat Pascha', Stenographischer Prozessbericht (1921), p. 121; cf. Schwartz (2013 (reprint of the 1914 edition)), p. 477; RGE (Collection of Decisions of the Reichsgericht) 1909, p. 260, Judgment of 26 March 1909; Liszt (1927), pp. 464–465.

third of the bottle, did he suddenly see *Taleat* on the balcony. At that moment, *Taleat's* appearance provoked him and the millennial suffering of his people, the death of his mother and the images of the crime that unfolded before his eyes. The will of the accused was, at that moment, dominated by these images or horror. This led to the fact that the illness, the cognac, the blow to the head that the defendant had suffered in 1915, the death of his mother and the images of the massacre led to the commission of the crime, which is why he was not be able to act of his own volition.[43]

Furthermore, the defence emphasised that the jury would not has to answer the question '*Did the defendant kill Taleat?*' with a 'yes' or a 'no' but rather the question '*Is the defendant guilty of killing Taleat?*'

3.3 Judgment

After deliberating for one hour, the chairman of the jury announced: '*I testify on honour and conscience as the verdict of the jury: Is the defendant Soghomon Tehliryan guilty of deliberately killing a person, Taleat Pascha, on March 15, 1921, in Charlottenburg? – No*'. Accordingly, *Soghomon Tehliryan* was acquitted on the grounds of temporary insanity. The prosecutor appealed against the verdict, but later withdrew the appeal. *Taleat's* criminal proceedings in Berlin took place at a very unfavourable time for Germany.[44] After massive protests against the Leipzig Trials, which had already begun in January 1921, Germany, as a former ally of the Ottoman Empire in the First World War, had no interest in criminal proceedings in Berlin, which were likely to further expand Germany's co-responsibility. The Leipzig Trials, the impending economic collapse, the reparations claim of the Entente, the political disputes in the Weimar Republic: all of this was already sufficient for the everyday political life of the Germany. In the east, the Ottoman Empire was trying to cope with the consequences of the defeat. Although the capital Istanbul had been occupied by the British, the Kemalists had created a new government in Ankara, which opposed the Istanbul government. The government in Ankara had declared the decisions of the Istanbul government null and void after the government in Istanbul was taken over by the Kemalists on 19 October 1922.

3.4 Summary

Soghomon Tehliryan's actions were only one part of 'Operation Nemesis'. Other people who were responsible were shot by the members of 'Operation Nemesis',

---

[43] Der Prozess 'Talaat Pascha', Stenographischer Prozessbericht (1921), pp. 110–115.

[44] Cmp. Hosfeld and Petrossian (2020); Hosfeld (2015), p. 233.

e.g. the Grand Vizier of the Ottoman Empire, *Said Halim Pascha*, in Rome on 5 December 1921, as well as the founder of the Committee for Unity and Progress and head of *Teşkilât-ı Mahsusa, Bahattin Şakir*, in Berlin on 17 April 1922. One year after *Soghomon Tehliyan's* acquittal, another member of the Ottoman Triumvirate, *Cemal Pasha*, who was sentenced to death *in absentia* in Istanbul, was shot in Tbilisi.[45] The third member of the triumvirate, *Enver Pasha,* was killed in battle with the Russian Red Army.

It is important to note at this point that the retaliation was a response to the failure of justice. Historical events today allow us to make the following comparison: During the First World War, the international community failed to condemn those responsible for the numerous crimes committed during the Great War. The reasons for this differ. The Entente had its own diverse political problems. The European states had been physically and economically exhausted by the war. The Istanbul judgments were not executed, and those responsible escaped both punishment under criminal law and a political or international 'punishment'. This provoked vigilante justice. Although, after the Second World War, Stalin and Churchill believed that retaliation should be in the form of simple shootings, they were later convinced into pursuing international criminal proceedings and enforcing the sentences. Thus, those responsible for the Second World War received both their criminal and political-international punishment. However, whoever tried to escape justice was forced to appear before the court in Jerusalem by the Israeli Mossad as part of the 'Operation Garibaldi'. A kidnapping comparable to that of Adolf Eichmann was inconceivable during 'Operation Nemesis'.

4 Political Justice

The details of *Soghomon Tehliryan's* trial were discussed at national and international levels. The young law student *Raphael Lemkin* at the University of Lviv and the young public prosecutor *Robert Kempner* in Berlin, were particularly interested in the trial. About 25 years later, both met as colleagues during the Nuremberg Trials in front of the International Military Tribunal and both were inspired by the 1921 trial. During a discussion with his professor, Lemkin expressed surprise that the person who had participated in so many murders had not been arrested. In response, he was told a parable referring to state sovereignty:

> Let us take the case of a man who owns some chickens. He kills them. Why not? It is not your business. If you interfere, it is trespass.[46]

[45] Hosfeld (2005), pp. 300 et seq.

[46] Cooper (2008), p. 15; Petrossian (2019b), pp. 95 et seq.; The professor seems to be Stanisław Starzyński, see Vardanyan (2017), p. 249.

But the Armenians were not chickens, thought Lemkin, and set himself the goal of radically changing international law. Although he did not succeed in integrating the new word 'genocide' into the indictment during the Nuremberg Trials, the Convention on the Prevention and Punishment of Genocide was passed in 1948 and came into force in 1951.[47] The prohibition of genocide is regarded as the minimum human rights standard of international law or as *ius cogens*. After the Nuremberg Trials, Kempner came to the conclusion that genocide could well be fought against by foreign states and that it was not impermissible interference in their internal affairs.[48]

However, while the recognition of suffering through legal instruments existed and those legal instruments were a consequence of the political recognition of such suffering, it was evident that this was insufficient in terms of bringing political justice to the communities of victims.

4.1 Victims

The Second World War, victims were generally considered '*forgotten men*'. The victims of mass atrocities did not receive appropriate international attention. Due to the massive refugee crises after the First World War, with millions of people migrating from Eastern Europe to Western Europe, the international community was compelled to find a solution for the refugees. This led to multiple international conventions, which were the building blocks for the refugee convention from 1951.[49]

Victims of war crimes or other macro-crimes did not receive much attention in the aftermath of a war of destruction. International law did not recognise any rights of the victims; instead, they were viewed as a powerless group unable to defend themselves. Politically, only a individuals who were 'strong' and could victimise were celebrated as war heroes. Attention was not given to the thousands of victims of colonial regimes and to the victims of genocide and mass destructions of the First World War.[50] Only very few victims were called to testify as witnesses in the Istanbul Trials in the aftermath of the First World War.[51] This perspective only shifted after the Second World War. In fact, at the Nuremberg Trials against the principal Nazi war criminals, as well as in the trials that followed both in Nuremberg and elsewhere against Nazi criminals, victims could not participate, and very few were even called as witnesses. The International Military Tribunal indeed focused on the crimes against peace, i.e. the charge of having conspired and instigated an

[47] Safferling (2011), pp. 159 et seq.; Volkmann (2009), pp. 153 et seq.

[48] Kempner (1980), p. 168.

[49] Cf. Makarov (1951), p. 432; cf. UNHCR (1951) or United Nations (1946).

[50] Schneider (1982).

[51] Dadrian and Akçam (2011), p. 210.

aggressive war.[52] The concept of crimes against humanity, which would have demanded a closer look at the millions of civilians killed, was still in its infancy and the concept of the crime of genocide was only developed after, and in reaction to, the flaws of the IMT judgment in this regard.[53] However, in the *Eichmann Trial* in Jerusalem[54] and the *Auschwitz Trial* in Germany,[55] the Holocaust and the victims were brought into the public conscience.[56] To hear the voices of the victims and to fully understand the suffering of those deprived of all human respect was only now made part of the prosecutorial task. Nevertheless, the demand that echoes from Nuremberg, to end impunity, laid down as Principle I of the Nuremberg Principles by the UN General Assembly in 1946,[57] is also a demand for respect for the victims of international crimes, to take alliance with the victim rather than the mass-murderer.[58]

4.2 Recognition

Generally, the victims of a mass atrocities expect recognition for the suffering and harm caused by the crimes. However, there is a problem with defining victims, especially concerning who victims are and how they can be identified.

The UN Declaration of Basic Principles of Justice for Victims and Abuse of Power 1985 recognises victims as persons who individually or collectively have suffered harm, including physical or mental injury, emotional suffering, economic loss or substantial impairment of their fundamental rights through acts or omissions that are in violation of the criminal law. Accordingly, the victim's recognition depends on three important characteristics: damage suffered, existence of a crime and causality. However, as long as there is no judgment on the existence of a crime, it is impossible to recognise the existence of victimhood based upon an alleged crime.[59] Claiming victimhood before the final judgment may contradict the presumption of innocence from the perspective of criminal law. Therefore, until the final verdict, the victims are merely *presumed* to be victims in criminal justice.[60] In contrast, victims have the right to believe that they have been victims of a crime. Each person can individually understand their harm and develop an approach or an opinion on how they became victims. This approach to victimisation can develop

52 Bloxham (2001), pp. 69–70; Safferling (2015), p. 1063.

53 Schabas (2010), pp. 19–35.

54 Bach (2010), pp. 275–285.

55 Dux (2010), pp. 287–298; Pendas (2010), pp. 53 et seq.

56 Priemel (2016), pp. 9 et seq.

57 UN General Assembly (1946); and United Nations (1957), para. 97.

58 Cf. Fletcher (2005), pp. 554 et seq.

59 See Safferling and Petrossian (2021), pp. 33 et seq.

60 See Pemberton and Vanfraechem (2015), pp. 31–33.

into a lifestyle and a doctrine. In this way, victimisation becomes a victim's identity.[61] Accordingly, the denial of victimisation may harm the dignity of a person and violate their corresponding human rights,[62] such as the individual right to personality (personal identity),[63] the right to freedom of thought, the right to the freedom to have or to adopt a belief (Article 18 ICCPR), the right to a private life (Article 8 ECHR), the protection of the family (Article 23 ICCPR), among others. Otherwise, this situation is known as secondary victimisation.[64] Given the physical and psychological suffering of victims of a mass crimes, it is their right to regard themselves as victims, regardless of whether the perpetrator is identified, arrested, prosecuted or convicted (A.2 UN Declaration of Basic Principles of Justice for Victims of Crime and Abuse of Power).

If it is considered that the victim is a victim, a further question is what the victim is a victim of? Victim status can have a variety of ramifications, either in international or criminal law, or even in politics. A differentiated assessment is made as to whether a victim has been the victim of genocide or of a robbery or whether it is a victim of an epidemic disease. Accordingly, the victims of the Holocaust and their families are on a very different level from the victims of a crime under national law. Again, this is the starting point of the circle in which the existence of a victim depends on the fulfilment of the elements of the alleged crime. One solution to this *'Zugzwang'* is to treat a victim with respect, as if the crime did indeed take place, unless it is proven to be otherwise.

4.3 *Satisfaction*

One further issue that follows the acknowledgment of suffering is compensating the victim. Even under Roman law, the person who committed a civil wrong was obligated to recover or repair the damage.[65] Recovering from the damage is one of the fundamental pillars of civil law. Mass crimes not only violate personal rights but also the safeguards of the community. Although the victim may be satisfied by material compensation, in most cases, however, the core of the victimisation is not material, but rather political and psychological. Sometimes even an apology by the perpetrator—*'I am sorry'*—is not sufficient for the victims.[66] The ICC is the first

---

[61] Cf. Hovhannisyan (2017), p. 174.

[62] Petrossian (2019a).

[63] Marshall (2014), p. 72.

[64] '*when a victim of a crime feels they have been subjected to inadequate, insensitive or inappropriate treatment, attitudes, behavior, responses and/or practices by criminal justice and social agencies that compound their original trauma*' in Gekoski et al. (2013), p. 308; Wemmers (1996), p. 20 et subs.

[65] Zimmermann (1996), pp. 902–903.

[66] '*I am really sorry, I am really remorseful and I regret all the damage that my actions have caused. I regret what I have caused to my family, my community in Timbuktu, what I have caused*

institution that considers reparation for the victims of international crimes.[67] The existing instruments for the reparation of the victims, however, cannot be enough for the complete satisfaction of the damage suffered by the victims.

Germany recently acknowledged its genocide against the Nama and Herero tribes from Namibia.[68] Since the 2000s, Germany has apologised several times for its crimes during the colonial regime,[69] however, not for genocide.[70] For the community of victims, this was not sufficient. With an unsuccessful application before the New York District Court[71] for the state responsibility of Germany, the victims' community sent out a political signal for their struggle for recognition and reparation. The recognition of the suffering was followed by compensation for the genocide to the tune of 1.1 billion euros, to be paid to Namibia for 30 years. However, the amount of compensation was criticised by the victims.[72]

4.4 Summary

Approximately forty (as of December 2023) states have officially recognised the genocide of the Armenians by various instruments, but this has no legal consequences for the mass crime and the reparation. While it is of political and moral support for the victims and helps to keep the memory of the events alive, it holds little importance for the legal consequences concerning reparations, as the Republic of Turkey has so far refused to recognise it. Other international legal instruments, such as the genocide convention or other international treaties, are not politically sufficient to 'force' Turkey to acknowledge the suffering and the damage caused to the Christian minorities of the Ottoman Empire.

---

my home nation, Mali, and I'm really remorseful about what I had caused the international community as a whole', see ICC (2016), p. 8.

[67] Based on the Van Boven principles, see more in Safferling and Petrossian (2020), p. 13.

[68] Ochab (2021).

[69] '*I ask you in the sense of the common, father our forgiveness of our fault. Without a deliberate memory, without deep grief, there can be no reconciliation. Reconciliation needs memory*'. Speech by Federal Minister Heidemarie Wieczorek-Zeul at the memorial celebrations of the Herero uprisings am 14 August 2004 in Okakarara, 2004, Audioportal Freier Radios (2012) 'Ein kleines Wunder' - Antrag im Bundestag zur Anerkennung des Völkermords in Deutsch-Südwestafrika. https://www.freie-radios.net/47201 (last accessed 1 December 2023).

[70] The request of the Fraction of the Left to the German Bundestag (1 July 2015) for reconciliation with Namibia and commemorating the genocide of the Herero and Nama in the former colony German-Südwestfrica on 17 March 2016, cf. Deutscher Bundestag (1 July 2015), Deutscher Bundestag (14 October 2015).

[71] Stephan (2018); Jaspert (2019).

[72] Die Zeit (2021) Herero und Nama fordern Nachverhandlung von Reparationszahlungen. Zeit Online, 31 May 2021. https://www.zeit.de/politik/ausland/2021-05/namibia-voelkermord-herero-nama-ablehnung-versoehnung-abkommen-deutschland (last accessed 1 December 2023).

In the 1970s, the political ignorance of the events of the First World War led again to vigilante justice by ASALA by the attacks on Turkish ambassadors for the recognition and reparation of the Armenian genocide.[73]

In the case of the Second World War and the Nama and the Herero, Germany was in a position to recognise the suffering and the damage of the victims of mass destruction, however, Turkey not only denies the crime committed, but also continues its aggressive behaviour towards the victims' communities. The recognition of the events of the First World War as genocide is in Republic Turkey officially criminalised.[74] Despite the fact that Turkey officially denies the events of the First World War as genocide and mass destruction, it officially supported the war against the Armenians in 2020,[75] which constitutes another psychological victimisation for the victims of Armenian genocide.

5 Conclusion

Compared to the trials in Nuremberg and Tokyo, the trials in Leipzig and Istanbul were not as successful; nevertheless, they were the first steps towards establishing international criminal justice. While the Leipzig Trials focused on violations of international law and the customs of war, the Istanbul trials were the first where state leaders were brought to justice for crimes against their own civilians. However, the main responsible state actors escaped criminal conviction for those actions that were manifested politically as crimes against humanity and civilisation.[76] The escape from criminal justice led to vigilante justice, whereby the convicted persons were tracked down and murdered. The political assassinations and, above all, the trial of *Soghomon Tehliryan* laid the foundation for rethinking the political and legal framework of that time. Raphael Lemkin also changed the legal understanding of minority rights and of the protection thereof. Nevertheless, this was not sufficient for the political recognition of the victims of the First World War, as the Republic of Turkey politically denies the events. After a century, it is still up to the perpetrator to decide whether to recognise the victims. There is no other legal instrument that enforces recognition unless the perpetrator wants to.

---

[73] The Armenian Secret Army for the Liberation of Armenia (ASALA); The intention of the ASALA was to force 'the Turkish Government to confess the responsibility for the genocide of the Armenians from 1915, to force to pay the reparations' see more United States Department of State (1990), p. 57.

[74] Petrossian (2019b), p. 226.

[75] Fraser (2020).

[76] See France, Great Britain, and Russia Joint Declaration (1915) Department of State, Washington, 29 May 1915. https://www.facinghistory.org/resource-library/totally-unofficial-raphael-lemkin-and-genocide/france-great-britain-and-russia-joint-declaration-1915 (last accessed 1 December 2023); see also Garibian (2008).

Documents

116th Congress (12 December 2019) United States Senate Resolution 150 - A resolution expressing the sense of the Senate that it is the policy of the United States to commemorate the Armenian Genocide through official recognition and remembrance

116th Congress (2019–2020) H.Res.296 - Affirming the United States record on the Armenian Genocide, 29 October 2019

Audioportal Freier Radios (2012) "Ein kleines Wunder" - Antrag im Bundestag zur Anerkennung des Völkermords in Deutsch-Südwestafrika. https://www.freie-radios.net/47201. Accessed 1 December 2023

Cassese A (2009) Affirmation Of The Principles Of International Law Recognized By The Charter Of The Nürnberg Tribunal

Der Prozess "Talaat Pascha", Stenographischer Prozessbericht (1921). Deutsche Verlagsgesellschaft für Politik und Geschichte, Berlin

Deutsche Welle (2021) US President Joe Biden recognizes Armenian genocide. Deutsche Welle, 24 April 2021, https://www.dw.com/en/us-president-joe-biden-recognizes-armenian-genocide/a-57324601. Accessed 1 December 2023

Deutscher Bundestag (1 July 2015) BT-Drucksache 18/5407

Deutscher Bundestag (14 October 2015) BT-Drucksache18/6376

Die Zeit (2021) Herero und Nama fordern Nachverhandlung von Reparationszahlungen. Zeit Online, 31 May 2021. https://www.zeit.de/politik/ausland/2021-05/namibia-voelkermord-herero-nama-ablehnung-versoehnung-abkommen-deutschland. Accessed 1 December 2023

France, Great Britain, and Russia Joint Declaration (1915) Department of State, Washington, 29 May 1915. https://www.facinghistory.org/resource-library/totally-unofficial-raphael-lemkin-and-genocide/france-great-britain-and-russia-joint-declaration-1915. Accessed 1 December 2023

ICC (2016) The Prosecutor v. Ahmad Al Faqi Al Mahdi. Transcript, 22 August 2016

UN General Assembly (1947) Resolution 177 (II). 21 November 1947

Treaty of Sèvres (1920). Sèvres

UN General Assembly (1946) Dec. 96/I of December 11, 1946

United Nations (1946) Constitution of the International Refugee Organization. United Nations, Treaty Series, vol. 18, p. 3. New York

United Nations (1957) Question of international criminal jurisdiction. In: Yearbook of the International Law Commission, 1950, Volume II. New York

United States Department of State (1990) Patterns of Global Terrorism Report, 1989

UNHCR (1951) Arrangements of 12 May 1926 and 30 June 1928. Conventions of 28 October 1933 and 10 February 1938. Protocol of 14 September 1939. In: Article 1.

References

Akçam T (2007) A shameful act. Constable, London

Anumyan M (2014) Հայոց ցեղասպանության իրողությունը երիտթուրքերի դատական վավերագրերում (1919-1921). The documentation of the Armenian Genocide in the judicial documents of the Young Turks. Akunq.net, 3 September 2014. https://akunq.net/am/?p=40919. Accessed 1 December 2023

Bach JG (2010) The trial of Adolf Eichmann and other genocide trials. In: Safferling C, Conze E-A (eds) The Genocide Convention sixty years after its adoption. T.M.C. Asser Press, The Hague, pp 275–286

Balint J (2013) The Ottoman state special military tribunal for the genocide of the Armenians: 'doing government business'. In: Heller KJ, Simpson G (eds) The hidden histories of war crimes trials. Oxford University Press, Oxford

Bloxham D (2001) Genocide on trial. Oxford University Press, Oxford, New York

Bogosian E (2015) Operation Nemesis, the assassination plot that avenged the Armenian genocide. Little, Brown and Company, Hachette Book Group, New York

Cooper J (2008) Raphael Lemkin and the struggle for the Genocide Convention. Palgrave Macmillan, Basingstoke, New York

Crowe D (2011) War crimes and genocide in history, and the evolution of responsive international law. In: Crowe D (ed) Crimes of state past and present. Routledge, London, New York

Dadrian V (1989) Genocide as a problem of national and international law: the World War I Armenian case and its contemporary legal ramifications. Yale J Int Law 14(2):221–334

Dadrian V, Akçam T (2011) Judgment at Istanbul. Berghahn Books, New York

Düx H (2010) The Auschwitz Trial at the Landgericht Frankfurt and its importance for the prohibition of genocide. In: Safferling C, Conze E-A (eds) The Genocide Convention sixty years after its adoption. T.M.C. Asser Press, The Hague, pp 287–298

Edmondson C (2019) Senate passes resolution recognizing Armenian genocide, in Defiance of Trump. The New York Times, 12 December 2019. https://www.nytimes.com/2019/12/12/us/politics/senate-armenian-genocide.html. Accessed 1 December 2023

Fletcher G (2005) Justice and fairness in the protection of crime victims. Lewis Clark Law Rev 9(3): 547–557

Fraser S (2020) AP explains: what lies behind Turkish support for Azerbaijan. APnews, 2 October 2020. https://apnews.com/article/turkey-territorial-disputes-azerbaijan-ankara-armenia-9a95d9690569623adedffe8c16f3588d (last accessed 1 December 2023 20 Jun 2021)

Garibian S (2008) Crime against humanity. Mass Violence & Résistance, 19 June 2008. https://www.sciencespo.fr/mass-violence-war-massacre-resistance/en/document/crime-against-humanity. Accessed 1 December 2023

Gekoski A, Adler JR, Gray JM (2013) Interviewing women bereaved by homicide: reports of secondary victimization by the criminal justice system. Int Rev Victimol 19(3):307–329

Hosfeld R (2005) Operation nemesis. Kiepenheuer & Witsch, Cologne

Hosfeld R (2015) Tod in der Wüste. C.H. Beck, Munich

Hosfeld R, Petrossian G (2020) Der Prozess gegen Soghomon Tehlirjan, Deutschland 1919–1921. In: Groenewold K, Ignor A, Koch A (eds) Lexikon der Politischen Strafprozesse. https://www.lexikon-der-politischen-strafprozesse.de/glossar/tehlirjan-soghomon/. Accessed 1 December 2023

Hovhannisyan H (2017) From enemy to neighbour?: The Armenian issue in Ottoman Turkey and the problem of 'de-victimisation' of Armenian society. In: Babie P, Savić V-I (eds) Law, religion and love. Routledge, London, New York, pp 166–180

Jacobs SL (2019) The complicated cases of Soghomon Tehlirian and Sholem Schwartzbard and their influences on Raphaël Lemkin's thinking about genocide. Genocide Stud Prev: Int J 13(1): 33–41

Jaspert F (2019) Setback for the descendants of the Nama and Ovaherero indigenous peoples. Völkerrechtsblog, 08 May 2019. https://voelkerrechtsblog.org/de/setback-for-the-descendants-of-the-nama-and-ovaherero-indigenous-peoples/. Accessed 1 December 2023

Kempner R (1980) Der Völkermord an den Armeniern. Recht und Politik 1980:167–169

Kevorkian R (2011) The Armenian Genocide. I.B.Tauris, London, New York

Kieser H-L (2020) Talaat Pasha. Father of Modern Turkey, architect of genocide. Princeton University Press, Princeton, Oxford

Kloian R (1985) The Armenian Genocide: news accounts from the American Press: 1915-1922. ACC Books, Richmond

Kramer A (2006) The first wave of international war crimes trials: Istanbul and Leipzig. Eur Rev 14(4):441–455

Lattimer M, Sands P (2003) Justice for crimes against humanity. Hart Publishing, Oxford

Liszt F (1927) Lehrbuch des deutschen Strafrechts. W. de Gruyter, Berlin und Leipzig

Liszt F (2018) Lehrbuch des deutschen Strafrechts. De Gruyter, Berlin, Boston

Makarov A (1951) Das internationale Flüchtlingsrecht und Rechtsstellung heimatloser Ausländer nach dem Bundesgesetz vom 25 April 1951. Zeitschrift für ausländisches öffentliches Recht und Völkerrecht 14(1951/52):431–462

Marshall J (2014) The legal recognition of personality: full-face veils and permissible choices. Int J Law Context 10(1):64–80

Ochab E (2021) Germany recognizes the atrocities against the Herero and Nama people as genocide and offers assistance. Forbes, 28 May 2021. https://www.forbes.com/sites/ewelinaochab/2021/05/28/germany-recognizes-the-atrocities-against-the-herero-and-nama-people-as-genocide-and-offers-assistance/?sh=6097a7c878ed. Accessed 1 December 2023

Papazyan AA, Sahakyan RG (1989) Der Völkermord an den Armeniern gemäß der Verfahren gegen die Jungtürken, 1988, die Protokolle des Verfahrens, Հայերի ցեղասպանությունը ըստ երիտթուրքերի դատավարության փաստաթղթերի. Haykakan SSH GA Hratarakch'ut'yun, University of Michigan

Paylan S, Klonowiecka-Milart A (2015) Examining the origins of crimes against humanity and genocide. In: Bergsmo M, Cheah WL, Song T, Yi P (eds) Historical origins of international criminal law: volume 3. Torkel Opsahl Academic Epublisher, Brussels, pp 557–585

Pemberton A, Vanfraechem I (2015) Victims' victimisation experiences and their need for justice. In: Vanfraechem I, Bolivar D, Aertsen I (eds) Victims and restorative justice. Routledge, London, pp 15–47

Pendas D (2010) The Frankfurt Auschwitz trial, 1963 – 1965. Cambridge University Press, Cambridge et al.

Petrossian G (2019a) Ist Negationismus eine Form der Fortsetzung des Völkermordes?. Grundundmenschenrechtsblog, 25. Juli 2019. http://grundundmenschenrechtsblog.de/ist-negationismus-eine-form-der-fortsetzung-des-voelkermordes/. Accessed 1 December 2023

Petrossian G (2019b) Staatenverantwortlichkeit für Völkermord. Duncker & Humblot, Berlin

Petrossian G (2020) Ein Strafverfahren als Ausgangspunkt der Entwicklung des Völkermordsbegriffes. Journal der Juristischen Zeitgeschichte 14(3):93–100

Priemel KC (2016) The Betrayal. Oxford University Press, Oxford

Rikhof J (2014) The Istanbul and Leipzig Trials. In: Bergsmo M, Cheah WL, Yi P (eds) Historical origins of international criminal law: volume I. Torkel Opsahl Academic Epublisher, Brussels, pp 259–298

Safferling C (2011) Internationales Strafrecht: Strafanwendungsrecht, Völkerstrafrecht, Europäisches Strafrecht. Springer, Berlin, Heidelberg

Safferling C (2015) Nürnberg und die Zukunft des Völkerstrafrechts. Juristen Zeitung 70(22): 1061–1068

Safferling C, Petrossian G (2020) Wiedergutmachung für Opfer von Makroverbrechen. MenschenRechtsMagazin 25 (2020) 1:20–31

Safferling C, Petrossian G (2021) Victims before the International Criminal Court. Springer, Cham

Schabas W (2010) Genocide in international law and international relations prior to 1948. In: Safferling C, Conze E-A (eds) The Genocide Convention sixty years after its adoption. T.M.C. Asser Press, The Hague, pp 19–35

Schneider H (1982) Opfer des Völkermordes. In: Schneider H (ed) Das Verbrechensopfer in der Strafrechtspflege. Walter de Gruyter, Berlin, New York, pp 305–318

Schwartz E (2013 (reprint of the 1914 edition)) Das Strafgesetzbuch für das Deutsche Reich: Mit Kommentar. Springer, Berlin, Heidelberg

Sondhaus L (2011) World War One: the global revolution. Cambridge University Press, Cambridge

Stephan F (2018) The first genocide of the 20th century before a domestic court, A New York Court about to decide on its jurisdiction in Rukoro et al. v. Germany. Völkerrechtsblog, 28 May 2018. https://voelkerrechtsblog.org/de/the-first-genocide-of-the-20th-century-before-a-domestic-court/. Accessed 1 December 2023

Tehlirian S (1993) S. Tehliryan, Memoirs (original in Armenian, Վահան Մինախորեան, Սողոմոն Թեհլիրյան, վերհիշումներ, Թալեաթի ահաբեկումը-, 1993). Հայաստանի ԳԱԱ Հրատարակչություն, 1993, University of Michigan

Vardanyan V (2017) The Armenian genocide and its influence to the development of Rafał Lemkin's concept. In: Bieńczyk-Missala A (ed) Civilians in contemporary armed conflict. Rafał Lemkin's heritage. Wydawnictwa Uniwersytetu Warszawskiego, Warszawa, p 249

Volkmann C (2009) Die Strafverfolgung des Völkermordes nach dem Weltrechtsprinzip im internationalen Strafrecht und im Völkerstrafrecht. Peter Lang, Frankfurt am Main et al.

Von Sanders O (1920) Fünf Jahre Türkei. Scherl, Berlin

Wemmers JA (1996) Victims in the criminal justice system. Kugler, Amsterdam

Yeghiayan V (1990) The Armenian Genocide and the trials of the Young Turks. American Armenian International College Press, La Verne, Calif

Zimmermann R (1996) The law of obligations. Oxford University Press, Oxford

Gurgen Petrossian LL.M. is a Senior Officer for International Criminal Law at the International Nuremberg Principles Academy and Lecturer at Friedrich-Alexander Erlangen-Nuremberg University. He consulted one of the largest German textile companies on German Due Diligence Act. He holds a Master degree in Law from Heidelberg University and a Bachelor degree in Law from Yerevan State University. He completed his PhD from the University of Erlangen-Nürnberg in 2018. Dr. Petrossian has successfully led and completed funded research projects on '*Victims before International Criminal Court*' and '*Length of the Proceedings at the International Criminal Court*'. His research interests lie mainly in international law, international criminal law and human rights. From 2016–2019 he was the one of the main organisers of the 'Nuremberg Moot Court' law competition. He has provided assistance to the Republic of Armenia and the Iraqi Kurdistan Autonomous Region on incorporating international criminal law into their respective legal system. He is the president of German-Armenian Lawyers' Association.

The Nuremberg Principles from Historical, Philosophical, and Contemporary Legal Perspectives

Adam Bosiacki

Abstract The procedures in Nuremberg and elsewhere for the prosecution of National Socialist acts of violence are now generally recognized as fair, despite a few critical points. In addition to the principle of criminal liability for international crimes, the basics of criminal proceedings were also developed in Nuremberg. However, these principles were never applied to communist crimes. This article discusses attempts to deal with human rights violations by the communist systems in the former Eastern Bloc countries, especially with the help of the EU. In the end it has to be stated that the decommunization process was not really carried out.

1 Contemporary Impact of the Nuremberg Principles

The 20th century turned out to be a century of totalitarian systems, which Alexis de Tocqueville rightly predicted[1] constituted despots, comparable only to the criminal components of antiquity. Fascism, National Socialism, and finally Communism have

[1] Alexiy de Tocqueville, *De la démocratie en Amérique*, 12th ed, Paris 2012, part IV, chapter VI: *Je veux imaginer sous quels traits nouveaux le despotisme pourrait se produire dans le monde : je vois une foule innombrable d'hommes semblables et égaux, qui tournent sans repos sur eux-mêmes pour se procurer de petits et vulgaires plaisirs, dont ils remplissent leur âme. Chacun d'eux, retiré à l'écart, est comme étranger à la destinée de tous les autres, ses enfants et ses amis particuliers forment pour lui toute l'espèce humaine ; quant au demeurant de ses concitoyens, il est à côté d'eux ; mais il ne les voit pas ; il les touche et ne les sent point ; il n'existe qu'en lui même et pour lui seul, et s'il lui reste encore une famille, on peut dire du moins qu'il n'a plus de patrie.*

Au-dessus de ceux-là, s'élève un pouvoir immense et tutélaire, qui se charge seul d'assurer leurs jouissances, et de veiller sur leur sort. Il est absolu, détaillé, régulier, prévoyant et doux. Il ressemblerait à la puissance paternelle, si, comme elle, il avait pour objet de préparer les hommes à l'âge viril ; mais il ne cherche, au contraire, qu'à les fixer irrévocablement dans l'enfance ; il aime que les citoyens se réjouissent, pourvu qu'ils ne songent qu'à se réjouir. Il travaille volontiers

A. Bosiacki (✉)
University of Warsaw, Warsaw, Poland
e-mail: abosiacki@wpia.uw.edu.pl

M.-E. Geis et al. (eds.), *Dealing with Totalitarian Regimes and Human Rights*, Interdisciplinary Studies in Human Rights 11,
https://doi.org/10.1007/978-3-031-57338-5_3

offered a selection in modern times of crimes, but also of social devastation on the huge charter predicted in modern times, from the time of the Jacobin terror, which in the 20th century was made possible by the development of technology. Genocide, crimes against humanity, and war crimes were also committed in the name of criminal ideologies, the indexes of which were set on the belief in the hegemony of one state, nation, and race, and the other on absolute egalitarianism and the belief that people could be liberated from poverty and deprivation by equating all in property and one common ideology. Italian fascism, German national socialism, and Soviet communism are just such social ideologies and doctrines. The first two of them were condemned after the defeat of the German Reich and fascist Italy in 1945. Communism in Europe survived not only until the collapse of the USSR—formally in 1991—but also as the only totalitarian system that went through an evolution in its life. It has the ability to show the "right" face after the elimination and building of a new system, and, implicitly, created a post-communist system in many countries after the fall of communism. They do not disguise themselves to overcome many of its mutants. Nowadays, the key concerns are the impossibility of building a stable civil society in these countries and the formation of a market economy more than 30 years after the uprising of the peoples of 1989. We cannot forget that there are still states in the world that practice genocidal practices.

This chapter will present attempts to work out the principles of overcoming communism in the context of punishing the perpetrators of crimes committed by the officials of the regime in the name of communist ideology, similar to the Nuremberg trials and the Tokyo trials, or more broadly the Nuremberg Principles that could be used in this case.

à leur bonheur ; mais il veut en être l'unique agent et le seul arbitre ; il pourvoit à leur sécurité, prévoit et assure leurs besoins, facilite leurs plaisirs, conduit leurs principales affaires, dirige leur industrie, règle leurs successions, divise leurs héritages ; que ne peut-il leur ôter entièrement le trouble de penser et la peine de vivre ? C'est ainsi que tous les jours il rend moins utile et plus rare l'emploi du libre arbitre ; qu'il renferme l'action de la volonté dans un plus petit espace, et dérobe peu à peu à chaque citoyen jusqu'à l'usage de lui-même. L'égalité a préparé les hommes à toutes ces choses ; elle les a disposés à les souffrir et souvent même à les regarder comme un bienfait.

Après avoir pris ainsi tour à tour dans ses puissantes mains chaque individu, et l'avoir pétri à sa guise, le souverain étend ses bras sur la société tout entière ; il en couvre la surface d'un réseau de petites règles compliquées, minutieuses et uniformes, à travers lesquelles les esprits les plus originaux et les âmes les plus vigoureuses ne sauraient se faire jour pour dépasser la foule ; il ne brise pas les volontés, mais il les amollit, les plie et les dirige ; il force rarement d'agir, mais il s'oppose sans cesse à ce qu'on agisse ; il ne détruit point, il empêche de naître; il ne tyrannise point, il gêne, il comprime, il énerve, il éteint, il hébète, et il réduit enfin chaque nation à n'être plus qu'un troupeau d'animaux timides et industrieux, dont le gouvernement est le berger.

J'ai toujours cru que cette sorte de servitude, réglée, douce et paisible, dont je viens de faire le tableau, pourrait se combiner mieux qu'on ne l'imagine avec quelques unes des formes extérieures de la liberté, et qu'il ne lui serait pas impossible de s'établir à l'ombre même de la souveraineté du peuple.

Established in 1945 on the initiative of the four victorious "powers"[2] of France, the USA, Great Britain, and the USSR, the International Military Tribunal with its seat in Berlin as a judicial body, of course, was aimed at trying the main war criminals of the German Reich from World War II, accused of war crimes, crimes against peace and against humanity (a similar court for the Far East was established a year later).[3] In the first and most important trial of the leaders of the German Reich, held in Nuremberg, the tribunal worked from 20 November 1945 until the judgment was announced on 1 October 1946 (Military Tribunal for Far East ruling until 1948), and then, as is known, its jurisdiction was extended over time. Accordingly, 12 additional trials were held,[4] including a separate trial of doctors and lawyers, as a result of which 185 people were indicted.

In addition to the criminal law, the Nuremberg trials, especially the first of these trials, were symbolic in character, judging the crimes of the Nazi system but also the members of the German elites who had been proven to have committed these crimes in their various forms of accountability (including, in particular, directing perpetration and superior responsibility).

From today's point of view, there is no doubt that the Nuremberg trials and the Tokyo trials were fair in essence. This conclusion was not changed by incidents during the trials best known from today's perspective, such as attempts by the USSR to put the responsibility for the Katyn massacre on the Germans, or participation of a judge in the Soviet delegation who had a very infamous past, similarly to the later long-time Prosecutor General of the USSR.[5] The democratic states also resisted pressure from the USSR to impose the death penalty on all defendants.[6] Thus, an undeniable belief prevailed that the main trial and subsequent trials were legal and conducted in a reliable manner not only on the basis of generally accepted principles of international law, but in addition pursuant to the so-called London Charter or Nuremberg Charter adopted at the Four Powers Conference in London on 8 August 1945, in which the issues of dispute were agreed on and the International Military Tribunal was established. Amplified through the United Nations Charter signed on 26 June 1945, which entered into force almost a month before the start of the main

[2]This term could have been, although it was not, already obsolete then, in accordance with the de jure proclaimed since the 1920s in normative acts adopted within the League of Nations, the concept of equality of states in international relations.

[3]It is also worth noting that there was no separate court for the crimes committed by the Italian fascists who ruled the country in 1922–1943.

[4]The subsequent proceedings were conducted according to the legal system of the United States (person vs. USA).

[5]As indicated, a judge on behalf of the USSR at the first and most important trial was Iona T. Nikitchenko (1895–1967), deputy chairman of the Military Chamber of the Supreme Court of the USSR. judge at the first (1936) and third (1938) Moscow trial, the prosecutor was Roman Rudenko (1907–1981), in the years 1953–1981 Prosecutor General of the USSR, known to have been part of the NKVD administrative convictions (*troika*) in 1937–1938 on the death penalty in the Donetsk region.

[6]Heydecker and Leeb (1979), p. 105.

trial (24 October 1945). Of course, this did not end the controversy over the retroactivity of the adopted provisions, but nowadays, as already stated, there is no doubt about the honesty of the Nuremberg trials and their basic decisions.[7]

A contrario, it could be argued that failure to judge some Nazi criminals, including the most important functionaries of the German Reich, would be contrary to a fundamental sense of justice or a gross injustice. In this sense, both the Nuremberg trials and the "local" proceedings against Germans or *Volksdeutsche* accused of crimes during the war, often taking place on the basis of separate courts created in these cases, to this day are considered "just," despite the fact that the then issued regulations were also applied to the anti-communist opposition in the territories occupied until 1945 by the German Reich (in this case, the judgments are of course considered "unjust," issued as a result of an abuse of law). The legitimate conviction of a just punishment for Nazi criminals was not changed, therefore, by the commonly used interpretation of the provisions, which obviously stated that the communists, also granted by those in power in many European countries of Central and Eastern Europe since 1944/1945, which should be considered very severe,[8] to be used against Nazi criminals. According to the available knowledge, not one of the judgments passed at that time (in communist Poland, ruled by the Supreme National Tribunal, Najwyższy Trybunał Narodowy, which existed in the years 1946–1948) was annulled, and none of the convicted Nazi criminals have been rehabilitated.

The Nuremberg trials have thus become a symbol of judging criminals who are important or the highest functionaries of a criminal totalitarian system and, above all, the criminal liability of such people. This is the first time that such persons have been accused of committing crimes and this could give cause to hope that crimes of a similar nature would be punished, at least symbolically, in the future. The Nuremberg trials also developed the rules of procedure in such cases (the so-called Nuremberg rules) and the so-called Nuremberg Code. Although not applied for almost 50 years, after the fall of communism in the countries of Central and Eastern Europe and the USSR, the Nuremberg rules and regulations seemed applicable again.

---

[7]It is also worth noting the imposition of lenient penalties for some defendants in the absence of evidence or sufficient evidence of their guilt, in accordance with the principles of humanitarianism and *in dubio pro reo*, applied in criminal law, despite the severity of provisions regarding such crimes in the criminal law systems of individual countries (the United States, USSR, Great Britain and France) at the time.

[8]In Poland it was in particular the Decree of the Polish Committee of National Liberation of 31 August 1944 on the punishment for fascist-Nazi criminals guilty of murdering and tormenting civilians and prisoners, and for traitors of the Polish Nation (Journal of Laws of 1946, no. 69, item 377, as amended), also used against soldiers of the anti-communist underground.

2 Application of the Nuremberg Principles to Communist Crimes

The Nuremberg principles stipulated that international law may penalize acts that have not been prosecuted in the domestic law of individual countries, international law may directly impose obligations on individuals, the state functions performed do not exempt from liability before international criminal courts, acting on orders is not a factor exempting responsibility for the committed acts, the catalog of crimes subject to prosecution will be established by acts of international law (the first such catalog is already found in the statute), or that individuals may be liable for these crimes under international law itself.[9] In the second trial in Nuremberg (of medical doctors, December 1946-August 1947), the so-called Nuremberg Code was established, which, contrary to the name, determines the conditions of admissibility of medical experiments on humans (above all, always with their knowledge and informed consent). All this, as indicated, was an incentive to initiate proceedings against state officials in the future, even though such actions had never taken place before the fall of communism in Europe.

The Nuremberg rules also prompted the establishment of international criminal courts in the 1990s. In particular, the International Criminal Tribunal in The Hague (and its prosecutor) and the International Criminal Tribunal for the former Yugoslavia were established then (1993). They supplemented the well-known International Court of Justice, also established after the war (in 1945), also based in The Hague. Contrary to the Nuremberg Tribunal established in 1945, however, both courts did not condemn the communist ideology or its repressive institutions for almost 30 years, and the International Criminal Court did not conduct spectacular proceedings against communist officials, not to mention the governing bodies of *real socialism* states.

Therefore, one does not need insight to say that the Nuremberg rules and regulations were not applied against the officials of the communist states. Poland is a good example to analyze in this case. Being the leader of the fight to overthrow communism among the countries that were dependent on the USSR as a result of World War II, it is perceived among these countries as a symbol of the fight against communist totalitarianism. A specific model, however, was Germany where, according to the common opinion of the supporters of decommunization,[10] the break with the totalitarian system (first with National Socialism, then with communism) was, in popular opinion, the most consistent.[11] As it turned out, this opinion

[9]UN General Assembly (February 1946).

[10]Kurski and Semka (1992), p. 68: Interview with then Minister of National Defense Jan Parys.

[11]The former Minister of National Defence Jan Parys, previously cited as a consistent supporter of complete decommunization and lustration, said in 1992 that we do not have two armies, as in Germany, one of which can be disbanded and the other will take over its tasks. We must use those people who are; see Kurski and Semka (1992), p. 68. The former minister admitted on the one hand that the officers were mostly ordinary Poles, regardless of whether they had Polish Union Workers

was not fully true, according to the proponents of the break with communism. The German state absorbed the former German Democratic Republic, with the dissolution of all its institutions. Over the years it was pointed out that for obvious reasons this could not be achieved in Poland. Regardless of the objective criteria, many political circles indirectly denied the need to settle accounts with the old system, pointing to a social conflict from the perspective of such solutions. In Poland and the former Soviet bloc countries, the reforms of the 1990s in terms of settling accounts with communism failed. The axis of the conflict were the demands of the so-called lustration and decommunization, which constituted the necessity to eliminate persons from public life who are registered as officials or secret collaborators of the communist secret services (*lustration*), or who performed appropriate leadership functions in the communist party. As an argument in favor of such solutions, the possibility of blackmail by foreign secret services (implicitly mainly Russian) and potential property or social privileges of former communist activists were indicated. The model was based on German solutions after World War II, carried out on the inspiration of the countries that won over the German Reich. As mentioned, lustration and decommunization were not carried out in Poland at that time. In contrast, it took place in Czechoslovakia before its collapse, and later in the Czech Republic and Hungary, as well as in Germany, but as it turned out, it was incomplete everywhere.

3 The Current Issues of *Decommunization*

Contemporary authors point out that decommunization has a broad social character encompassing many elements, ranging from social attitudes towards many institutions in the material sense and ending with formal attitudes towards many current issues of the social system, state system, and normative solutions. In Germany, attempts were made to limit the settlement of the past of the former German Democratic Republic, thus such settlements were not carried out in many respects.

> Two social and political attitudes often converge on this issue. A quarrel over the past, wrote radically the German author, is often a dispute over the future of democracy and its institutions. There are, however, two fundamental attitudes that could be seen in both parts of Germany after 1945. On the one hand, integralists from all political camps, for the sake of social peace, try. In fact, there is an alliance of conservative integralists, leftist conciliators, and Protestant social ethics. Thanks to this, a Bavarian CSU politician (...) can simultaneously oppose the "Wehrmacht exhibition" and demand "chivalry" towards the communist torturers. An SPD politician (...) suddenly discusses Adenauer's integration policy towards the former Nazis and demands an end to the settlement of communist grievances. Leading Protestant columnists (...) demand reconciliation, forgiveness and amnesty. On the other

---

Party (Polish: PZPR) identification cards or not (noting in another place that they were all in the party, which does not mean that they are the same), on the other hand while stating that he dismissed incompetent, discredited people (including members of the so-called Military Council of National Salvation, introducing Martial Law in the People's Republic of Poland on December 12/13, 1981) and who owed their promotion to their career in the party (ibid.).

> side are former opponents and leaders of organizations fighting for civil rights and the politicians who support them. They are looking for an absolute explanation and are not afraid of social conflicts. Due to the fact that neither side has a clear advantage, specific political and legislative decisions are made under the influence of one or the other side.[12]

The cited diagnosis corresponds to the situation of settlements with the communist system and decommunization in Poland. The same attempts were made to work out decommunization at the level of European institutions. In the years 1992–2014, the issues that I defined as decommunization were introduced into the debates of the Parliamentary Assembly of the Council of Europe and in the European Parliament. They investigated in particular the limits of lustration and, in a broader sense, the restoration of the state violated by crimes committed by states and communist officials. These are widely known elements of the so-called restorative justice, such as reparations, restitution, or rehabilitation. This was possible thanks to the opening of the archives of the former communist secret services and the disclosure of former secret collaborators. The comparison of the scope of decommunization, from broad (in Czechoslovakia, defined by the laws of 1991 and 2000), through late (in Hungary and Poland) and apparent (obstructed, in the Baltic states, Romania and Bulgaria), and partial (in Slovenia or Slovakia), is only a typology of a phenomenon that has not yet been fully conducted.[13] At the national level, however, sanctions have been developed for people (including the ban on holding public office for a period of no less than four years) as a result of the so-called lustration (discussed in more detail in another chapter). The declarations and recommendations resulting from the discussion on the international forum, which are semi-imperative regulations and therefore require the application of specific solutions, have only been defined in general terms in the case of decommunization.[14]

By contrast, at the level of national legal order many countries have developed concepts that make it possible to prosecute the perpetrators of a crime. The starting point was constitutional regulations. The current constitution of the Republic of Poland of 1997 states in particular that the statute of limitations regarding actions connected with offences committed by or by order of public officials and which have not been prosecuted for political reasons, shall be extended for the period during which such reasons existed (Art. 44). Political parties and other organizations whose programs are based upon totalitarian methods and the modes of action of nazism, fascism, and communism, as well as those whose programs or activities sanction racial or national hatred, promote the use of violence for the purpose of obtaining power or to influence the State policy, or provide for the secrecy of their own structure or membership, shall be prohibited (Art. 13). The preamble to the Polish constitution in force also states the existence and functioning of the Third Republic, which shows that, similarly to the times of the partitions of Poland (1795–1918), the state that existed during the communist system (1944–1989) was not a sovereign

[12] Neubert (2001).

[13] Neumayer (2019); reviewed: Bosiacki (2020).

[14] Neumayer (2019); reviewed: Bosiacki (2020).

state that can determine its policy. Granted that, the preamble to the constitution does not have direct legal effects.

Furthermore, a regulation of significant importance in the implications of the Nuremberg law is the development of the concept of communist crimes in the Polish legal order and, above all, the communist crime and its qualified form on a mass scale. The concept of the communist crime was then reiterated in limited form in Hungary, Lithuania, the Czech Republic, Latvia, Bulgaria, and Romania. All these countries submitted proposals for the criminalization of communist crimes at the level of secondary EU law. However, the proposals were rejected by the Commission.[15]

Under Polish law, a communist crime is an act committed by an officer of the communist state against a Polish citizen in the period from November 8, 1917 to July 31, 1990, consisting of the use of repression or other forms of violation of human rights against an individual or group of people, or in connection with their commission, being punishable according to the Polish criminal law in force at the time[16] and with a sentence of not less than three years' imprisonment. Such a law was in particular the Criminal Code of the Republic of Poland of 1932 and the Criminal Code of the Polish People's Republic of 1969. The scope of the hallmarks of a communist crime, however, did not include specific penal acts, most often very repressive, of the communist state. Due to the impediment to punishing communist crimes, they were excluded from the statute of limitations, as well as from the amnesty laws still in use in the Polish People's Republic (the first one was applied in 1947, when the Polish People's Republic did not exist under this name yet).[17]

The time scope of the communist crimes coveres the period from the Soviet aggression against Poland under the pact with Hitler of 23 August 1939, to the enactment of the laws on the police and special services of the Third Republic, as well as the crimes committed against Poles in the USSR until 1939, or the acts committed by the Communist Party of Poland on the territory of the Republic of Poland before that date. It was pointed out that the broad significance of the scope of communist crimes included, for example, participation in the verification committees of employees under martial law (1981–1982) in workplaces, especially journalists, or the forgery of documents to the detriment of other people. Similar arguments were applied by the political forces opposing decommunization to the deprivation of retirement privileges from persons serving in communist bodies of repression (the list of such bodies was much shorter in the act than the catalog of repressive bodies committing communist crimes).[18]

---

[15] Witoń (2020). More in: Neumayer (2019).

[16] Article 2 sec. 1 of the Act of 18 December 1998 on the Institute of National Remembrance - Commission for the Prosecution of Crimes against the Polish Nation.

[17] Koj and Piątek (2010).

[18] The latter included 14 organs of repression in the years 1944–1990 (Article 5 (1) of the Act on the Institute of National Remembrance - Commission for the Prosecution of Crimes against the Polish Nation, Instytut Pamięci Narodowej (1998).

Contrary to the provisions of the Nuremberg laws, the cognition did not cover the organizations of the repression apparatus mentioned in the act, which, unlike in Germany after World War II, were not considered criminal in any country. The number of communist functionaries tried after the change of the political system (and after the entry into force of the Act on the Institute of National Remembrance of 1998) was minimal. This applies to the leading bodies of the communist state who were accused of being the perpetrators of mass communist crimes (the massacre on the Polish coast in December 1970, the massacre at the "Wujek" mine on 16 December 1981, and many others). As well as to the perpetrators of separate political killings, including priests in the 1980s. The attempt to relegate the members of the so-called Military Council of National Salvation backfired in the same fashion, not to mention the unplanned degradation of other officers and generals of the communist armed forces. In 2016–2018, the names of streets, squares and other forms of public space were not fully decommunized in Poland. The abolition of the names of all monuments, streets and squares with communist origins was successful, the remaining names were not changed by local self-governmental units, which had to be done by law and passed to government administration bodies (after 2018). In some places, the names of communist organizations, holidays, and lesser-known communist activists were left behind, some of them were allegedly controversial, others, in contrast, did not refer to such cases.[19] Moreover, the attempts to prohibit former communist officials or secret collaborators from performing functions at universities have failed. On the contrary in the latter case the so-called lustration was undermined (?) in Poland on a large scale (see also below in Part III and Chapter "Polish Property Transformations in the Context of Transitional Justice (Since 1988)" of this volume).

Summing up, it can be said that the large-scale decommunization in the countries of the former Soviet bloc was not carried out. Its individual stages were developed largely thanks to the experience of the so-called Nuremberg principles after World War II. Contrary to the situation in Germany after 1945, in none of the communist countries a spectacular judgment of communist crimes was delivered, starting with the trial of the highest officials of this system, and even a legal condemnation of communist organizations was missing (except for the organs of repression). Formal settlements—apart from the Baltic states—did not take place in the territories of the former Soviet Union.

Fortunately, a departure from the methods and the totalitarian system of government took place. Similarly to Germany, there were obstacles to punishing the perpetrators of the crimes of such a system. Over the more than 30 years the scale of judicially imposed penalties is small, as is the number of people prohibited from

[19]In Warsaw, the issue of retaining the name of *The People's Army Avenue* (Aleja Armii Ludowej), the armed organization of Polish communists in the years 1944–1945, is particularly famous, instead of replacing it with the street of Poland's President, Lech Kaczyński, who died tragically in 2010. The last name was revoked by a final judgment due to procedural reasons by the Supreme Administrative Court. However, as the name of Aleja Armii Ludowej, it continued to exist constantly after 1989.

holding public office. A surprising conclusion is that many political forces, including political parties of modern non-communist countries, take up the defense for the functionaries of the old order and postulate the liquidation of the institution of settlements with communism. This of course influences, at least indirectly, the political culture of the former communist states. Discussions in this area often do not have a legal character, but only a political dimension. Consequently, this discussion penetrates into an area which is no longer the subject of the presented text.

Documents

UN General Assembly (1946) Resolution 3(I), Extradition and Punishment of War Criminals, 13 February 1946, 3(I),

UN General Assembly (1946) Affirmation of the Principles of International Law recognized by the Charter of the Nürnberg Tribunal General Assembly resolution 95(I). New York

Instytut Pamięci Narodowej (1998) The Act on the Institute of National Remembrance – Commission for the Prosecution of Crimes against the Polish Nation, 18 December 1998

References

Bosiacki A (2020) Laure Neumayer: the criminalization of communism in the European political space after the cold war. Polski Przegląd Dyplomatyczny (Polish Diplomatic Review) nr 2/2020:168–171

Heydecker JJ, Leeb J (1979) Trzecia Rzesza w świetle Norymbergi. Bilans tysiąca lat (The Third Reich in the light of Nuremberg. Balance of a thousand years). Książka i Wiedza, Warsaw

Koj E, Piątek P (2010) Zastosowanie amnestii wobec sprawców zbrodni komunistycznych, Instytut Pamięci Narodowej (Application of the amnesty to the perpetrators of communist crimes, Institute of National Remembrance), https://ipn.gov.pl/pl/aktualnosci/602,Zastosowanie-amnestii-wobec-sprawcow-zbrodnikomunistycznych.html. Accessed 1 December 2023

Kurski J, Semka P (1992) Lewy czerwcowy. Editions Spotkania, Warsaw (The Left June, an interview with the then Minister of National Defense, Jan Parys)

Neubert E (2001) "Dekomunizacja" instytucji politycznych, ("Decommunization" of political institutions). Ośrodek Myśli Politycznej, Polish edition http://www.omp.org.pl/artykul.php?artykul=105. Accessed 1 December 2023 (text published in Poland in: Kuglarz P (ed) (2001) Od totalitaryzmu do demokracji (From totalitarianism to democracy). Ośrodek Myśli Politycznej, Krakow)

Neumayer L (2019) The criminalization of communism in the European political space after the cold war. Routledge, London, New York

Witoń D (2020) Komisja odrzuca projekt penalizacji negacji zbrodni komunistycznych (The Commission rejects the project to penalize the negation of communist crimes)

Adam Bosiacki is a full professor at the University of Warsaw, Faculty of Law and Administration, Chair of the Department of Political and Legal Doctrines. Editor-in-chief of the semi-annual journal Warsaw University Law Review, advocate. Collaboration with some Polish and foreign academic universities (Hoover Institution at Stanford University CA, with his individual web side, University of Zurich, Friedrich-Alexander University Erlangen-Nürnberg, formerly Moscow and St. Petersburg). In his research activity, Bosiacki deals with the history of Russia and the USSR, the history of Central and Eastern European law, the history of administration, including local and corporate self-government, the history of legal thought (especially modern), comparative law (mainly public), and the history of science. Author of several monographs and more than a hundred scientific articles, scientific editor of the publishing series and thematic editor and member of the editorial boards of some scientific journals.

Criminal Defence at the Nuremberg Trial of the Major War Criminals: Strategies and Impact

Christoph Safferling and Philipp Graebke

Abstract While there is an abundance of literature on the Nuremberg Trial of the Major War Criminals in general, little has been written on the role of the defence before the International Military Tribunal (IMT). The following is intended as an introduction to the situation of the defence at the Nuremberg Trial of the Major War Criminals. By way of example, some individual biographies and specific situations will be presented in order to convey an impression of the various strategies used and the difficulties the defence counsel had to struggle with. Finally, the most important arguments advanced by the defence counsel are being discussed. This investigation takes into account not only the comments made by defence counsel and other people involved in the trials, using the relevant literature, but it also refers to the official record of the Nuremberg Trials. Furthermore, it evaluates the 100 Minutes of closed sessions in which the Nuremberg judges passed decrees giving direction to the proceedings during the trial.

1 Legal and Factual Framework

1.1 The Legal Provisions

The defendants' rights concerning their defence during the trial were set out in Articles 16 and 23 of the London Charter of the IMT as well as in Rule 2d of the

C. Safferling
Friedrich-Alexander University of Erlangen-Nuremberg, Erlangen, Germany
e-mail: christoph.safferling@fau.de

P. Graebke (✉)
Friedrich-Alexander University of Erlangen-Nuremberg, Erlangen, Germany
e-mail: philipp.graebke@fau.de

M.-E. Geis et al. (eds.), *Dealing with Totalitarian Regimes and Human Rights*, Interdisciplinary Studies in Human Rights 11,
https://doi.org/10.1007/978-3-031-57338-5_4

Tribunal's Rules of Procedure.[1] According to Article 16d of the IMT Charter, each defendant had the right to defend themselves or to have the assistance of counsel.[2] Article 23 of the Charter stipulated that the function of counsel for a defendant could be discharged by any person who was professionally qualified to conduct cases before the courts of his country or by any other person who could be specifically authorised by the Tribunal. Rule 2d of the Rules of Procedure further stated that the Tribunal would designate counsel for any defendant who failed to apply for particular counsel. The same power would be conveyed to the Tribunal where particular counsel requested could not to be found within a period of ten days or was not available, unless the defendant elected in writing to conduct his own defence. Furthermore, only one counsel was permitted to appear at the trial for any defendant, unless by special permission of the Tribunal. While, of course, this numeral restriction can be explained by the large number of defendants and the need to speed up the trial, it also bears eloquent witness to the structural imbalance between the excellently staffed prosecution teams and the 'lone warriors' of the defence.

A total of 27 main defence counsel with 54 deputies and 67 secretaries were employed in Nuremberg,[3] not only for the individual persons indicted, but also for the indicted organisations (Table 1).[4]

1.2 Appointment of Defence Counsel

Contact to defence counsel was established in different ways. In his memoirs, Albert Speer wrote that together with the indictment, he was handed a long list of German lawyers.[5] From their ranks he could choose his attorney, if he had no options of his own. One of the lawyers, Alfred Seidl, in a book published later, described that in October 1945, two American officers had appeared in his offices to deliver the

[1] For biographical details of various defence counsel see Seliger (2015), passim, as well as Scheerer and Lorenz (2006), p. 436, on the biography of Franz Exner. For an analysis of some strategies employed by the defence, cf. Kastner (2005), pp. 67–71 as well as pp. 133 ff., in which the defence is repeatedly addressed. Weinke (2006), pp. 38 f., briefly dwells on individual motives for taking on the defence and believes that she can discern at least "patriotism" and "saving the honour of German soldiers" as motives among the defence counsels. In modern international criminal law, the situation has hardly changed; cf. Robinson (2005), p. 113.

[2] Cf. Harris (1999), p. 24.

[3] Heydecker and Leeb (2003), p. 118.

[4] Cf. the list in TMWC I, p. 5, where, however, only those deputy defence counsel who actually spoke in court are listed.

[5] Speer (1970), p. 511; cf. also Conot (1983), p. 78 and Taylor (1992), p. 132; Lippe (1951), p. 13 states that Dr Siemers was appointed defence counsel for the trial by the British Military Government in Hamburg and by the Hamburg Bar Association. He suggests that the fact that Raeder chose him as his defence counsel was to be attributed solely to the fact that Raeder wanted to be defended by a Hamburg lawyer, ibid. p. 163.

Table 1 Defence Counsel for the Defendants at the IMT

Defence Counsel	Defendant/Organisation
Babel, Ludwig (1881–1952), Nuremberg	SS and SD [defence counsel for the SS and SD until 18 March 1946, defence counsel for the SS until 1 June 1946, Associate counsel for the SS until 27 August 1946]
Ballas, Dr Walter (1887–1969), Essen	Krupp von Bohlen und Halbach, Gustav [until 15 November 1945]
Bergold, Dr Friedrich (1899–1983), Nuremberg	Bormann, Martin
Böhm, Georg (1900–1952), Nuremberg	SA
Dix, Dr Rudolf (1884–1952), Berlin	Schacht, Hjalmar
Exner, Prof. Dr Franz (1881–1947), Munich	Jodl, Alfred
	General Staff and High Command of the German Wehrmacht [until 27 January 1946]
Flaechsner, Dr Hans (1986–1985), Berlin	Speer, Albert
Fritz, Dr Heinz (1902–1992)	Fritzsche, Hans
Gawlik, Dr Hans (1904–1983), Nuremberg	SS and SD [defence counsel for the SD from 18 March 1946]
Haensel, Dr Carl (1889–1968), Freiburg	SS and SD [with H. Pelckmann from 1 April 1946]
Horn, Dr Martin (1911–1960), Munich	von Ribbentrop, Joachim [from 5 January 1946]
Jahreiss, Prof. Dr Hermann (1894–1992), Cologne	Jodl, Alfred
Kauffmann, Dr Kurt (1902–1993)	Kaltenbrunner, Ernst
Klefisch, Dr Theodor (1880–1951), Cologne	Krupp von Bohlen und Halbach, Gustav [until 15 November 1945]
Kranzbühler, Navy Judge Otto (1907–2004), Hamburg	Dönitz, Karl
Kraus, Prof. Dr Herbert (1884–1965), Göttingen	Schacht, Hjalmar
Kubuschok, Dr Egon (1902–1981)	von Papen, Franz
	The Reich Cabinet
Laternser, Dr Hans (1908–1969), Wiesbaden	General Staff and High Command of the German Wehrmacht [from 27 January 1946]
Loeffler, Dr Martin (1905–1987)	SA
von Lüdinghausen, Dr Otto Freiherr, Berlin (1881–1948)	von Neurath, Constantin
Marx, Dr Hanns (1882–1973)	Streicher, Julius
Merkel, Dr Rudolf (1905–1987), Nuremberg	Gestapo
Nelte, Dr Otto (1887–1957)	Keitel, Wilhelm

(continued)

Table 1 (continued)

Defence Counsel	Defendant/Organisation
Pannenbecker, Dr Otto (born 1907) Düsseldorf	Frick, Wilhelm
Pelckmann, Horst (1904–1975)	SS and SD [associate counsel for the SS until 27 August 1946, defence counsel for the SS from 1 June 1946]
von Rohrscheidt, Dr Günther (born 1888)	Heß, Rudolf [until 5 February 1946]
Sauter, Dr Fritz (1884–1958), Munich	Funk, Walter
	von Ribbentrop, Joachim [until 5 January 1946]
	von Schirach, Baldur
Schilf, Dr Alfred (1901–1972)	Fritzsche, Hans
Seidl, Dr Alfred (1911–1993), Munich	Heß, Rudolf [from 5 February 1946]
	Frank, Hans
Servatius, Dr Robert (1894–1983), Cologne	Sauckel, Fritz
	Leadership Corps of the National Socialist German Workers' Party [Nazi Party]
Siemers, Dr Walter (1902–1990)	Raeder, Erich
Stahmer, Dr Otto (1879–1968)	Göring, Hermann
Steinbauer, Dr Gustav (1889–1961), Vienna	Seyß-Inquart, Arthur
Thoma, Dr Alfred (born 1887), Nuremberg	Rosenberg, Alfred

request by several defendants to be represented by the owner of the law firm, Dr Fritz Sauter.[6]

The appointment of defence counsel, however, did not only depend on the wish of the defendants and the consent of the requested lawyers.[7] The tribunal also had to agree to the admission of a defence counsel.[8] The Russian judges, in particular, adopted a very critical view of the fact that some of the defence counsel had been members of the NSDAP (National Socialist Workers' Party),[9] but in a closed

[6]Seidl (1988), pp. 26–27.

[7]Kraus (1964), p. 233 writes that it was suggested to him that he could be forced to take over the defence of Kaltenbrunner or Streicher, this did not in fact happen; some lawyers flatly refused to represent any of the defendants. Thus, reports say that Munich lawyer von Scanzoni, who had emigrated to Switzerland simply did not react to the request by nine defendants to take over their defence so that they had to look for defence counsel elsewhere; cf. Conot (1983), pp. 81–84; Taylor (1992), p. 132.

[8]Which, for example, did not happen when Rosenberg requested to have his co-defendant Frank as defence counsel, Minute No. 20 (31 October 1945); cf. also Conot (1983), p. 83 f.

[9]Figures concerning this vary: while Minute No. 38 (17 November 1945) speaks of eight defence counsel who were thus burdened, Czapski (1946), talks about six defence counsel, and according to

session,[10] the opinion of the remaining judges prevailed that these, too, had to be admitted as defence counsel, pursuant to Article 23 of the London Charter.[11]

From a strategic point of view, it would certainly have been sensible to appoint a lawyer with experience in the Anglo-American trial tradition, at least to support the leading defence counsel. In a later trial, Alfried Krupp attempted this. However, he did not succeed.[12]

1.3 Relationship to the Defendants

The relationships of the defence counsel to their respective clients varied greatly. On the one hand, quite constructive relations developed. Thus, it is reported that Frank said his legal counsel was 'priceless'.[13] Speer, too, described[14] his defence counsel as a circumspect, tactful lawyer who displayed a sensible, unhistrionic attitude. In addition, Speer stated that his counsel felt sympathy towards him out of which a real mutual affection developed which lasted far beyond the end of the trial. Correspondingly, Viktor Frh. von der Lippe, who assisted Dr Siemers in the defence of Raeder, described the latter as the most agreeable client imaginable.[15]

There were also various changes of defence counsel. Seidl, who later defended Rudolf Heß, did not make any explicit statements about his client's reasons for changing counsel, but expressed the opinion that Heß had not been able to establish an 'inner relationship' to his assigned counsel.[16]

Taylor (1992), p. 627, the number was at least 14. At a press conference held by defence counsel on 24 November 1945, this question was deemed irrelevant and not answered, Lippe (1951), p. 37.

[10]The *Minutes* of these closed sessions can be accessed in the library of the Peace Palace in The Hague but have not yet been published. The documents were available to the authors in digital form at the Research and Documentation Centre for War Crimes Trials of the University of Marburg.

[11]Cf. Minute No. 28 (13 November 1945), then Minute No. 38 (17 December 1945); cf. also Conot (1983), p. 83; Gründler and Manikowsky (1967), p. 99.

[12]Cf. Kronstein (1953), pp. 139, 142; cf. also Taylor (1953), p. 197 ff.; Taylor writes that Krupp's request for this lawyer came too late, and he had been unavailable for other reasons. In addition, he underlines that von Buelow and von Weizsäcker had been defended by American lawyers. Also in late February 1946, six defence counsels requested the assistant of an American lawyer to advise them on questions of Anglo-American law, Minute No. 60 (4 March 1946), Lippe (1951), pp. 121, 147. In addition, Dönitz requested that a British or American submarine admiral defend him in case Kranzbühler could not be reached, Cf. Conot (1983), p. 83.

[13]Gilbert (1947), p. 276.

[14]Speer (1970), p. 511.

[15]Lippe (1951), p. 347.

[16]Seidl (1988), p. 26.

There was, however, also major friction. At the beginning of his hearing, Streicher accused his defence counsel[17] of not having conducted his defence, or of being incapable of conducting his defence according to his, Streicher's, instructions. Dr Marx then explained to the tribunal that he did not want to justify Streicher's anti-Semitism, and hence had lost his client's confidence.[18] He asked the Tribunal to decide whether in these circumstances he was to continue to defend his client. The Tribunal confirmed to Marx that his explanation was in accordance with the traditions of the legal profession and asked him to proceed with the case. When in the further course of the trial, Streicher again viciously attacked his defence counsel,[19] the Tribunal admonished him and told him to stop being insolent and threatened to suspend the hearing of his case.[20]

Overall, it is reported that towards the end of the trial, increased tensions arose between individual defendants and their defence counsel because of the final statements,[21] for example between Kaltenbrunner and Dr Kauffmann. It was reported that von Ribbentrop conducted a regular running battle with his counsel.[22]

2 The Defence in the Course of the Trial

2.1 Question of Joint Defence

First, the question arose as to the areas in which a joint defence might be possible and fruitful. On 19 November 1945, before the proceedings had actually started, the lawyers submitted a motion to the Tribunal (Motion Adopted by All Defence Counsel) in which they stated their joint objections to the proceedings.[23] In this motion, they asked that the Tribunal request an independent legal opinion on the legitimacy of the International Military Tribunal and on the issue of the prohibition of ex post facto legislation.[24] The Tribunal, however—as is known to be quite usual in international trials[25]—relied on its own competence to answer those questions and rejected the motion two days later, with reference to Article 3 of the London Charter.

[17] TMWC XII, pp. 306–307; before the beginning of the trial, Streicher had already declared that he wanted an anti-Semitic lawyer, Taylor (1992), p. 133; Minute No. 17 of 30 October 1945 could also refer to this.

[18] TMWC XII, pp. 306–307; cf. Gilbert (1947), p. 301.

[19] TMWC XII, p. 336.

[20] TMWC XII, p. 336.

[21] Lippe (1951), pp. 46, 364. Conversely, Kauffmann was very disappointed about Kaltenbrunner's final statement, Lippe (1951), p. 477.

[22] Lippe (1951), p. 346.

[23] Text in TMWC I, pp. 168–170; cf. also Harris (1999), pp. 33–34.

[24] TMWC I, p. 170.

[25] Cf. ICTY Prosecutor v. Tadic, IT-94-1, Appeals Chamber Decision of 2 October 1995, Decision on the Defence Motion for Interlocutory Appeal on Jurisdiction.

Apart from this attempt at establishing a joint defence, Professor Jahrreis' statement can be attributed to all defence counsel.[26] In this statement, the Cologne professor of international law objected mainly to the existence of a crime of aggression which might trigger individual responsibility, but, as is well known, he did not manage to convince the judges. A similar statement by Dr Klefisch concerning general legal issues in the trials of the organisations was refused a hearing,[27] but was nonetheless considered by the Tribunal[28] and the prosecution.[29]

Furthermore, individual defence counsel were commissioned to deal generally with specific specialist legal fields.[30] Other than this, despite frequent defence counsel meetings, usually in the evenings,[31] there was hardly any serious cooperation.

At all events, a joint approach became increasingly difficult in the course of the trial, when arguments and strategies, even fundamental interests of the individual defendants started deviating or even turned out to be mutually contradictory.[32] Each defence counsel had to take into account his own client. Thus, Schacht outrightly rejected any common cause with Göring. Such conflicting interests showed up even more clearly, when e.g., Hans Bernd Gisevius, a witness we will come back to later on, on the one hand was summoned for the defence of Schacht and Frick, and on the other hand, during his hearing,[33] very seriously incriminated Göring.[34]

This issue was summed up by one of the Nuremberg defence counsels, when, after a colleague's suggestion to organise a joint approach by all defence lawyers, he laughed and replied: 'By the time we get such a joint action together, the trial will be over. Here, you can only get somewhere on your own!'[35]

2.2 *Selected Defence Counsel and Their Strategies*

On 8 March 1946, when the prosecution had finished presenting its evidence, the hearing of witnesses for the defence began. In particular, the defendants, who

[26]Cf. TMWC XVII, p. 458; Lippe (1951), p. 67 and Harris (1999), p. 522.

[27]TMCW XXI, p. 175; for content cf. Lippe (1951), pp. 444–445.

[28]TMWC XXI, p. 175.

[29]In its reply, the prosecution makes concrete reference to this statement, TMWC XXII, pp. 197 f.

[30]Lippe (1951), pp. 67 and 73.

[31]Lippe (1951), passim.

[32]Haensel (1980), p. 93; also, with numerous examples: Lippe (1951), pp. 22, 46, 130, 136, 140, 143.

[33]TMWC XII, pp. 167 ff.

[34]E.g. TMWC XII, pp. 170 ff.

[35]Quoted in Haensel (1980), p. 113.

according to Anglo-American procedural criminal law were admissible as witnesses,[36] testified on their own behalf.

2.2.1 Hermann Wilhelm Göring

The first defendant to get the opportunity to testify in his defence, between 13 and 21 March 1946, was Hermann Wilhelm Göring. He was indicted on all four counts pursuant to Article 6 of the London Charter: (1) crimes against peace, (2) conspiracy to wage aggressive war, (3) war crimes, and (4) crimes against humanity.[37] Essentially, Dr Otto Stahmer tried to depict Göring as a man who was no typical Nazi, but as someone who had rather joined the 'Movement' as a revolutionary, and not for the sake of its ideology.[38] In particular, he argued that Göring had known nothing about the atrocities and had not supported them either. As far as the war was concerned, he had always tried to prevent it.[39] Göring himself, when talking to Gilbert, even repeatedly doubted the technical feasibility of the Holocaust.[40] He had to dismiss this, however, after the testimony of Rudolf Höß who described the extermination process in Auschwitz concentration camp in great detail.[41]

Among the witnesses summoned by Stahmer, it was mainly Karl Bodenschatz, Göring's former adjutant, and Birger Dahlerus, a Swedish engineer and businessman, who were to contribute to the exoneration of the defendant. Pointing out that in 1939, the German Air Force had not been prepared for the war, Bodenschatz tried to argue that Göring had pressed for negotiations and had even tried to negotiate with England behind the backs of Hitler and Ribbentrop.[42] In other ways as well, he testified that the former 'Reichsmarschall' had been a nice man, that he had made sure that his friends and acquaintances were released from concentration camps, such as the two Ballin married couples who, in 1923, when Göring was wounded during the 'March on Feldherrenhalle', had taken him in from the street and looked

---

[36] Trüg (2003), p. 55; U. S. Supreme Court *Rock v. Arkansas* 483 U.S. 44 (1987). After a closed session, the majority of the Tribunal voted for the defendants' opportunity to testify on their own behalves, Minute No. 58A (20 February 1946), and this decision was then publicly announced by the presiding judge, TMWC VIII, 159–161; earlier on, it had been decided that in the course of the defence of a defendant, any other defendant could testify; cf. also Taylor (1992), p. 321 with further references.

[37] On the counts of the indictment cf. Safferling (2009), pp. 148, 158.

[38] TMWC IX, p. 236 ff.

[39] TMWC IX, p. 675 ff.

[40] Gilbert (1947), p. 251.

[41] On the person of Rudolf Höß and his trial in Poland, cf. Harris (2007); Harris was the first to interrogate Höß as a representative of the US-American prosecution.

[42] TMWC, IX, p. 11.

after him.[43] During the cross-examination, however, Jackson succeeded in proving inaccuracies and contradictions in Bodenschatz's testimony.[44]

Dahlerus was the main witness for the defence. He stated that, immediately before the attack on Poland and at Göring's behest, he had made attempts at negotiating with England.[45] He said that he used his connections in English government circles, in particular with Lord Halifax, and had in the course of these negotiations repeatedly flown from Berlin to London and back. According to him Göring had in fact only wanted access to Danzig and even at the last minute had tried to prevent the outbreak of the war.[46] However, during the following cross-examination, he also stated that Göring had warned him that Ribbentrop might try to sabotage the negotiations or even to shoot down his Dahlerus' plane.[47] Dahlerus described how Hitler had raged like a madman and threatened to annihilate his enemies. He said he had gained the impression that Göring who had witnessed this furious outbreak without turning a hair, was in a state of deranged intoxication.[48]

In the course of his own testimony, Göring mainly pointed out that for military leaders to hold and express an independent opinion would have defied understanding,[49] and that he received his orders from Hitler. He also confirmed that he still remained loyal to him.[50] While Göring had to admit that he had set up the first concentration camps in Prussia, he pointed out that he had already handed these two or three camps over to the SS in the spring of 1934.[51] Whenever evidence was unambiguous, he took responsibility, at least partially, for example, concerning German rearmament,[52] the annexation of Austria[53] and the transport of some clergy to concentration camps.[54] He also conceded that he had already considered the attack on Russia in 1940.[55] In testimony in court, however, he resorted to the statement that he had known nothing about the atrocities committed and that he did not approve of them now. In the matter of the accusation of the art thefts instigated by him, he defended himself with the explanation that he had intended to establish an art collection for the future cultural interests of the state.[56] However, in the issue of the handing over of the Sagan prisoners of war to the Gestapo he had to evade the

[43] TMWX IX, 14, on the Ballin married couples cf. TMWC IX, pp. 19 ff.

[44] TMWC IX, pp. 16 ff.

[45] TMWC IX, pp. 460 ff.

[46] TMWC IX, pp. 465 ff.

[47] TMWC IX, pp. 482 ff.

[48] TMWC IX, pp. 481–482.

[49] TMWC IX, p. 311.

[50] E.g. TMWC IX, p. 440.

[51] TMWC IX, pp. 257–258.

[52] TMWC IX, pp. 279 ff.

[53] TMWC IX, pp. 293 ff.; particularly 454 ff.

[54] TMWC IX, pp. 271–272.

[55] TMWC IX, p. 623.

[56] TMWC IX, p. 327.

question.[57] He could not provide any response to the various pieces of evidence for his support of anti-Semitic measures. In the course of Göring's testimony on 19 March 1946, there was a fierce verbal exchange between Jackson and the defendant; this shall later be dealt with in greater detail.

After Göring's lengthy interrogation, the Tribunal made it clear,[58] that there was to be a change in future procedure. It expressed the view that German history had now been dealt with extensively, and that the Tribunal did not propose to allow any of the other defendants to go over the same ground in their evidence except insofar as it was necessary for their own defence.

2.2.2 Rudolf Heß

Rudolf Heß was also indicted on all four counts. Up until 5 February 1946, Heß was defended by Dr Günter von Rohrscheidt;[59] followed by Dr Alfred Seidl.[60] Heß was one of only two defendants, who did not testify on their own behalf. While Seidl states[61] that this had been due to Heß' negative attitude to the Tribunal, others report[62] that Heß had refrained from testifying at the insistence of Seidl and Göring in order not to be exposed to the embarrassing situation of not being able to answer questions as a result of memory loss.

This memory loss had a procedural prelude, since, on 7 November 1945, Dr von Rohrscheidt had at first stated that the defendant was not fit to stand trial and that, therefore, his client's mental competence first needed to be examined by a neutral expert.[63] In its decision of 24 November 1945, the Tribunal set up a commission to examine the mental fitness of the accused Heß.[64] Following the findings of these experts taken from the victorious nations[65] to the effect that Heß could indeed participate in the hearings, on 30 November 1945, his defence counsel had submitted a request for an additional expert report,[66] the objective being for the proceedings against his client to be suspended due to his inability to stand trial. But when this was discussed during the trial, Heß declared that he had simulated loss of memory for tactical reasons and that now his memory would 'again respond to the outside

[57] TMWC IX, pp. 571–572.

[58] TMWC IX, p. 673.

[59] For further biographical details see also: Seliger (2015), pp. 135 f.

[60] After Dr Stahmer had rejected the defence offered to him by the Tribunal. Cf. Lippe (1951), pp. 111, 117.

[61] Seidl (1988), p. 148.

[62] Gilbert (1947), p. 217; also Lippe (1951), p. 196.

[63] Motion on behalf of defendant Hess for an examination by a neutral expert with reference to his mental competence and capacity to stand trial, in TMWC I, pp. 155–156.

[64] Order of the IMT of 24 November 1945, in TMWC I, pp. 157–158.

[65] Report of commission to examine defendant Hess, in TMWC I, p. 159.

[66] Cf. TMWC II, pp. 478–479.

world'.[67] The psychologist at the Nuremberg court, Gilbert, indeed confirmed[68] the functioning of Heß's memory immediately after this statement, but on 19 January 1946 again observed memory failure in Heß.[69] He gave his opinion that Heß had made his declaration during a short period of recovery and later had not been able to retract without appearing ridiculous.[70] A further request for a renewed examination of the mental competence of the defendant, submitted by Seidl on 31 August 1946, was rejected by the Tribunal on the afternoon of the same day.[71] In its verdict the Tribunal still adhered to its opinion that Heß was indeed fit to stand trial.[72]

Seidl based the defence of his client mainly on the fact that Heß' power had actually been limited and that he had not used the little power he had to act in support of the indicted crimes, but rather had tried to achieve the opposite of those crimes. Thus, for example, he maintained that the 'Instruction of the Civilian Population on the Proper Attitude in Case of Landings by Enemy Aircraft or Parachutists' of 13 March 1940 was not to be understood as a call to commit war crimes, but rather as an instruction to the civilian population to conform with the Hague Convention.[73] With reference to territorial claims made by Germany before the war, he stated that Heß had in no way committed a criminal act. He only referred to the right of self-determination of nations,[74] the Munich Conference[75] and the supposed refusal of Polish Foreign Minister Beck to hold serious negotiations with the German Reich.[76] Furthermore, Seidl contested the jurisdiction of the Tribunal[77] and emphasised the violation of the *nullum crimen* principle, at least with respect to crimes against peace and to conspiracy.[78]

Among the witnesses for Heß, those of particular importance for the defence were Ernst von Bohle, Secretary of State and Gauleiter, and head of the NSDAP Auslands-Organisation (Overseas Branch), as well as Alfred Heß, the defendant's brother. Seidl read out the affidavit sworn by von Bohle,[79] which stated that the only purpose of the Auslands-Organisation of the NSDAP had been 'to hold together in an organised way the approximately 3300 Party members living outside the boundaries of Germany at the time of the seizure of power'.[80] He maintained that the

[67]TMWC II, 496. Cf. also Harris (2007), p. 32.

[68]Report of Prison Psychologist, in TMWC I, p. 166.

[69]Report of Prison Psychologist, in I, 166; Gilbert (1947), pp. 126 ff.

[70]Gilbert (1947), p. 217.

[71]TMWC XXII, p. 395.

[72]Judgment of the IMT, in TMWC I, pp. 171, 284 f.

[73]TMWC XIX, p. 384.

[74]TMWC XIX, pp. 359–360.

[75]TMWC XIX, p. 361.

[76]TMWC XIX, p. 364.

[77]TMWC IX, pp. 692–693.

[78]TMWC XIX, pp. 381–384.

[79]For the way this written statement was used see below, III, 2, d.

[80]TMWC X, pp. 12–13.

organisation had been entirely peaceful, and all its activities had been completely public and legal.[81] This was basically confirmed in the affidavit sworn by Alfred Heß who also pointed out that Heß had always emphasised the necessity of the principle of non-interference with the internal affairs of foreign states and had also enforced this principle.[82]

A reading of the affidavit sworn by Secretary of State Gaus initially failed on account of the Russian prosecutor's veto.[83] Seidl wanted to read out this affidavit because it could provide information about the secret additional protocol to the German-Soviet Non-Aggression Pact of 23 August 1939.[84]

The defence counsel of the Führer's former deputy made considerable efforts to introduce the Treaty of Versailles into the trial, in the form of evidence on the fairness and legal validity of this treaty.

2.2.3 Wilhelm Keitel

Field Marshall General Wilhelm Keitel was indicted on all four counts. He stated that he was a soldier by inclination and conviction,[85] and, although he had hesitated for some time,[86] managed to bring himself to make at least a partial admission of guilt during the trial.[87] Göring commented that Keitel in his defence tactics answered 'each and every one of the charges directly to forestall the cross-examination'.[88]

While placing the main responsibility with Hitler[89] and stating that he had always only followed orders, he nevertheless admitted that he had been aware of the unlawfulness of certain orders.[90] He stated that sometimes he had even protested to Hitler, for example about the shooting of British pilots.[91] Nevertheless, he said that he had always been completely loyal to his commander-in-chief,[92] and tyrannicide would have been unthinkable for him. Among the witnesses, Dr Hans-Heinrich Lammers was of particular importance for the former chief of the Wehrmacht's Upper Command. He supported Keitel's assertion that he had known nothing about Hitler's plans of aggression by stating that Hitler had never talked about war,

[81] TMWC IX, p. 13.

[82] TMWX IX, p. 76.

[83] On this see below III. 2. c.

[84] For further information see: Schulmeister-André (2016), pp. 475–478.

[85] TMWC X, p. 470.

[86] Kempner (1969), pp. 95 ff.

[87] TMWC X, pp. 470–471.

[88] Gilbert (1947), p. 242.

[89] TMWC X, pp. 626–627.

[90] TMWC X, p. 471.

[91] TMWC X, p. 567.

[92] TMWC X, p. 483.

particularly not about preventive war, as a means of achieving foreign political aims.[93]

2.2.4 Ernst Kaltenbrunner

Ernst Kaltenbrunner was indicted on counts 1, 3, and 4. As reported,[94] Dr Kurt Kauffmann clearly wanted to persuade his client to make a confession in view of the overwhelming evidence. Kaltenbrunner, however, insisted on his tactics of constant evasion and denial of all accusations.[95] In the course of his hearing he accepted responsibility for everything that had happened with his 'knowledge',[96] but at the same time denied any knowledge of crimes.[97] If he was to blame at all, as he planned to say in his final statement, he had been swept away by a mightier destiny.[98] Several times he denied his own signature, pointing out that under the aegis of his predecessor, Heydrich, it had been common to automatically create copy signatures of superiors [as facsimile].[99] With reference to the order to kill all the inmates of Mauthausen concentration camp, he claimed to have given the order to surrender the entire camp and all internees to the enemy.[100] He maintained that the so-called 'Special Treatment' had been nothing but a luxury vacation,[101] and that anyway in the Reichssicherheitshauptamt [Reich Main Security Head Office] he had only dealt with Departments III and IV, but by no means with the Gestapo [Secret State Police] and he therefore knew nothing about the extermination process.[102] Kaltenbrunner even claimed that, in October 1944, the persecution of the Jews which he maintained he had only found out about at that time had been completely stopped—on his intervention with Himmler and Hitler.[103]

As far as witness statements were concerned, in view of the testimony of Rudolf Höß who stated that the extermination of human beings had been treated with utmost secrecy and that the death commandos comprised just sixty people,[104] the defence tried to prove that there was hardly a person who had knowledge of this. But of course, Höß was a direct subordinate of Müller who in turn was a direct subordinate of Kaltenbrunner.

---

[93] TMWC XI, 36.

[94] Haensel (1980), p. 139.

[95] Gilbert (1947), pp. 255 f.

[96] TMWC XI, 232.

[97] For example in TMWC XI, 269–270; TMWC XI, 318.

[98] Haensel (1980), p. 153.

[99] For example in TMWC XI, 346.

[100] TMWC XI, 329.

[101] TMWC XI, 338–339.

[102] TMWC XI, 318.

[103] TMWC XI, 275–276.

[104] TMWC XI, 399–400.

During the trial, a letter which Dr Kauffmann had written to the Mayor of Oranienburg was of particular interest for the defence. In this, he had asked for information as to whether everybody in the Oranienburg area had known about the things happening in the concentration camp. The Mayor had then sent his reply to this letter—which had been positive, moreover,—both to the lawyer and to the prosecutor's office. And now in the cross-examination, the prosecution wanted to use precisely this reply against Kaltenbrunner on 13 April 1946.[105] After Dr Kauffmann's objection[106] the Tribunal, however, ruled[107] that the prosecution would not be permitted to use this document.

2.2.5 Hans Frank

On 18 April 1946, Hans Frank entered the witness box. He was indicted on counts 1, 3, and 4. The former Governor General of Poland who had been Hitler's lawyer in the early 'fighting days' and had turned back to his Catholic faith shortly before the trial,[108] showed himself penitent from then on. In particular, when he was arrested, he handed over extremely comprehensive notes to the Allied troops, notes taken by several historians employed by him for just this purpose, his so-called diary.[109] In these documents, all of his activities in the service of the German Reich were very precisely highlighted.

Nevertheless, he too attached great value to justifying himself. He testified that he had never participated in far-reaching political decisions,[110] and that above all he had never been guilty of stealing art treasures.[111] The defence, with the help of Frank's diary, also tried to show Frank's care for the Polish population[112] and his aversion to the creation of concentration camps.[113] Nonetheless, he accepted responsibility for the total sequence of events, in particular for the extermination of the Jews, as a member of the government which in his opinion bore collective responsibility.[114]

Among Frank's witnesses, Dr Josef Bühler in particular, Frank's deputy in the Government General, reported on disputes his superior had had with Himmler and other SS and Police chiefs.[115] He stated that Frank considered resettlement undesirable, if only because it would lead to unrest in the population and a consequent drop

---

[105] TMWC XI, 374–375.
[106] TMWC XI, 375.
[107] TMWC XI, 378; Minute No. 70 (13 April 1946).
[108] Gilbert (1947), p. 19.
[109] On this cf. also below IV. 2. a.
[110] TMWC XII, 6.
[111] TMWC XII, 14.
[112] TMWC XII, 19–20, 22–23.
[113] TMWC XII, 17–19.
[114] TMWC XII, 7, 13.
[115] TMWC XII, 85.

in agricultural production.[116] Furthermore, he stated that Frank had been opposed to the increasing legal uncertainty and the elimination of independent judges.[117] In addition, Bühler made some remarks on the creation of Frank's diaries.[118]

2.2.6 Julius Streicher

Julius Streicher indicted on counts 1 and 4, was admonished several times during the hearing of his case, for example for insulting a witness[119] or, as mentioned above for hostility towards his defence counsel, Dr Marx.[120]

His remarks consisted solely in a denial of guilt. He stated that he was 'predestined by fate to be the apostle of anti-Semitism', and while he admitted having demanded the annihilation of the Jews, he claimed he had not meant this literally.[121] Furthermore, he excused his rabble-rousing as poetic licence[122] and supposedly a wish to seek retaliation for attacks made by the foreign press.[123] He maintained that the synagogues had only been destroyed for 'reasons of urban architecture'.[124]

2.2.7 Hjalmar Schacht

Hjalmar Schacht's hearing started on 30 April 1946. He was indicted on counts 1 and 2. The defence concentrated their efforts on demonstrating his opposition to Hitler. They maintained that he was a patriotic democrat,[125] that he only entered an alliance with Hitler as an expedient for the purpose of setting aside the Treaty of Versailles.[126] He maintained that he had vehemently protested against any anti-Semitic, illegitimate or brutal measures.[127] He testified that it had become clear to him in 1938 that Hitler had betrayed him, that Hitler wanted war[128] and that consequently, he, Schacht, had then played a leading role in the attempt on Hitler's life on 20 July

[116] TMWC XII, 67.

[117] TMWC XII, 82; TMWC XVIII, 132–133.

[118] TMWC XII, 86–87.

[119] TMWC XII, 311.

[120] TMWC XII, 306; TMWC XII, 336; See also above in A. III; for further biographical details also see: Seliger (2015), p. 154f.

[121] TMWC XII, 357, 367.

[122] TMWC XII, 375.

[123] TMWC XII, 314–315.

[124] TMWC XII, 325.

[125] TMWC XII, 419.

[126] TMWC XII, 451.

[127] TMWC XII, 448–450.

[128] TMWC XII, 452–453.

1944.[129] With reference to his Frankfurt speech of 9 September 1936 in which he had claimed 'Lebensraum' [living space] for Germany, he stated that he had been 'solely concerned with the restoration of Germany's colonial rights'.[130] He testified that rearmament, insofar as he had been informed about it at all, had been necessary and justified,[131] for after all Germany's neighbours had refused to disarm as the Treaty of Versailles had stipulated.

The defence was then able to call a surviving resistance fighter of 20 July 1944, Hans Bernd Gisevius, to testify for Schacht. This witness had already been called by Dr Pannenbecker in the course of his defence of Frick and was then questioned by Dr Dix. He effectively confirmed Schacht's oppositional attitude,[132] his contacts to Admiral Canaris and Major General Oster,[133] and his involvement in the events of 20 July.[134]

2.2.8 Karl Dönitz

On the anniversary of the capitulation, Karl Dönitz, indicted on counts 1, 2 and 3, took to the witness box. His defence pointed out that Dönitz had first attained political power on 1 May 1945.[135] They stated that before this time he had been just a soldier and had followed the orders of his supreme commander[136] and that any coup against this commander during a war would always have been considered high treason.[137]

Referring to the accusations concerning naval warfare, i.e. the sinking of ships without warning and the failure to assist those who were shipwrecked, he pointed out on the one hand that the orders relevant to submarine war stemmed from his predecessor, Raeder,[138] and on the other hand that the British and American navies acted in exactly the same way.[139] Also, because the merchantmen were armed, he had had no other choice anyway, unless he wanted to endanger his own crews.[140] Relating to the accusation that he had unduly prolonged the war, he stated[141] firstly, that as a soldier he had been obliged to obey, secondly, that particularly after hearing

[129] TMWC XII, 547–549.
[130] TMWC XII, 430.
[131] TMWC XII, 472.
[132] TMWC XII, 188.
[133] TMWC XII, 195.
[134] TMWC XII, 221.
[135] TMWC XIII, 296.
[136] TMWC XIII, 298–299.
[137] TMWC XIII, 303–304.
[138] TMWC XIII, 253.
[139] TMWC XIII, 254.
[140] TMWC XIII, 255.
[141] TMWC XIII, 306–308.

about the Yalta Conference, it had been his duty to provide some more time for the refugees from the east, and thirdly, that he was confronted with an entirely different situation on 1 May 1945 when the refugees needed only very few days to reach the west, the boundaries of the east and west fronts having moved so much closer together. Admiral Godt testified as a witness for Dönitz, stating that the Commander-in-Chief of the Navy had issued orders that, if possible, survivors of ships sunk by submarine attacks were to be rescued.[142]

The reading of an affidavit sworn by US Admiral Nimitz caused a major stir; this document actually confirmed the defence's claim that the British and American navies had waged their naval war using the same methods as the Germans. In his statement, the Commander-in-Chief of the American navy in the Pacific admitted that American submarines had attacked enemy and neutral merchantmen without prior warning.[143] He also confirmed that no rescue measures were carried out for the passengers and crews of those ships if these measures might have endangered the safety of their own ship.[144] As far as German submarine warfare against enemy merchantmen was concerned, therefore, the *tu-quoque* argument[145] could be applied, convincing the Tribunal that the German navy's practice had been in keeping with international law.[146] As far as submarine warfare against neutral merchantmen was concerned, the violation of international law by one's own actions could not be argued away in the same manner, but at least one could deny the opponent the right to punish these actions. In this aspect too, the *tu-quoque* argument managed to convince the judges.[147] The *tu-quoque* argument was not, however, accepted by the Tribunal beyond this point.[148]

---

[142] TMWC XIII, 534.

[143] TMWC XVII, 378.

[144] TMWC XVII, 379–380.

[145] On the *tu-quoque* principle in international law in general, cf. representative: Verdross and Simma (1984), § 67. In international law the *tu-quoque* principle is not recognised as a general justification but may be taken into account in the context of an equity decision.

[146] Judgement of the IMT, in TMWC I, 171, pp. 311–312; in fact, the Tribunal found that the British armed their merchant vessels, made them attack [enemy vessels] and integrated them in their navy intelligence system, and that therefore in this context Dönitz could not be accused of a war crime for German submarine warfare. The Tribunal might have accepted as proof for the compliance of this behaviour with international law the fact that Nimitz (as quoted) had admitted that the USA had conducted unlimited submarine warfare against the Japanese merchant navy which had proceeded exactly like their British counterpart, since it, the Tribunal, overruling the objections of the prosecution (TMWC VIII, pp. 547–548) and following the defence's arguments (TMWC VIII, p. 549), had admitted the sending out and reading of the interrogatory in order to construe the international law of submarine warfare by determining what actions were taken by the powers during the war, Minute No. 69 (10 April 1946); for the entire topic cf. also Kranzbühler (1949), p. 16; Taylor (1992), pp. 399–401 and 408–409.

[147] Judgement of the IMT, in TMWC I, 171, 313–314; cf. also Kranzbühler (1949), p. 16; Kraus (1947), p. 16; Lippe (1951), p. 516.

[148] Kauffmann (1987), pp. 537, 549, points out that while the "natural sense of justice" would have required the punishment of war crimes committed by the victors, the inclusion of such crimes would have changed nothing in the condemnation of the German defendants in Nuremberg.

2.2.9 Albert Speer

Albert Speer entered the witness box on 19 June 1946; he too expressed penitence. He was indicted on all four counts. In his defence, he stated that it had not been up to him to check what violent measures had been taken to procure his workforce.[149] Furthermore, he stated that in the spring of 1945, he had come out against Hitler who wanted to continue a meaningless fight, and had even planned to assassinate him with poison gas in his bunker.[150] He maintained that he had known nothing of the extermination of the Jews.[151] However, he admitted to an overall responsibility of all government ministers for crimes on such a scale.[152]

2.2.10 Martin Bormann

The case against Martin Bormann was tried in absentia. He was indicted on counts 1, 3 and 4. While today we know with certainty that Borman was already dead at that time, this particular fact had not been established at the time of the trial. When the Borman case was first heard in any substantial manner on 28 May 1946, the defence counsel pointed out his particularly difficult situation. Dr Bergold[153] stated that he had questioned many witnesses but had not been able to find anything exonerating.[154] In his opinion, one main problem was that all other defendants hated Borman and were trying to incriminate him in order to exonerate themselves.[155] Furthermore, he added that his client was probably dead and therefore could not give him any information.[156] In order to take this into account and to give the defence some more time, the Tribunal first postponed the hearing of the Borman case. On 29 June 1946, the Tribunal came back to Borman again. Then Dr Bergold submitted an application for another postponement,[157] pointing out that he wanted to question only the witness Klöpfer, who had just been brought to Nuremberg that morning. Therefore, he did not yet know what this witness would be able to say. The Tribunal, however, adhered to the time schedule and rejected the application.[158] During the same

---

[149] TMWC XVI, 457; Kastner (2001), p. 172.

[150] TMWC XVI, pp. 493–495.

[151] Up until the new millennium the myth of Speer as the "noble Nazi" was upheld in Germany. Heinrich Breloer managed to publicly deconstruct this myth by his film "Speer und Er" ["Speer and He"] in 2005. A complete analysis of Albert Speer's life and his career after his release from Spandau is now available by: Brechtken (2017).

[152] TMWC XVI, 483.

[153] For further biographical details also see: Seliger (2015), pp. 80–82, 183 f., 278 f.; Salleck (2016), pp. 28–32.

[154] TMWC XIV, 569.

[155] TMWC XIV, 569.

[156] TMWC XIV, 569.

[157] TMWC XVII, 246–247.

[158] TMWC XVII, 247.

morning session, Bergold dispensed with this witness, stating that Klöpfer could not testify as to Borman's guilt or innocence.[159]

In fact, Bergold voiced fundamental objections to trying a case in the absence of the defendant.[160] He said that he could only attempt to prove, on the basis of the documents presented by the prosecution, that the defendant did not play the important part that was now attributed to him. As a lawyer, he was, however, opposed to this type of speculation. And anything he could present had to be speculation, since he was unable to find anything positive in the available documents without the assistance of the defendant.[161]

At this point, the defence tendered evidence that Borman was in fact dead. They tried to prove this by calling the witness Kempka. He was Adolf Hitler's former driver and the only available witness to testify to having seen Bormann die. But his statement to have observed Borman's death in an explosion[162] did not manage to convince the Tribunal. Thus, the accusations made by the prosecution against Borman remained ultimately uncontradicted.[163]

2.2.11 Indictments of Organisations

Apart from the individual indictments, the Tribunal also tried indictments of various organisations. The proceedings against the Schutzstaffeln (the SS) of the NSDAP stand out in this respect. However, this can only be dealt with briefly here. These organisations were tried without representatives of such organisations being present.[164] The Tribunal appointed defence counsel, sometimes several of them, for their defence.[165] Apart from Dr Pelckmann, Ludwig Babel[166] was yet another lawyer representing the SS; he will be of further interest later. After his resignation, he was replaced by Dr Carl Haensel.[167]

As the latter reported,[168] following remarks made by French judge Donnedieu de Vabres on 1 March 1946, there had been no doubt that the Tribunal foresaw a

[159] TMWC XVII, 261.

[160] TMWC XVII, 261; Bergold had already submitted an application for terminating the proceedings against Borman due to his absence before the start of the trial on 17 November 1945, and then again on 22 July 1946, which was, naturally, rejected in both cases.

[161] TMWC XVII, 261.

[162] TMWC XVII, 448.

[163] Kastner (2001), p. 177.

[164] Excepting those defendants who were members of the relevant organisations, cf. Art. 9 IMT Charter.

[165] TMWC IV, pp. 1–2.

[166] For further biographical details also see: Seliger (2015), pp. 193–195, 197–199.

[167] For further biographical details also see Seliger (2015), pp. 197f., 274 f., 283–286.

[168] Haensel (1980), pp. 275–276; Lippe (1951), pp. 96–97, 153–155 up to this date reported repeated confusion and lack of clarity for all parties involved concerning the trial of the organisations.

two-part process for the punishment of individual members of organisations. First, the criminal nature of an organisation was to be determined by the Tribunal, and then, a further trial was to check whether individuals had voluntarily joined the relevant organisation and had had knowledge of its criminal goals.[169] In view of the fact that, as the defence stated,[170] the number of SS members ran into millions, they pointed out that in the event that the SS was found to be a criminal organisation, 80 to 90% of the cases then to be expected would have to end with acquittals.[171]

In this context, of course, the problematic question arose as to whether there is a causal relationship between an individual person becoming a member of the SS and their responsibility for this organisation's crimes. Variously during the trial, it had been said that the Führer had given order to 'the SS ... to carry out' the 'final solution of the Jewish question'.[172] It was important, therefore, to obviate individual responsibility being ascribed simply because of SS membership,[173] particularly since this—in a wider sense—also had repercussions for the evaluation of the knowledge the German people as a whole had of these crimes.[174]

After the Tribunal had refused the request for an expert psychological report on mass phenomena,[175] the defence requested that Hermann Rauschning[176] be summoned. The Tribunal refused this request too, pointing out that the witness was now living abroad;[177] the interrogatory sent to him by post was never answered by Rauschning.[178] Furthermore, point 6b of the decision of 12 March 1946[179] restricted the court to summoning only higher-ranking SS officers. Nevertheless, the Tribunal gave the defence permission[180] to visit prisoner of war camps and talk to the arrested

[169] IMT judgement, in TMWC I, 171, pp. 255–257.

[170] TMWC VIII, p. 392; in contrast the prosecution considered any even approximately precise estimate to be impossible, TMWC VIII, 373–374. Cf. also the numbers stated in the judgement, TMWC I, pp. 171, 268–269.

[171] Haensel (1980), p. 276.

[172] Such as in TMWC XI, p. 39.

[173] Haensel (1980), p. 230.

[174] In fact, it was thought after the pronouncement of the judgement that the thesis of collective guilt had anyway been disproved, Haensel (1980), p. 304; Kraus (1947), p. 7; likewise Laternser (1986), pp. 557, 562, who, however also noted that the Tribunal did not explicitly establish this; cf. however likewise Kauffmann (1987), pp. 537, 543, who stated that the IMT refrained from any statement concerning collective guilt. On the guilt principle in the Nuremberg Judgement cf. also Safferling (2009), pp. 161–163.

[175] Minute No. 78 (22 May 1946); cf. also Haensel (1980), p. 278.

[176] TMWC XIX, p. 256.

[177] TMWC XIX, p. 268.

[178] Haensel (1980), p. 279.

[179] Minute No. 63 (12 March 1946), decision was not read out in court. On this cf. Haensel (1980), p. 269.

[180] Minute No. 63 (12 March 1946), point 1 of the decision; cf. also Haensel (1980), p. 218; Kauffmann (1987), pp. 537, 549; Lippe (1951), pp. 172–174 and 226.

SS members. In this manner 136,213 individual and collective affidavits were given.[181]

Witnesses testifying included Dieter Wisliceny and Wolfram Sievers. Wisliceny confirmed that only individual people and not an entire organisation such as the SD had been given the task of exterminating the Jews.[182] Likewise, Sievers greatly narrowed down the group of people who had had knowledge of the medical experiments.[183]

2.3 *Structural and Actual Difficulties of the Defence*

2.3.1 Restrictions Contained Within the Charter

The scope of action for the defence was already materially limited by the Charter for the International Military Tribunal.

2.3.1.1 Article 3

Article 3 of the Charter explicitly prohibited the defence from objecting to one or several judges for reasons of partiality. Thus, any dispute about the critical question of appointments to the judges' bench was ruled out right from the start. It would be worth discussing why only judges from the victorious powers had been appointed to the IMT judges' bench.[184] German judges or judges from neutral countries were not called on.

A further irritant was the fact that four persons who had been involved in the negotiations for the London Charter where now also immediately involved in the trial, namely Justice Robert H. Jackson and Sir David Maxwell-Fyfe as prosecutors, General Iona Nikitchenko as judge and Robert Falco as French alternate judge. It was remarked that this violated the principle of the division of powers and that the independence and impartiality of the judges was not given.[185] In particular, the

[181] Judgement of the IMT, in TMWC I, pp. 171, 172; on this cf. also Haensel (1980), p. 285; Lippe (1951), p. 255.

[182] TMWC IV, pp. 372–373.

[183] TMWC XX, pp. 556–557.

[184] Kastner (2001), p. 216; cf. also Haensel (1963–1964), pp. 248, 259.

[185] This was already pointed out in the motion adopted by all defence counsel of 19 November 1945 in TMWC I, pp. 168, 169–170; Kranzbühler (1949), p. 12; Kranzbühler (1965), pp. 333, 338; Laternser (1986), pp. 557, 564. Kraus (1964), pp. 233, 246 however attested that nevertheless the judges had been impartial; likewise Pannenbecker (1965), pp. 348, 352; Kauffmann (1987), pp. 537, 538 and 550–551, considered the judgement to be pondered and differentiated and stated that there could not have been any other composition of the Tribunal, that it was rather an advantage for the defendants, since in the case of German judges being appointed, the bench would have had to be staffed with opponents of the regime.

USSR judges who were appointed aroused indignation.[186] The defence stated that the defendants were tried for preparing and waging a war of aggression against Poland which, however, had been waged together with the Soviet Union, according to the secret additional protocol to the German-Soviet Non-Aggression Pact. In looking back, Seidl stated that the Tribunal ought to have been dissolved after this fact became known, or ought at least to have closed the proceedings concerning counts 1 and 2 and restricted itself to dealing with ‘genuine’ war crimes.[187]

2.3.1.2 Article 7

Likewise, Article 7 of the IMT Charter excluded any reference to the official position of a defendant within the government of a state, i.e. immunity. Particularly in view of the ‘sovereignty of the princes’, which was deemed of particular importance by the League of Nations, this was of course rather problematic.

2.3.1.3 Article 8

Article 8 of the IMT Charter ruled out any reference to orders from a superior as grounds for exemption from punishment. The defence considered this to be new law which invalidated a hitherto admissible defence plea.[188] When looking back on the trial, however, at least two of the defence counsel stated that the court had in principle acknowledged the possibility of exoneration due to a difficult predicament which had in turn been caused by a command emanating from a superior, only had not considered that any of the defendants had been in such a situation.[189]

2.3.1.4 Article 24(c)

Finally, the defence took exception to Article 24(c) of the IMT Charter which, in contrast to Anglo-American procedural law, granted the prosecution but not the defence the right to make an opening statement.[190] In their opinion, the prosecution had been able to explain its goals to the Tribunal, and therefore the evidence

---

[186] Kastner (2001), p. 218; Pannenbecker (1965), pp. 348, 351–352.

[187] Seidl (1988), p. 198.

[188] Kranzbühler (1949), p. 13; Laternser (1986), pp. 557, 576 ff.

[189] Kraus (1964), pp. 233, 238; Kauffmann (1987), pp. 537, 548.

[190] Cf. e.g. for Britain: Sprack (2008), marginal note 20.57; for the USA in general: Hay (2005), marginal note 623. Likewise this was the procedure in the Yugoslavia Tribunal, according to Rule 84 of the Rules of Procedure and Evidence of the International Criminal Court; cf. the “Opening Statement” in the case Prosecutor v. Thomas Lubanga Dyilo, Case: 01/04-01/06, session minutes of 27 January 2009, ICC-01/04-01/06-T-109-ENG WT 27-01-2009 1/59 NB T. Justly, the defence, before making its opening statement, deplored the fact that the chief prosecutor, after making his

proffered by the prosecution had always been seen in the right context by the judges.[191]

2.3.2 Restrictions Due to Procedural Decisions Taken by the Tribunal

2.3.2.1 Disputes About Closing Statements

On 13 June 1946, the first dispute about the closing statements by the defence arose. Since the taking of evidence took more and more time, thereby lengthening the trial, the Tribunal considered limiting the defence's speaking time, referring to Article 18 of the IMT Charter. The Tribunal considered an overall period of 14 days for all defence counsel as a whole, excluding, however, the statements for the indicted organisations.[192] Dr Nelte,[193] Dr Kubuschok[194] and Dr von Lüdinghausen,[195] in particular, rose to object to this proposal. This time could in no way be sufficient, they maintained, particularly due to the delays caused by the complicated interpreting mechanism, and the time necessary for such closing statements could not be foreseen in advance.

Another political reason for not creating further problems for the defence at this late stage of the proceedings is mentioned by Gilbert when he observes how Göring[196] repeatedly shouted out during the course of the discussions that they [the defence] should let the Tribunal do what they wanted; the German people would then see for themselves how fair this trial was. In this respect, the IMT saw itself under pressure from the public and—to phrase it in modern terms—it was sitting in a 'human rights glass house'.[197] It is not known whether this consideration influenced the Tribunal's decision, but with its decision of 20 June 1946, it ruled that the duration of individual closing statements should be limited to seven hours, i.e. one day.[198]

---

opening statement the day before, failed to attend the proceedings on the day the defence made its opening statement.

191 Laternser (1986), pp. 557, 566; Lippe (1951), p. 59.

192 TMWC XVI, p. 141.

193 TMWC XVI, p. 142.

194 TMWC XVI, p. 144.

195 TMWC XVI, p. 143.

196 Gilbert (1947), p. 377.

197 Lagodny (2001), pp. 800, 823, with reference to the International Criminal court in The Hague and its adherence to human rights.

198 TMWC XVII, pp. 1–2; even in retrospect, Laternser (1986), pp. 557, 567 considered this an extraordinary restriction. Cf. Lippe (1951), pp. 318–319, 322–323, 340 however also thought that the defence counsel had not done well in this question and insofar had got off rather lightly. It should be pointed out that the Tribunal only permitted half a day for the closing statements on behalf of the indicted organisations. TMWC XIX, p. 353 and XX, p. 104.

Dr Alfred Seidl's closing statement was even interrupted by the Tribunal,[199] and all passages referring to the fairness and legal validity of the Treaty of Versailles on the one hand and the legal repercussions of the secret pact between Germany and the Soviet Union of 23 August 1939 on the other hand were deleted.[200] The defence counsel then had to make his closing statement without the objectionable passages.[201] He himself in retrospect called this 'control of substance' a 'restriction of the defence as is probably to be found only very rarely in the history of law'.[202]

2.3.2.2 On the Rules of Cross-Examination

One event which happened on 19 March 1946 during Jackson's cross-examination of Göring was to be of importance for the entire defence. In the course of a heated exchange which had lasted for quite some time, Göring, who often answered the prosecutor's questions in very harsh tones,[203] replied to Jackson's accusation that the German mobilisation measures had been preparing for a war of aggression and had, therefore, been kept secret, that he did not think he could recall reading beforehand about any mobilisation preparations of the United States.[204]

Jackson, who was running the risk of suffering a rhetorical as well as a political defeat at the hands of the former second highest man of the Third Reich, turned to the Tribunal for help,[205] trying to achieve a situation where the defendants should only be permitted to answer with 'yes' or 'no' when under cross-examination and only be permitted to give any further explanations later on when being questioned by their own counsel. Stahmer argued against this by saying that the defendant had in no way intended to make propaganda or make an accusation against the USA, and that Göring's statement had to be seen merely as a reference to the practices of other nations.[206] He stated that this was quite justified since the witness should be given the possibility of giving short reasons for his answers. The Tribunal upheld this argument[207] and continued to give all defendants the possibility of giving a short explanation after their direct answers. Of course, this personal 'victory' of Göring over Jackson was only of short duration.[208] Starting the very next day, Jackson took

[199]TMWC XVII, p. 554.

[200]TMWC XIX, p. 331.

[201]TMWC XIX, p. 353 f.; for further information see: Schulmeister-André (2016), pp. 490–492.

[202]Seidl (1988), p. 195; Lippe (1951), p. 401 talks of pre-censoring; Kauffmann (1987), pp. 537, 549, however, states that, quite apart from the question of the closing statements, overall the defence had not been restricted by the Tribunal.

[203]Kastner (2001), p. 138; Lippe (1951), p. 181.

[204]TMWC IX, p. 507.

[205]TMWC IX, p. 507 ff.

[206]TMWC IX pp. 511–512.

[207]TMWC IX, p. 512.

[208]Kastner (2001), p. 139.

to quoting from documents so that Göring was occasionally refuted by his own signature. For the defence in general, however, the impression of a weakening chief prosecutor remained.

2.3.2.3 Submissions of Evidence to the Prosecution

When on 23 February 1946 the Tribunal decided[209] that, to save time, any exonerating evidence should first be submitted to the prosecution for comment, a threat which had already existed for quite some time now became more concrete:[210] that the evidence proffered by the defence would be unjustifiably rejected as irrelevant. Dr Horn[211] in particular, Ribbentrop's defence counsel, objected to this strongly.[212] He argued that the defence had not yet been able to question some of the witnesses and therefore often did not know themselves what a witness would be able to contribute. The Tribunal did then make some concessions to the defence.[213] They stated that they would act in a very liberal way in allowing evidence, as they had already acted very liberally in this respect anyway. The formal obstacle of having to inform the prosecution in advance remained though.

2.3.2.4 The Role of Affidavits

The extensive use of affidavits was a further peculiarity of the trial in Nuremberg. Clearly, the presenting of such sworn statements instead of questioning witnesses would present a problem with regard to the principle of immediacy. On the one hand, such affidavits were used when witnesses were to be questioned but were too far away from Nuremberg, on the other hand, if their testimony would be less relevant for the judgement, in order to avoid long oral testimonies.[214]

When on 28 November 1945 a fierce dispute arose about the admissibility of this approach, the Tribunal, after a short deliberation and with reference to Article 19 of

[209] TMWC VIII, pp. 159 ff.

[210] The prosecution had already made a similar suggestion to the Tribunal on 11 February 1946, but the first point of this had been rejected in a closed session on 16 February 1946, minute No. 56 (16 February 1946), the remaining points in the session of 21 February 1946, minute No. 59 (21 February 1946). These decisions were made public on 18 February 1946, TMWC VII, p. 567, and on 23 February 1946, TMWC VIII, p. 159; cf. Taylor (1992), pp. 321–322; Lippe (1951), pp. 131 f. Nevertheless, the Tribunal, immediately after refusing this request by the prosecution proclaimed the decision which is of interest here.

[211] For further biographical details see also: Seliger (2015), pp. 168, 319.

[212] TMWC VIII, pp. 161–163.

[213] TMWC VIII, p. 163.

[214] On this cf. also Pannenbecker (1965), pp. 348, 352–353, who considers this approach by the Tribunal as well balanced and striving for fairness; Lippe (1951), pp. 35, 43 f., 64 f.; Taylor (1992), pp. 241 ff.

the IMT Charter, decided to permit the presentation of affidavits in principle, while compared to a testimony given under cross-examination, they were to be given a different probative value. In addition, the Tribunal stated that the defence could apply to summon the witness according to the usual regulations and, if the Tribunal permitted this summons, question this witness at the appropriate time.[215] Dr Kubuschok had argued that an affidavit did not have sufficient probative value to be admitted as evidence, if the witness whose statement it contained was alive and could be reached by the Tribunal.[216] The prosecution, however, believed that, despite its inherent weakness, the reading of an affidavit was admissible, and that the Tribunal could then decide on its view of the evidential value of this statement.[217] However, in this particular concrete case, the affidavit concerned had been sworn by the 70-year-old American ambassador to Mexico, resident in Mexico City who indeed seemed not to have been reachable by the Tribunal.

In fact, during the afternoon session of the same day, the Tribunal, after some deliberation, refused the prosecution's reading of an affidavit sworn by the former Austrian chancellor, Kurt von Schuschnigg, after the defence pointed out that Schuschnigg had been questioned in Nuremberg only nine days previously and therefore must also be easy to reach now.[218] In a closed session at the end of the day in which Robert Jackson as a representative of the prosecution and Rudolf Dix as a representative of the defence counsel took part, it was agreed to consider these matters further, but that a decision would not be made at this time.[219]

But by 14 December 1945 at the latest, the whereabouts of a witness was no longer considered to be the decisive criterion for the admissibility of the reading of an affidavit. The defence had requested the Tribunal to generally prohibit the reading of affidavits in the course of the hearing of evidence for the indicted crimes against humanity, if the relevant witness was resident in Germany and was able to appear in court. They pointed out that maybe several months would pass until a potentially imprecise statement could be corrected by summoning a witness; and that this period of time was particularly crucial, since until this time the Tribunal remained influenced by a statement dealing with the tortured lives and deaths of people, and that for this reason alone the statements would affect everyone deeply.[220] In this case the interest of a speedier trial would have to take second place to the interest of establishing the truth.[221] At the start of the afternoon session, the Tribunal denied the defence's motion and at the same time permitted the reading of two affidavits, one of which contained the testimony of a prisoner kept in custody in Nuremberg.[222]

---

215 TMWC II, pp. 350–351.

216 TMWC II, p. 350.

217 TMWC II, p. 350.

218 TMWC II, p. 385.

219 Minute No. 43, (28 November 1945).

220 TMWC III, p. 542.

221 TMWC III, p. 548.

222 TMWC III, pp. 571–572.

In the further course of the trial, as presumably has become clear from the presentation of the individual examples, the defence too learnt how to make use of the instrument of affidavits to introduce statements into the trial.

2.3.2.5 On the Necessity to Read Out Documents

A further problem, closely related to the one above, consisted in the threat of a restriction to the principle of oral proceedings. While the Charter prescribed an oral trial, it also contained, in Article 18, the obligation for the Tribunal to accelerate the proceedings. Reacting to a presentation of evidence which was dragging on longer and longer, Justice Jackson made the suggestion[223] on 22 March 1946 that in the interest of time the documents which were already translated into all four trial languages should be taken as read, without being read out in open court. Pointing out that the prosecution's documents had been read out in court for months, the defence objected to this procedure which they considered unfair.[224] At the beginning of the afternoon session, the Tribunal declared[225] that whenever a document was introduced, introducing counsel 'could summarize it or otherwise call its relevance to the attention of the Tribunal, and read such brief passages as were strictly relevant or deemed important'. In addition, any objection to documents submitted would be heard. In this context, the Tribunal also confirmed the abovementioned obligation for the defence to make any exonerating evidence known to the prosecution in advance.

2.3.2.6 The Legal Status of the Treaty of Versailles

Another decision which posed problems for the defence was the Tribunal's decision[226] that evidence concerning the injustice and legal validity of the Treaty of Versailles was inadmissible. This issue was first raised in the context of the prosecution's objection[227] to volume III of the documents for the defendant Heß. In this, Dr Seidl had collected a number of statements by foreign statesmen, economists and others concerning the genesis of this treaty. The prosecution insisted that the problems concerning the conditions of this treaty were irrelevant as evidence for the Tribunal.[228] Seidl then explained[229] that by using these documents he wanted to establish a *culpa in contrahendo* of the opposite side, i.e. the non-compliance of the

[223] TMWC IX, p. 658 f.

[224] TMWC IX, pp. 661 ff.

[225] TMWC IX, p. 673.

[226] TMWC X, p. 90.

[227] TMWC X, pp. 79 ff.

[228] TMWC X, pp. 78 ff.

[229] TMWC X, pp. 81 ff.

opposite side with the treaty and the causal link between the treaty and the alleged conspiracy. Since the prosecution had repeatedly referred to violations of the treaty with reference to the point of conspiracy, the relevance of documents concerning the treaty had all the more to be acknowledged for the defence, too.[230] In addition, Dr Dix argued[231] that regarding the subjective aspect of the facts of the case, in particular, these statements were important, for a defendant might have engaged in rearmament acting out of pure and decent beliefs, which in many cases were also held abroad. The Tribunal, however, would not be convinced and after a closed session proclaimed its abovementioned decision. At the same time, it rejected volume III of the documents submitted for Heß.

2.3.3 Difficulties Arising from the External Circumstances of the Trial

2.3.3.1 The Application of Common-Law Procedures

The German defence counsel also had problems with the adversarial system employed in the Tribunal. On the one hand, they were simply not used to it, on the other it further strengthened the prosecution's already stronger position.[232] Although the Anglo-American system demands equality of arms between prosecution and defence, it does not, like the German system, oblige the prosecution to objectivity in the sense of a proactive search for exonerating evidence.[233] This had particularly negative repercussions for the defence, since, in spite of several applications, they were not permitted access to the archives of documents held by the prosecution.[234] The Tribunal adhered to this decision right through to the end.[235] This was felt all the more strongly in a document trial, such as that before the IMT, and considering the pre-determined restriction to allow strictly German evidence only, since foreign archives remained barred.[236] In view of such a prevalence of the prosecution, Kranzbühler noted, it could be no surprise if the prosecution supressed evidence, even intimidated witnesses by threatening them with substantial

[230] TMWC X, p. 82.

[231] TMWC X, p. 83 f.

[232] Kastner (2001), p. 134; Kranzbühler (1949), pp. 6 f.; Seidl (1988), pp. 20 f.; Laternser (1986), pp. 557, 561; Taylor (1992), p. 396. However, cf. also Pannenbecker (1965), pp. 348, 350, who at least states that the defendants had not had any disadvantages due to the adversarial system.

[233] Safferling (2003), pp. 74 ff.; Trüg (2003), p. 341; however, on this also cf. the statement by the Tribunal's President, Judge Lawrence, who said that the prosecution had certainly disclosed to the defence any document or any witness . . . who would assist the defence, TMWC XVII, p. 498. How strange this procedure seemed to lawyers brought up in the Anglo-American system, can be seen when Jackson, in a dispute concerning this issue, stated that he would not in any instance serve two masters, TMWC III, p. 551.

[234] Haensel (1963–1964), pp. 248, 256; Kranzbühler (1949), p. 7; Laternser (1986), pp. 557, 561 f.

[235] Cf. e.g. TMWC XX, pp. 280 ff.

[236] Kranzbühler (1949), p. 7; id., Laternser (1986), pp. 557, 561 f.

hardship.[237] In fact, the secret additional protocol which Seidl tried to introduce into the trial over a period of months had already been in the possession of the prosecution before the start of the trial. This was confirmed to Seidl during the trial by the British chief prosecutor, Sir David Maxwell-Fyfe,[238] while General Zorya, a member of the Soviet prosecution team, when asked whether the additional protocol could be introduced into the trial, tersely replied[239] that such a conversation was irrelevant.[240] As far as access to the prosecution's evidentiary archives was concerned, Telford Taylor, the deputy of the American chief prosecutor, also conceded[241] that basically the defence ought to have had unrestricted access to all documents. But he also points to the special circumstances of the concrete case which had justified at least a certain degree of suspicion as regards the defence.[242]

2.3.3.2 Testimonial Issues

But it was not only the lack of access to documents which presented difficulties for the defence. Finding exonerating witnesses also turned out to be a major problem. While on the one hand these persons often could not be found or brought to Nuremberg because German infrastructure had been destroyed by the war,[243] on the other hand every witness had to be admitted by the Tribunal.[244] According to Article 19 of the Charter, the judges could reject the admission of witnesses without stating reasons. In the matter of the hearings of the indicted organisations the Tribunal even established a commission which heard some defence witnesses with the result that the judges only received a summary of these statements without having heard or seen the witnesses in person.[245]

---

[237] Kranzbühler (1949), p. 11; Laternser (1986), pp. 557, 561 f.

[238] Seidl (1988), p. 174.

[239] Seidl (1988), p. 175.

[240] Schulmeister-André (2016), pp. 486 f.

[241] Taylor (1992), p. 627.

[242] Taylor (1992), p. 627.

[243] Kastner (2001), p. 135; there are also reports about people being afraid to be named as witnesses, Lippe (1951), p. 15.

[244] Kastner (2001), p. 135; Laternser (1986), pp. 557, 566; Lippe (1951), p. 99.

[245] Minute No. 63 (12 March 1946), point 4 of the decision which was not read out in court. The Tribunal later on determined the further procedures: the president of the commission, Colonel Neave, was to summarise the results for the Tribunal. Whatever the defence wanted to introduce from the findings for the organisations, had to be introduced as evidence by them in their respective document volumes, Minute No. 87 (27 June 1946). On the entire issue, cf. also Laternser (1986), pp. 557, 566; Lippe (1951), pp. 311, 345 ff., 415; Taylor (1992), pp. 502 f.

2.3.3.3 The German-Soviet Non-Aggression Pact

The prevalence of the prosecution may be rather vividly demonstrated by the defence's attempts to introduce the secret additional protocol to the German-Soviet Non-Aggression Pact as evidence in the trial. It was mainly the resistance of the Soviet prosecution which made things difficult for the defence.[246] During his defence of his client Heß, Dr Seidl had already attempted to prove the existence of this secret additional protocol by means of an affidavit sworn by the former ambassador of the German Reich to Moscow, Dr Friedrich Gaus.[247] Since this affidavit was not available in translation, it was not permitted to be read out in court.[248] The hearing of the witness Margarethe Blank at least enabled the existence of the additional protocol to be established.[249] The witness did, however, not have any knowledge as to its content.

On 1 April 1946, Seidl was permitted to read out the above Gaus' affidavit during the hearing of Ribbentrop,[250] but in this presentation the conflict between Germany and Poland was only described as an imminent possibility.[251] A simple, uncertified copy which the defence counsel had received from an unknown source was not admitted as evidence in the trial. But, in a second affidavit by ambassador Gaus, the conformity of this copy with the original could be confirmed. This second affidavit was, however, not submitted by the defence counsel who instead waited for the witness von Weizsäcker who had been summoned for the defendant Raeder. On 21 May 1946, von Weizsäcker, the former German ambassador to Moscow, was able to give the Tribunal a very accurate description of the content of the additional protocol which was indeed known to him.[252] Of course, as an observer remarked in his memories of the trial,[253] due to the weeks of disputes during which more and more had gradually become known about the secret additional protocol, this was something of an anti-climax. In the end the secret additional protocol did not find its way into the Tribunal's judgement.

2.3.3.4 Financial Aspects

Finally, there were occasional financial problems. All in all, each of the main defence counsels was paid 9500 RM by the IMT for his first client and an additional payment of 50% [of this sum] for each further client, where this sum also had to pay the fee for

---

[246] For further information also see: Schulmeister-André (2016), p. 478.

[247] TMWC X, pp. 7 f.

[248] TMWC X, p. 96; likewise in a later attempt, TMWC X, pp. 46 ff.

[249] TMWC X, p. 190.

[250] TMWC X, p. 312 f.

[251] Number IV of the affidavit, TMWC X, p. 316.

[252] TMWC XIV, p. 283 ff.

[253] Gilbert (1947), p. 227.

the respective assistant counsel.[254] This fee was also intended to cover any expenses incurred in the search for exonerating material.[255] Occasional delays in payment significantly hampered the defence's work.[256]

When the Tribunal learnt in the summer of 1946 that Dr Babel, defence counsel for the SS, had collected money for the purposes of the defence in various internment and POW camps, this lawyer was discharged without further payment at the end of August 1946 for a gross breach of defence counsel regulations.[257]

2.4 *Main Emphases of Arguments for the Defence*

2.4.1 Substantive Arguments

Again and again the German defence counsel attempted to introduce, in favour of their clients, the prohibition of ex post facto legislation as a basic principle for criminal trials under the rule of law. With particular reference to the criminal offence of aggression, it was pointed out that neither the Covenant of the League of Nations nor the Kellogg-Briand Pact or any other similar treaty contained a corresponding penal norm.[258] They maintained that neither were conspiracy against world peace nor the crimes of the indicted organisations existing international criminal offences or concepts.[259] In addition, the Nuremberg defence counsel criticised the broad interpretation of the count of war crimes,[260] even though they did not want to dispute the IMT's competence in its function as 'occupation court'.[261] The crimes against

[254] Minute No. 41 (21 November 1945) and Minute No. 72 (17 April 1946); on this also Kastner (2001), p. 136; Lippe (1951), pp. 70 f., 93, 133, 242, 486, 537.

[255] Kastner (2001), p. 136.

[256] Weinke (2006), p. 38.

[257] Minute No. 97 (27 August 1946); cf. Also Kastner (2001), pp. 136 f.

[258] Motion adopted by all defence counsel of 19 November 1945 in TMWC I, pp. 168 ff., 168; TMWC XVII, p. 480; TMWC XIX, p. 381; cf. also Kranzbühler (1949), p. 13; Kraus (1964), pp. 233, 244 f.; Laternser (1986), pp. 557, 572 ff.; Pannenbecker (1965), pp. 348, 350 f.; Taylor (1992), p. 581.

[259] TMWC XVII, pp. 508 f.; TMWC XIX, pp. 381 f.; TMWC VIII, p. 390; TMWC XXI, p. 581; cf. also Haensel (1963–1964), pp. 248, 254; Kastner (2001), p. 134; Kraus (1964), pp. 233, 245; Kraus (1947), pp. 6 f. and 17 ff., who even, referring to talks given by IMT judges after the trial, states that basically the Tribunal had also been opposed to this count Taylor (1992), p. 628.

[260] TMWC XVII, p. 589 f.; Kranzbühler (1949), p. 13; Kraus (1947), pp. 23 f.

[261] Seidl (1988), p. 20.

humanity were partly considered as a count within the competence of the IMT,[262] but partly[263] also as retroactive criminal law.[264]

2.4.2 Procedural Law Arguments

There were frequent disputes about the admissibility of certain questionable exhibits. In a trial where arguments were essentially based on documents,[265] it is particularly important to pay attention to the compatibility of exhibits with the principles of the rule of law.

One piece of evidence which merits mention here is the diary of the defendant Frank, 43 volumes with around 12,000 pages. As Bühler reported,[266] Frank started keeping this diary in 1939. For this purpose, he had recruited an entire team of historians who used stenography to create accurate records of all his statements and activities. Of course, this type of diary is not necessarily comparable with the collections of private thoughts as they are commonly found in a 'diary'.[267] In any event, the Tribunal at no time considered not admitting this diary in the trial. After all, Frank had himself handed over the document to the soldiers who arrested him.[268]

On the other hand, two declarations were introduced in the trial which had come about under questionable circumstances from a rule of law point of view. They are first of all the so-called Moscow Declaration by Erich Raeder, as well as a declaration which Fritzsche signed in Moscow in September 1945. Both, by the way, were the only defendants who had become Soviet prisoners at the end of the war, and both signed the said declarations in captivity.[269]

---

[262] Seidl (1988), p. 20.

[263] TMWC XXII, p. 37; cf. also Kranzbühler (1949), p. 13; slightly more restrained: Kraus (1964), pp. 233, 242; Kraus (1947), pp. 19 ff. However, Kranzbühler (1965), pp. 333, 343, states that this step corresponded to a necessary development.

[264] However, on the entire issue also cf. Kauffmann (1987), pp. 537, 546 ff., who in looking back, takes the stance that the IMT with the London Charter applied law which had been created ad hoc, but had nevertheless been positive law, since it had corresponded to international law as well as natural law at the time when the crimes were committed. In those areas where in fact, as in the area of Article 9 of the IMT Charter, natural law had been further developed, he states that the Tribunal implemented comprehensive measures for the protection of innocent people.

[265] Haensel (1980), p. 83.

[266] TMWC XII, p. 86.

[267] On the entire issue cf. Kastner (2001), pp. 148 f.; Lippe (1951), pp. 66, 92 f.

[268] At least this is what Frank testified, TMWC XII, p. 7; the American assistant prosecutor, Baldwin, however reported to the Tribunal that the books had only been found on 18 May 1945, i.e. after Frank's arrest, TMWC V, p. 68.

[269] Kastner (2001), p. 174; Lippe (1951), p. 21; Taylor (1992), p. 132.

Raeder, who first acknowledged the declaration when it was presented to him,[270] could then only attempt to qualify the statements made in this document, these being mainly defamations of other Nazi leaders.[271] When, on the following day, the Soviet delegation wanted to read out the declaration in its entirety,[272] Dr Siemers managed to convince the Tribunal that this document should not be read out completely.[273] Dönitz explained Raeder's defensive attitude on this point through the fact that Raeder's family was still in Russian hands and that he feared reprisals.[274]

Fritzsche's behaviour was much more aggressive[275] when mention was made of the declaration which he had signed and in which he had testified to his close association with National Socialism.[276] While he admitted having signed the document, he pointed out that this had happened while he was in 'very severe solitary confinement'.[277] For clarification, he added that there had never been violence, but the conditions of his confinement had put pressure on him. He pointedly declared that at the time of signing the document he had made it clear that nobody would believe what was written down there because this record 'did not contain his language'.[278]

2.4.3 Mitigating Circumstances

Most defendants pleaded that they had known nothing. In particular the military[279] and leading politicians[280] stated that they had had no idea of Hitler's aggressive intentions; they maintained that they themselves had always understood the wars waged by them as defensive or preventive wars. Rosenberg and Streicher claimed to have known nothing about the effect of their propaganda writings. As a matter of course, they had also known nothing about the extermination of the Jews. The blame for this was shifted firmly onto Hitler, Himmler and a very few insiders within the SS. Many SS leaders who had directly witnessed the killings, such as in Auschwitz or Buchenwald, were interrogated.[281] Using their statements that the exterminations

[270]TMWC XIV, 225; the prosecution had already wanted to use this declaration during Göring's cross-examination, TMWC IX, p. 615, which, following an objection by Dr Stahmer, was not permitted by the Tribunal TMWC IX, p. 617.

[271]TMWC XIV, pp. 225 ff.

[272]TMWC XIV, p. 242.

[273]TMWC XIV, p. 243; on the entire issue cf. Lippe (1951), pp. 281 ff.

[274]Gilbert (1947), p. 346.

[275]Cf. Kastner (2001), p. 175.

[276]TMWC XVII, p. 202.

[277]TMWC XVII, p. 204.

[278]TMWC XVII, p. 203; for further information also see: Schäfers (2012), p. 154.

[279]Such as Keitel, Jodl, Dönitz, Raeder.

[280]Such as Ribbentrop, von Papen.

[281]E.g. testimony by Höß, TMWC XI, pp. 397 ff.; testimony by Morgen, TMWC XX, pp. 487 ff.

in the camps had always been implemented in strict secrecy and that the individual death commandos had been kept as small as possible, for example the one in Auschwitz had only consisted of 60 men, they sought to convince the Tribunal that even the highest-ranking officials in the state and in the Nazi party did not have any knowledge of the systematic extermination of human beings.

In any case—such was the basic attitude of many defendants—the SS had been a state within a state.[282] Himmler and his subordinates had always caused problems and had seized power whenever and wherever they could. In any case, only a fantasist such as Himmler could have seriously considered the extermination of six million people. They themselves would never have had such a thought. The peak of this dubious line of reasoning was ultimately reached when a man like Kaltenbrunner, who reported to only one superior, Himmler, actually accused his subordinates of these crimes while claiming to have known or suspected absolutely nothing at all.

Whenever defendants were faced with proof of their personal involvement in anti-Semitic measures, they declared that they had only obeyed the Führer, but had not been anti-Semites themselves.[283] Those who did not consider the 'overlord of extermination' to be Himmler identified him in the person of Adolf Hitler. Again and again Hitler's omnipotence in the Führer state was referred to in order to demonstrate the lack of knowledge and the powerlessness of even the highest-ranking Nazi leaders.[284] It was repeatedly stated that it had been impossible to contradict him, for he always asserted his will, and if anyone had opposed him, they would have been shot immediately.

But not all defendants invoked the absolute power of Hitler. From time to time the defendants also argued that in truth they had been opponents of Hitler and the entire regime. In particular Schacht, who had indeed been imprisoned in a concentration camp after the events of 20 July 1944, argued in this way. He was especially supported in this by the testimony of witness Gisevius who had undoubtedly been an opponent of the regime. In the cross-examination, Gisevius testified that the resistance group he had also belonged to had considered the defendants, except for Schacht, to be the men responsible for the unspeakable misery which that government had brought upon Germany and the world.[285]

Speer too, who together with his counsel Flächsner managed to satisfy the Tribunal that by suspending Hitler's 'Nero commands' at the end of the war, he had actually been active against Hitler, benefited from this opposition stance in the Tribunal's final judgement.[286] Whether in fact, as he reported later[287] and had

[282] Such as Göring, Seyß-Inquart.

[283] Such as Ribbentrop, Schacht, von Papen.

[284] Such as Göring, Heß, Kaltenbrunner.

[285] TMWC XII, pp. 250 f.

[286] IMT judgement, in TMWC I, pp. 189, 333 f.

[287] Speer (1970), p. 517.

already claimed during the trial,[288] it was only with considerable reluctance that he talked about his assassination plans of wanting to kill Hitler with poison gas is something that will most probably remain an unsolved mystery.[289] In any case, he and his defence counsel did not in fact use this part of his testimony in their final statement.

3 Final Review

After all this, the question arises as to what the defence actually achieved in Nuremberg. An answer to this question will, of course, also be an answer to a question about the purpose and meaning of any defence in a criminal trial.[290]

If the number of acquittals is to be considered an indicator of effective criminal defence, then the acquittals of Fritzsche, Schacht and von Papen, must be noted as positives. Nonetheless, even this success was of short duration only, since, shortly afterwards, the acquitted persons were re-arrested by the German authorities and two of them were sent to prison again.[291] In contrast, half of the defendants were executed by hanging and seven were sentenced to long terms of imprisonment, some to life. In view of the severity of the charges as well as the fact that victors judged the vanquished, this differentiated result may nonetheless be considered a success in this sense.

On another point, the defence counsel at the Nuremberg Trial managed to come across as convincing in support of the general tenet that any accused person should take a lawyer,[292] because the accused tends to lack in neutrality towards his problem as well as in competence to solve it. An objective perception of the facts of the case and the sophisticated application of legal norms is what defence lawyers can contribute to the trial in support of their clients. The Nuremberg defence counsel succeeded in doing that. Without any theatricality, they dealt with the accusations made by the prosecution and with the legal issues posed by them.

At this point, a further aspect of the Nuremberg Trial shall be considered. In this pioneer trial of international criminal law, standards were set which continue to have repercussions for contemporary international criminal procedural law. The untiring

[288] TMWC XVI, pp. 494 f.

[289] Cf. Brechtken (2017), pp. 303 f.

[290] This section is not intended to deal with the dispute between "Organ Theory" and "Contract Theory". On this issue, for a brief summary cf. Meyer-Goßner (2009), § 137 marginal note. 1; Beulke (2008), marginal note 20 ff. The various theories, however, ought to be re-examined against the background of international criminal procedural law.

[291] Kastner (2001), p. 356 (Footnote 334); Taylor (1992), pp. 612 ff.; Schacht was acquitted in an appeal hearing on 02 September 1948 and in the course of an appeal in a renewed trial in late 1950, after he, too, had before been assessed as a Major Offender.

[292] Volk (2008), § 11 p. 90; Peters (1985), p. 212; Roxin and Schünemann (2009), § 19, marginal note 1.

activities of the Nuremberg lawyers have demonstrated, and continue to demonstrate, the necessity of granting a defence counsel to each person indicted in a court of law. As a consequence of Nuremberg, the right to legal assistance was guaranteed in all major human rights conventions.[293] It is only with the assistance of their defence counsel that the defendant can find their way around the trial proceedings.[294] This applies especially to the complicated proceedings of an international criminal trial. And the Tribunal was undoubtedly concerned with safeguarding the function of the defence for the future when the president of the Tribunal, Lord Justice Lawrence, referred in his final statement to the significance of the defence in this trial:

> Before doing so, the Tribunal wishes to express its appreciation of the way in which Counsel for the Prosecution and Counsel for the Defence have performed their duties. The Tribunal has been informed that the defendants' counsel have been receiving letters from Germans improperly criticising their conduct as counsel in these proceedings. The Tribunal will protect counsel insofar as it is necessary so long as the Tribunal is in session, and it has no doubt that the Control Council will protect them thereafter against such attacks. In the opinion of the Tribunal, Defence Counsel have performed an important public duty in accordance with the high traditions of the legal profession, and the Tribunal thanks them for their assistance.[295]

References

Beulke W (2008) Strafprozessrecht. Nomos, Baden-Baden

Brechtken M (2017) Albert Speer. Eine Deutsche Karriere. Siedler Verlag, Munich

Conot R (1983) Justice at Nuremberg. Harper & Row, New York

Czapski S (1946) Rechtsanwälte in Nürnberg. DANA-Bericht v. 08.06.1946. Wetzlarer Neue Zeitung, 12.06.1946

Gaede K (2006) Fairness als Teilhabe – das Recht auf konkrete und wirksame Teilhabe durch Verteidigung nach Art. 6 EMRK. Duncker & Humblot, Berlin

Gilbert GM (1947) Nuremberg diary. Farrar Straus Giroux, New York

Gründler G, Manikowsky A (1967) Das Gericht der Sieger. Gerhard Stalling Verlag, Oldenburg

Haensel C (1964) The Nuremberg Trial revisited. DePaul Law Rev 13(2):248–259

Haensel C (1980) Das Gericht vertagt sich – Tagebuch eines Verteidigers. Limes, Wiesbaden

Harris WR (1999) Tyranny on Trial. The trial of the major German war criminals at the end of World War II at Nuremberg, Germany, 1945-46. Texas A&M University Press, Dallas

Harris WR (2007) Murder by the millions: Rudolf Hoess at Auschwitz. Oxford University Press, Oxford

Hay P (2005) US-amerikanisches Recht. C. H. Beck, Munich

Heydecker JJ, Leeb J (2003) Der Nürnberger Prozess. Kiepenheuer & Witsch, Cologne

Kastner K (2001) Von den Siegern zur Rechenschaft gezogen. Hofmann Verlag, Nuremberg

Kastner K (2005) Die Völker klagen an. Der Nürnberger Prozess 1945-1946. Wissenschaftliche Buchgesellschaft, Darmstadt

Kauffmann K (1987) The Nuremberg Trial in retrospect. Whittier Law Rev 9:537–549

[293] Cf. only Article 6 section 3 lit. c) ECHR; Article 14 section 3 lit. d) International Covenant on Civil and Political Rights.

[294] In this cf. also Gaede (2006).

[295] TMWC XXII, p. 410.

Kempner R (1969) Das Dritte Reich im Kreuzverhör: aus den unveröffentlichten Vernehmungsprotokollen des Anklägers. F. A. Herbig, Munich
Kranzbühler O (1949) Rückblick auf Nürnberg. Zeit-Verlag, Hamburg
Kranzbühler O (1965) Nuremberg eighteen years afterwards. DePaul Law Rev 14(2):333–348
Kraus H (1947) Gerichtstag in Nürnberg. Gesetz u. Recht Verlag, Hamburg
Kraus H (1964) The Nuremberg Trial of the major war criminals: reflections after seventeen years. DePaul Law Rev 13(1):233–242
Kronstein H (1953) Book Review of Frhr. von Wilmowsky T (1950) Warum wurde Krupp verurteilt? Friedrich Vorwerk Verlag, Stuttgart. Columbia Law Rev 53(2):139–144
Lagodny O (2001) Legitimation und Bedeutung des Ständigen Internationalen Strafgerichtshofes. Zeitschrift für die gesamte Strafrechtswissenschaft 113(4):800–823
Laternser H (1986) Looking back at the Nuremberg Trials with special consideration of the process against military leaders. Whittier Law Rev 8(2):557–580
Lippe V (1951) Nürnberger Tagebuchnotizen. November 1948 bis Oktober 1946. Fritz Knapp, Frankfurt/Main
Meyer-Goßner L (2009) Strafprozessordnung. Gerichtsverfassungsgesetz, Nebengesetze und ergänzende Bestimmungen. C. H. Beck, Munich
Pannenbecker O (1965) The Nuremberg war crimes trial. DePaul Law Rev 14(2):348–353
Peters K (1985) Strafprozeß. C. F. Müller, Karlsruhe
Robinson P (2005) So you want to be an international criminal lawyer? In: Kirsch S (ed) Internationale Strafgerichtshöfe. pp. 113–128
Roxin C, Schünemann B (2009) Strafverfahrensrecht. C. H. Beck, Munich
Safferling C (2003) Towards an international criminal procedure. Oxford University Press, Oxford
Safferling C (2009) Lernen von Nürnberg. Rechtsgeschichte 14:148–167
Salleck B (2016) Strafverteidigung in den Nürnberger Prozessen. Duncker & Humblot, Berlin
Schäfers B (2012) Freispruch in Nürnberg. Peter Lang, Bern
Scheerer S, Lorenz D (2006) Zum 125. Geburtstag von Franz Exner (1881-1947). MschrKrim 89: 436–454
Schulmeister-André I (2016) Internationale Strafgerichtsbarkeit unter sowjetischem Einfluss. Der Beitrag der UdSSR zum Nürnberger Hauptkriegsverbrecherprozess. Duncker & Humblot, Berlin
Seidl A (1988) Der Fall Rudolf Heß 1941 – 1987. Dokumentation des Verteidigers. Universitas, Berlin
Seliger H (2015) Politische Anwälte? Die Verteidiger der Nürnberger Prozesse. Nomos, Baden Baden
Speer A (1970) Inside the Third Reich. Macmillan, London
Sprack J (2008) A practical approach to criminal procedure. Oxford University Press, Oxford
Taylor T (1953) The Krupp trial. Fact v. fiction. Columbia Law Rev 53(2):197–210
Taylor T (1992) The anatomy of the Nuremberg Trials. Knopf, New York
Trial of war criminals before the Nuernberg Military Tribunals under Control Council Law No. 10 Nuernberg, October 1946 – April 1949 (1949), Vol. 1-5, 7-14 and 16-22. Washington D.C.
Trüg G (2003) Lösungskonvergenzen trotz Systemdivergenzen im deutschen und US-amerikanischen Strafverfahren. Mohr Siebeck, Tübingen
Verdross A, Simma B (1984) Universelles Völkerrecht. Duncker Humblot, Berlin
Volk K (2008) Grundkurs StPO. C. H. Beck, Munich
Weinke A (2006) Die Nürnberger Prozesse. C. H. Beck, Munich

Christoph Safferling studied law in Munich and London. He received his doctoral degree at the University of Munich in 1999 and passed the bar exam in 2000. From 2006 to 2015 he was professor at the Philipps-University of Marburg, and the director of the International Research and Documentation Centre for War Crimes Trials. Since 2012 he is a member of the Independent Academic Commission at the Federal Ministry of Justice for the Critical Study of the National Socialist Past. Since 2015 he holds the chair for criminal law, criminal procedure, and international law at the Friedrich-Alexander-University Erlangen-Nuremberg and he is the current director of the International Nuremberg Principles Academy (as of December 2023).

His main fields of research are: international criminal procedural law, the mental elements of the crime, and the history of international criminal law. He is co-editor of the German Law Journal. He is the author of 'International Criminal Procedure' (OUP 2012), and is the co-author of the studies 'Die Akte Rosenburg. Das Bundesministerium der Justiz und die NS-Zeit', Munich, C.H. Beck 2016, and 'Staatsschutz im kalten Krieg. Die Geschichte der Bundesanwaltschaft zwischen NS-Vergangenheit, Spiegel-Affäre und RAF', Munich, dtv 2021).

Philipp Graebke is a research associate with professor Christoph Safferling who holds the chair for criminal law, criminal procedure, international criminal law and public international law at Friedrich-Alexander-University Erlangen-Nürnberg. He studied law in Marburg, Germany, and passed the bar exam in Frankfurt am Main, Germany. He worked as a researcher for the Independent Academic Commission at the Federal Ministry of Justice for the Critical Study of the National Socialist Past, initially at Philipps-University Marburg, and later at Friedrich-Alexander-University Erlangen-Nuremberg. He is currently finalising his PhD thesis on the contemporary history of German criminal law.

Part II
Observing and Restructuring: Institutional Emancipation

The Long Shadows of the Past: The Federal Ministry of Justice and the Nazi Era

Christoph Safferling

Abstract In 1947, eighteen lawyers were called to account under the provisions of Control Council Law No. 10, specifically for crimes against humanity and war crimes; not because of an act of judicial perversion but because of the effects of their actions on people or humanity as a whole. The remarkable thing about the overall complex of the 'Nuremberg Trials' is that, on the one hand, responsibility has been found not only in lawyers, but also among other professional sectors, such as doctors, industrialists, and other bureaucrats, e.g. members of parliament and employees of ministries. On the other hand, however, a further dynamic could be observed: a lawyer was appointed to assist each defendant with a view to ensuring a fair trial. The victorious powers thus deliberately applied a standard contrary to the one in the Nazis' own proceedings.

1 The Role of the Defence

Almost without exception, the defenders were German lawyers.[1] Although they did not necessarily have an impeccable Nazi past,[2] they were not always experienced in criminal law and certainly not in comparative law or American criminal procedural law. They therefore gathered in groups to analyse and discuss problems and develop defence strategies; that system continued into the early Federal Republic. This way,

[1] An exception in the Krupp trial is the US lawyer Joseph S. Robinson, who represented Friedrich Bülow, and Warren. Magee, who worked for Ernst von Weizäcker in the Wilhelmstrasse trial, cf. Seliger (2016), p. 232 ff., p. 171.

[2] Cf. Seliger (2016), p. 83; individual monographic representations also: Luber (2018); Salleck (2016).

C. Safferling (✉)
University of Erlangen-Nuremberg, Erlangen, Germany
e-mail: christoph.safferling@fau.de

M.-E. Geis et al. (eds.), *Dealing with Totalitarian Regimes and Human Rights*, Interdisciplinary Studies in Human Rights 11,
https://doi.org/10.1007/978-3-031-57338-5_5

narratives of exculpation were developed, whose decrepit strength can still be felt today.[3]

The so-called Heidelberger Juristenkreis led by Heidelberg professor Eduard Wahl would meet and advocate the amnesty of war criminals as well as an early release of those arrested and convicted.[4] There was also massive lobbying—with success, as we know today. The Federal Ministry Justice monitored this group of lawyers by sending the ministerial councillor Alfons Wahl to the meetings.[5] The relevant documents can be found at the Max Planck Institute in Heidelberg, but they have not yet been processed.

2 Criminal Prosecution Structure

Roughly estimated, there have been around 7000 convictions since 1945: a strikingly small number compared to the approximate 100,000 investigative proceedings initiated in Germany.[6] Despite proceedings still taking place today, it can be said that the years between 1945 and 1949 represented the high phase of judicial processing with around 5000 proceedings and convictions.[7] In other words, from the establishment of the Federal Republic of Germany to present day, a total of around 2000 convictions have been recorded.[8] Conclusions can be drawn from this: The main burden of prosecution was borne by the Allies. Insofar as German courts and public prosecutors were involved,[9] a majority of them discontinued prosecution activities with the establishment of the Federal Republic of Germany.[10] The reason for this were the early amnesties of 1949 and 1954.[11] Konrad Adenauer, in particular, wanted to create a new beginning with the Basic Law and the establishment of the Federal Republic while letting the crimes of the past stay in the past.[12]

---

[3] Cf. Görtemaker and Safferling (2016), p. 51.

[4] Cf. Frei (2003), pp. 163 ff.; Seliger (2016), pp. 393 ff.; Herbert (2001), pp. 454 ff.; Görtemaker and Safferling (2016), pp. 145 ff.

[5] Cf. Görtemaker and Safferling (2016), pp. 147 ff.

[6] Detailed figures can be found in Eichmüller (2012); Eichmüller (2008), p. 621.

[7] Eichmüller (2008), pp. 621, 638.

[8] An analysis with reference to the reappraisal in the Soviet occupation zone/the German Democratic Republic can be found in Jasch and Kaiser (2017).

[9] For details on the reconstruction of the judicial system in Germany: Raim (2013).

[10] Miquel (2004), p. 146.

[11] Regarding these laws: Safferling (2013), pp. 169, 176 ff.; on their effect: Eichmüller (2012), p. 41.

[12] Frei (1996), pp. 484, 487; Safferling (2013), pp. 169 ff.

Only in 1958, a small increase was recorded thanks to the Ulm Einsatzgruppen Trial,[13] followed by the Auschwitz Trials[14] under considerable media attention, and the establishment of the central office in Ludwigsburg. All of them had been provided with significant resources to ensure preliminary investigations could be carried out with focus and commitment, but also with fortitude against substantial resistance, especially in relation to criminal enterprises that had taken place in Eastern Europe,[15] which was difficult to access due to the Iron Curtain.[16]

In 1960, manslaughter had already been made subject to statute of limitations without much discussion.[17] Then, with the passing of the Introductory Law of the Act of Regulatory Offences (EGOWiG) in 1968 and through the judgement of the 5th Criminal Senate of the Federal Court of Justice from 20 May 1969, the statute of limitations for assisted murder was created, which basically led to a complete standstill in further prosecution through the so-called 'cold amnesty'.[18] Thus, the ominous cooperation between the Federal Ministry of Justice and the Federal Court of Justice achieved what conservative circles had already demanded in the course of the 1965 limitations-statute debate in the Bundestag but without succeeding: Only acts of excess would continue being punished, whereby only those who could be proven to have unilaterally killed or arbitrarily shot people in the course of e.g. ghetto evacuations were convicted as 'murderers'.

3 Exculpation Strategies

What is remarkable, however, is the failure of the German judiciary to deal with judicial injustice. Only one lawyer was convicted by a German court of participating in national-socialist systemic miscarriages of justice.[19] For the murder of von Dohnanyi, Canaris, Osten, Bonhoeffer, and others in the Sachsenhausen and Flossenbürg concentration camps, a public prosecutor, SS-Standartenführer Walter Huppenkothen, was sentenced to an imprisonment of seven years.[20] Huppenkothen is not even suitable as a fig leaf for the judiciary, since, as a member of the Einsatzgruppe and department head at the Reich Security Main Office, he was

[13] Details also in Eichmüller (2012), pp. 188 ff.

[14] Werle and Wandres (2015), pp. 24 ff.; Finally, on the other Auschwitz trials: Renz (2018) as well as Steinke (2013).

[15] Cf. Weinke (2008); Hofmann (2018).

[16] On these issues cf. Renz (2001), pp. 63 ff.

[17] Safferling (2017), pp. 19, 30.

[18] For details, Görtemaker and Safferling (2016), pp. 399 ff.

[19] In addition: Vormbaum (2013), pp. 142, 151.

[20] Bundesgerichtshof (BGH), Federal Court of Justice ruling, 19 June 1956, 1 StR 50/56, published in Neue Zeitschrift für Strafrecht (1996), p. 485; also Hirsch (2013), pp. 56 ff.; In detail on this convoluted process and the changes in the case law of the BGH cf.: Koch (2017), p. 131.

closely connected to the Nazi terror and was personally involved in the murder of thousands in Poland.

The reason for this inadequate processing of systemic miscarriages of justice were in particular the exculpation strategies developed in the Nuremberg Trials. Fritz Bauer described the dogmatic subtleties of the Federal Republic of Germany's judiciary as a 'guild rampart' that was erected against the punishment of judicial murders.[21]

One slogan read, for example, 'if I had given up my office between 1933 and 1945, then a real Nazi would have taken my place'. The assertion that 'if I hadn't carried out the Nazi orders, I would have ended up in a concentration camp' could be interpreted as a kind of coercion. One (for lawyers particularly evident) defence was: 'I only applied the laws'. Another defence, crucial for the self-image that could be observed in the post-war period until well into the 1960s, was: 'I only served to maintain order, especially order during war'. This required a tough crackdown, otherwise society would have collapsed; in any case the war could not have continued. In general, all this 'only prevented worse things'. Moreover, one often hears and reads the claim that 'an anti-Nazi spirit lived in office'. These protective claims can be found repeatedly in one way or another in the corresponding documents.

The way in which these exculpation strategies are used and how they work will be exemplified below using certain Federal Ministry of Justice employee biographies from 1957.

3.1 Heinrich Ebersberg

It shall begin with Heinrich Ebersberg. Ebersberg, born in 1911 and already active in the SA since 1933, was a personal advisor at the Reich Ministry of Justice since 1936. Initially, he accompanied the State Secretary Schlegelberger to the 1941 conference of Higher Regional Court Presidents and Chief Public Prosecutors on the suppression of prosecuting euthanasia murders linked to the so-called *T4-Aktion*,[22] and he later became the advisor of the Ministers Gürtner and Thierack. The conference at the 'Haus der Flieger' in Berlin with the leading criminal prosecutors of the Third Reich manifests the very profound attachment to the Führer as the incarnated will of the people and supreme legislator, and thus to the fundamental premise of the National Socialist ideology.[23]

[21] Quoted from Koch (2017), pp. 131 f.

[22] Görtemaker and Safferling (2016), p. 342 with further references. On this conference and the T4 campaign as a whole: Burckhardt (2015).

[23] Cf. most recently Ambos (2019), pp. 36 ff.

As a personal advisor to the Minister, Ebersberg was responsible for the programme called 'Correction of Inadequate Judgements'.[24] This agreement of 18 September 1942 involved Reich Justice Minister Otto Thierack, State Secretary Curt Rothenberger, SS Leader Heinrich Himmler and Hitler's Secretary Martin Bormann. Its gist was that if there was a suspicion at the Reich's Ministry of Justice that a criminal judgement at any court in the great Reich was too mild, then it could be examined, and a decision could be made as to whether the execution of this judgement should be handed over to the Gestapo. This meant that convicts would end up in concentration camps and thus be subject to the programme of extermination through forced labour.[25]

Heinrich Ebersberger's task was to present the relevant files to the minister.[26] Although he later admitted having held this office—which he could hardly deny in any event—he of course asserted that by doing so he had prevented worse from taking place. After all, so goes his justification, his reports consisted of simply presenting the files to the Minister; he would never have voted and therefore would not have made a proposal for a decision.[27] Considering the fact that the moral standards of the Ministry were difficult to reconcile with this statement, the argument proves to be nothing short of outrageous.[28] At the Nuremberg Trials, the defendants were not believed their alleged lack of knowledge about what was hiding behind this programme: 'One man can keep a secret, two men may, but thousands, never'.[29]

Ebersberg's employment with the Federal Ministry of Justice did not happen all too smoothly, but once he was employed, doubts concerning his qualifications soon evaporated.[30] In the course of the Braunbuch Campaign, Heinrich Ebersberg was initially suspected of having incurred serious guilt. Ultimately, however, the Federal German authorities gave Ebersberg unreserved faith. There were disciplinary proceedings initiated against him in this context, but only due to the ongoing criminal proceedings based on voluminous allegations.[31] After all, hundreds of files had passed his desk, as a result of which countless people were unjustly taken to concentration camps and had to work themselves to death there.

Interestingly, there was a letter from the defence attorney Behling from Berlin found in his personal file regarding the denazification processes. Behling issued a

[24] Cf. Görtemaker and Safferling (2016), pp. 48 ff.

[25] Cf. Safferling (2019), p. 70.

[26] Cf. Safferling (2019), p. 70.

[27] Cf. RGBl. 1936, S. 89.

[28] See Görtemaker and Safferling (2016), p. 341.

[29] US Government Printing Office, Trials of War Criminals before the Nuremberg Military Tribunals under Control Council Law No. 10, Vol. III, Washington 1951, p. 1081; on the legal process in Nuremberg also: Safferling and Luber (2017), p. 881.

[30] On the attitude of Ebersberg in the Federal Ministry of Justice, see also Apostolow (2019), pp. 239 ff.

[31] Cf. Görtemaker and Safferling (2016), p. 342.

kind of testimony for Ebersberg which reads thus: 'Yes, if one sought to achieve anything at all at the Ministry in cases that concern handing someone over to the Gestapo, Mr Ebersberg would be the one to talk to. With him, one could maybe have a word, and maybe it would lead to a favourable decision'.[32] Here, the contradiction to Eberberger's previous assertion that he only discussed but never voted[33] becomes clear; A call would have been obsolete in such a case, because Ebersberg could not have done anything.

Despite such discrepancies, policymakers in the late 1940s and 1950s through the early 1970s failed to see justice done. Criminal proceedings were discontinued due to the statute of limitations pursuant to EGOWiG. Disciplinary proceedings were consequently also discontinued on the instruction of State Secretary Maassen, despite the limitation period being irrelevant there. Although Ebersberg was, contrary to the original plan, not promoted to the sub-department head of Division III,[34] he did govern the department for business administration law and energy law until his retirement in 1973.

3.2 *Heinrich Grützner*

A second case in point: Heinrich Grützner. Grützner was not at the Reich Ministry of Justice; he was a Public Prosecutor in Potsdam. Dr Heinrich Grützner, a pastor's son, had already joined the NSDAP on 23 February 1933, before the so-called seizure of power.[35] Around that time, he became part of a vastly interesting incident: On 30 June 1934, Kurt von Schleicher and his wife were murdered in their villa in Babelsberg by the Gestapo during the Röhm Putsch.[36] Subsequently, the responsible constabulary came to the crime scene including Grützner as the responsible investigating public prosecutor. The scene he found there led him to the conclusion that it was clearly a politically motivated murder. He therefore called the Reich Ministry of Justice and reported his suspicion. Fatally, though, he was only able to leave a telephone note since the responsible sub-department head or head of unit were not present at the time, so it occurred that the house management also became aware of it.

---

[32] Before Ebensberg was hired, the lawyer Behling had already been asked at the Rosenburg; Apostolow (2019), p. 240.

[33] Cf. Safferling (2019), p. 71.

[34] About the activities of Department III and the continuities in commercial law: Thiessen (2013), p. 204.

[35] Personnel file Grützner at the Federal Ministry of Justice, PA P 11-G 12.

[36] Cf. Gruchmann (2001), pp. 442 ff.; as well as the very early description in Eschenburg and Rothfels (1953), p. 71. The author also had the opportunity to ask Grützner about the incident. The incident also emerges from the annex to the denazification questionnaire (Entnazifizierungsfragebogen) dated 3 January 1949 of the State Prosecution personnel file at the OLG (Higher Regional Court) Celle as part of the PA Grützner P 11-G 12.

Contemporaneously, the Prussian Prime Minister, Hermann Göring, had already spread his theory of state emergency on the radio. He announced that the last Chancellor of the Weimar Republic, Kurt von Schleicher, resisted arrest and was shot dead by a police officer in self-defence during this arrest attempt. When inspecting the crime scene with the assistance of a forensic doctor and interviewing witnesses, the young public prosecutor Grützner apparently found something different had happened, which did not correspond to the self-defence killing account nor could it have been the case of von Schleicher's suicide. He was, however, strictly prohibited from publicly repeating this version of the sequence of events: According to his personal file, at the late hour of 11:30 p.m. that night a delegation from the Reich Ministry of Justice led by the then State Secretary, Roland Freisler, visited Grützner's home and threatened him that he would end up in a concentration camp if he ever professed that von Schleicher had been murdered.

Incidentally, Hans von Dohnanyi, the personal advisor to Reich Justice Minister Gürtner, also happened to be present during this night visit. It was probably thanks to Gürtner that this atrocious event was put on record at all and that it remained there.[37] The Heinrich Grützner case is thus an example of how one could later say: 'If I had not followed the Nazi ideology faithfully, I would have ended up in a concentration camp'. There is certainly no evidence that such threats ever materialised in any particular case, but Grützner was instrumentalised by the said defence lawyers to appear as a witness in various trials with the Ministry's corresponding permission to testify in favour of that line of defence.[38]

Also interesting from a personal point of view is the fact that Grützner's doctorate was rated with the average grade '*rite*', but when he applied to the Federal Ministry of Justice, he alleged having a doctorate '*summa cum laude*' and only omitting a habilitation due to the outbreak of the war.[39] Because of his mediocre final grade, he had difficulty getting accepted into the Justice Department. However, the party was able to see him through this, in particular the FDP connections to Dehler, which then paved the way for Grützner to enter the Ministry with a small detour via the State Justice Administration.[40] There he was responsible for international criminal law, admittedly, in an operational unit and not in one of the large substantive policy units. He is, however, certainly a figure of considerable renown, also due to his later publications and the editorial work for the journal 'Goltdammer's Archive'.[41] In the

---

[37] Gruchmann (2001), p. 446.

[38] Cf. the summons in Grützner's personnel file: summons LG Düsseldorf, 8 April 1965, PA Grützner P 11-G 12, p. 174; Summons LG Cologne, 9 April 1965, PA Grützner P 11-G 12, p. 177; Summons LG Essen, 3 December 1965, PA Grützner P 11-G 12, sheet 194; Summons LG Düsseldorf 4 May 1966, PA Grützner P 11-G 12, p. 199.

[39] Personnel file in the BMJV, PA P 11-G 12; cf. also letter from Grützner to Dehler, 4 October 1949, BMJV BEW 60, sheet 1.

[40] Personnel record of the Prosecution Service OLG Celle, Bl. 2 - Part of the personnel file in the BMJV, PA P 11-G 12.

[41] 'Goltdammer's Archive' is the oldest German-written criminal law journal. It was founded in 1853 by the Royal High Tribunal Councilor Theodor Goltdammer as the 'Archiv für Preußisches

case of Grützner, the Federal Ministry of Justice was not particularly enthusiastic about these part-time activities;[42] still, the famous commentary on international criminal law bears his name to this day.[43]

3.3 *Eduard Dreher*

Even beyond the context of the 'cold amnesty' of the EGOWiG, for which he has to take a large part of responsibility, Dr Eduard Dreher became especially visible through his strongly positivistic attitude epitomised by the statement that what was right then could not be wrong today. Dreher, born in 1907, was the first Public Prosecutor at the Innsbruck Special Court.[44] He was by no means forcibly moved there; rather, he applied for the post to the Special Court in Tyrol in 1940 on his own initiative as a then-Public Prosecutor in Dresden. According to his own statement, he did this out of 'affection for the mountains', but in reality, it was for career reasons.[45] He was an incredibly hardworking, highly diligent Public Prosecutor, and almost drew the cases to himself to process them. Toward the end of the war, he was promoted to the office of the Attorney General in Innsbruck, where he worked as a kind of deputy head of the authorities. After the war, Dreher would only be expelled from Austria on 3 July 1945. The letter from the Innsbruck Attorney General, Dr Grünewald, reads as follows:

> Your dismissal is only put down to the fact that the requirements for further disposition in a public office as a German citizen are not met. The review of your official work at the Public Prosecutor's Office and the Chief Public Prosecutor's Office did not give rise to any complaints.[46]

He repeatedly referred to this letter later in the course of denazification to prove that he had carried out his work in accordance with the law and not in the service of the inhuman Nazi ideology. His position met with some success:[47] He was 'denazified' and placed to the Rosenburg in Bonn after a short period as an attorney in Stuttgart.

Strafrecht' and was known from 1880 as 'Archiv für Strafrecht'. During the Nazi era, the 'Archiv' was also brought into line and appeared between 1935 and 1944 as a supplementary journal for criminal legal studies of the 'Deutsche Justiz', the organ of the Academy for German Law, edited by Karl Klee, Roland Freisler and Otto Thierack. In 1953, the journal was supposed to be resumed on its 100th birthday. The editorial offered Grützner to become a publisher.

[42] Note made by Winners, 5 September 1952, BMJ PA P 11-G 12, pp. 90 and 93.

[43] Cf. Grützner et al. (2019).

[44] Cf. Safferling (2019), p. 66.

[45] Cf. Görtemaker and Safferling (2016), p. 331.

[46] PA Dreher P 11-D 14 p. 20.

[47] Cf. e.g. Lackner and Horstmann (2006), pp. 149, 166.

From the mid-1950s, accusations were raised that, as a public prosecutor in Innsbruck, he had secured death penalty rulings for petty crimes.[48] The three cases of Anton Rathgeber, Josef Knoflach, and Karoline Hauser became relevant in this context. The allegations were made from the German Democratic Republic and were reiterated in the 1960s Braunbuch Campaign. However, the full extent of his activities was not known until the Rosenburg study, despite Dreher having been active in many more cases in Innsbruck. He did not express his attachment to the National Socialist legal thinking only by applying for death penalties though: along the 'broadcasting crimes' (a total of 44 cases, 34 with Dreher's involvement) and proceedings due to the so-called 'Ordinance against Pests Harmful to the Common Good of the Country' (59 cases in total, 41 with Dreher's involvement), the proceedings for illegal animal slaughter, i.e. criminal offences under the War Economy Ordinance (135 cases, 87 with Dreher's involvement) were on the agenda also. For rural Tyrol, this is not surprising. Dealing with it was also comparatively mild: There were no death penalties[49] and in the course of the execution of sentences there used to be extended generous reprieves in individual cases in order to maintain agriculture.[50] Conversely, crackdowns were taken in other areas, especially cases of looting and multiple perpetrators. In the period from 1940 to 1944, Dreher applied for the death penalty a total of 17 times as a representative before the Special Court. The court acceded to the request nine of those times.

In the three cases that had already become known in the 1950s and 1960s, Dreher had applied for the death penalty for simple looting, in some cases under a rather adventurous interpretation of the 'Ordinance against Pests'.[51] Dreher interpreted the extensive Nazi law in an even broader manner and went so far as to apply it analogously. When confronted with this, he would invoke memory gaps. Even after the files from Vienna were requested at Bonn's Rosenburg and presented to him, he stated that he had only been applying the law.

This claim is significantly vitiated when it becomes clear that Dreher had secured the conviction through analogous application of law according to § 2 RStGB and that there had been no plunder at all. A 'plain application of the law' as claimed by Dreher thus appears at least questionable.[52] The analogous application of law had been introduced into criminal law by the National Socialists, which was immediately repealed by the Allies in 1945 as part of a wholesale denazification of the laws.[53] It remains highly doubtful to what extent this interpretation had been actually

[48] Cf. Safferling (2019), p. 66.

[49] In contrast to this, the colleague from Vienna, Karl-Heinz Nüse, demanded the heaviest punishment and, if necessary, to deter the common betrayal and the low sentiment of the '*Schwarzschlachters*' complete eradication, cf. Nüse (1940), pp. 958 ff. Nüse was later also active in the Federal Ministry of Justice in the field of state security, cf. Farthofer (2019), pp. 74 ff.

[50] See for example the case of Maria Mayrhofer and Alois Gertl, Landesarchiv Innsbruck KLs 161/1942.

[51] Cf. Safferling (2019), p. 67.

[52] Cf. note by Lüttger, 18 November 1960, in: PA Dreher P 11-D 14., pp. 85 ff.

[53] Cf. Safferling (2013), pp. 169, 172 ff.

mandatory upon Dreher. The department head of the Federal Ministry of Justice, Joseph Schafheutle, provided legitimation for this in a specially prepared report, where he came to the conclusion that Dreher could only have possibly applied for the death penalty.[54]

What is also interesting, however, is Dreher's reaction to the assessment of his superior, in which he made interesting statements in 1957 on the question of the relevance of the prohibition of analogy in criminal law. He stated that it was not legally binding, and that he could have as well come to this conclusion through an expanded interpretation—as lege artis was done in the Federal Republic of Germany after 1945—but his chosen way of analogy appeared 'dogmatically cleaner' to him.[55] In truth, the public prosecutor in Innsbruck, who was doggedly pursuing an ambitious career, showed a turn to the material concept of injustice, i.e. to the idea of a 'total criminal law', and followed the increasing de-formalisation of criminal law. In that respect, he was fully committed to the National Socialist ideology of criminal law.[56] It is noteworthy that Dreher had decisive influence on substantive criminal law in the Federal Republic of Germany. He did this not only as a sub-department head of the criminal law department on the Rosenburg, but above all as the author of the leading commentary on the Criminal Code used by any magistrate.[57]

3.4 *Wolfgang Fränkel*

Another person, not in the inner circle of the Federal Ministry of Justice, but still employed in the division of the Federal Ministry of Justice, is Wolfgang Fränkel. He was in the Federal Prosecutor's Office in Karlsruhe from 1950 and was later the Public Prosecutor General from 3 March 1962 to 24 June 1962 being the shortest period to hold that office. The reason for this was the presentation of a brochure with the title 'From Reich Prosecutor to Federal Prosecutor' on 23 June 1963 in East Berlin by Greta Kuckhoff, a member of the Rote Kapelle resistance group, who was sentenced to ten years in prison by the Reich Court-Martial in 1943. The 130-page brochure consisted of facsimile copies from the relevant procedural files provided meticulously accurate documentation of the pastor's son Wolfgang Immerwahr Fränkel, born in 1905, being responsible for the so-called annulment complaints.

As the assistant at the Reich Attorney General's office, he would *en masse* aggravate judgements in proceedings by means of special revision and thus 'help' many to a death sentence.[58] The aim of this measure, introduced throughout the German Reich in 1940 at the insistence of the State Secretary of the Reich Ministry

[54] Cf. report Schafheutle v. September 22, 1959, BEW 65 / I p. 178.

[55] Cf. supplementary statement by Dreher, 6 November 1959, BEW 65 / I p. 188.

[56] On this topic also: Ambos (2019), p. 38 et seq.

[57] Cf. Görtemaker and Safferling (2016), p. 330.

[58] In summary with examples: Wilke (2015), pp. 149 ff.

of Justice Roland Freisler, was to secure the National Socialist claim to power 'by deterring' and 'defanging' while maintaining a semblance of formality.[59] Thus, Fränkel had to be put into temporary retirement by Wolfgang Stammberger, the Federal Minister of Justice at the time.

It is further noteworthy that Fränkel had already worked for the 'Oberbundesanwalt' (the former term for the Federal Public Prosecutor[60]) since 1951, before he became equally prominent as the head of the authority. Fränkel initially, in the first confrontation, offered the Minister his immediate resignation due to the allegations, but later portrayed himself as a victim of intrigue, hostile, communist attacks.

The Federal Ministry of Justice established a supra-factional tripartite commission consisting of Thomas Dehler (FDP), Hans Wilhelmi (CDU), and Gerhard Jahn (SPD) to examine the allegations and to give a recommendation.[61] The tripartite committee came to the conclusion that, regarding his role in the systemic injustice of the Nazi regime, Fränkel was not suitable as a federal prosecutor for general political and judicial reasons, even though he was not accused of any misconduct during his service at the Reich Attorney's Office. It is worth mentioning that Fränkel's former superiors at the Reich Public Prosecutor's Office, who incidentally also recommended him to the Federal Prosecutor's Office, Carl Kirchner and Hans Richter, were federal judges at the Federal Court of Justice and were never prosecuted as responsible Reich attorneys after 1945. In the aforementioned disciplinary proceedings, he defended himself with the exculpation myth: 'It was necessary to maintain order'. The actual extent of his radicalism, however, becomes clear in the assertion he made in an original case, namely that if a Czech man rapes a German woman while all the German men are at the front, he deserves death penalty already because the German women are unprotected. In 1964 he still proclaimed: 'I would do the same today'.[62]

Maintaining state order was the credo and persons like Fränkel believed in it. It is not just the (supposed) state emergency that they believed justified their actions though.[63] Additionally, the attitude towards criminal law as something that must be used to protect the 'German national community' and to eliminate 'racially harmful elements' could also be seen in action. This typical National Socialist conception of criminal law[64] can be witnessed in numerous places and can be substantiated by the statements of Fränkel in the disciplinary proceedings.

---

[59] Cf. Gruchmann (2001), p. 1088.

[60] In this context, the chair of Prof Dr Christoph Safferling, LL.M. (LSE) at the Friedrich-Alexander-Universität Erlangen-Nürnberg in cooperation with the historian Prof Dr Friedrich Kießling of the Catholic University of Eichstätt-Ingolstadt are currently historically processing the authority of the Attorney General's Office.

[61] Cf. PA BMJ P 41 - F3, disciplinary proceedings special file copy for the BMJ, p. 291.

[62] PA BMJ P 41 - F3, disciplinary proceedings special file copy for the BMJ, p. 286.

[63] PA BMJ P 41 - F3, files of investigator Marquordt, p. 70.

[64] On this topic also Ambos (2019), pp. 57 ff.

3.5 Walter Römer

The Ministry Director Walter Römer only prevented worse. The catholic Römer, born in 1902, was the first public prosecutor at the Munich Regional Court from 1933 through 1945, where he was the head of the 'Law Enforcement and Pardon Department' and thus responsible for the execution of all sentences 'from death sentences to small fines' as well as appeals for clemency.[65]

Römer was not a member of the NSDAP and the position of an enforcement attorney was not a particularly desired one, so it can be assumed that his twelve-year tenure in this position is also an expression of a stunted career. Although assessments emphasised that 'The political reliability of the public prosecutor Dr Walter Roemer raises no concern',[66] he did not stand out through political commitment to the National Socialist regime either. His actions concerning the Night and Fog Decree could have been fatal for him. That decree mandated that dissidents, especially from the northern and western occupied territories, be collected during 'Night and Fog' and brought into the Reich. Due to secret procedures, the persons concerned were taken to concentration camps, and their relatives were not informed of their whereabouts. (This 'disappearance' phenomenon was later made infamous by the 1970's Latin American military dictatorships as a crime against humanity.) Römer was responsible for law enforcement and imprisonment of people who were incarcerated in Munich under this Decree.

During the Nuremberg Trials, in which he testified as a witness for the prosecution[67] on 24 April 1947, he was able to present a bundle of letters that he had collected from persons convicted under the Night and Fog Decree. This was strictly forbidden as they were letters to relatives and, as such, not allowed to reach the public under any circumstances. After the end of the war, he decided to hand them over to the Allies in order to at least give the relatives something. Römer moreover claimed to have delayed the execution of death sentences from December 1944 onwards. In fact, the transfer of 147 prisoners from Stadelheim in Munich to the correctional facility in Nuremberg is on record; these persons did indeed escape an execution and survived the war due to this transfer.[68]

Even if his work does not appear particularly honourable at this point, he nonetheless contended that he had prevented something worse and thus perhaps saved someone's life. Römer was reinstated in the judicial service via the Bavarian Ministry of Justice. From there, he came to the Rosenburg together with Dehler, the then-President of the Bamberg Higher Regional Court and became head of

[65]BMJ PA Roemer P11-R12, Vol. 1, Roemer to State Commissioner Auerbach, 15 October 1947 [sic!].

[66]BMJ PA Roemer P11-R12 - Files of the State Ministry of Justice; this is an example of Römer's misnomer as 'Doctor' by third parties.

[67]BMJ PA Roemer P11-R12, Vol. 1, Roemer's interrogation protocol from 24 April 1947 in the context of the Nuremberg Trials; also, Görtemaker and Safferling (2016), pp. 57 ff.

[68]Cf. Görtemaker and Safferling (2016), p. 349 with further references.

Department IV for public law and constitutional law for years. The development of democracy and basic rights under the Basic Law were thus in the hands of a person who—albeit without a Party membership—had played a key role in the Bavarian judiciary during National Socialism.

The false claim prominently made by Simon Wiesenthal at regular intervals about Römer murdering the Scholl siblings, followed the department head throughout his life, so that in the end, after Römer's death in 1985, the Federal Minister of Justice Engelhardt abstained from the publication of an obituary. It was feared that such an appreciation would again cause turmoil about the matter.

3.6 *Wilhelm Dallinger*

Wilhelm Dallinger, born in 1908, was a prototype Bavarian lawyer. In the oral examination of the 2nd state exam on 3 July 1935, he was directly recruited by the chamber judge Dr Hoche for civil service at the Reich Ministry of Justice[69] where he began to work as an assistant two months later. There he was employed in the areas of criminal law, criminal procedure law and juvenile criminal law in particular.[70] Prominent were his writings in this subject area, where he extolled fascist youth education based on the example of Italy. He also worked on the reform of the Reich Juvenile Court Act of 1943. As a typical opportunist, he joined the NSDAP on 1 July 1937, right after the record stop was lifted,[71] but he then took up the position of a 'Blockhelfer', which made the concern of potential difficulties in the denazification process entirely justified. Finding access to judicial service again could also be difficult.

The way to the Bavarian Justice service and then to the Federal Ministry of Justice[72] was paved for him by Section 131 of the Basic Law together with the letter of recommendation from his patron, Professor Franz Exner.[73] In his letter, Exner only emphasised Dallinger's legal skills and did not address his political views. That could be viewed with some skepticism, being that ten years earlier he had declared Dallinger a 'thoroughly politically reliable and National-Socialist-minded young man' who was only prevented operating in National Socialist associations by his invidious financial situation.

[69] KGRat Dr Hoche (Chairman of the examination commission for state examinations) declares to D. that he will lobby for the call-up to the Reich Ministry of Justice, as Dallinger had achieved the best result so far in Bavaria. Personnel file OLG Munich A 514, no sheet, note from 12 July 1935.

[70] Details can be found in Safferling and Dallinger (2017), p. 603.

[71] Rückert (2013), pp. 60 ff.

[72] Certified copy of Exner's statement from 02/10/1946; State Archives Munich, SpkA K2530 Dallinger, Wilhelm, p. 30.

[73] On the forensic biologist Franz Exner and his controversial attitude towards National Socialism, cf. Scheerer and Lorenz (2006), pp. 436–454; cf. also Fuchs (2009); cf. Ambos (2019), pp. 29 ff.

In his denazification proceedings, Dallinger himself repeatedly emphasised what an anti-Nazi spirit he was. He received support from Toni Schäfer, then widow of the former head of department Dr Ernst Schäfer, who died in July 1945. In a letter, she tells about Dallinger's visits at the Schäfers' with numerous table discussions of a 'downright anti-Nazi spirit' which Dallinger also shared.[74] Ernst Schäfer had already gotten into the Reich Ministry of Justice during Radbruch's period of office and was promoted to head of the criminal law department. He left the Ministry together with Franz Schlegelberger when Otto Thierack took office. In any case, these two letters made it possible for Dallinger to re-enter the Bavarian judiciary and subsequently pursue a ministerial career in Bonn.

4 Consequences

The biographies briefly presented here chart the legal functions of the concerned individuals during National Socialism. All these persons were greater or lesser cogs in the National Socialist terror regime and contributed to its overall functioning. Josef Schafheutle and Wilhelm Dallinger, for example, assisted at the Reich Ministry of Justice in the formulation of the 'Gewaltverbrecher' Act in 1934 but also in other National Socialist laws such as the Treachery Act or the 'Ordinance against pests harmful to the common good of the country' and even the 'Night and Fog Decree'. Their extensive commentary on the concerned laws as well verifies their influence on the application of the law in National Socialist sense. The specific application in individual cases was then carried out by Eduard Dreher in Innsbruck or perhaps Heinrich Grützner in Potsdam. On this legal basis, they procured death penalties and harsh and discriminatory sentences, which in turn were executed by Walter Römer in Munich. If the desired goal was not achieved, i.e. the deft public prosecutors were not successful at trial, then one could turn to the Reich Ministry of Justice, such as to Heinrich Ebersberg as part of the project 'Correction of inadequate judgements', or to Wolfgang Fränkel who was able to contribute to an aggravation of a judgement in the course of the nullity complaint.

Each of these individuals, who later met at the Rosenburg under various circumstances, had contributed to the National Socialist injustice. They were part of this system and ultimately ensured that the Nazi terror actually lasted as long as it did. None of the above individuals showed remorse or contrition. Instead, they referred to exculpation narratives in a mantra-like manner: They only applied the laws, they stayed in office to prevent even worse things happening, they were constantly threatened with being sent to a concentration camp, and they secretly lived with an anti-Nazi spirit inside. However, they could not live completely unmolested in their highest offices in the Federal Republic. Time and again they were overtaken by the shadows of the past. However, none of the criminal and disciplinary proceedings that

[74] Cf. also BMJ PA Dallinger P 11-D 1, p. 5.

were (late and somewhat reluctantly) initiated against some of them resulted in conviction. They were instead all able to live a quiet retirement with full state pensions. They themselves probably earnestly believed that they had done nothing wrong.[75]

References

Ambos K (2019) Nationalsozialistisches Strafrecht. Nomos, Baden-Baden

Apostolow M (2019) Der "immerwährende Staatssekretär". Vandenhoeck & Ruprecht, Göttingen

Burckhardt A (2015) Das NS-Euthanasie-Unrecht vor den Schranken der Justiz: eine strafrechtliche Analyse. Mohr Siebeck, Tübingen

Eichmüller A (2008) Die Strafverfolgung von NS-Verbrechen durch west-deutsche Justizbehörden seit 1945. Vierteljahrshefte für Zeitgeschichte 56:621–638

Eichmüller A (2012) Keine Generalamnestie. Die Strafverfolgung von NS-Verbrechen in der frühen Bundesrepublik. Oldenbourg Verlag, Munich

Eschenburg T, Rothfels H (1953) Zur Ermordung des Generals Schleicher. Vierteljahreshefte für Zeitgeschichte 1953(1):71–95

Farthofer H (2019) Neuausrichtung des Staatsschutzes nach 1945? Die Beispiele Bundesrepublik Deutschland, Italien und Österreich. Vandenhoeck & Ruprecht, Göttingen

Frei N (1996) Amnestiepolitik in den Bonner Anfangsjahren. Die Westdeutschen und die NS-Vergangenheit. Kritische Justiz (KJ) 1996:484–487

Frei N (2003) Vergangenheitspolitik. Die Anfänge der Bundesrepublik und die NS-Vergangenheit. Dtv Verlagsgesellschaft, Munich

Fuchs W (2009) Franz Exner (1881–1947) und das Gemeinschaftsfremdengesetz: Zum Barbarisierungspotenzial moderner Kriminalwissenschaft. LIT Verlag, Berlin

Görtemaker M, Safferling C (2016) Die Akte Rosenburg. C. H. Beck, Munich

Gruchmann L (2001) Justiz im Dritten Reich 1933-1940. De Gruyter, Munich

Grützner H, Potz PG, Kreß C, Gazeas N (2019) Internationaler Rechtshilfeverkehr in Strafsachen, Sammlung und Kommentar. C. F. Müller, Munich

Herbert U (2001) Best – Biographische Studien über Radikalismus, Weltanschauung und Vernunft, 1903-1989. J. H. W. Dietz Nachfolger, Bonn

Hirsch G (2013) Die bundesdeutsche Justiz und die Aufarbeitung von NS-Unrecht. In: Bundesministerium der Justiz and UWK-BMJ (eds) Die Rosenburg. 2. Symposium. Die Verantwortung von Juristen im Aufarbeitungsprozess. Bundesministerium der Justiz, Berlin, pp. 56–70

Hofmann K (2018) "Ein Versuch nur – immerhin ein Versuch". Die Zentrale Stelle in Ludwigsburg unter der Leitung von Erwin Schüle und Adalbert Rückerl (1958-1984). Metropol-Verlag, Berlin

Jasch HC, Kaiser W (2017) Der Holocaust vor deutschen Gerichten. Amnestieren, verdrängen, bestrafen. Reclam, Ditzingen

Koch A (2017) Der Huppenkothen-Prozess. Die Ermordung der Widerstandskämpfer um Pastor Dietrich Bonhoeffer vor den Schranken der Augsburger Justiz. In: Koch A, Veh H (eds) Vor 70 Jahren – Stunde Null für die Justiz?, Die Augsburger Justiz und das NS-Unrecht. Nomos, Baden Baden, pp 131–158

Lackner K, Horstmann T (2006) An den Grenzen des Rechts. Campus Verlag, Frankfurt

Luber M (2018) Strafverteidigung im Nürnberger Juristenprozess am Beispiel des Angeklagten Oswald Rothaug. Duncker & Humblot, Berlin

[75] Cf. Stolleis (2013), pp. 327, 328.

Miquel M (2004) Ahnden or Amnestieren? Westdeutsche Justiz und Vergangenheitspolitik in den sechziger Jahren. Wallstein Verlag, Göttingen
Nüse KH (1940) Zur Behandlung der "Schwarzschlachtung" im Kriege. Deutsche Justiz 1940:958–960
Raim E (2013) Justiz zwischen Diktatur und Demokratie. Wiederaufbau und Ahndung von NS-Verbrechen in Westdeutschland 1945-1949. Oldenbourg Verlag, Munich
Renz W (2001) Auschwitz als Augenscheinsobjekt. Anmerkungen zur Erforschung der Wahrheit im ersten Frankfurter Auschwitz-Prozess. Mittelweg 36(1):63–72
Renz W (2018) Auschwitz vor Gericht. Fritz Bauers Vermächtnis und seine Missachtung. CEP Europäische Verlagsanstalt, Hamburg
Rückert J (2013) Einige Bemerkungen über Mitläufer, Weiterläufer und andere Läufer im Bundesministerium der Justiz nach 1949. In: Görtemaker M, Safferling C (eds) Die Rosenburg. Das Bundesministerium der Justiz und die NS-Vergangenheit – eine Bestandsaufnahme. Vandenhoeck & Ruprecht, Göttingen, pp 60–87
Safferling C (2013) "...daß es sich empfiehlt, generell tabula rasa zu machen..." Die Anfänge der Abteilung II – Strafrecht im BMJ. In: Görtemaker M, Safferling C (eds) Die Rosenburg. Das Bundesministerium der Justiz und die NS-Vergangenheit – eine Bestandsaufnahme. Vandenhoeck & Ruprecht, Göttingen, pp 169–176
Safferling C (2017) Verfolgung der Täter durch Täter? Ein Versuch zu erklären, warum es nach dem großen Frankfurter Auschwitzprozess ein halbes Jahrhundert gedauert hat, bis Oskar Gröning verurteilt wurde. In: Frank Lüttig F, Lehmann J (eds) Die letzten NS-Verfahren. Nomos, Baden-Baden, pp 19–40
Safferling C (2019) Lex Rosenburg: Überfällig oder überflüssig? Zeitschrift für Didaktik der Rechtswissenschaft (ZDRW) 6(1):62–75
Safferling C, Dallinger W (2017) NS-Kontinuität in der frühen Bundesrepublik und die Auswirkungen auf die Reform des Jugendstrafrechts. In: Safferling C, Kett-Straub G, Jäger C, Kudlich H (eds) Festschrift für Franz Streng zum 70. Geburtstag. C. F. Müller, Munich, pp 603–616
Safferling C, Luber M (2017) Der Tempel der deutschen Justiz muss wieder eingeweiht werden. Juristische Arbeitsblätter (JA) 2017(49):881–887
Salleck B (2016) Strafverteidigung in den Nürnberger Prozessen. Duncker & Humblot, Berlin
Scheerer S, Lorenz D (2006) Zum 125. Geburtstag von Franz Exner (1881–1947). Monatsschrift für Kriminologie und Strafrechtsreform 89:436–454
Seliger H (2016) Politische Anwälte? Die Verteidiger der Nürnberger Prozesse. Nomos, Baden-Baden
Steinke R (2013) Fritz Bauer oder Auschwitz vor Gericht. Piper, Munich
Stolleis M (2013) Concluding remarks. In: Görtemaker M, Safferling C (eds) Die Rosenburg. Das Bundesministerium der Justiz und die NS-Vergangenheit – eine Bestandsaufnahme. Vandenhoeck & Ruprecht, Göttingen, pp. 327, 328
Thiessen J (2013) Wirtschaftsrecht und Wirtschaftsrechtler im Schatten der NS-Vergangenheit. In: Görtemaker M, Safferling C (eds) Die Rosenburg. Das Bundesministerium der Justiz und die NS-Vergangenheit – eine Bestandsaufnahme. Vandenhoeck & Ruprecht, Göttingen, pp 204–295
US Government Printing Office (1951) Trials of War Criminals before the Nuremberg Military Tribunals under Control Council Law No. 10, Vol. III. Washington D.C.
Vormbaum T (2013) Die "strafrechtliche Aufarbeitung" der nationalsozialistischer Justizverbrechen in der Nachkriegszeit. In: Görtemaker M, Safferling C (eds) Die Rosenburg. Das Bundesministerium der Justiz und die NS-Vergangenheit – eine Bestandsaufnahme. Vandenhoeck & Ruprecht, Göttingen, pp 142–151
Weinke A (2008) Eine Gesellschaft ermittelt gegen sich selbst. Die Geschichte der zentralen Stelle in Ludwigsburg 1958-2008. Wissenschaftliche Buchgesellschaft, Darmstadt
Werle G, Wandres T (2015) Auschwitz vor Gericht. C. H. Beck, Munich
Wilke M (2015) Staatsanwälte als Anwälte des Staates. V&R Unipress, Göttingen

Christoph Safferling studied Law in Munich and London. He received his doctoral degree at the University of Munich in 1999 and passed the bar exam in 2000. From 2006 to 2015, he was professor at the Philipps-University of Marburg, and the Director of the International Research and Documentation Centre for War Crimes Trials. Since 2012 he is a member of the International Academic Commission at the Federal Ministry of Justice for Critical Study of the National Socialist Past. Since 2015, he holds the chair for criminal law, criminal procedure, and international law at the Friedrich-Alexander-University Erlangen-Nuremberg and is the current president of the International Nuremberg Principles Academy (as of December 2023).

His main fields of research are: international criminal procedural law, the mental elements of the crime, and the history of international criminal law. He is co-editor of the German Law Journal. He is the author of 'International Criminal Procedure' (OUP 2012), and is the co-author of the studies 'Die Akte Rosenburg. Das Bundesministerium der Justiz und die NS-Zeit', Munich: C.H. Beck 2016, and 'Staatsschutz im kalten Krieg. Die Geschichte der Bundesanwaltschaft zwischen NS-Vergangenheit, Spiegel-Affäre und RAF', Munich: dtv 2021).

Protecting the Democratic State Through Criminal Law: Legislation History and the Role of the Federal Public Prosecutor

Jana Kuhlmann

Abstract This chapter will expound how modern German law has conceptualised its legal framework to protect the state by tracing the historic development of the laws regarding political crimes with a focus on High Treason and Subversion. Alongside the provision of the social and political context, the special role of modern Germany's Federal Public Prosecutor as the highest prosecutory authority will be examined as it emerged from the predecessing organisational structures of Imperial Germany, the Weimar Republic and the National Socialist Regime. In the process, passed-on values and possible ideological relics shall be exposed facilitated by recent research on the history of the Federal Public Prosecutor's forming years. As a brief outlook, the most urgent challenges the German state and its authorities face in terms of state protection nowadays will be touched at the end.

1 Introduction to Modern Terminology and Institutions

> In a totalitarian state, the idea of 'protecting the state' is misused to protect the ruling structures from the people. Protecting a liberal state on the contrary means to protect the constitution, which includes freedom of protest, religion and opinion as well as the rights of minorities, but also ensuring the absence of violence in the political discourse.[1]

I want to express special gratitude towards Prof. Dr. Martin Heger, Humboldt-Universität zu Berlin, for kindly providing the manuscript of a talk he gave at 2018's KOSMOS Conference on Combating Terrorism in Europe even before the accompanying publication was printed.

[1] Klink Manfred, speech upon the 60th anniversary of the Federal Criminal Police Office of Germany titled 'Vom Staatsterrorismus zum islamisitschen Terrorismus/Auswirkungen unterschiedlicher terroristischer Bedrohung in Deutschland' (convenience translation); The presentation was held at the BKA's anniversary conference '60 Jahre Staatsschutz im Spannungsfeld zwischen Freiheit und Sicherheit', Bonn, 17 June 2011. German transcript available via https://www.bka.de/DE/DasBKA/Historie/STVeranstaltung/stVeranstaltung node.html (last accessed

J. Kuhlmann (✉)
Friedrich-Alexander University of Erlangen-Nuremberg, Erlangen, Germany
e-mail: jana.kuhlmann@fau.de

M.-E. Geis et al. (eds.), *Dealing with Totalitarian Regimes and Human Rights*, Interdisciplinary Studies in Human Rights 11,
https://doi.org/10.1007/978-3-031-57338-5_6

1.1 Concepts

Regardless of legal tradition, High Treason and Subversion are typically understood as criminal disloyalty to one's state.[2] This however can take on many forms: Participating in a war against one's native country, attempting to overthrow its government, spying on its military, its diplomats, or its secret services for a hostile and foreign power as well as attempting to kill the head of state, to name only the most obvious. To defend the state against this kind of menace, Germany decided to use the 'sharp sword of criminal law'.[3] The corresponding set of regulations is known as *Staatsschutzstrafrecht*—'State Protection Criminal Law'. When stipulating the prohibited behaviour as clearly as possible—as demanded by the rule of law— German law distinguishes between the 'direction' and the 'means' of the act of disloyalty. The direction component asks whether the state is threatened by internal or external agitation. Within those two categories, threats can manifest themselves in violent or non-violent execution. That is why the *Strafgesetzbuch* (StGB, 'German Criminal Code') works with the concepts of *Hochverrat* as the literal translation for High Treason and *Staatsgefährdung* as the term for non-violent acts of subversion on the one hand and *Landesverrat* as a general term for evoking or supporting exterior threats to the state, for example by whistleblowing and espionage, on the other hand. Due to the nature of *Landesverrat* affecting Germany's relation to foreign states, only the Federal Government is in charge for the matter.[4] When it comes to the threats from the inside, the fact that Germany is organised as a federal republic adds complexity to the subject. The Federal Government and the federal states share responsibilities for preventive and repressive measures against terrorism and attacks against the constitutional order. Consequently, different authorities are involved in State Protection as the antidote to such threats and a specific framework of competence has evolved.

1 December 2023). Klink was *Erster Direktor* ('First Director') of the BKA and as such head of the departments *Sicherungsgruppe* ('Personal Security'), *Staatsschutz* ('State Protection') and *Technische Dienste* ('Technical Services') from May 1970 until November 2003.

[2] C.f. Lee (2012), pp. 299–342.

[3] For the use of the term *'Das scharfe Schwert des Strafrechts'* c.p. Kett-Straub and Kudlich (2017), Rn. 7; for the related terms *'fragmentarischer Charakter des Strafrechts'* and *'Strafrecht als ultima ratio'* see Maiwald (1972), pp. 9ff.

[4] Article 73 Abs. 1 Nr. 9a, 10 *Grundgesetz der Bundesrepublik Deutschland* (GG, 'Basic Law').

1.2 The Federal Public Prosecutor at the Federal Criminal Court

1.2.1 Functions and Responsibilities

The Federal Public Prosecutor, in German *Generalbundesanwalt* (GBA) or, as a body, *Bundesanwaltschaft*, holds the highest prosecutory authority in Germany and was basically installed as a traditional prosecution unit, with its special responsibility being crimes against the state. In this role, the GBA has the same tasks as every regional prosecution office: to conduct investigation proceedings and to press charges against people suspected of terrorism, high treason, subversion or of having committed an offence under the International Criminal Code. In fact, the GBA shares this substantive competence with regional prosecution offices,[5] as the *Oberlandesgerichte* (OLG, 'Higher Regional Courts') function as the trial courts in state protection matters.

At the same time, since 1969 the GBA also represents the state in appeal trials before the *Bundesgerichtshof* (BGH, 'Federal Criminal Court').[6] In general, every crime or combination of offences that leads to an expected sentencing of more than four years imprisonment (including capital offences such as murder or manslaughter) will be tried in first instance at the Regional Courts;[7] the Higher Regional Courts will judge crimes against the state.[8] If in those cases either the pleading prosecutor or the defendant appeals to the BGH, the Office of the Federal Public Prosecutor takes over the part of the regional prosecution, although they are free to decide whether they agree with the regional prosecution's position on the appeal arguments or not. By this mechanism, the votes of the GBA are prone to heavily influence top-level jurisdiction in all matters of severe criminality, which itself decisively shapes the interpretation of the inner-most principles of the StGB and *Strafprozessordnung* (StPO, 'Code of Criminal Procedure').

1.2.2 Integration in the Federal Executive Apparatus and Internal Organisation

In German law, the prosecution as a body is an independent judicial organ that has a major impact on investigation proceedings and law enforcement. It is therefore not part of the judiciary authority of the court, but holds executive powers. In general, any local prosecution will reside at the same location as the corresponding court, but despite the connection through jurisdiction and venue, the prosecution is neither sub-

[5] As laid down in § 120 *Gerichtsverfassungsgesetz* (GVG, 'Judicature Act') in conjunction with § 142a GVG.

[6] § 142 Abs. 1 Nr. 1 GVG.

[7] § 74 GVG.

[8] § 120 GVG.

nor superordinate to the court, and a judge is not authorised to give instructions to a prosecuting attorney. Every prosecutor is, however, bound to directives from their superiors, and the rank order goes up to the ministries of justice at the federal state level. The same principles apply to the Office of the Federal Public Prosecutor as Germany's highest prosecutory authority: its headquarters are located in Karlsruhe, hometown of the BGH, and the Public Prosecutor General is subject to the supervision of the Federal Minister of Justice and integrated into the budget of said Ministry. Because the office of the Federal Public Prosecutor is politically charged in nature, he has a special status under civil service law:[9] The head of the office, the Prosecutor General, must at all times be aligned with the crime policy objectives and foundational opinions of the Government. He can be suspended at any time without further explanation. This monocratic and hierarchical structure has in the past been criticised by the European Court of Justice in its ruling concerning the European arrest warrant in May 2019.[10]

1.2.2.1 Relation to Other Federal Authorities

In their role as appeal prosecutor, the *Bundesanwaltschaft* can work with the material passed on to them by the local prosecution offices and will never initiate new investigations due to the nature of the appeals held at the BGH. Those trials are based on the evidence collected for the initial trial and only re-asses the legal interpretation, that is, the application of substantial or procedural norms in the case as summarised by the trial court.

However, being concerned with investigating state protection matters, the GBA stands on the forefront of federal law enforcement—although they are not alone at the top. To understand the importance and special role of Germany's Federal Prosecutor, one must be aware of the system of top tier authorities concerned with state protection matters in which the Office is incorporated. As the GBA is a purely bureaucratic body with no genuine investigation forces at their disposal, they inevitably depend on the flow of information generated by actual investigation authorities on the different ends of their respective responsibility.

Because of its jurisdiction, the Federal Intelligence Service (*Bundesnachrichtendienst*, BND) is suited to provide the GBA with information concerning exterior threats to the state's security, like espionage or international terrorism. The BND's domestic secret service counterparts are the Federal Office for the Protection of the Constitution (*Bundesamt für Verfassungsschutz*, BfV), and its 16 correlating authorities at the state level.[11] The GBA relies on their information

[9] § 54 Abs. 1 Nr. 5 *Bundesbeamtengesetz* (BBG 'Federal Civil Servants Act').

[10] ECJ C-508/18 and C-82/19 PPU – Judgement of the ECJ (Grand Chamber) 27 May 2019 (OG and PI).

[11] There is also a separate military intelligence organisation, the *Militärischer Abschirmdienst* (MAD, which means 'Military Counterintelligence Service').

regarding cases of subversion, High Treason etc. On the executive branch, the Federal Criminal Police Office of Germany (*Bundeskriminalamt*, BKA) marks the top of the law enforcement hierarchy as the federal investigative police agency of Germany, directly subordinated to the Federal Ministry of the Interior. The federal state police offices are in charge for emergency response and general risk prevention in the realms of their respective territory. To equip the GBA with some sort of a standard investigational and executing unit, the *Sicherungsgruppe* ('Protection Division')[12] at the BKA was originally assigned to carry out executive orders in the GBA's name. This arrangement dates back to the Offices' early days in 1952. Additionally, the GBA relied on the police divisions that assist local prosecution offices; this is the standard today,[13] where the GBA shares the investigational responsibilities for state security matters anyway.

Federal laws regulate the crucial cooperation of all these listed authorities to treat the typically supra-regional or national menaces accordingly. The cooperation between those bodies is, however, a source of consistent disagreement and uncertainty. Not to speak of a downright turf war, the discrepancies have led to a couple of scandals of varying dimensions, the NSU-scandal of 2011 being the most prominent.[14]

1.2.2.2 Structure

When it was founded in 1951, the Office of the Prosecutor General only had one department with six branches covering both trial and appeal proceedings at the same time, each for a certain group of accused persons, apparently following the idea that enemies of the state can be categorised sociologically. Fortunately, the Office distanced itself from this one-dimensional concept in the years following. With good faith, this development could be attributed to critical self-observation and reflection upon the imprints of one's own past; after all, this early structure features unmistakable parallels to the perpetrator typology coined by Nazi scholars like Exner and Mezger. This apparent continuity naturally rings the alarm bells against the background of findings in the Office's general records that contain hints of that

[12] BKA organizational chart, https://www.bka.de/EN/TheBKA/OrganisationChart/organisationchart_node.html (last accessed 11 October 2019).

[13] While the BKA's Protection Division focuses on what their name implies: protecting constitutional organs and foreign high officials on state visits, https://www.bka.de/EN/TheBKA/OrganisationChart/OrganisationalUnits/ProtectionDivision/protectiondivision_node.html (last accessed 1 December 2023).

[14] In an effort to mend the critical situation at least with respect to Islamist terrorism, in December 2004 the 'Joint Counter-Terrorism Centre' was created as an initiative that brings together over 40 partner services, including all of the afore-mentioned plus the Military Counter-Intelligence, Federal Office for Migration and Refugees and representatives of the Federal Prosecutor General. The inclusion of the prosecution authority is a novelty internationally and intensifies the co-operation between law enforcement and prosecution.

very mindset. It is more likely, however, that the Federal Ministry of Justice incentivised the restructuring into a more elaborate and (most importantly) transparent form in order to make it easier to monitor the activities of the GBA. Evidence for that hierarchical interrelation was found in the form of written correspondence between the Ministry and the Prosecutor General at that time, Carlo Wiechmann, including drafts and suggestions made by the Federal Ministry of Justice. The Ministry seemingly was absolutely ready to dictate an organisational structure to the Office of the Federal Public Prosecutor, if they did not sort themselves out in a satisfying way—quickly. The GBA managed to file an organisation suggestion that was approved by the Ministry after a series of vastly creative drafts. Finally, by 1974 the Office exhibited a structure already very similar to today.

Mirroring the dichotomy of responsibilities, the GBA's organisational structure these days differentiates between the Office's role in the Federal Criminal Court's appeal jurisdiction and the role of a 'traditional' trial prosecutor in cases of crimes concerning state security. To further divide the latter competence, traceable crimes against the state are categorised by the 'direction' of the act of disloyalty against the state that has manifested itself in an offence, leaving the GBA with the three substantial departments 'Appeals', 'Espionage/International Criminal Law' and 'Terrorism' respectively. This structure pays tribute to the historic heritage of the evolution of state protection legislation, as the Department Espionage covers the idea of *Landesverrat* as a general term for evoking or supporting exterior threats to the state; thus, the relevant crimes share an international relevance with the field of International Criminal Law, which is why both categories are intertwined. As the first shaking experiences with the phenomenon of terrorism were national, the Department that deals with the concept of *Staatsgefährdung*—that is, domestic threats and subversion—goes under the label 'Terrorism', which admittedly does not quite fit the modern interpretation of the term.

2 Historical Developments of Germany's Penal Legislation for the Protection of the State and the Parallel Evolution of the Highest Prosecuting Authority

2.1 Before the National Socialists' Regime: Empire and Weimar Republic

In 1871, the *Reichsstrafgesetzbuch* (RStGB, 'Criminal Code of the Empire') came into force, and it already contained the crimes of High Treason and Subversion in the form of *Hochverrat*—the actus reus being 'to threaten the inner order of the state'—and *Landesverrat*—threatening national security externally.[15] The other norms that

[15] Gutfleisch (2014), p. 33.

penalised acts of 'political crime' can be roughly grouped into organisation crimes (such as forming a rebel group or a conspiratorial secret society), uttering or demonstrating subversive content (like incitement or challenging the public to disobey the law) and disparagement of state institutions, official orders or the Emperor himself. In 1877, the *Reichsanwaltschaft*, so to speak the 'Imperial Public Prosecutor', was founded to prosecute those offences, of which initially offending His Majesty the Emperor was the most relevant before the courts. Before the outbreak of the First World War, *Hochverrat* and *Landesverrat* were of rather less practical significance.[16] However, coming up to the November Revolution of 1918, several laws came into action that augmented the landscape of High Treason and subversive crimes, most importantly the *Verratsgesetz* (VerratsG, 'Treason Law') of 1893[17] and the *Spionagegesetz* (SpionageG, 'Espionage Law') of 1914.[18] Their various norms widened criminal liability by proscribing even preliminary acts of subversion as well as expanding the concept of 'passing on information to the enemy'.[19] The *Sozialistengesetz* (SozialistenG, 'Socialist Law')[20] and the *Sprengstoffgesetz* (SprengstoffG, 'Explosives Law')[21] were meant to counteract social democrat, socialist and communist agitation as well as anarchist aggression in the run-up to the First World War.

In the authoritarian Prussian state, the Imperial Public Prosecutor acted as a preserver of the conservative governmental system. Therefore, in 'defending the Emperor and the Empire' the focus was on prosecuting socialists suspected of High Treason and Subversion.[22] In fact, the second *Oberreichsanwalt* Hermann Tessendorff became namesake to a wave of excessive persecution of members of the labour movement, unionists and politicians. According to contemporary sources, 2200 trials were conducted exclusively against social democrats in the years after the Empire's founding.[23] In *Tessendorffs* opinion, 'there is no substantial difference between the social democrats and the so-called anarchists'.[24] However, *Tessendorff's* and his successor's efforts in counter-socialism did not really pay off.

After the downfall of the German Empire, the republic was proclaimed in November 1918. The Criminal Code as well as all the special State Protection

[16] Schroeder (1970), p. 5.

[17] *Reichsgesetzblatt* (RGBl. 'Reich Law Gazette') 1839, p. 205.

[18] *Gesetz gegen den Verrat militärischer Geheimnisse* ('Statute Against the Betrayal of Secrets'), RGBl. 1914, p. 195.

[19] Schroeder (1970), p. 96.

[20] *Gesetz gegen die gemeingefährlichen Bestrebungen der Sozialdemokratie* ('Statute Against the Dangerous Endeavours of Social Democrats'), RGBl. 1878, p. 351, valid from 1878–1890.

[21] RGBl. 1884, p. 61.

[22] Wilke (2016), p. 35.

[23] Bernstein (1907), p. 293.

[24] Quoted after v. Treutlein-Moerdes (1904), p. 113.

Laws remained in force in their original wording,[25] but their interpretation had changed due to the new conceptions of state and constitution.[26] State protection by means of criminal law became increasingly important, as the new order was not as politically stable as its imperial predecessor was: political violence, both from reactionary leftist and far-right movements, overshadowed the Weimar Republic during all its existence.[27] As a consequence of various attempted murders, coups and riots, it became a habit that the President of the Reich used 'emergency decrees' to amend the legal tools to 'protect the state'. Article 48 of the constitution of the Weimar Republic (WRV) allowed the President, under certain circumstances, to take emergency measures without the prior consent of the Reichstag and included the promulgation of such 'emergency decrees'. The laws created in this manner resulted in cutbacks on freedom of the press, assembly and association as well as genuine proscriptions. On 21 June 1922, the first *Gesetz zum Schutze der Republik* (RepublikschutzG, 'Law for the Protection of the Republic')[28] was adopted. It criminalised favouring or approving violent acts against members of the government and attacks aimed against the political system itself, which means the choice of the republican form of state. In practice, there even existed a Special Tribunal for State Protection Cases on the federal level from 1922 to 1926. The RepublikschutzG however was complemented by ever-new emergency decrees,[29] including for example the obligatory death penalty for High Treason and manslaughter with 'political motivation[30] eventually. In 1932, a rush of events affecting both state organisation and legislation led up to the seizing of power by the National Socialist Party. As far as state protection regulation was concerned, the previous sets of rules were modified or abolished in favour of the National Socialists,[31] while basic rights of the political opposition were gradually restricted more and more.

After World War I, the Office of the Prosecutor General kept its jurisdiction. From the day of the proclamation of the republic on, the *Reichsanwaltschaft* was obliged to defend the Democratic principles of the new form of state—only that this new state was actually governed by the very same social democrats that had been prosecuted as public enemies shortly before. What would have required profound changes in the views of the officials only lead to the formation of an esprit de corps amongst the members of the *Reichsanwaltschaft*, who predominantly shared inner reservations against democracy and liberalism. Proof of their ideological inertia was

[25] According to Art. 178 *Weimarer Reichsverfassung* (WRV, 'Constitution of the Weimar Republic').

[26] Schroeder (1970), p. 115.

[27] Gutfleisch (2014), p. 36.

[28] RGBl. I 1922, p. 585.

[29] E.g. RGBl. I 1931, p. 79, p. 699; RGBl. I 1932, p. 133.

[30] § 4 *Verordnung betreffend die Wiederherstellung der öffentlichen Sicherheit in Groß-Berlin und in der Provinz Brandenburg* ('Regulation Regarding the Restoration of Public Security in Berlin and Brandenburg') RGBl. I 1932, p. 377.

[31] *Verordnung gegen politische Ausschreitungen* ('Regulation Against Political Riots'), RGBl. 1932 I, p. 297.

the collective failure of the German Judiciary in the 'Leipzig Trials'. The *Reichsanwaltschaft* was responsible for prosecuting war crimes committed by Germans on foreign ground[32]—the trials ended with only ten convictions, with a maximum sentence of five years imprisonment, and seven acquittals. All the remaining cases against approximately 900 persons were dropped.[33] With the entitled feeling of victimisation through the treaty of Versailles and thus encouraged in their national sensibility, the judiciary saw themselves as the old elite. So it was that the rapidly growing *Reichsanwaltschaft*, which was led by national-conservatives throughout the Weimar Republic, became critically receptive for the ideology of the Nazi Party that took over in 1933.

Though state protection legislation and its execution was continually being extended in the days of the Weimar Republic, it already struck contemporaries as imbalanced[34] and in hindsight did not take sufficient action against far-right forces—but not because of overly liberal laws, but due to lenient application of the actually rather strict rules (e.g. in the case of the Hitler-Ludendorff-coup).[35]

2.2 *During the National Socialists' Regime*

Political prosecution during the Nazi regime was far more than what written law implied, as the substantial rule of law has been set aside completely. Nevertheless, classical state protecting laws were still developed further per regulated legislative procedures, maintaining an absurd state of formal legality.

For that matter, the established traditions of passing new laws mainly via emergency decrees continued in the transitional period at the end of the Weimar Republic, with the *Reichstagsbrandverordnung* ('Emergency Decree after the Burning of the Reichstag')[36] having outstandingly radical effects. It permanently narrowed civil liberties, tightened punishment for High Treason and other classical subversive crimes and allowed the retroactive application of new rules to past actions.[37] Hitler had urged President Paul von Hindenburg to pass this emergency decree in order pursue a 'ruthless confrontation' with the Communist Party of Germany. After passing the decree, the government instituted mass arrests of communists, including all of the Communist Party parliamentary delegates.

The next exceptional Nazi decree, dedicated to *Verrat am Deutschen Volke und hochverräterische Umtriebe* ('Subversive Activities and Treason to the detriment of

---

[32] RGBl. 1919, p. 2125.

[33] C.f. Hankel (2003).

[34] Gutfleisch (2014), p. 39.

[35] C.f. Schwend (1954), pp. 242–260.

[36] *Verordnung des Reichspräsidenten zum Schutz von Volk und Staat* ('Regulation by the President for the Protection of People and State'), RGBl. I 1933, p. 83.

[37] *Lex van der Lubbe*, RGBl. 1933, p. 151.

the German People') of 1933,[38] worked in a similar way. For example, it added the death penalty for *Landesverrat* by passing secret information to external forces and stated that for the requisite mens rea, even negligent ignorance of the subversive nature of a piece of writing was enough to justify punishment. This helped the Nazis to get rid of their bitter rivals, the communists, and with their seats empty, the Nazi Party went from being a plurality party to the majority, thus enabling Hitler to consolidate his power.

From the passing of the *Gesetz gegen die Neubildung von Parteien* ('Law against the Reformation of Political Partys') in May 1933[39] onwards, state protection also meant protecting the one and only 'Party of the State', which by then was the National Socialist German Workers' Party (Nazi Party), by any cost. This again led to plenty of stricter laws regarding High Treason and Subversion, entering even the private sphere by proscribing every 'false' or 'inflammatory' statement about the Nazi Party independent of the place where it has been uttered.[40] The deluge of new regulations finally was incorporated into the Criminal Code in 1934 with the so-called *Verratsnovelle* ('Treason Amendment'),[41] which marked the temporary end of the drastic changes in state protection legislation. The 'core crimes', High Treason and Subversion, were separated into two sections of the code, their preparation and attempt being punishable from very early stages on. Death penalty became the generally intended sentence, although custodial sentences were possible in minor cases.[42]

As every other public organ, the *Reichsanwaltschaft* as executing authority of those very laws was subject to measures of enforced conformity and 'racial purging' after the seizing of power through Hitler. The only prominent victim to those operations amongst the *Reichsanwaltschaft* was the prosecutor Dr. Richard Neumann. Because of his Jewish descent, he was removed from office in 1935. He had been kept in duty both for his reputation as an unyielding prosecutor of Communist Party members and as a so-called 'alibi jew', but was incarcerated in the concentration camp Theresienstadt eventually.[43] Nevertheless, his colleagues at the *Reichsanwaltschaft* supposedly appreciated the new government as it marked the abandonment of democracy and fuelled the fire of the authority's communist hunters.[44] With the installation of the Special Tribunals and the *Volksgerichtshof*

[38] RGBl. I 1993, p. 85.

[39] RGBl. I 1933, p. 479.

[40] *Heimtückegesetz* ('Treachery Act'), RGBl. 1934, p. 1269. See also Dörner (1998), p. 30 f.

[41] *Gesetz zur Änderung von Vorschriften des Strafrechts und Strafverfahrens* ('German Criminal and Criminal Procedural Code Amendment Act'), RGBl. I 1934, p. 341.

[42] Gutfleisch (2014), p. 43.

[43] He survived the war, worked as a prosecutor in Berlin afterwards and became president of a Penal Senate at the Federal Criminal Court.

[44] C.p. Kaul (1971), p. 58 f.

(VG, 'People's Court'),[45] the *Reichsanwaltschaft* became even more influential in terms of supporting the Nazi objectives. Both elements of the *Reichsanwaltschaft's* jurisdiction have been affected by Nazi legislation: On the one hand, it was the *Volksgerichtshof's* primary goal to speed up the penal processing of subversives and political enemies (such as communists and social-democrats). The court was therefore created in such a way that its mechanisms were extremely 'efficient'; additionally, the state representatives involved were increased in staff. On the other hand, the Prosecution had been given additional tools to work with: first, the so-called 'invalidity appeal'. This special legal remedy allowed the Federal Prosecutors to appeal any decision within a year in case a verdict was 'unjust'—therefore invalid—in the underlying application of law to the facts as they were established in trial. Similarly, the 'extraordinary objection' not only referred a case back to a trial court like a successful invalidity appeal, but enabled special senates to decide directly upon a case that previously had been allegedly handled the wrong way. Those tools were used to mitigate convictions of those loyal to the Nazi leadership and to draconically exacerbate sentencing against people that were considered 'parasites to the German people'.[46] With this powerful and obviously abusive legal toolkit, it comes as no surprise that some of the worst legal professionals of the Nazi era were members of the Public Prosecutor General: Ernst Lautz, for example, who received a ten-year sentence in the Nuremberg Judge's Trial[47] in 1947. For Wolfgang Fränkel, his fanatical ambition in making use of this very toolkit should later suddenly end his post-war career as soon as his past was uncovered.

The later Federal Prosecutor Walter Wagner has described the machinery of the *Volksgerichtshof*, of which the *Reichsanwaltschaft* was an essential part, as an 'instrument of terror outside the ordinary jurisdiction'.[48] Through involvement in political criminal law—which for that matter also included 'racial defilement cases'—in the role of the initial prosecuting authority and their inflammatory influence on appeal proceedings, the *Reichsanwaltschaft* helped to permeate the German judicial system with the national-socialist world view.

With the dreading of the Second World War, state protection legislation was tightened once more. The focus was then laid on further criminalising 'undermining of military morale', 'subversion of the war effort' and 'weakening the faith of the people' (the umbrella term was *Wehrkraftzersetzung*, translating to 'decomposition

[45] Article. 3 *Gesetz zur Änderung von Vorschriften des Strafrechts und des Strafverfahrens* ('German Criminal and Criminal Procedural Code Amendment Act', in effect as of 2 March 1934), RGBl. I 1934, p. 341, introduced the VGH as a form of special tribunal; it became a so-called *ordentliches Gericht* ('regular court of law') by the *Gesetz über den Volksgerichtshof und über die fünfundzwanzigste Änderung des Besoldungsgesetzes* ('Statute for the *Volksgerichtshof* and the 25th Amendment of the Salary Act'), RGBl. I 1936, p. 369.

[46] *Volksschädlingsverordnung* ('Ordinance on Antisocial Parasites'), RGBl. I 1939, p. 1679.

[47] Part of the Subsequent Nuremberg Trials.

[48] Wagner (1974), p. 861.

of the power of the defence'). New laws[49] also prohibited any interaction with external forces, be it by simply listening to foreign radio stations[50] or through the actual betrayal of secrets.

Evaluating the application of the set of rules for the protection of the state, it is to be emphasised that the courts—including the introduced *Sondergerichte* (Special Tribunals)—interpreted the law in conformity with the new order. The abolition of the basic prohibitions of retroactivity and against reasoning by analogy[51] made this fairly easy though, and modifications of the Code of Criminal Procedure detrimental to the interests of the accused topped that off.

2.3 After the Second World War: The Federal Republic of Germany ('Western Germany')

After the end of the Second World War, the German Reich within its original borders before the Nazis' expansion campaign fell into four occupation zones as well as the divided city of Berlin, the Saar region and the areas lost due to the war. Initially, the legislative power rested with the Joint Control Council of the Allied Commanders-in-Chief and in principle, the laws of the German Reich remained in full force in all occupied zones as well as Berlin. To abolish the whole body of law or even all of the laws passed since 1933 was never seriously taken into consideration.[52] Instead, the Commanders-in-Chief repealed those rules that struck them especially influenced by radical ideology with the Allied Control Council Acts No. 1, 11 and 55. This affected special laws assigned to political crime (like for example the *Heimtückegesetz*—'Treachery Act'—of 1934[53]) as well as the state protection regulation sections of the Criminal Code. To protect their German personnel and whistleblowers from prosecution, the Allies did not only reset state protection norms to their pre-Nazi editing, but revoked them altogether, so that the newly formed federal states of 1945 lacked any form of state protection regulations. The idea that defending the state (or the federal states respectively) might be necessary by means of the law was then developed in the shape of the 'well-fortified democracy' concept that was installed in the federal states' constitutions. As the British, French and American decision-makers prepared the constitution for the future German state at

[49] *Kriegssonderstrafrechtsverordnung* (KSSVO, 'Wartime Regulations for Criminal Procedures'), RGBl. 1939, p. 1455; *Verordnung zur Ergänzung der Strafvorschriften zum Schutz der Wehrkraft des Deutschen* ('Additional Criminal Provisions for the Protection of German Military Strength Act'), RGBl. I 1939, p. 2319.

[50] *Verordnung über außerordentliche Rundfunkmaßnahmen* ('Regulation for Exceptional Broadcasting Measures'), RGBl. 1939 I, p. 1683.

[51] *Gesetz zur Änderung des Strafgesetzbuches* ('German Criminal Code Amendment Act'), RGBl. I 1935, p. 839.

[52] Vormbaum (2009), p. 219.

[53] RGBl. 1934, p. 1269.

the Herrenchiemsee conference, they discussed the reintroduction of state protection laws, but only implemented High Treason in Art. 143 of the *Grundgesetz* (GG, 'Basic Law [of the Federal Republic of Germany]') as a temporary solution. The GG itself was created as an interim constitution: with the reunification in mind as the clearly set goal, the writers purposefully did not name the set of rules *Verfassung* = 'constitution', but chose a neutral term to mark its transitional character, as stated in the historic version of the preamble. However, the name has not been changed even after 1990.

2.3.1 The First Years of the Federal Republic (1951–1974)

2.3.1.1 General Idea of State Protection (Society and Politics) and Self-Conception of the Bureau of the Federal Prosecutor: Effects of the German 'Red Scare'

The re-organisation of state protection legislation took place in 'Western' Germany as intended per the *Erstes Strafrechtsänderungsgesetz* (1. StRÄG, 'First Criminal Law Amendment Act') in 1951,[54] but the people responsible had not been sure from where to expect the main threat for the young democracy. The radical right had quickly reactivated their political commitment under new flags, resulting in parliamentary representation. The left presence became prevalent though due to exceptional results of the German Communist Party (KPD), which intermediately was part of all federal state governments, and, of course, due to the general developments in world politics and the accompanying alienation of the Sowjet Occupation Zone. The rising tension between the 'two Germanys' primarily characterised the state protection efforts in the following years.

In 1951, the German Criminal Code (*Strafgesetzbuch*, StGB) (re-)introduced *Hochverrat* (High Treason), *Staatsgefährdung* (Subversion) and *Landesverrat* into the legal framework for protecting the state and its foundations. *Hochverrat* and *Staatsgefährdung* are meant to protect the domestic integrity of the state—which means its constitutional and territorial foundations—against attacks from the inside. *Hochverrat* is committed violently or by the threat of force whereas Subversion is always non-violent. *Hochverrat* is also more extensive, because it protects the constitutional order as a whole, while *Staatsgefährdung* only shields the very existence of the Federal Republic and some of its most basic principles. *Landesverrat* is geared to protecting the Federal Republic's position of power with respect to foreign governments. It penalises attacks of foreign states against Germany's legal assets and therefore criminalises leaking state secrets and espionage; it is therefore used as a general term for evoking or supporting exterior threats to the state.

[54] *Bundesgesetzblatt* (BGBl. 'Federal Law Gazette'), I 1951, p. 739.

Mechanisms of distancing oneself from negatively perceived concepts from the past played a big part in developing a new German self-image of the state and its protection. In the context of the act of compiling the state's constitutional basis, German scholars like to speak of the 'lessons learned from Weimar and the NS-injustice'. Not only because of the repeal of most of the legal framework for state protection,[55] it was obviously necessary to turn ones back on the legal and conceptual structures that had facilitated the Nazi regime. At the same time, under US-American influence the opposition to communism became, although textually a constant to National Socialism, an integral part of the early leadership's objectives. Especially in matters of state security legislation and policy, German self-definition can be described as having happened through a negative demarcation to the Soviet Occupation Zone and the principles it stood for.[56] In terms of the Federal Public Prosecutor's investigation responsibility, this became apparent in the prosecution of (alleged) communists for general subversive activities, treason in journalism or membership in a prohibited organisation after the ban of the Communist Party of Germany (KPD).[57] Contemporaries claimed that Germany experienced a similar 'Red Scare' as the United States under President McCarthy from 1947 to 1956. The numbers indicating such a phenomenon vary widely, though. As an example, the following figures shall be quoted, supposedly referring to investigational proceedings because of crimes against the state in 1963: the journalist Lutz Lehmann came forward with the publicity-effective number of 10.222 on television; the Federal Public Prosecutor's statistics for the Federal Ministry of Justice imply 2.190 and the GBA's general files state only 591. It has yet to be examined further how these numbers come together. In any case, it can be said that the state protection legislation of the young Federal Republic unburdened the prosecution of people with a communist mindset by letting it be enough that an otherwise legal endeavour is supported or linked to an anti-constitutional organisation to make an individual action a punishable crime. This led to extended prosecution of leaflet, journalistic activity or joining meetings or gatherings in certain suspicious contexts.

2.3.2 Formative Experiences

During the formative years of the Federal Public Prosecutor, the sheer number of proceedings against communists had a significant imprint on the agency's self-image. However, to further illustrate the 'coming of age'-story of the *Bundesanwaltschaft*, three incidents of the 60s up until the 90s are especially worth telling: First, the dismissal of the third Public Prosecutor General Wolfgang Fränkel, second, the Office's legal defeat in the so-called SPIEGEL-affair and third the year-long fight against the leftist terror group RAF.

---

[55] Allied Control Council Acts No. 1, 11 and 55.

[56] In depth: Farthofer (2019).

[57] Foschepoth (2017), pp. 99; 284.

2.3.2.1 Causa Fränkel: Tainted by the Nazi Past, Exposed by the Socialist Neighbour

After the prominent head of the Office Max Güde changed to parliamentary work for the Christian Democrats in 1961, the position of Prosecutor General was vacant. Following the natural order of things, the agency's senior prosecutor took over for the time being. This longest serving employee in the rank of a Federal Prosecutor was Wolfgang Fränkel, born in 1905. He was offered the office by also only recently appointed Minister of Justice Wolfgang Stammberger and accepted with effect as of 23 March 1962. He was suspended only four months later, after allegations brought forward by an East German propaganda brochure were found to be true: During the Nazi reign, Fränkel was verifiably involved in appeal trials that ended with the death sentence for already harshly punished convicts.[58] His role at the *Volksgerichtshof* was exposed by the 'Committee for German Unity' of the *Deutsche Demokratische Republik* (DDR, 'Democratic Republic of Germany'). The meticulously researched paper was based on original documents of *Reichsgericht* and *Reichsanwaltschaft*, which have been stored in Leipzig. It elaborated Fränkel's lack of professional ethics on 130 pages in painful detail, with the intent to call out what the DDR leadership saw as political hypocrisy and inconsistency in applying democratic principles to the task of filling the state's highest offices. The incident was therefore acrimonious to the Federal Public Prosecutor in two ways: it not only confronted the Office with its own tainted history, but the justified criticism came from the socialist neighbour that was the primary cause for investigation activity of the *Bundesanwaltschaft* at the time. However, it was not humbling enough of an experience yet. Other than his dismissal, the exposure did not lead to any legal consequences for Fränkel: the Court for Public Service at the Federal Criminal Court acquitted him of employment fraud in 1965[59] and the criminal case charging him with aiding in murder was dropped in 1967.[60] He had successfully pleaded loss of memory.

2.3.2.2 SPIEGEL Affair: A Victory for Liberal Media

Only a few months after the scandal revolving around Wolfgang Fränkel and his Nazi past, the so-called 'SPIEGEL affair' stirred up West Germany again, when the weekly political magazine 'DER SPIEGEL' published an article about the nation's

---

[58] Ausschuss für Deutsche Einheit/Vereinigung Demokratischer Juristen Deutschlands (ed.), '*Von der Reichsanwaltschaft zur Bundesanwaltschaft*' (1962) (booklet edited by organs of the Soviet Occupation Zone about the development from the *Reichsanwaltschaft* to the Federal Prosecutor's Office).

[59] *Bundesgerichtshof* (BGH 'German Federal Supreme Court'), judgement delivered on 16 July 1965, RiSt 2/64.

[60] Fieberg (2004), p. 116; Kaul (1971), p. 221; Podewin (1968), p. 121 (the date given for the decision is incorrect); c.p. also Panorama Deutschland, In: Spiegel-Ausgabe 32/1963 vom 07. August 1963, p. 12.

defence forces.[61] The piece broached the issue of German military policy and strategy in comparison to the NATO's fundamental choices under US-American influence, in particular nuclear armament.[62] Federal Prosecutor Siegfried Buback pressed charges against the journalists responsible, had them arrested and the editorial offices raided. The accusation: treason by the media. The Federal Criminal Court however rejected the opening of the main proceedings and the constitutional complaint issued by the two indicted editors was not successful only by a tied vote.[63] Post-war West Germany had thus passed this first test of freedom of the press. The Federal Public prosecutor, on the contrary, suffered considerable damage to its reputation as an agency. The Office had revealed 'restorative structures',[64] and in its compliant execution of orders from then-Minister-of-Defence Franz-Joseph Strauß indicated a conservative mind-set gravitating towards instrumentalisation of the argument of state protection for shutting down critique. In the further course of time, the Federal Republic experienced a political change towards shared government responsibility between the Christian Democrats and the Liberals or rather the Social Democrats. This also provided the framework[65] for the crucial reform of procedural criminal law in 1964[66] and the restructuring of state protection legislation as part of the reform of the German Criminal Code in 1969,[67] when state protection legislation was reorganised once again. Reflecting the distinction between threats from the inside and threats from the outside, the Criminal Code got two sections dedicated to state protection: The first one was called 'Betrayal of Peace, High Treason and Subversion of the Democratic State' and the second one was about *Landesverrat* and other general threats to external security. Both sections contained multiple variants of the crimes that captioned them. *Friedensverrat* ('Betrayal of Peace') for example was established as a new crime in two paragraphs. It penalised preparation of and call for war of aggression. Other crimes of internal subversion are sabotage, the violation of decisions of the Federal Constitutional Court, sharing of propaganda or displaying emblems of anticonstitutional organisations. Disparagement and undermining military morale still exist in slightly modified form. Betrayal of secrets, espionage, jeopardising peace and working for a foreign secret service are all modern variants of the second section dedicated to *Landesverrat* that still exist today.

[61] Ahlers and Schmelz (1962).

[62] For more detail see also Grosser and Seifert (1966), p. 56 ff.

[63] *Bundesverfassungsgericht* (BVerfG 'Federal Constitutional Court'), judgement delivered on 5 August 1966, BVerfGE 20, 162; 1 BvR 586/62. 610/63 and 512/64.

[64] Wilke (2016), p. 272.

[65] Acknowledging the extension of the 'rule of law'-principles and, consequently, both the rather liberal tendency of the two reforms and their substantial parallelism Rieß (2009), p. 466.

[66] *Gesetz zur Änderung der Strafprozessordnung und des Gerichtsverfassungsgesetzes* (StPÄG 'German Criminal Procedural and Judicature Amendment Act'), BGBl. I, 1964, p. 1067 (under Cabinet Erhard, economic-liberal/conservative).

[67] *Erstes Gesetz zur Reform des Strafrechts* (1. StrRG 'First Criminal Reform Law'), BGBl. I 1969, p. 645.

2.3.2.3 The 'German Autumn': Leftist Terror in the 70s

Scandals such as the employment of a critical individual like Wolfgang Fränkel or the acquittal of Hans-Joachim Rehse,[68] Judge at the *Volksgerichtshof* and colleague of the infamous Roland Freisler, triggered protests in West Germany by leftist youth in the late 60s. The movement identified issues such as racism, women's liberation and anti-imperialism and denounced that both Eastern and Western German denazification efforts had failed; the demonstrators remembered the harsh treatment of the SPIEGEL's investigative journalists and criticised that the rest of the predominantly conservative media landscape was biassed. It was from those riots that the RAF emerged. West German Government and Western media almost unanimously considered the 'Red Army Faction', also known as the Baader-Meinhof Gang,[69] a far-left terrorist organisation as they engaged in a series of violent subversive acts between 1970 and 1998.[70] As the RAF threatened national security, they quickly determined the Federal Public Prosecutor's daily business. In total, the RAF has been held responsible for at least thirty-three deaths, including important representatives of the constitutional state or symbol figures like the President of the Employers' Association Hanns-Martin Schleyer. Their activity peaked in late 1977 in a national crisis known as the 'German Autumn'. In the process, they got rid of their most persistent persecutor: Siegfried Buback. He had studied law during the Nazi regime and was therefore trained in national-socialist legal methodology; he also had joined the Nazi party in 1940. He came to the Bundesanwaltschaft in 1963, entered the rank of a Federal Prosecutor in 1971 and was appointed Prosecutor General in 1974. A RAF task force assassinated him on his way to work on 7 April 1977.

[68] BGH, judgement delivered on 30 April 1968, (the prior conviction was quashed and referred back to the district court), acquitted by Landgericht Berlin (LG 'district court'), judgement delivered on 6 December 1968, (500) 3 P (K) KS 1/67.

[69] The translation into 'faction' rather than 'fraction' depends on the exact understanding of the German term *Fraktion*, that can both stand for 'a small group within a larger group, consisting of people with different opinions from the rest' (as in 'fraction') as well as for 'a division or part of a whole' in the mathematical sense ('faction'). While the idea of the RAF as 'extra-parliamentary opposition' was predominant in the German reception, the RAF itself considered its name to be an expression of their belonging to a global communist, anti-imperialist guerilla movement, following Leninist terminology; compare for example 'Theses on the Structure of Communist Parties, submitted to the Third Congress of the Comintern' from 12 July 1921. The program states under section III. paragraph 11 that 'For the purpose of carrying out day-to-day work, each Party member should belong to a smaller working group: a committee, commission, board, group, fraction or cell'. Cited from https://www.marxists.org/history/international/comintern/3rd-congress/party-theses.htm (last accessed 8 June 2020) after Adler (1980). Employing a common media practice, officials referred to the group also as *Baader-Meinhof Bande* ('gang/group') after its most prominent leaders Andreas Baader and Ulrike Meinhof instead of publicly accepting the self-given, propagandistic battle name.

[70] For the RAF's history c.f. Horchem (1974); Winkler (2007); Hoffmann (1997); Weinhauer et al. (2006).

To respond to the threats evoked by the violent and inciting aggression of the group, since 1974 special regulations for counterterrorism have been enshrined in the Code of Criminal Procedure and the formation of terrorist organisations was implemented as a crime in § 129a of the German Criminal Code.[71] This ended the short-lived trend of decriminalisation, that in the years prior had led to, for example, the mitigation of demonstration regulations and the abolition of the criminal liability for 'morality offences'.[72] The procedural amendments included measures like 'veiled' and 'patterned' investigations, contact bans between the accused and their lawyers and later the leniency programme regarding terrorist crimes ('whistleblowing'). However, the 'new' crime of forming a terrorist organisation must be interpreted to some extent as token politics, because the establishment of § 129a StGB only enabled more severe punishment for politically motivated perpetrators (the term 'terrorist' itself was never defined). Forming a 'criminal' organisation—and every terrorist organisation usually is also a criminal organisation—has already been prohibited by § 129 StGB before. Primarily, the substantial counterterrorism laws of that period were created to justify extended pre-trial interventions. Other than substantial laws, the procedural rules that came with the new proscriptions could be applied to past acts, so that the authorities could demonstrate their ability to cope with the situation.

Not only the search for RAF members and the attempts to stop attacks from happening shaped the Office's activity in those troublesome days, but also the dispute with individual captured terrorists in court. Members of the GBA once had shown little enthusiasm in the face of novelties like the compulsory appointment of a defence lawyer during hearings in the pre-trial phase.[73] In internal notes they referred to this concept, that was introduced in 1964, as 'potentially hindering to the effectiveness of the investigation proceedings'.[74] Little did they know that soon, they would be confronted with an even more uncomfortable presence of the defence. In the legal treatment of the RAF crimes, the Bundesanwaltschaft entered into open hostility to the defence that spawned a new strategy and type of defence counsel by merging in the phenomenon of 'conflict defence'. Though aggressive tension in the courtroom, disturbances at the trial and the abuse of the defendant's rights have been known forever, they had previously remained a rare occasion in German proceedings. The adversary conduct of negotiations only developed into a proven method in the political trials of the 60s, 70s and 80s, where the accused questioned the order of

[71] *Gesetz zur Änderung des Strafgesetzbuches, der Strafprozeßordnung, des Gerichtsverfassungsgesetzes, der Bundesrechtsanwaltsordnung des Strafvollzuggesetzes* ('German Criminal Code, Criminal Procedural Code, Judiciary Act, Federal Lawyers Act and Penal Code Amendment Act'), BGBl. I 1976, p. 2181.

[72] C.f. Heger (2019).

[73] *Gesetz zur Änderung der Strafprozessordnung und des Gerichtsverfassungsgesetzes* (StPÄG 'German Criminal Procedural and Judiciary Amendment Act' so-called 'small criminal law reform' particularly the amendment of § 130 German Criminal Procedural Code), BGBl. I 1964, p. 1074 – entry into force on 1 April 1965.

[74] General Records of the Federal Public Prosecutor (archive in Karlsruhe), GenA 410 SH II p. 144.

the state and wished to demonstrate their rejection of the status quo.[75] At the same time, it was the goal of the defence not only to positively make political statements, but also to destructively ridicule the prosecution and the court. This made it necessary (and still provides material for discussions today) to differentiate between legitimate defence and improper exercise of rights of defence. Understandably, this demeanour also provoked a more sworn in and likewise outgoing attitude and generally high identification with the purpose of the trial on the side of the involved prosecutors. The experience of those trials and the trauma of being directly victimised by the public enemy changed the self-image of the Federal Public Prosecutor. However, it did not lead to a long-lasting radicalisation or entrenched anti-liberalism. It seems plausible to attribute this to the already consolidated constitutional framework in which this state protection crisis unfolded.

2.3.3 Modern Legislation (Reunification Until Today)

Despite his functional responsibility, the Federal Public Prosecutor was not engaged in the series of post-war trials for National Socialist Crimes of Violence (*NSG-Verfahren*), but those proceedings were left to the OLGs and their local Prosecution Offices. Nothing to little steered the GBA's focus away from prosecuting communists and leftist extremists up until the German reunification. The 1990s were characterised by xenophobic crimes and an increase in extremist activities of foreigners and state-facilitated terrorism.[76] The shift towards Islamist terror as the GBA's main concern was also already on the horizon at that time and finally peaked on 11 September 2001—an event of worldwide significance, which raised awareness for the danger of terrorist attacks from abroad amongst German authorities as well.

The legislation reforms following the 9/11 attacks—unlike previous legislative amendments in post-Nazi Germany—criminalised behaviour that has not been punishable through any other law before. To unburden legal actions against supporters of, for example, Al Qaeda, in 2002 it became a punishable crime to be part of a criminal or terrorist group, even if it is based in a foreign country (§§ 129, 129a, 129b StGB).[77] The idea however dated back to the attacks against the US embassies in Kenia and Tanzania in 1998 and was actually an EU directive.[78] The liberal

[75] Heinrich (2013), p. 1 f.

[76] C.f. Heger (2019).

[77] *34. Strafrechtsänderungsgesetz* (34. StrÄndG '34th Criminal Code Amendment Act') BGBl. I 2002, p. 3390.

[78] 98/733/JHA: Joint action of 21 December 1998 adopted by the Council on the basis of Article K.3 of the Treaty on European Union, on making it a criminal offence to participate in a criminal organisation in the Member States of the European Union, 98/733/JHA: Joint action of 21 December 1998 adopted by the Council on the basis of Article K.3 of the Treaty on European Union, on making it a criminal offence to participate in a criminal organisation in the Member States of the European Union, OJ L 351, 12/20/1998, pp. 1–3.

government of the time had been hesitant to bring it into action, but international and public pressure led the decision makers to pass the law eventually.

The latest trend in state protection legislation was the extension of criminal liability in preliminary stages of violent subversion even beyond the dogmatics of attempt and completion.[79] In June 2015, § 89a was amended[80] to proscribe the outward voyage from Germany to another country, if this is done in order to prepare acts of violent subversion by receiving instructions on how to use, produce or acquire rifles, explosives, poison etc. Unlike the legal innovation might suggest, this was by no means a new phenomenon: The first generation of the infamous RAF did exactly that when they went to Jordan in 1970 to train with guerrillas and looked to the Palestinian cause for inspiration and guidance. The 2015 amendment of § 89a got the unofficial name 'Terror Camp Paragraph' and the BGH recently confirmed that it could be interpreted in accordance with the Constitution despite its wide formulation.[81]

3 Current Challenges

Germany's turbulent past with regards to state protection legislation was influenced by the ever-alternating backgrounds of hostility against the state. With the NSU-scandal and most recent events like the murder of District President of Kassel, Dr. Walter Lübcke,[82] or the attack on a synagogue in Halle on 9 October 2019,[83] the Federal Public Prosecutor is more involved in investigations against the radical right than against the radical left.

[79] Generally about the idea of and legal dealing with inchoate offences in Germany, England and the Netherlands c.f. Keiler and Roef (2016), pp. 203–234.

[80] *Gesetz zur Änderung der Verfolgung der Vorbereitung von schweren staatsgefährdenden Gewalttaten* (GVVG-ÄndG 'Law Amending the Prosecution of the Preparation of Serious Acts of Violence Against the State'), BGBl. I 2015, p. 926.

[81] BGH, judgement delivered on 6 April 2017, BGHSt 62, 102.

[82] Pressemitteilung Nr. 23 des GBA vom 17.06.2019 (press declaration no. 23 given by the GBA on 17 June 2019), https://www.generalbundesanwalt.de/SharedDocs/Pressemitteilungen/DE/2019/Pressemitteilung-vom-17-06-2019.html?nn=478310 (last accessed 18 February 2020).

[83] Pressemitteilung Nr. 42 des GBA vom 10.10.2019 (press declaration no. 42 given by the GBA on 10 October 2019), https://www.generalbundesanwalt.de/SharedDocs/Pressemitteilungen/DE/2019/Pressemitteilung2-vom-10-10-2019.html?nn=478310 (last accessed 18 February 2020).

3.1 The Scandal Around the Investigations Leading up to the 'NSU'-Trials: Inefficiency of Domestic Intelligence Due to 'Bund-Länder'-Frictions

The neo-Nazi terrorist organisation *Nationalsozialistischer Untergrund* (NSU, 'National Socialist Underground') committed ten murders, three bomb attacks, and 15 bank robberies in the years between 1998 and 2011. They did not claim responsibility for their crimes and were not discovered by law enforcement until 4 November 2011. Politicians and the mainstream media since have titled the so-called NSU case one of the biggest 'failures' of the German law enforcement and the secret services. These failures were allegedly caused by individual 'mistakes' as well as competition and a lack of coordination between the responsible authorities. The Prosecutor General was in charge of the investigations only since the end of 2011, after the organisation had proclaimed their existence publicly. The Domestic Intelligence Services however have been watching supporters in the sphere of the NSU before. The so-called '*Operation Rennsteig*' became the centre of the NSU scandal: As it turned out in 2012, '*Operation Rennsteig*' was a cooperation between The Domestic Secret Service of the federal state of Thuringia, the BfV and the MAD. During the course of the secret mission, the far-right extremist scene of Thuringia was supposed to be infiltrated and eventually taken over by the states' agents to keep it controllable in the long run. This was harshly criticised as it supposedly aided the rise of the radical right underground forces that eventually fuelled the NSU attacks. Among other sensitive revelations, this lead to a *Verfassungsschutzreform* ('Amendment of Laws regarding the Protection of the Constitution') in 2015,[84] which regulated the use of state's agents, granted more budget and personnel to the BfV and enhanced joint data and information administration between the authorities. It is still discussed though whether the BfV should be allowed to interfere on the federal state level even against the will of the State Offices for the Protection of the Constitution.

3.2 Terrorism Department at the Office of the Prosecutor General

As per 3 January 2019,[85] the GBA's Department Terrorism has initiated a total of 1168 investigation proceedings in 2018, of which

[84] *Gesetz zur Verbesserung der Zusammenarbeit im Bereich des Verfassungsschutzes* ('Law on Improving Cooperation in the Field of the Protection of the Constitution'), BGBl. I 2015, p. 1938 ff.

[85] Bundestagsdrucksache 19/6904, Terrorismusverfahren in der Generalbundesanwaltschaft [sic] im Jahr 2018, (BT-Drs. 19/6904, printed matter of the Bundestag regarding prosecution of terrorism by the Federal Prosecutor's Office 2018; answer by the Federal Government regarding the 'small

- 305 are regarding international, non-Islamist terrorism
- 855 regarding Islamist terrorism (but none with regards to international far-right extremist terrorism)
- six purely national investigations were connected to far-right extremist terrorism
- and one investigation was held each for international and national radical left terrorism.

The Federal Ministry of Justice and Consumer Protection boosted the Federal Public Prosecutor's budget more than any of its other authorities in 2020s financial plans.[86] This extra money will most likely be spent for fighting the crime type usually referred to as 'the repatriates from Syria': individuals with German citizenship that leave the country to radicalise and then return to either support their terrorist organisation or plan attacks themselves.

3.3 Resume

Konrad Adenauer, 1st chancellor of The Federal Republic of Germany, assured in his first governmental statement on 20 September 1949:

> While the Federal Government is dedicated to let the past be past where it appears to be objectively justifiable, it is, on the other hand, even more dedicated to draw the right conclusions from the past, confronting all those who are up to shaking the very existence of our state, may they be extremist left-wing or extremist right-wing.

In the same speech, Adenauer commented rather condescendingly on press statements from foreign countries that had uttered concerns about far-right machinations in Germany. Those perceptions for sure must be exaggerated, the Chancellor was convinced. In the public eye, the already re-organising far-right was insignificant compared to the far-left, whose threatening aura grew in accordance with the escalating east-west conflict, both through a global and the uniquely German perspective. Under Adenauer, members of the communist party that had been persecuted by the Nazi-regime during 1933 and 1945 were disallowed their status as victims of the NS-injustice. The decision of the Federal Constitutional Court to ban the Communist Party of Germany in 1956 has been upheld until today. According to reports by the Federal Office for the Protection of the Constitution, the succession party DKP and seven sub-organisations of DIE LINKE (the left-wing party elected to the current parliament) still impose a threat to the basic democratic order of the state. The relationship of the German state to the political conviction that can be described as communism, is therefore similarly tense today as it is to national-

---

inquiry' by the representatives Martina Renner, Dr. André Hahn, Gökay Akbulut, additional representatives and the fraction DIE LINKE).

[86] LTO (ed.) (2019), 17 Millionen Euro mehr für die Justiz, https://www.lto.de/recht/nachrichten/n/justiz-bundeshaushalt-2020-etat-17-millionen-euro-zuwachs-anstieg/ (last accessed 17 October 2019).

conservative attitudes. Whether it is justified to speak of a ‘communist hunt’ in the young Federal Republic has been, amongst other issues, one of the research subjects in the project investigating the Federal Public Prosecutor’s formative years, presented in the book “Staatsschutz im Kalten Krieg” by Kießling and Safferling (2021). The question is directly linked to the self-discovery of a young democratic state in the unrest of history that affected developments in legislation, foreign politics and the public appearance of executive authorities. The political climate has definitely influenced especially the amendments in the legislation for state protection of the last 50 years in the form of stricter and further criminalisation, usually shortly before a federal election.[87] The population’s need for security turned out to be a main driver for voting behaviour, so naturally the parties do not take risks to neglect concerns triggered by threatening events like terrorist attacks. This has traditionally been true for the conservative parties, but also for the more liberal ones, that, after a short period of decriminalisation attempts, jumped on the bandwagon of anti-terror-legislation for example in the 1976 election campaign of Helmut Schmidt or the Social Democrat-Green-Government in 2002. Protecting the democratic state through criminal law is thus a very delicate topic deserving of further historical revision as well as future critical analysis.

References

Adler A (ed) (1980) Theses Resolutions and Manifestos of the First Four Congress of the Third International (trans: Holt A, Holland B). Ink Links, London

Ahlers C, Schmelz H (1962) “Bedingt abwehrbereit”, In: Spiegel-Ausgabe 41/1962 vom 10. Oktober 1962, pp. 34–53

Bernstein E (1907) Die Geschichte der Berliner Arbeiterbewegung. Ein Kapitel zur Geschichte der deutschen Sozialdemokratie, Teil I. Buchhandlung Vorwärts, Berlin; reprint by Detlev Auvermann, Glashütten (1972)

Dörner B (1998) “Heimtücke”: Das Gesetz als Waffe. Ferdinand Schöningh, Parderborn et al.

Farthofer H (2019) Neuausrichtung des Staatsschutzes nach 1945? V&R, Göttingen

Fieberg G (2004) Wolfgang Fränkel. In: Justizministerium des Landes Nordrhein-Westfalen (ed) Zwischen Recht und Unrecht – Lebensläufe deutscher Juristen, Justizministerium des Landes Nordrhein-Westfalens, Düsseldorf

Foschepoth J (2017) Verfassungswidrig!. Das KPD-Verbot im Kalten Bürgerkrieg. V&R, Göttingen

Grosser A, Seifert J (1966) Die Spiegel Affäre 1 – Die Staatsmacht und ihre Kontrolle. Walter, Olten

Gutfleisch U (2014) Staatsschutzstrafrecht in der Bundesrepublik Deutschland 1951-1968. BWV, Berlin

Hankel G (2003) Die Leipziger Prozesse. Deutsche Kriegsverbrechen und ihre strafrechtliche Verfolgung nach dem ersten Weltkrieg. Hamburger Edition, Hamburg

Heger M (2019) Ein Ende der Kriminalisierung – Die Strafgesetze zur Bekämpfung des Terrorismus in der Bundesrepublik der 1970er Jahre. In: Petzsche A, Heger M, Metzler G

[87] C.f. Heger (2019).

(eds) (2006) Terrorismusbekämpfung in Europa im Spannungsfeld zwischen Freiheit und Sicherheit. Nomos, Baden-Baden, pp 47–64
Heinrich J (2013 [2016]) Konfliktverteidigung im Strafprozess. C.H. Beck, München
Hoffmann M (ed) (1997) Rote-Armee-Fraktion: Texte und Materialien zur Geschichte der RAF. ID-Verlag, Berlin
Horchem HJ (1974) West Germany's Red Army anarchists. Institute for the Study of Conflict, London
Kaul FK (1971) Geschichte des Reichtsgerichts 1933 – 1945 Band IV. Detlev Auvermann KG, Glashütten i. Taunus
Keiler J, Roef D (2016) Inchoate offences. In: Keiler J, Roef D (eds) Comparative concepts of criminal law. Intersentia Ltd, Cambridge et al.
Kett-Straub G, Kudlich H (2017) Sanktionenrecht. C.H. Beck, München
Kießling F, Safferling C (2021) Staatsschutz im Kalten Krieg, dtv München
Lee Y (2012) Punishing disloyalty? Treason, espionage, and the transgression of political boundaries. Law Philos 31(3):299–342
Maiwald M (1972) Zum fragmentarischen Charakter des Strafrechts. In: Schroeder FC, Zipf H (eds) Festschrift für Reinhart Maurach zum 70. Geburtstag. C.F. Müller, Karlsruhe, pp 9–23
Podewin N (ed) (2002) Braunbuch: Kriegs- und Naziverbrecher in der Bundesrepublik und in Berlin (West). Das neue Berlin, Berlin (reprint 1968)
Rieß P (2009) Entwicklungstendenzen in der deutschen Strafprozessgesetzgebung seit 1950. ZIS (Zeitschrift für Internationale Strafrechtsentwicklung) 10(2009):466–483
Schroeder FC (1970) Der Schutz von Staat und Verfassung im Strafrecht. C.H. Beck, München
Schwend K (1954) Bayern zwischen Monarchie und Diktatur. Pflaum, München
v. Treutlein-Moerdes J (1904) Die Staatsanwaltschaft bei dem Reichsgerichte. In: Die ersten 25 Jahre des Reichsgerichts, Sonderheft des Sächsischen Archivs für Deutsches Bürgerliches Recht zum 25-jährigen Bestehen des höchsten Deutschen Gerichtshofs. Rossberg, Leipzig
Vormbaum T (2009) Einführung in die modern Strafrechtsgeschichte. Springer, Berlin
Wagner W (1974) Der Volksgerichtshof im nationalsozialistischen Staat. Oldenbourg, München
Weinhauer K, Requate J, Haupt HG (eds) (2006) Terrorismus in der Bundesrepublik: Medien, Staat und Subkulturen in den 1970er Jahren. Campus Verlag, Frankfurt am Main
Wilke M (2016) Staatsanwälte als Anwälte des Staates? Die Strafverfolgungspraxis von Reichsanwaltschaft und Bundesanwaltschaft vom Kaiserreich bis in die frühe Bundesrepublik. V&R, Göttingen
Winkler W (2007) Die Geschichte der RAF. Rowohlt Berlin Verlag, Berlin

Jana Kuhlmann Dipl.-Jur. (Univ.) has worked as Research Assistant until 2022 at the chair for Criminal Law, Criminal Procedure and International Criminal Law and Public International Law held by Prof. Dr. Christoph Safferling LL.M. (LSE), Friedrich-Alexander-Universität Erlangen-Nürnberg. She is currently a Legal Trainee in Hamburg. Her doctorate revolves around issues of German contemporary legal history. The essay was originally created as a two-part presentation at the workshop 'Policy of Dealing with the Past: a German-Polish Dialogue' on 10/30/2018 in Erlangen and 10/09/2019 in Warsaw, respectively. The lecture form and content has essentially been retained for this chapter.

The Combat of Communist Ideology and Propaganda in the Legal Order of the Second Republic of Poland, 1918–1939

Kamil Słomiński

Abstract In this chapter, the author analyses the combat of communist ideology and propaganda in the legal order of the Second Republic of Poland from the legal and historical perspective. The 'combat' included in the title refers to actions undertaken by legislative, executive and—most essentially—judicative branch of power towards communists. This chapter seeks to examine several judicial decisions including soft-law acts. The forms of combatting communism are captured in the context of fundamental rights as well as the diversity of legal and political doctrines. The author undertakes a comprehensive study of this phenomenon, taking into account the historical point of view as well as the development of legal research from the Second Republic of Poland until present day.

1 Introduction

The term 'ideology' may be interpreted from different scientific standpoints. It may be described as a set of ideals or demands which are more concrete than pure 'idea'. According to the Cambridge Dictionary, ideology is a set of beliefs or principles, especially those on which a political system, party, or an organisation is based, e.g. socialist/capitalist ideology.[1] In case when the political and legal demands are concretised, they are expressed in a corresponding doctrine. Political and legal doctrine should be interpreted as a consistent and structured set of views regarding social life, which has its own ideological and philosophical basis.[2] Political agenda is based on specific doctrines. Additionally, in the European history of legal and

[1] Meaning of ideology in English, https://dictionary.cambridge.org/dictionary/english/ideology (last accessed 1 December 2023).

[2] Izdebski (2017), p. 16.

K. Słomiński (✉)
Faculty of Law and Administration, University of Warsaw, Warsaw, Poland
e-mail: k.slominski@uw.edu.pl

M.-E. Geis et al. (eds.), *Dealing with Totalitarian Regimes and Human Rights*, Interdisciplinary Studies in Human Rights 11,
https://doi.org/10.1007/978-3-031-57338-5_7

political thinking, other autonomous visions of ideology are at stake. Namely, it may be perceived as an element of state repression, which is responsible for reproduction of social relations and subordination of an individual to the state.[3] In this chapter, the term 'ideology' shall be used and understood as a set of concepts which is more precise than an idea but not as explicit as a legal and political doctrine. When the terms communism or doctrine of communism will be mentioned in this work, it will be so with the concrete postulate of this paradigm being taken into consideration.

The phenomenon 'propaganda' has changed its meaning throughout centuries. Initially, propaganda was a term not burdened with negative connotations. Thus, its meaning may be understood neutrally and not necessarily as a method of indoctrination.[4] The main functions of propaganda are: integration, agitation, information and disinformation.[5] In the two murderous totalitarian regimes, nazism and Stalinism, propaganda bore its own crucial role in underpinning the prevalent social relations. After these experiences, it was necessary to radically change the meaning of the term. L. Fraser, in 1957, highlighted, that propaganda should be defined as 'the activity, or the art, of including others to behave in a way in which they would not behave in its absence'.[6] The propaganda was perceived as a crucial element in 'manufacturing consent'.[7] However, in this chapter, propaganda will be understood as ways and methods of promotion of political and legal doctrine. That is to say—as a neutral term.

2 Origins of the Polish Communist Movement in the Interwar Period

Political communist structures in Poland were created simultaneously with the constitution of the independent Polish state within new borders after the First World War. Earlier, at the time of the partitions, political organisations referring to Marxism were active on the Polish territory. Among such groups were i.a.: the International Social Revolutionary Party 'Proletariat' (The First Proletariat), the Social Revolutionary Party 'Proletariat' (The Second Proletariat), the Social Democracy of the Kingdom of Poland and Lithuania (SDKPIL) and the Polish Socialist Party – Left. These organisations had different views concerning the independence of Poland and the social and economic status of the peasantry.

Polish social democrats perceived revolution very similarly to the original Marxists. The outburst of the revolutionary process was supposed to appear inevitable and necessary. The main thinker of Polish Marxism before 1918 was Rosa Luxemburg.

[3] Cf. Althusser (1971), pp. 127–186.

[4] Zwoliński (2003), pp. 238–255.

[5] Cf. Kuśmierski (1980), p. 108.

[6] Fraser (1957), p. 1.

[7] Herman and Chomsky (2002), pp. 1–112.

She was an active member of SDKPIL. Luxemburg explained that the class struggle should be based on mutual aid and cooperation between the broad masses. Furthermore, the role of the social democratic party was thought to be crucial; its actions should concentrate on propaganda and pointing at the inevitability of revolution.[8] Revolution was supposed to be an effect of multiannual social democratic agitation. SDKPIL denied that there was any point in the struggle for an independent Polish state. According to the Party leaders, the aim was to conduct revolution, after which it would be possible to gain full national and social liberation, within the form of an international republic.[9] Luxemburg rejected Lenin's policy concerning the self-determination of nations. She highlighted that, 'under the reign of capitalism, there is no self-determination'.[10] SDKPIL and the Polish Socialist Party – Left criticised the Bolsheviks for the realisation of the dictatorship of the proletariat as an element of the party's dictatorship as well as for the liquidation of citizens' freedoms.[11] Predecessors of the Communist Party of Poland projected the abolition of private property in agriculture. They planned the creation of huge collective farms.[12]

Undoubtedly, Marxism and Leninism had a huge impact on Polish communists. European Marxists were active in the First and Second Internationals which constituted a platform of cooperation between labour and socialist organisations. The idea of a European labour movement may be perceived as an external inspiration for Polish socialists before the First World War. According to Trembicka, the essential consequences of Marxist thought were immense social costs and the need to create a 'new man', which was being realised in Russia after 1917 by the Bolsheviks.[13] The Russian socialist movement had especially strong links with Poland. The Leninist revolution certainly made an impact on communist groups in Polish territory. Lenin rejected any legal battle for gaining power and introduced a centralist rule in the Party. He significantly changed philosophical and political fundamentals of Marxist ideology. Lenin accepted the concept of a revolution in individual countries, even those which were not highly developed. Moreover, he supported cooperation between the peasantry and the proletariat in order to gain power. The Leninist legal and political thought rejected pluralism, the separation of powers and the rule of law. Bosiacki considered that the Bolsheviks created a new system based on intuitive unwritten rules. The law was reduced to a system of penal codes and served as a regulator of repression combined with the sphere of power.[14]

[8]Kochański (1976), pp. 185–186.

[9]Trembicka (2007), pp. 13–49.

[10]Ciołkosz (1961), pp. 198–199.

[11]Ciołkosz (1961), pp. 206–207.

[12]Trembicka (2007), p. 29.

[13]Trembicka (2007), p. 16.

[14]Bosiacki (1999), pp. 15–42.

3 Activity of Polish Communists in the Interwar Period

On 16 December 1918, the Communist Workers' Party of Poland (KPRP) was created, thanks to the unification between SDKPIL and Polish Socialist Party – Left. In 1925, the Party was renamed to 'Communist Party of Poland (KPP)'. KPP belonged to the Third International, which was created upon Lenin's request. The Party constituted the backbone of communism in the interwar Poland. KPP coordinated and supervised the activity of organisations like Polish Communist Youth Association or the section of International Red Aid (MOPR). 'Bund'—leftist and anti-zionist Jewish party was also treated as a communist organisation.[15]

Polish leftist movement was divided into social democratic Polish Socialist Party (PPS) and communists (KPP). Both parties strove for gaining power for the labour class and building a socialist society. PPS approved of parliamentarian system and political pluralism. Fundamentally, this party rejected the Leninist model of power. On the contrary, the KPP proposed revolting and gaining power through violence. This factor ultimately led to KPP being regarded as an illegal organisation.[16] Polish communists disagreed with the concept of Polish independence and worked for the international community. The Revolution in Poland was supposed to be a part of a universal revolution.[17]

It is noteworthy that members of the Polish communist movement actively opposed to institutions of the new Polish state. They boycotted the first general elections in 1919. On 13 January 1919, S. Wojciechowski, Polish minister of internal affairs, highlighted that it is necessary to fight with anarchy and Bolshevism.[18] In 1920, during the Polish-Russian war, creation of the new Polish state was planned. Polish communists joined the Provisional Polish Revolutionary Committee (Polrewkom), which was created in Moscow. During the war, many Polish citizens in the East collaborated with the Soviet power. In Poland, their activity was perceived as betrayal. After the Russian's defeat, communists changed their tactic and decided that Polish proletariat has to act 'as a leader and spokesmen of the whole nation'.[19] It was found that the real independence of Poland can be realised only as an effect of workers' revolution. In its program from the 1932, KPP promoted the dictatorship of proletariat and the confiscation of the land property.[20]

Communist movement in the interwar period was focused around a few factors: approval for political changes in Russia and aspiration for the creation of 'Polish Soviet Republic'; objection to the state apparatus of new Poland; aspiration for

[15]Cf. Collection of the Supreme Court's rulings. Rulings of the Second Criminal Chamber [next: CSCR.RSC(C)], Warsaw 1923, pp. 324–325, pos. 215, Szpajzer and others case.

[16]Cf. CSCR.RSC(C), Warsaw 1924, pp. 93–99, pos. 46, Toeplitz case.

[17]Tomicki (1987), p. 118.

[18]Ławnik (1979), p. 72.

[19]Daniszewski (1954), p. 19.

[20]Tomicki (1987), pp. 136–137.

revolutionary coup, which could possibly be committed thanks to a collaboration with foreign states.

4 Freedom of Speech in the Second Republic of Poland

The problem regarding freedom of speech in a young state is combined with a 'transitional justice' issue. The level on which this freedom is guaranteed, very often depends on stability and security of a newly created state. One can say, that power which is endangered tends to radicalise its punitive side. Freedom of speech may be a neglected value because the core of statehood itself is insecure and requires exceptional regulations which interfere with the area of citizens' freedoms.

Polish state which regained its independence after 123 years of partitions had to struggle with external enemies and shaped its new borders in a very complicated process. Already in 1918, workers' committees were being created in Poland. These political organisms were associated with the Soviets. Polish politicians reacted very sharply against creation of communist organisations on the Polish territory. Polish Prime Minister J. Moraczewski announced harsh repressions against those who use freedom of speech to 'undermine the authority of a state power'.[21] As a way to prevent communist ideas from spreading, there were restored parts of the Russian, Prussian and Austrian criminal acts which criminalised political and state crimes. But one of the more important measures, which helped in the fight against communist propaganda, was a press law.

A system of press law, which was used in order to combat communist propaganda, was really complicated and multi-level. In February 1919, the Decree on provisional press provisions[22] was enacted upon Paderewski's government request. This act formally declared the freedom of press (Article 1). Other regulations concerned limitations of this freedom. Censorship was prohibited, but press publishers and editors had to be aware of the possibility of application of repressive measures towards them. According to the Article 27 of the aforementioned Decree, administrative authorities had competence to confiscate press materials if they contained a content which breached criminal law. Moreover, courts were eligible to suspend a newspaper as a preventive measure.

Polish government often used legislation concerning the state of emergency. In January 1919, the Decree on the introduction of state of emergency[23] was enacted. This act and law, originating from ex invaders, constituted comprehensive legal measures which could strongly affect the freedom of press. The minister of internal

[21] Appeal to citizens, 'Monitor Polski', 3 December 1918.

[22] Decree on temporary press regulations, Journal of Laws of the Polish State, 1919, No. 14, pos. 186.

[23] Decree on the introduction of a state of emergency, Journal of Laws of the Polish State, 1919, No. 1, pos. 79.

affairs was entitled to issue regulations in order to maintain public order. It was legal to prohibit public assemblies and rallies. The minister of internal affairs was also empowered to confiscate and suspend releases which endangered the public security. In 1918 and 1919 the state of emergency was introduced in Zagłębie Dąbrowskie and Galicia. The legislation which contains powers for the executive to limit the freedom of press and assemblies was necessary because of the speed and flexibility of executive actions. The provisions included in criminal law were not sufficient because they transferred all cases to courts which were limited by strict procedures and norms.[24] In these conditions, according to S. Wojciechowski, Polish minister of internal affairs: 'the only legal measure to fight against communist agitation was the state of emergency and possibility of neutralisation of dangerous entities'.[25]

One of the main goals of legal regulations concerning limitation of freedom of speech and assemblies was to combat Communist political organisations and radical leftist press. The rules contained in aforementioned Decrees were relatively effective in the fight against communism. The legal measures, e.g. confiscation, were applied quite often against labour press. Since 1919 many communist magazines had been closed, e.g. 'Sztandar Socjalizmu' ('Socialist Banner'), 'Komunista' ('Communist'), 'Nowe Społeczeństwo' ('New Society') or 'Robotnik Miejski' ('Urban Worker').[26] Administrative authorities were often suspending leftist newspapers, e.g. 'Przełom' ('Breakthrough'), 'Nowiny' ('News').[27] The legal provisions concerning the state of emergency were used as a tool to combat KPRP—communist party. The places and newspapers associated with KPRP were being closed. The Party was forced to act in hiding, illegally. The society tended to accept many limitations, which were directed against communist organisations, because of the fact that Poland was in the state of war against Soviet Russia between 1919–1921. Communist organisations collaborated with Soviets and on this background more than one criminal case against communists was led. Criminal law provisions and at the same time press law were used in the young Polish state in order to maintain a political and legal stability. The communist organisations were perceived as a force which cooperates with foreign powers and, therefore, as enemies. That being said, it is easy to understand why leftist press or KPRP were victims of repression from the Polish state. The methods which were used between 1919–1921 should be judged in the context of the lack of basic law and codified fundamental rights of an individual.

Through the next years repressions, which were directed against communists, became present in yet another legal and political situation. On 17 March 1921 the March Constitution[28] was enacted. This act accepted parliamentarian system,

---

[24] Cf. Pietrzak (1956), p. 106.

[25] Statement presented by the Minister of Internal Affairs in the Administrative Commission in the Sejm. Transcript from 17th session of the Sejm, 21 March 1919.

[26] Pietrzak (1956), p. 108.

[27] Pietrzak (1956), p. 108.

[28] Act of March 17, 1921 – The Constitution of the Republic of Poland, Journal of Laws, 1921 No. 44, pos. 267.

separation of power and enumerated human rights. Article 104 of the March Constitution stipulated the freedom of convictions. Article 105 of the March Constitution should be cited *in extenso*: 'Freedom of the press is guaranteed. Censorship, or the system of licensing printed matter, may not be introduced. The daily papers and other matter printed in the country may not be debarred from the mails, nor may their dissemination on the territory of the Republic be restricted. A special statute will define the responsibility for the abuse of this freedom'. This provision strongly influenced issues concerning legality of censorship and press freedom limitations. The crucial issue is how this constitutional regulation really worked, especially in the context of repressions towards the communist movement.

In the legal doctrine, the priority of the constitution was questioned. Article 126 of the March Constitution brought serious doubts: 'This constitution has binding force from the day of its publication, or in so far as the realisation of its individual provisions is dependent on the issuing of special statutes on the day of their going into force'. The rights guaranteed by the March Constitution were sometimes treated as pure declarations.[29] The Supreme Administrative Court decided that rights guaranteed by the Constitution shall apply as programme declarations unless legislation concerning these rights will be enacted.[30] In dispute situations, statute had priority over the Constitution. The Supreme Court ordered that the Constitution has priority only over the prior legislation, which is clearly contradictory to the Constitution.[31] Norms which stipulated rights and freedoms were illusory in character. Of course, centralised review of constitutionality was not present in interwar Polish legal order. The judiciary accepted this interpretation of constitutional norms. The freedom of speech and assemblies were sanctioned if realisation of these rights was in accordance with the specific statutory norms.[32] The Supreme Court concluded that preaching slogans like 'Long live the Third International' or 'Long live revolution' are crimes according to the criminal law.[33] Moreover, belonging to the communist party was treated through the whole interwar period as a crime—being a part of conspiracy. After the March Constitution had been enacted, a system of confiscations was also used. In the 1920s many newspapers were being closed or suspended, e.g. 'Inwalida' ('Invalid'), 'Die Woche', 'Kultura Robotnicza' ('Worker's Culture'), 'Das Leben' or 'Walka Robotnicza' ('Worker's struggle'). In 1924 only one daily paper run by radical leftists was distributed—'Trybuna Robotnicza' ('Worker's Tribune').[34] In the next parts of this chapter, it will be demonstrated that the aforementioned interpretation of the Constitution, as well as

[29] Sobolewski (1954), p. 39.

[30] Collection of the Supreme Administrative Tribunal's rulings 1924, pos. 453; Collection of the Supreme Administrative Tribunal's rulings 1928, pos. 1363.

[31] CSCR.RSC(C), Warsaw 1924, pos. 1.

[32] Cf. Decree on temporary press regulations (1919), Decree on the introduction of a state of emergency (1919).

[33] CSCR.RSC(C), Warsaw 1930, pos. 140.

[34] Pietrzak (1956), p. 115.

the use of norms which limited political freedoms, were quite often used as tools in the battle against the communist movement.

5 Legal Grounds for Penalisation of Communism

5.1 Before the Enactment of the Makarewicz Code

In the Second Republic of Poland, until 1932, criminal provisions deriving from ex-invaders' regulations were binding. Especially norms concerning crimes against the state, included in the Russian Tagancev Code[35] (next: T.C.), were in force. In pre-revolutionary Russia, T.C. was quite often used as a tool in the battle against communists. Polish courts, after 1918, applied T.C. norms in order to combat anti-state communist organisations.[36] Criminal norms contained in T.C. penalised major betrayal. Moreover, the Article 102 of T.C. stated that participation in conspiracy, which purpose is to perform infringement upon the state system, is a crime according to the law. This provision also penalised creation of such conspiracy, an attempt at performing such an act, joining a conspiracy and an incitement to conspiracy.[37] The interpretation of the Article 102 of T.C. allowed one to consider being active in communist organisations, e.g. political parties as a crime. The legal doctrine declared that in order to accuse someone of such crime, it is essential that such conspiracy reveal an intention to commit an infringement upon the state system.[38] It is worth to highlight that not only concrete acts aiming at overthrowing the system were punishable, but also participation in conspiracy. Articles 125 and 126 of T.C. considerably limited the freedom of association in order to prevent anti-state activity. Participation in an organisation, with the knowledge that such an organisation aimed to overthrow the existing state system, inciting workers to strike or inciting to disobedience to the legislation or state power was a punishable act. It is clear that this regulation could be applied against political and social activity in communist organisations which directly opposed to the existing political and economic system in the Second Republic of Poland. The legal doctrine approved the thesis that being active in organisations which purpose was overthrowing the state system, even if the only activity was exchanging views and paradigms, qualified as a crime described in the Article 126 of T.C.[39] The responsibility prescribed in the criminal norm derived from the Article 126 of T.C. was independent from the place in which the organisation was established. In cases concerning communist political

[35]Criminal Code of 22 March 1903 with amendments and additions in force in the Republic of Poland on 1 May 1921, Warsaw 1922, Ministry of Justice Publishing House.

[36]Koredczuk (2012), pp. 122–123.

[37]Tagancev (1922a), p. 25.

[38]Tagancev (1922a), p. 25.

[39]Tagancev (1922a), p. 67.

crimes in the Second Republic of Poland, the Articles 129 and 130 of T.C. were applied rather often. These provisions limited freedom of speech, prescribed by the Article 104 of the March Constitution. Delivery, reading, spreading or making public in any form works such as speeches and images which incited to overthrow the state system, disobedience to the legislation or state power as well as to hatred between different social groups was treated as a serious crime. Moreover, aforementioned actions were punishable even when they were not committed publicly.

Incitement to an action against the law and state system was perceived as a dangerous, antisocial act which should be punished. Incitement was not the same act as instigation. The instigation was interpreted as urging concrete people to commit an act. The incitement, on the contrary, could be directed at an indefinite mass or group.[40] Articles 367 and 368 of T.C. introduced prohibition of strike. It was prohibited to organise or participate in the strike and to incite to a strike action. These regulations became a significant obstacle which interfered with efficient socialist or communist political activity. Communists and socialists who did not try to maintain contact and support for the working class were deprived of their rudimentary social base. The criminal law treated such an occurrence as a social danger which demanded sanctions. The norms included in the Articles 367–368 of T.C. protected an employer from breaking a labour contract.[41] The criminal norms which penalised actions expressing communist political thought served a really important purpose in a young state –reinforcing public order and stability. On the other hand, it is important to see that in many cases these provisions served as a base for judicial activity which led to the limitation of political pluralism. Later in this chapter, judicial application of these norms will be demonstrated.

5.2 *Under the Rule of the Makarewicz Code*

In 1932, the President issued the Criminal Code[42] (next: C.C.), which unified the criminal law in the whole state. C.C. is also known as the Makarewicz Code, because J. Makarewicz[43] was one of the main authors of the Code's regulations. Certain norms included in C.C. were applied in order to combat communist ideology and propaganda. The Article 93 Subsection 1 of C.C. penalised an attempt to deprive Polish state of independence or a part of Polish territory. This crime was described as a state crime. Article 93 Subsection 2 of C.C. criminalised an attempt to violently change the Polish system of the state. These two types of crimes were very specific

[40] Tagancev (1922a), p. 75.

[41] Tagancev (1922b), p. 356.

[42] Ordinance of the President of the Republic of Poland of 11 July 1932 - Criminal Code, Journal of Laws, 1932, No. 60 pos. 571.

[43] Makarewicz was a professor of criminal law at the Lviv University, main author of Polish criminal codification.

because an attempt was treated as the commission of a crime, so an attempt at an attempt was not possible.[44] The purpose of the norm included in the Article 93 Subsection 2 of C.C. was to prevent a violent change of the system—that is—to prevent a revolution. The change of the political system was not prohibited but it was supposed to be conducted peacefully. Moreover, the two elements of communist activity were really controversial in the context of this provision. Communists inherently opposed to private property and were proponents of strike actions. Abolishment of private property should be conducted by revolution (class struggle). These elements prove that the activity of radical communist organisations may be perceived as revolutionary and, therefore, as a crime. It was highlighted in legal doctrine that forcible transfer of property in factories from employers to employees with the intention to conduct such transfer in the whole territory of the state could be qualified as a crime from the Article 93 Subsection 2 of C.C.[45] All kinds of assaults against the rule of private property were interpreted as crimes against the system of the state.[46] The preparation of a crime from the Article 93 of C.C. was also penalised (Article 96 of C.C.). Makarewicz Code considered entering in an arrangement in order to commit a crime from the Article 93 as a crime (Article 97 Subsection 1 of C. C.). The legislator accepted a conspiracy construct. The Supreme Court considered that entering into Red Aid should be qualified as a crime from the Article 97.[47] An arrangement was not interpreted as an organisation. Informal arrangements without specific structure were also subjected to the Article 97 of C.C.[48] Article 154 Subsection 1 of C.C. criminalised public incitement or praise of a crime. The public incitement should be differentiated from instigation. One can instigate a determined person or group of people. The incitement consists in expressing an encouragement to commit a crime *ad incertam personam*. The distribution of leaflets, works or images which incited to a crime constituted as a form of this crime. The court should determine the act to which one incited. The Article 154 Subsection 2 of C.C. penalised incitement or praise if the act was considered a state crime. This regulation was quite often used against communist activists who incited to rebellion or a strike. Carrying a transparent with communist-revolutionary slogans could be qualified as a crime from the Article 154 Subsection 2 of C.C.[49] Public incitement to an occupational strike should be qualified as a crime.[50] Communist propaganda would become a state crime if there occurred an intention to use violence at the time

---

[44] Makarewicz (2012), p. 303.

[45] Makarewicz (2012), p. 304.

[46] Makarewicz (2012), p. 306.

[47] Judgment of the Supreme Court of 5 February 1935, 1 K. 1081/34, CSCR.RSC(C), Warsaw 1935, pp. 655–666, pos. 397.

[48] Makarewicz (2012), p. 311.

[49] Makarewicz (2012), p. 409; Judgment of the Supreme Court of 20 September 1934, 1 K. 549/34, CSCR.RSC(C), Warsaw 1934, pp. 172–173, pos. 107.

[50] Makarewicz (2012), p. 410.

or in the future.[51] Other regulations stipulated sanctions for participating in secret associations or public assemblies which aimed at committing a crime. Moreover, public blasphemy was a crime, according to the Article 172 of C.C.

What was pivotal for the interpretation of C.C. provisions concerning communist propaganda, was delivered in an important article[52] written by J. Makarewicz and published in 'Gazeta Sądowa Warszawska'.[53] The author concluded that the basis of communism is abolishment of private property.[54] The roots of communist thinking are situated in Plato's and early Christian thought.[55] These views were in contrary with the Polish system of state which stipulated a principle of private property in economy. The crucial issue raised in this article concerns defining when communist propaganda becomes a crime according to the Polish law. The author clearly saw a difference between spreading certain ideas—propaganda of thought; and agitation aiming at making change in the world—propaganda of action. The praise of collective property cannot be interpreted as a crime.[56] The system of state may be changed in a parliamentarian manner. Propaganda of action is interpreted as a criminal incitement to a crime or praise of a crime.[57] The author considered that beginning of a revolution is often modest, so criminalisation of communist propaganda is necessary.[58] The most important issue was to check whether one incited to changing the system violently. Disrespecting constitutional principles is the same as disrespecting the system of state.[59] So, assaults against private property, individual freedom or protection of labour are assaults against the whole state. A crime against the state was perceived as one of the serious crimes.[60] The author highlighted that incitement, described in the Article 154 Subsection 2 of C.C. should be interpreted differently in comparison with instigation.[61] An agitator wants to create specific public mood. The author fully supported criminalisation of communist propaganda. Communist activity was perceived to be dangerous. This fact should not raise doubts, bearing in mind that J. Makarewicz observed phenomena which happened in the Soviet Russia after 1917.

---

[51] Makarewicz (1937b), p. 366.

[52] Makarewicz (1937a), pp. 349–351; Makarewicz (1937b), pp. 365–370.

[53] Gazeta Sądowa Warszawska (Warsaw Judicial Newspaper) was a magazine which contained legal articles, judicature, announcements etc.

[54] Makarewicz (1937a), p. 349.

[55] Makarewicz (1937a), p. 349.

[56] Makarewicz (1937b), p. 365.

[57] Makarewicz (1937b), p. 366.

[58] Makarewicz (1937b), p. 367.

[59] Makarewicz (1937b), p. 368.

[60] Makarewicz (1937b), p. 368.

[61] Makarewicz (1937b), p. 369.

6 Penalisation of Communism in Jurisprudence of the Supreme Court

6.1 Before the Enactment of the Makarewicz Code

The court judgment in the case Szpajzer and others[62] constitutes an illustration on how the courts perceived revolutionary activity within the Polish soil in the twenties. The case concerned activists of 'Bund'—Jewish anti-zionists and socialists. The Supreme Court proceeded with the Article 126 of T.C.—participation in an organisation, with the knowledge that such organisation aims at overthrowing existing state system. The judges concluded that 'Bund' should be described as an organisation hostile to the Polish state. Moreover, activists of 'Bund' aimed at 'creating a dictatorship of the proletariat and social soviet republic'.[63] It was raised that such activity should be qualified as a crime from the Article 126 of T.C. Szpajzer and other activists were sentenced.

Another important example of combat against communist ideology within the judicature of the Polish Supreme Court is the judgment in the case of Toeplitz.[64] The Court gave the judgment in 1924 as a consequence of cassation. Toeplitz was accused of membership in the Polish Communist Youth Association, which aimed to overthrowing the existing state system. The activity of the accused was qualified as a participation in an organisation with the knowledge that such organisation aims at overthrowing existing state system. Toeplitz was accused of committing the following crimes: organising communist circles in the army, spreading communist literature through the youth and collecting information about number of Polish army towards foreign state.[65] The Supreme Court analysed the statute of the Association and confirmed that provisions about 'consideration that it is necessary to overthrow bourgeois class violence and bourgeois state by organised forces of proletarians and lay the basis for new society through dictatorship of revolutionary proletariat', undoubtedly mean that Polish Communist Youth Association considered overthrowing the Polish system of state, using violence as the aim of activity. Advocacy argued that Association is significantly different in comparison to the KPRP.[66] It was argued that Polish Communist Youth Association only 'considers overthrowing the state system to be necessary' and does not 'strive to overthrow'. The Supreme Court rejected this argumentation and concluded that 'the ultimate goal is the same (. . .) the difference is like during war between troops being in trenches and those who train in order to start the fight'.[67] Advocacy raised the issue that the Association is not

[62] CSCR.RSC(C), Warsaw 1923, pp. 324–325, pos. 215.

[63] Excerpts from court decisions translated by the Author.

[64] CSCR.RSC(C), Warsaw 1924, pp. 93–99, pos. 46.

[65] Koredczuk (2012), p. 125.

[66] Belonging to KPRP was considered a crime in the Supreme Court's judicature.

[67] CSCR.RSC(C), Warsaw 1924, p. 96, pos. 46.

different from other legal socialist organisation and compared Polish Communist Youth Association to the Polish Socialist Party (PPS). The Supreme Court highlighted that there was a huge difference, not in the programme but in the method of activity. 'If an association does not aim at gaining a majority by peaceful evolution, but by overthrowing the existing political system using violence (...), then all rationally organised social systems must fight against such association, not excluding criminal repression'.[68] In the justification for the judgment, the Court explicitly indicated which aims and activities communist parties can adopt. As a model of legal socialist party, the Supreme Court pointed British Labor Party.

The Supreme Court's approach to combat communist propaganda emphasises the judgment from 1923 in the case of Kuziemska and Szymczakowski.[69] The defendant was accused of inciting to overthrow the existing social system using violence (Article 129 of T.C.). Szymczakowski stood trial as a result of the act he made in 1922 in Żyrardów, during 1st May procession. He was carrying a banner with an inscription: 'Long live polish Soviet republic K.P.R.P.'. First, the Supreme Court interpreted the notion 'incitement' from the Article 129. The Court highlighted that it was crucial to distinguish between instigation and incitement. To consider an act as an incitement, it was enough to prove that the act has 'all kinds of influence on listeners, viewers or readers which aims at inculcating a readiness to act in a determined direction'.[70] It was not needed to create an intention with which one would commit a crime or bring such crime about. The Supreme Court approved a very wide interpretation of incitement—'a single phrase, single cry, single image, single emblem and even single gesture is able to express criminal, intentional agitation'.[71] As examples of penalised incitement, the Court enumerated, i.a. cries 'Down with the Constitution, long live for imperial dictatorship', banner with the inscription 'Break away from Poland!' The Supreme Court concluded *expressis verbis* that words 'speaker', 'piece', 'image', used in the Article 129 of T.C., shall be interpreted widely.[72] So, the Supreme Court accepted the thesis that inscription which propagates communist soviet republic should be understood as an incitement to overthrow the existing social system.

One should agree with the thesis that in Poland, through the interwar period, courts were in a very difficult situation. On the one hand, members of communist organisations criticised courts for being very harsh, on the other hand, representatives of the government accused them of excessive liberalism.[73]

Expressions which included communist propaganda were harshly punished between 1919 and 1921 because of the Polish-Soviet war. Polish citizens who sympathised with Bolshevism helped Russians in creating political institutions on

[68] CSCR.RSC(C), Warsaw 1924, p. 96, pos. 46.

[69] CSCR.RSC(C), Warsaw 1923, pp. 142–147, pos. 93.

[70] CSCR.RSC(C), Warsaw 1923, p. 143, pos. 93.

[71] CSCR.RSC(C), Warsaw 1923, p. 144, pos. 93.

[72] CSCR.RSC(C), Warsaw 1923, p. 144, pos. 93.

[73] Koredczuk (2012), p. 124.

the Polish soil. Moreover, important activity of Polish communists was expressed in anti-Polish propaganda. After Soviet failure, courts convicted those people as guilty of treason and incitement to overthrow the existing social system using violence. Srul Grabie was one of the accused in such cases. He organised pro-Soviet processions with cries 'Down with Poland!' The Supreme Court concluded that his acts were crimes.[74] Judges highlighted that one who incites to crime does not have to indicate concrete, specific ways to overthrow the state system and does not have to give a guidance on how to conduct a treason.

The judicature in the cases of Szpajzer and others, Kuziemska and Szymczakowski and Srul Grabie illustrates how the Supreme Court intervened to stop communist propaganda in the young Polish state. It is clear that positive law and judicature were set to protect Polish statehood and prevent it from hostile interventions, especially Soviet intervention. Communist propaganda and ideology in those times were perceived as a danger for Polish state and legal system. Judicial interpretation of provisions which penalised anti-state propaganda was set to cover as many different acts as possible. The important question, which remains, is whether the Polish model of legal combat of communism included 'propaganda of thought'.[75]

6.2 Under the Makarewicz Code

Under the rule of the Makarewicz Code, a crucial role in fighting communist agitation was played by the Article 154 Subsection 2 of C.C. which penalised public incitement to a state crime. The Supreme Court stressed that incitement does not require simultaneous indication of a positive change in the state system.[76] A destructive call with an intention to change the system was sufficient to be qualified as a crime. In the judicature it was decided that 'Carrying a transparent with communist-revolutionary slogans may be qualified as a crime from the Article 154 Subsection 2 of C.C.'.[77] The Supreme Court highlighted that the form of incitement to a crime is irrelevant; carrying a banner proves a sympathisation with the slogans written in the banner.[78] What is more, there is no difference between raising cries by participants of an assembly and repeating them by others.[79] In this case, it was about a slogan: 'Long live KPP, USSR'. Interestingly, it was raised in

[74] CSCR.RSC(C), Warsaw 1921, pp. 214–217, pos. 136.

[75] The issue is raised in the Sect. 5.2.

[76] Judgment of the Supreme Court of 15 December, 1937, 1 K. 1331/37.

[77] Judgment of the Supreme Court of 9 December 1932, II. 1 K. 1333/32, CSCR.RSC(C), Warsaw 1933, pp. 61–62, pos. 30.

[78] Judgment of the Supreme Court of 20 September 1934, 1 K. 549/34, CSCR.RSC(C), Warsaw 1934, pp. 172–173, pos. 107.

[79] Collection of the Supreme Court's rulings. Criminal Department, Cracow 1934, p. 65, pos. 245.

the legal doctrine that believing in communist values or even belonging to the communist party is not a crime as long as one does not undertake direct action or show support for a crime.[80]

Under the rule of the C.C., it was adopted that the KPP is a subversive organisation which aims at depriving Poland of its independence.[81] Belonging to KPP was qualified as a crime. Legal grounds for such treatment constituted of provisions in Article 93 and 97 of the Makarewicz Code. These articles penalised conspiracy which purpose was to commit a state crime. Activists of communist parties in the interwar period really often incited to change of the social and political system of the state. Such incitement was punishable if change of the system was supposed to be achieved using violence. The mentioned articles were applied in judicature in the case concerning members of the Communist Party of Western Belorussia.[82] Involvement in this party was qualified as a crime (Article 97 of C.C.). In the judgment from 5th February 1935, the Supreme Court concluded that entering into the Red Aid corresponds to the crime from the Article 97 of C.C.[83] Distance of the goal and the variety of used means do not exclude application of the Article 97 C.C.[84] Everyone who enters such an organisation takes responsibility, regardless of whether one takes real actions aiming at committing a state crime or not. Joining a criminal association may be expressed not only by formal membership, but also by real involvement, without formal membership. Such involvement may be expressed especially by direct help for people who are members of organisation which aims at a committing a state crime.[85] Such active involvement shall be interpreted as a crime (Article 93 of C.C. in connection with Article 97 of C.C.). In the prior judicature, the Supreme Court accepted the thesis that the legal political party may transform itself into the anti-state association.[86]

The rudimentary aim of the mentioned provisions and judicature was the maintenance of durability of the Polish state and reinforcing public order. The spirit of judicature created by the Supreme Court before the enactment of the Makarewicz Code was approved. The communist doctrine and propaganda were treated as public danger and activists were consequently punished. The large number of court's verdicts in cases concerning communist activity in twenties and thirties is a proof that communists were active in the public sphere and had their own social basis. This reality was perceived by the Polish elite as a highly undesirable state.

---

80 Peiper (1936), p. 224.

81 Koredczuk (2012), p. 130.

82 Judgment of the Supreme Court of 20 March 1935, 2 K. 116/35, CSCR.RSC(C), Warsaw 1935, pp. 543–546, pos. 462.

83 Judgment of the Supreme Court of 5 February 1935, 1 K. 1081/34, CSCR.RSC(C), Warsaw 1935, pp. 655–666, pos. 397.

84 Judgment of the Supreme Court of 5 February 1935, 1 K. 1081/34, CSCR.RSC(C), Warsaw 1935, pp. 655–666, pos. 397.

85 Judgment of the Supreme Court of 13 January 1937, I K 1038/36.

86 Judgment of the Supreme Court of 13 April 1931, II K 205/31.

7 Polish Parliament's Approach to Combating Communism

Since the beginning of the Polish parliamentarianism after the First World War, the Polish Parliament adopted a definite attitude toward communist ideology and propaganda. Between 1919 and 1922 the Legislative Sejm worked to enact the new Constitution. Since 1922 until September 1939, the Polish Parliament consisted of two Chambers—Sejm (the lower house) and Senat (the upper house). The priority in legislative policy and shaping new Polish state had the Sejm, so acts made by this chamber will be included. Polish Sejm adopted a strict, anti-communist agenda, which expressed itself not only in strict law, but also in soft law declarations like parliamentarian resolutions. Among many political options, two main views toward combating communism should be highlighted. The right wing of the political scene was represented by 'endecja',[87] which endorsed republicanism, the idea of a catholic state and national solidarity. The left-wing parties, excluding communists, were dominated by Polish Socialist Party and PSL 'Wyzwolenie'.[88]

The right-wing parties adopted a radical anti-communist approach. Already in 1919, there were requests concerning 'combating Bolshevik agitation and the annihilation of Bolshevik centers in Poland'.[89] In this notion, deputies appealed for preventing from printing and spreading criminal communist-Bolshevik propaganda calling for unrests. Interestingly, leftist deputies supported the fight against communism and stated that there is no exception in combating communism in the Polish Sejm.[90] However, leftist parties were against criminal repressions against communism. They stated that combating communism should be performed by moderate social reforms that should help the poorest.[91] Right-wing deputies were more radical in their statements. The deputy and priest Styczyński highlighted:

> I recognise communist agitators as traitors... and for them the only method is gallows. If the government hanged communist provocateurs, we would free our good-hearted workers from Bolshevism.[92]

Politicians who represented right-wing parties proposed to enact a project which qualified communist activity as a state crime. The Article 1 of this project sounded: 'All kinds of communist activity or communist agitation on Polish soil, in print or in words, qualifies as treason'.[93] This proposal was not the most strict one. Mr. Lutosławski—a radical right-wing deputy and a priest—appealed for the

[87] The shortcut is from N—national, D—democracy.

[88] Polish People's Party 'Liberation' endorsed radical agricultural reforms and supported peasants' movement.

[89] Pietrzak (1956), p. 130.

[90] Pietrzak (1956), p. 131.

[91] Pietrzak (1956), p. 131.

[92] Transcript from 72nd session of the Sejm, 18 July 1919, citation translated by the Author.

[93] Transcript from 247th session of the Sejm, 27 September 1921.

enactment of a special criminal legislation concerning communism. He considered that even membership in the Third International should be treated as a crime; all kinds of communist crimes should be harshly punished, including depravation of electoral rights.[94] This view is really important because between 1919 and 1921 many proposals concerning a special 'anti-communist Act' appeared. Most radical projects provided a possibility for administration to arrest 'anti-state' criminals for three months or penalisation of communist propaganda in private talks.[95] Interestingly, projects of amnesties prepared by government and deputies did not include convicted communist activists.

In 1919, the KPRP boycotted the general election. This decision was later considered as a mistake. Communists strove to be active in the next elections. However, they witnessed repressions that prevented them from effective rivalry.[96] KPRP could not participate in the election in 1921 under its name. The administration censored calls made by communists. Confiscations were applied. Rallies were blocked and the violence against communists was allowed. Moreover, some candidates were arrested during campaign.

Despite invoked repressions, communists had few representatives in the Parliament and in local authorities. They tried to express publicly their views in parliamentarian procedure. According to the March Constitution, deputies to the Sejm had many formal rights concerning public speeches or parliamentary interpellations. The authorities of the Parliament consequently sought to limit rights enjoyed by the communists.[97] The deputies of left-wing and right-wing democratic parties did not oppose many practices which resulted in exclusion of communist deputies from parliamentary activity. The communists were perceived by both parliamentarian sides as anti-state and anti-parliamentarian politicians. The parliamentarian activities against communists concentrated on three aspects: limitations of interpellation rights; limitations of deputies right to public speech; direct violence against communist MPs. The Government Commissioner in Warsaw issued a regulation which prohibited releases of communists' interpellations, calls and applications from printing houses.[98] Moreover, dissemination of a communist deputy's interpellation was qualified as a crime.[99] The Marshal of the Sejm had competence to accord a right to speak and to interrupt speeches. It sometimes happened that the Marshal scratched off fragments of speeches or did not allow reading an interpellation.[100] Mr. Dąbal—a communist deputy to the Sejm, was forcibly expelled from the tribune and

[94] Pietrzak (1956), p. 134.

[95] Pietrzak (1956), pp. 134–136.

[96] Pietrzak (1956), pp. 140–144.

[97] Pietrzak (1956), pp. 144–152.

[98] See: transcript from 129th session of the Sejm.

[99] Transcript from 172nd session of the Sejm.

[100] Transcript from 130th and 198th session of the Sejm.

subsequently beaten by other MPs. Interestingly, deputies from the left side of the Sejm were the most active during this event.[101]

8 Conclusion

In my opinion, the thesis that the combat of communism was a *raison d'etat* of the Second Republic of Poland, can be easily defended. The young Polish state was geopolitically and legally insecure. The legislation and judicature responded to the urgent need to prevent the Polish state from disintegration. Activity and ideology of Polish communists clearly indicated that the independence of Poland was not a value for the KPP and other communist organisations. On the contrary, direct cooperation with the Soviets and an anti-institutional attitude showed that the Polish state was an obstacle to the international (or at least pan-European) revolution. The stance adopted by Polish communists during the Polish-Soviet war was remembered for years. So, between 1918 and 1939, the communist ideology and propaganda were considered in Poland a real danger to public order.

The legislative, executive and judicial powers were interconnected in the fight against communism. Almost every state institution served as a tool for combating communism. The judiciary was put in a particularly difficult situation. Courts were under pressure because of communist reactions to judicature concerning anti-state activity. But the main centre of pressure was the political power (before and after the 1926 *coup d'etat*). Actually, the judiciary was very active in combating communism. Perhaps, actions performed by the executive branch had a strong influence on the courts. It is needed to quote a circular from 1921 directed to judges and prosecutors. 'It is necessary to immediately and strongly oppress and absolutely neutralise criminal bodies, which can be realised by proper application of the articles 126, 129, 367, 368, 509 T.C. (. . .) Every careless move, especially the mild application of preventive or repressie measures, brings incalculable damage to the state. I ask the Presidents (of courts—K.S.) and prosecutors for immediate disclosure of this letter for judges and prosecutors, who act in application of criminal repression concerning indicated articles, information'.[102] This circular undoubtedly constituted a serious interference with the independence of judges.

The law became a tool for fighting communism, especially through *ad hoc* legislation and the harsh judicial actions. It is important to highlight that the mechanism that led to communist propaganda being perceived as a serious crime was, in part, due to an extending interpretation. Provisions that prohibited belonging to communist organisations or spreading communist views, were interpreted to the disadvantage of communist defendants. Polish criminal legislature was perceived in the legal doctrine as 'manifesting the pursuit to cover citizens (. . .) with a network of

[101] Pietrzak (1956), p. 146.

[102] 'Wyzwolenie Robotnicze', No. 9, 25 September 1921, citation based on Pietrzak (1956), p. 127.

prohibitions and requirements accompanied by criminal sanctions'.[103] Legal framework which purpose was to combat communism may be seen as efficient and stable. Possibly, one can agree with this. However, the application of criminal and administrative norms may raise doubts related to the *nullum crimen sine lege* rule and the proportionality of measures. The sentence invoked above confirms such doubts from the perspective of the twenties.

Documents

Act of March 17, 1921 – The Constitution of the Republic of Poland, Journal of Laws, 1921 No. 44, pos. 267

Collection of the Supreme Administrative Tribunal's rulings 1924

Collection of the Supreme Administrative Tribunal's rulings 1928

Collection of the Supreme Court's rulings. Rulings of the Second Criminal Chamber. Warsaw, 1921

Collection of the Supreme Court's rulings. Rulings of the Second Criminal Chamber. Warsaw, 1923

Collection of the Supreme Court's rulings. Rulings of the Second Criminal Chamber. Warsaw, 1924

Collection of the Supreme Court's rulings. Rulings of the Second Criminal Chamber. Warsaw, 1930

Collection of the Supreme Court's rulings. Rulings of the Second Criminal Chamber. Warsaw, 1933

Collection of the Supreme Court's rulings. Rulings of the Second Criminal Chamber. Warsaw, 1934

Collection of the Supreme Court's rulings. Rulings of the Second Criminal Chamber. Warsaw, 1935

Collection of the Supreme Court's rulings. Criminal Department, Cracow 1934

Criminal Code of 22 March 1903 with amendments and additions in force in the Republic of Poland on 1 May 1921, Warsaw 1922, Ministry of Justice Publishing House

Decree on temporary press regulations, Journal of Laws of the Polish State, 1919, No. 14, pos. 186

Decree on the introduction of a state of emergency, Journal of Laws of the Polish State, 1919, No. 1, pos. 79,

Józef Piłsudski's appeal to citizens, "Monitor Polski," No. 201, 3 December 1918

Ordinance of the President of the Republic of Poland of 11 July 1932 - Criminal Code, Journal of Laws, 1932, No. 60 pos. 571

Rulings of the Polish Supreme Court. Criminal Department, R. IX, Cracow 1934

Supreme Court judgment of April 13, 1931, II K 205/31

[103] Mogilnicki (1928), p. 723.

Supreme Court judgment of December 15, 1937, 1 K. 1331/37
Supreme Court judgment of January 13, 1937, I K 1038/36
Transcript from 17th session of the Sejm, 21 March 1919
Transcript from 72nd session of the Sejm, 18 July 1919
Transcript from 129th session of the Sejm, 27 September 1921
Transcript from 130th session of the Sejm, 14 June 1924
Transcript from 172nd session of the Sejm, 18 December 1924
Transcript from 198th session of the Sejm, 25 April 1925

Press

"Wyzwolenie Robotnicze," No. 9, 25 September 1921

References

Althusser L (1971) Ideology and ideological state apparatuses. In: Althusser L (ed) Lenin and philosophy and other essays. Monthly Review Press, New York/London, pp 127–186
Bosiacki A (1999) Utopia, władza, prawo: doktryna i koncepcje prawne "bolszewickiej" Rosji 1917-1921. Liber, Warsaw
Ciołkosz A (1961) Róża Luksemburg a rewolucja rosyjska. Instytut Literacki, Paris
Daniszewski T (ed) (1954) KPP - uchwały i rezolucje. T. 1, I-II zjazd (1918-1923). Książka i Wiedza, Warsaw
Fraser L (1957) Propaganda. Oxford University Press, London
Herman ES, Chomsky N (2002) Manufacturing consent: the political economy of the mass media. Pantheon Books, New York
Izdebski H (2017) Doktryny polityczno-prawne. Fundamenty współczesnych państw. Wolters Kluwer, Warsaw
Kochański A (1976) Róża Luksemburg. Książka i Wiedza, Warsaw
Koredczuk J (2012) Zwalczanie działalności ugrupowań komunistycznych w polskim prawie karnym okresu międzywojennego. Prawo CCCXIV Studia Historycznoprawne, pp. 119–139
Kuśmierski S (1980) Teoretyczne problemy propagandy i opinii publicznej. Państwowe Wydawnictwo Naukowe, Warsaw
Ławnik J (1979) Represje policyjne wobec ruchu robotniczego 1918-1939. Książka i Wiedza, Warsaw
Makarewicz J (1937a) Propaganda komunizmu a kodeks karny. Gazeta Sądowa Warszawska 24: 349–351
Makarewicz J (1937b) Propaganda komunizmu a kodeks karny (dokończenie). Gazeta Sądowa Warszawska 25:365–370
Makarewicz J (2012) In: Grześkowiak A, Wiak K (eds) Kodeks karny z komentarzem. Lublin, Wydawnictwo KUL
Mogilnicki A (1928) Prawo karne w pierwszem dziesięcioleciu odrodzonego Państwa Polskiego. Gazeta Sądowa Warszawska 46:723–728
Peiper L (1936) Komentarz do kodeksu karnego, prawa o wykroczeniach, przepisów wprowadzających obie te ustawy. Leon Frommer, Krakow
Pietrzak M (1956) Zagadnienie wolności słowa w Polsce burżuazyjno-obszarniczej w latach 1918-1926. Czasopismo Prawno-Historyczne VIII(2):99–155

Sobolewski M (1954) Prawa i wolności obywatelskie i praktyka sądów przedwrześniowych. Kwartalnik Historyczny 61(2):35–60
Tagancev N (1922a) Criminal Code (Kodeks karny), 22 March 1903 [Vol. 2, Articles 73-197], trans. J. Dąbrowo & R. Lobman
Tagancev N (1922b) Criminal Code (Kodeks karny), 22 March 1903 [Vol. 3, Articles 198-408], trans. L. Konic
Tomicki J (1987) Wizje socjalizmu w Polsce do roku 1948. Książka i Wiedza, Warsaw
Trembicka K (2007) Między utopią a rzeczywistością: myśl polityczna Komunistycznej Partii Polski (1918-1938). Wydawnictwo Uniwersytetu Marii Curie-Skłodowskiej, Lublin
Zwoliński A (2003) Słowo w relacjach społecznych. Wydawnictwo WAM, Cracow

Kamil Słomiński PhD student at the Faculty of Law and Administration of the University of Warsaw. In his research activities, he specialises in criminal law. During his studies, he was awarded a scholarship by the Minister of Education and Science for significant achievements.

Towards Totalitarian Regime: Legal and Organisational Aspects of Transformation of Defence and Security Forces

Andrzej F. Piątkowski

Abstract Within this chapter, the author tries to point out certain constant legal and organisational benchmarks of an impending totalitarian regime that manifest themselves within the state security institutions, such as security forces and armed forces. The aim of the conducted reasoning is to separate the abnormalities within those structures that could be tolerated in a democratic state from those that are clear signs of arising totalitarian tendencies.

1 Transition Towards Totalitarian Regimes

During the 20th century, we could observe the rise to power of a number of totalitarian regimes. Despite major differences in their motives, ideology and political systems they have adopted, it is rather clear that armed forces and security forces played a vital role in both assuming and maintaining the rule by totalitarian governments. It is therefore reasonable to ask why and how those institutions supported or were persuaded to support the regimes, and what changes in their legal and organisational framework were necessary to adapt them to the totalitarian framework.

In this chapter, it will be argued that there are several benchmarks that forecast the upcoming shift from a democratic state to a totalitarian one that can be observed in the regulations (or lack thereof) and functioning of the governmental security structures. Those benchmarks, amongst others, are: the mandatory duplication of defence and security institutions, lack of legal basis for their functioning and operational activity as well as extensive use of lethal force outside wartime conditions.

Given the extent of the subject and the number of legal and organisational characteristics related to all the countries and agencies that are present in this article, the above thesis should be treated as a result of preliminary inquiry, which ought to

A. F. Piątkowski (✉)
Faculty of Law and Administration, University of Warsaw, Warsaw, Poland

M.-E. Geis et al. (eds.), *Dealing with Totalitarian Regimes and Human Rights*, Interdisciplinary Studies in Human Rights 11,
https://doi.org/10.1007/978-3-031-57338-5_8

be deepened by further scientific research and a much more detailed, separate analysis of individual institutions. Hence, a softer term 'benchmarks' was used instead of a more categorical phrase.

While the term 'defence and security forces (institution)' will be widely used in this chapter, it has to be explained exactly which types of subjects are being considered when using this phrase. Defence forces will refer primarily to the state military (armed forces) and the paramilitary formations (such as Waffen-SS, or Soviet Border Troops). The term 'security institutions' will be applicable to the civilian and military intelligence and counter-intelligence as well as the secret police.

The focus of the study will be aimed at the initial period in which the totalitarian state is formed in order to observe the most severe changes to the defence and security institutions. The earlier period (before rise to power) will also be taken into account, but in reference to Sect. 2, the level of inquiry will heavily depend on the means by which the totalitarian power is assumed. The period subsequent to the initial establishment of the regime will be cited only when an extreme example will present itself.

The study will pay particular attention to the analysis of defence and security institutions in Soviet Russia (Union of Soviet Socialist Republics), Nazi Germany (German Reich or Greater German Reich[1]) and Communist Poland (Polish People's Republic), which translates for a period of 1918 to 1991. To keep scientific relevance and impact on current research in this field, conclusions from those totalitarian regimes will be drawn to present modern examples of (possible) totalitarian tendencies in western democracies. Since a great number of decisions, regulations and procedures within defence and security institutions within totalitarian states lacked any legal basis, it will be necessary to refer to informal or customary examples of deterioration of democratic provisions regarding those entities.

For this chapter, the totalitarian regime will be defined[2] as a political system in which the state power is based on unlimited prerogatives of a ruler (or ruling group), that holds full executive, legislative and judicial competence in their hands. Within such political system, only a single party exists, while all others are outlawed together with any other forms of civil society.

It should be noted that this chapter was written during the global coronavirus pandemic, which resulted in rather limited access to written sources. Therefore, the author used mostly the written materials in his possession and the online ones (including eBooks).

---

[1] The official name of the state was changed in 1943.

[2] Pytlik (2011), pp. 118–125.

1.1 Different Paths Towards Totalitarian Regimes

The means by which a totalitarian movement has risen to power weighs heavily on how its relations with defence and security institutions are formed. Obviously, if the transition was legal or almost legal, there is no need to tame them prior to assuming power. However, in other cases, it is hard to imagine that the main instruments of state coercion will just stay indifferent to the illegitimate attempts to remove the current government. While this issue is only partially relevant to the thesis of this article, which deals with the actions that are taken after the totalitarian power has been asserted, the assumption is that the path towards this transition will greatly affect what changes the new rulers deem necessary to enforce in defence and security institutions. Therefore, a brief analysis of those specific paths with the relevant historical examples is required to trace the impacts of the subsequent relations between the regime and forces in question.

1.2 The Illegal Path

At the core of this type of transformation lies the need to assume forceful control over the state coercion. This is associated with several issues that will have impact on how the new order will shape defence and security institutions. Firstly, the illegitimacy of the rise to power means that all the previous organisations have to be removed and replaced. This reinforces the claim that that past regime was somehow ‘unworthy of power’, but in more practical terms it directly results from the fact that the old institutions will usually ally themselves with legitimate government and actively defy the revolutionists. Secondly, a large part of the staff will be either killed or imprisoned, creating a void in the command structure. This will present a challenge to the totalitarian government, as it will lack personnel with necessary competence and experience to fill the vacancies. This is usually countered either by appointing unprepared bureaucrats to high-ranking positions or promoting junior officers several ranks above their capabilities. Also, some members of the ‘old guard’ will join the new order for either ideological or selfish reasons. Third, the newly established institutions will either lack or have limited legal frameworks as the old regulations are revoked, and the totalitarian government will rarely see the need to replace them. This is mostly true for intelligence, counter-intelligence and secret police as the armed forces and police cannot operate without legal basis that will allow maintaining hierarchy and order, even if the provisions are only a façade.

The primary example of a totalitarian dictatorship gaining power by illegal means is communist/Soviet Russia. Capitalising on the success of the February Revolution, which has overthrown the autocratic monarchy in October 1917, the Bolsheviks started a second revolt to remove the infant democracy that was being established by the provisional government. This almost immediately started a civil war which lasted, in varying intensity, until 1922.[3] The circumstances of these events were far from usual or stable. The ongoing First World War (which fortunately for the communists soon ended), the struggle with the opposing White Army and the clash with newly formed Ukraine and Poland had a substantial impact on the formation of the defence and security institutions.

By default, any totalitarian regime should make its primary goal to seize absolute control over the police or military branch of the old regime to ensure its loyalty and suppress any organised form of armed counter-revolution. The pursuit of this objective usually leads to a temporarily reduced effectiveness of such institutions, as experienced staff is removed and the command structure is shattered. The Bolsheviks did not have such priviege, as they needed not only a loyal but also an effective army and intelligence, due to the ongoing war. Initially, the Red Army was formed from the ashes of the Imperial Russian Army both in terms of troops and commanders[4] (although the majority of the higher-ranking imperial officers joined the White Army), reinforced by a hastily organised conscription. The intelligence and counter-intelligence was almost entirely built from scratch, forming the infamous Cheka (All-Russian Extraordinary Commission, *Всероссийская Чрезвычайная Комиссия*, VChK).[5] This soon proved to be unreliable as during the most heated moments of the civil war, the security force was heavily involved in a witch-hunt within the army frontline reconnaissance units.[6] Perceiving them as a potential competitor, they all but removed the ability to perform combat duties of those units. Lew Trocki, who at that time assumed command of the military, demanded that Lenin establish a separate military intelligence that would be independent of Cheka. This request was fulfilled by creating an organisation later known as the Main Reconnaissance Directorate (*Главное Разведывательное Управление*, GRU).

One of the lessons that the Soviet leaders learned from this initial period was that all the branches of the government, including defence and security, should be duplicated. Therefore, the Red Army was balanced by the paramilitary branch of the VChK (later transformed, after many changes to its name, into the Committee for State Security—*Комите́т госуда́рственной безопа́сности*, KGB) and Border Troops, while the KGB itself was balanced with GRU (which also changed its designation several times).

[3] Hanchett (2019), pp. 1–18.

[4] Abramovitch (1962), pp. 28–33.

[5] Larecki (2007), pp. 726–729.

[6] Suworow (2010b), pp. 24–25.

1.3 The Legal Path

When a totalitarian party assumes governance by legal means (which usually involves winning an election), the changes to the defence and security apparatus are far more subtle than in the previous path. The old institutions are usually left unchanged, as per the teachings of Niccolo Machiavelli,[7] although new ones are created to supplement them, mostly for the purpose of formally accommodating party militias or other paramilitary organisations. Previous cadre is also allowed to stay, as the new government seeks to utilise their experience and authority. Legal framework will be changed at constitutional level, but this will rarely have an impact on the acts regulating functioning of the defence and security institutions. This assumption is, however, mostly derived from the example of Nazi Germany, which was particularly thorough in regulating every aspect of its existence, even when it meant preserving the evidence of its crimes.[8]

The most prominent example of a legal rise of a totalitarian party is Germany in the thirties of the twentieth century. After gaining a foothold in the Reichstag in January 1933, the leader of the National Socialist German Workers' Party (*Nationalsozialistische Deutsche Arbeiterpartei*, NSDAP), Adolf Hitler, was appointed by the president of the Weimar Republic to the position of Chancellor. A few months later, the Reichstag adopted the Enabling Act of 1933[9] which in a legally sound fashion provided Hitler with the dictatorial power. The body of the armed forces remained unchanged, although the *Reichswehr*, which operated in Weimar Republic, with accordance to the Treaty of Versailles,[10] was transformed into *Wehrmacht* in 1935. This was a direct violation of said treaty, as it reinstated conscription, but no purge within the armed forces was conducted. The same cannot be said about the Storm Detachment (*Sturmabteilung*, SA)—the party militia, which had its higher leadership killed or imprisoned in 1934 during an event that become later known as the Night of the Long Knives.[11] Similarly to the Soviet Union, all major security and defence institutions were duplicated. The SA, was shadowed by the Protection Squadron (*Schutzstaffel*, SS), which also duplicated the Wehrmacht once the war had started (with the military branch known as Waffen-SS), while the armed forces' intelligence, the *Abwehr*, shared some of its duties with the *Reichssicherheitshauptamt* (RSHA). It must be noted at this point that within defence and security institutions constant changes to the organisational structure are natural and frequent even in democratic states. Therefore, it is advised to closely analyse any such alterations before labelling them as 'totalitarian'.

What became evident during the Nurenberg Trials, most of the defence and security establishment remained loyal to the Nazi leaders until the end of the war,

---

[7] Machiavelli (1984), pp. 143–148.

[8] Gilbert (2012), 13–14. Kwietnia.

[9] The Guardian (1933), p. 1.

[10] The Treaty of Peace with Germany (Treaty of Versailles), Military Clauses, Part V, Section 1.

[11] Gilbert (2012), 15. lutego.

although it is not clear how widespread the knowledge and responsibility for most serious Nazi crimes (especially the Holocaust) was outside the inner circle of power and the SS. This could have impacted the loyalty of at least some members of defence and security institutions, though on the other hand it is rather clear that the *Wehrmacht* was involved in those atrocities.[12] Nevertheless, it is certain that some officers were regarded as a threat to the regime and the future conquest. Most notably, the cases of general Werner von Blomberg, who opposed the Nazi war plans and was discharged from service under dubious accusations,[13] and Werner von Fritsch, whose removal was the direct impulse for the preparation of the coup staged by admiral Wilhelm Canaris and Hjalmar Schacht.[14]

1.4 The Semi-Legal Path

This type of regime change is very similar to the legal path. The core difference is that while the legal framework for the changes is fairly maintained, practical employment of the rule of law is superficial at best. Since the semi-legal shift of the regime usually occurs when the situation of State is chaotic (as was the case with post-war Poland), it is difficult to track or assess how much the arising totalitarian government deviated from the democratic procedures during the initial period.

Near the end of the Second World War, under the directions of Stalin, Polish communists established a Polish Committee of National Liberation (*Polski Komitet Wyzwolenia Narodowego*, PKWN) which was in direct competition with the internationally recognised government-in-exile. Following the progress of the Red Army, the Committee (later known as the Temporary Government) started formally organising the state structures, seemingly accepting the legal framework of the Second Polish Republic. However, the newly created Citizens' Militia (Milicja Obywatelska) and Security Office (Urząd Bezpieczeństwa, UB), as well as the new armed forces, were new, communist-style entities, entirely disconnected from the legacy of the pre-war Polish State. The façade of recognising the traditions of the Second Polish Republic continued until 1952, when the new political construct, the Polish People's Republic, was formally established. The future of the state was theoretically to be decided by the citizens in the referendum of 1946 and elections of 1947, but both of those were rigged by the communists.[15] To some extent this became possible based on the understanding of the three world powers in Yalta, which recognised the Temporary Government,[16] effectively ruining any prospects of continuity of the former Polish state.

[12] Gilbert (2012), 25. kwietnia.

[13] Gilbert (2012), 25. kwietnia.

[14] Gilbert (2012), 25. kwietnia.

[15] Mac (1990), pp. 9–10.

[16] Roszkowski (2002), pp. 44–46.

The traces of legality present in the creation of the communist state did have some impact on the future of Poland. While it would be faulty to assume that this was the only factor, the semi-legal road to the totalitarian state could be considered one of the reasons for the relatively (in comparison to the other members of the Eastern Block) looser grip of Soviet Union on the country as well as its more liberal approach to communist ideals (i.e. lack of collectivisation of agriculture).

2 Institutions Necessary for a Successful Establishment of a Totalitarian State

Once the totalitarian dictatorship feels its position relatively well secured, there are always three areas of states apparatus that need to be immediately seized. The armed forces, the internal affairs and the justice system. The other branches of the government can be temporarily left in the hands of the opposition (if there is any), to be taken under control once the coercion institutions become unconditionally loyal. This scheme was especially visible in Eastern Europe just after the Second World War, when the local communists (with the aid of the Red Army) were installing pro-soviet governments in 'liberated' countries.

The importance of those three branches can be summed up in two parameters: the danger they pose to the regime itself and the level at which they are able to exercise totalitarian power over the general population.

2.1 Justice System

While the justice system was intentionally left out of the detailed analysis of this article, it is undoubtedly one of the core pillars of the totalitarian power. It is therefore desirable to assess its general role in this setup, at least in comparison to the other two actors (defence and security).

The justice system poses the least danger to the regime, as it has no substantial force at its disposal. Judges and prosecutors can slow down the advance of the totalitarian dictatorship when the democratic legal framework is still in effect, but once that is removed or ignored, the justice system has no effective means to oppose the system, except for individual defiant acts of the lawyers who refuse to follow the totalitarian legal guidelines.[17]

On the other hand, the justice, amongst the armed forces and the internal affairs, plays the biggest role in maintaining control over the population. As the totalitarian regimes should be regarded as an aberration of democracy and not as unique political systems, the judicial administration within them usually tries to mimic that of a

[17] Mac (1990), pp. 17–18.

democratic one. This implies that unlike in, for example, patrimonial monarchy, the illusion of due process has to be maintained and most civil or criminal law provisions are very similar to those of the previous system. Otherwise, the totalitarian regime would soon plunge into anarchy and chaos. Therefore, the justice system has to function effectively, maintaining the illusion of its legitimacy, while the totalitarian regulations or procedures will only present themselves in politically relevant cases. This of course is true in a theoretical model, as millions of people sent to Soviet Gulags,[18] many of which found themselves there based on the court rulings in criminal cases, can hardly be called politically involved.

2.2 *Defence Forces*

The defence forces (the armed forces and various paramilitary units) are on the other side of the spectrum, with their formal separation from the civilian branches of the government and parallel regulations in a number of areas.

By contrast to the justice system, the military has very little impact on the control of the population, at least in its day-to-day operations (that is, excluding suppression of demonstrations or uprisings). Those two groups simply do not interact with each other in any meaningful manner, be it in a totalitarian state or in a democratic one.

The military poses however the biggest threat to the regime. This assumption is based on several key factors that have more to do with how the armed forces are constructed, rather than the type of political system in which they operate. First, the armed forces are a self-contained state, with all the elements needed to operate without the help of the other branches of the government (except perhaps the ability to generate income). If the structure of any modern or historical armed forces is analysed,[19] it will soon become apparent that except combat units and command structures, the military has at its disposal its own: justice system (military courts), police (gendarmerie), intelligence and counter-intelligence, transportation and logistic capabilities, communication network, medical support and many more. The biggest significance of this finding is that when the armed forces are attempting to overthrow the current government, they do not need to initially take control of its branches—they can simply replace them.

The second more obvious reason is the sheer potential of the military, both in terms of manpower and armament. Once the government finds itself facing armoured and mechanised units, there is really not much it can do. It is therefore necessary in a totalitarian state to have an equivalent (perhaps not in numbers but in capabilities) force that could, to a limited degree, oppose such attempts by the military. This was especially true for the Soviet Union, where a large portion of the mechanised, naval or air force units was attached to either Border Troops or KGB

[18] Christie (1993), p. 17.

[19] Kozaczuk (2004), pp. 149–152.

paramilitary units.[20] Similarly, in the communist Poland, Border Protection Forces were subordinated to Ministry of Internal Affairs (although between 1965 and 1971 they were briefly attached to the Ministry of Defence).[21] By the same token, the Waffen-SS divisions were usually better equipped than their Wehrmacht counterparts (especially the elite '*Leibstandarte*', '*Das Reich*' and '*Totenkopf*' panzer divisions), although it would be faulty to assume this was exclusively out of fear of the regular military (as the mentioned Waffen-SS formations preformed the role of frontline units, not a palace guard).

The third factor is the hierarchy and chain of command[22] of the military. Unlike in the other branches of the government, the totalitarian rulers would find it exceptionally difficult to appoint their civilian supporters to high-ranking positions within the armed forces. They would lack the knowledge, experience and most importantly the respect of their subordinates to effectively perform command and control duties. As shown by the evidence of the early stages of the Russian Civil War, the Bolsheviks, despite their voiced will to demolish the previous class system, needed the support of some imperial officers to ensure the minimal level of competence within the Red Army.[23] This means that the totalitarian government can never be sure of the complete loyalty of the armed forces, as it never has a chance to remove the top of the previous military hierarchy without compromising the effectiveness of the entire organisation.

2.3 Security Forces

Intelligence, counter-intelligence and secret police lie between the defence forces and the justice system in terms of their ability to control the population and the danger they pose to the regime. Depending on the type of service, the security forces can control the population to a varying degree, depending on what is their operational speciality, which is also true for the level of danger they pose to the regime. Therefore, with the security forces it is necessary to spilt them into more detailed subcategories which should include intelligence and counter-intelligence (including secret police). It must be noted that while in modern democratic states those institutions are usually separate in organisational sense, within totalitarian regimes the division is usually drawn between civilian and military services which both conduct intelligence and counter-intelligence as a single institution. The intelligence, however, is always a separate entity regardless of the organisational framework, which is best summarised by the words of Franciszek Szlachcic, the Minister of Internal Affairs in communist Poland: 'the Department I - intelligence, was the elite

[20] Suworow (2011), pp. 186–188.

[21] Mac (1990), p. 33.

[22] NATO Glossary of terms and definitions, AAP-06 Edition 2019, pp. 24–25.

[23] Walsh (2009), pp. 13–18.

of the security structure. Completely different people work there, who by definition don't deal with internal matters, other officers or vice-ministers don't have access there. It can be said that while the Ministry of Internal Affairs is a state in a state, then such a state within the Ministry itself is the Department I and in the Ministry of Defence - Directorate II of the General Staff'.[24]

While the intelligence will usually have no direct impact on the society (as in similar fashion to the military, it does not interact with general population) it will have a considerable potential to overthrow the regime. The first threat to the government is connected to how the flow of the information is organised. As the international relations with other states are far from open and the freedom of movement is very limited, the intelligence (as diplomacy is usually also overrun with intelligence officers) becomes the main source of international information for the regime. Withholding or manipulating information is therefore a relatively easy method to throw a spanner in the works of the government (as famously the Admiral Canaris did[25]), reinforced by the fact the services will simply have the important data before the politicians. While this may not bring down the totalitarian government as such, it may accelerate its demise. As mentioned earlier, the regime tries to counter this threat by duplicating the intelligence services, so when one is providing misinformation, the other should pick this up. The second threat is the position of the heads of the intelligence within the structure of power. They are consulted and informed about most of the high-profile decisions and have to ability to utilise them to their advantage while also having physical access to the inner circles of the governmental structure. The last issue is the questionable loyalty of the officers of those services. Whatever ideological brainwashing they are subjected to, it is hard to negate their personal traits (intelligence, social skills, independent thinking are the usual requirements for recruitment) and their training (familiarity with culture and customs of their target country). This is further strengthened by their unavoidable exposure to other (usually democratic) states in which they conduct espionage activities. While this does not make them disloyal by default, it likely has an impact on their susceptibility to the official ideology.[26]

The counter-intelligence (which if coupled with secret police can also be referred to as security service) in the totalitarian state deals not only with foreign espionage, but more importantly for the regime, with any forms of opposition in the society. This implies that the security services are much larger in terms of manpower than the intelligence. As those organisations provide security for the governmental officials (in form of bodyguards and palace guard) and have control over governmental communication network, transport capabilities (planes, cars) and sometimes VIP medical services, they pose a substantial physical threat to the leaders. In a broader sense, secret police are essential in ensuring that the totalitarian ideology is, if not accepted, then at least not contested. This of course is related to the long-term

[24] Mac (1990), p. 34.

[25] Lowe (2008), pp. 46–52.

[26] Pillar (2010), pp. 472–484.

stability of the regime, regardless of any faction-related struggle in the upper echelons of the ruling 'caste'. The ability to control the population relies on several operational activities that are present in most totalitarian states, which include especially: large network of informants, invigilation of correspondence and a number of repression tools (concentration/internment camps, gulags, etc.), some of which rely on lethal force (executions, assassinations).

As stated before, in totalitarian regimes the intelligence and counter-intelligence are usually combined into one organisational structure (this was the case with *Abwehr*, KGB and GRU) which probably results from the assumption of the totalitarian rulers that it is easier to fuel the natural animosities between the civilians and soldiers in order to apply the 'divide and conquer' rule. This however created a dangerously powerful organisation that could attempt to seize power for itself. With the information of the intelligence, the manpower and the terror apparatus, it was much more viable, than it would be if those institutions have been split between separate organisational structures. It comes as no surprise that in the Soviet Union the contenders of Stalin came mostly from the security forces (first Genrikh Yagoda, then Nikolai Yezhov and finally, successfully—although only for brief period—Lavrentiy Beria[27]), while in Nazi Germany it was the head of the military security force who conspired to overthrow Hitler.[28] Interestingly, while it is unclear if the execution of Nikolai Yezhov had anything to do with plotting against Stalin, one of the possible explanations of his downfall, proposed by Victor Suvorov, is that he managed to gain control over both civilian and military intelligence services, which broke the *divide et impera* principle.[29]

2.4 *Legal and Organisational Aspects of Defence and Security Forces in a Totalitarian Regime*

As described in the previous section, the first apparent characteristic of the defence and security institutions is their duplication across most functional areas (which should be understood as tasks and capabilities). In Soviet Russia, the civilian intelligence and counter-intelligence (KGB) was duplicated by the military one (GRU), while the Red Army was duplicated by the KGB and Border Troops paramilitary units. In Nazi Germany the *Gestapo* (within RSHA) had similar responsibilities to the *Abwehr* and the *Wehrmacht* fought alongside the elite *Waffen-SS*. The Polish communist regime also created Border Protection Forces to rival the military, while the SB was shadowed by the Directorate II of the General Staff. This is of course only a general observation, as a detailed analysis of the

[27] It is very unclear how true the accusations that those three wanted to usurp power in the Soviet Union were and how much was it just a convenient excuse to remove them.

[28] Lowe (2008), pp. 46–52.

[29] Suworow (2010a), pp. 95–96.

activity of all the above institutions would be required to show how much those organisations competed with each other. What is important for the topic of this study is that in the mentioned totalitarian states, there were at least two forces similar in general purpose and task (armed force, intelligence or counter-intelligence).

The other sign of the upcoming totalitarian shift in the regime is the lack of legal framework for some of the defence or security institutions. As was mentioned in earlier sections, the armed forces are thoroughly regulated, as it is required for their proper functioning. The different case is with the security forces, however. While in some regimes they may have a legal basis, it usually only applies to the structure or personnel regulations. Such was the case with Polish SB, whose officers were formally part of the Militia Force, hence subject to the regulations which applied to them (The Decree on the Citizens' Militia).[30] However, there was no actual mention of the SB as such in the text of any legal act until 1983, when a law was passed that briefly mentioned the tasks of this security institution (essentially duplicating them with those of the Militia[31]). This essentially meant that the secret police was, in legal terms, hidden behind another organisation and its real tasks remained completely unregulated. This said, a lack of proper legal framework is not exclusive to the totalitarian regimes and is present in some democratic states even today (as will be described in Sect. 3.2). What is, however, unique to the totalitarian security forces is their disregard for the entirety of the legal framework, regardless of any acts regulating their own functioning. This resulted in the lack of responsibility and accountability in any form, not only in relation to the citizens, but also the totalitarian government itself. To once again quote F. Szlachcic: 'For the consecutive Presidents of the State Council – Zawadzki, Spychalski, Jabłoński – it would be the biggest surprise for themselves, if it came into their mind to ask what was happening in the internal affairs. There was an unwritten understanding – in the State Council, in the Parliament and in the Supreme Audit Office - that they should stay away from that. And from 1945 on everyone complied to this'.[32]

The third and the least debatable benchmark is the extreme rise in violence used by the security forces (and incidentally, also the armed forces). The extensive scientific studies and judicial inquires in this field leave no doubt about the extent of the Nazi and Communist crimes. During the Nuremberg Trials the Military Tribunal has accounted for 6 million dead in the Holocaust alone[33] (so this number can be entirely attributed to the activities of the security forces) and while it is impossible to present any credible number of victims of terror in the Communist Block, the estimates range anywhere between 7 and 20 million for the Soviet Union alone.[34] While such methods are rather unsurprising in a totalitarian state (even if the numbers are staggering), the important fact here is that mass terror becomes the

[30] Decree on the Prison Service, 'Dziennik Ustaw', 1954, No. 34, pos. 144.

[31] Act on the national archival resource and archives, 'Dziennik Ustaw', No. 38, pos. 173, Art. 6.

[32] Mac (1990), p. 24.

[33] Gilbert (2012), 10. Czerwca.

[34] Wheatcroft (1996), p. 1322.

primary task for the security forces (mostly counter-intelligence and/or secret police) even before the supremacy of the totalitarian leaders is fully established. Considering the example of Poland after the Second World War, the terror started immediately in 1945, even before the rigged elections of 1947 were conducted.[35]

The last thing to note are the similarities in changes to the organisational structure that the security forces were undergoing in Nazi and Communist regimes. With regard to the operational cells, the usual counter-intelligence and crime prevention was being supplemented by structures designed to combat the specified enemies of the regime. For example, within the RSHA, the Department IV (*Gestapo*) was responsible for combating marxists, communists, liberals, reactionists (all under Directorate IV A), Church, Jews, religious sects, and masonry (IV B). Section 4 in the Directorate IV B was responsible for organising the extermination of the Jewish population.[36]

3 Modern Examples of Totalitarian 'Red Flags'

In modern history, there are a number of examples of military or security services actions which were questionable at best or plainly illegal. There have been several cases of security agencies and armed forces functioning in a manner that contradicts the rule of law or taking actions that could be considered undemocratic by standards.

3.1 Targeted Killing

While the so-called 'black ops' of the democratic states were not uncommon in the Cold-War era (especially performed by Israeli intelligence services), the proliferation of such methods came with the War on Terror, which started after the Al-Qaida attacks on the World Trade Center. The most controversial actions taken by the United States against the terrorists' organisation took the form of 'targeted killing' which in simplified terms is a planned action taken by a subject of an international law (a state actor) aimed at the physical elimination of an individual who is considered a threat to the national security,[37] which usually takes form of a special forces operation or an air strike.

The most modern example would be the assassination of an Iranian general Qasem Soleimani, who was killed in a drone strike on the orders of president Donald Trump.[38] From the legal standpoint, more controversial are targeted killing

[35] Mac (1990), p. 5.

[36] Delarue (2011), pp. 353–356.

[37] Melzer (2009), pp. 3–6.

[38] Doucet (2020), p. 1.

conducted against a publicly unknown individual (like rank-and-file Al-Qaida members), where the public opinion, the courts or the relevant governmental committees (i.e. The United States Senate Select Committee on Intelligence) have virtually no ability to verify the identity of such persons.[39] This is because with targeted leaders, the threat they pose to the national security can be assessed and their deaths confirmed, while with the rank-and-file personnel this is largely impossible, leaving rather a lot of room for error or deliberate elimination of innocent individuals[40] (while not suggesting that such cases did take place). The issue of legality of targeted killing was widely discussed after the operation Geronimo (against Osama Bin-Laden), with the official position of the US government being that such actions are legal, based on the Executive order 11905, issued in 1976[41] and the presidential prerogatives.

Comparison of targeted killing with the assassinations/executions performed by totalitarian regimes is not easy. The first ones are directed against external enemies of the state and are put into a framework of a military operation. While the legality of such actions is always questionable in terms of methods used, their justification usually relies on a constitutional basis (the defence of the independence and integrity of the country). In totalitarian regimes such actions are directed against the states own citizens, although they are very often justified in the same way as in democracies (as an elimination of a threat to the state/regime).

The biggest difference between a modern democratic state and a totalitarian one in this regard is the issue of accountability. In the first one, the targeted killings are approved by the government and the knowledge about them is made available to the general public. This makes such actions subject to either political (in a form of elections) or legal (from questioning by various committees to a criminal trial) responsibility. This is not present in a totalitarian state, which allows the regime to use such methods frequently and without restrain.

3.2 Legal Framework for the Intelligence Communities

The two most notable cases for the lack of proper legislation in regard to intelligence and counter-intelligence agencies in modern democratic states apply to Israel and Great Britain, where the attempts to legislate the security forces were made decades after establishing those institutions and only after a substantial pressure from the public opinion and the justice system.

In Israel, out of three security agencies—the AMAN (military intelligence and counter-intelligence), the MOSSAD (civilian intelligence) and the Shin-Bet (the civilian counter-intelligence)—only the last one was up to this date put into a legal

---

[39] Report of the Select Committee on Intelligence, p. 10.

[40] Mayer (2009), p. 1.

[41] Executive Order 11905, pp. 23–25.

framework.[42] This was due to the rising number of leaks to public and media about the questionable practices of this organisation. Recently, even this legislation was found to be inadequate. During the ongoing global COVID-19 pandemic, the Shin-Bet conducted surveillance activities, which utilised operational techniques used for counter-terrorism, to monitor the citizens movement and contain the spread of the virus. However, the Israeli High Court ruled that such use of those techniques requires a new legal basis.[43]

Likewise, for the most part of the twentieth century, the British Intelligence Community lacked any formal basis for its activities. This was only changed near the end of the Cold War with the introduction of the Security Service Act of 1989[44] and Intelligence Services Act of 1994,[45] which put the Secret Intelligence Service (former MI6) to the Security Service (former MI5) legal framework.

The basis for legislating the intelligence community (or its elements) was the complete lack of the legal venue for transgressions of those services against the citizens of their own state. As long as their legally dubious activities were directed against foreign spies or terrorists, this state of affairs was tolerated in political circles and the public knew little about their operations. However, as more frequently the Israeli and British citizens found themselves treated by those services in a manner far from the standards of the democratic state, with no ability to seek justice in courts, the political process to remedy this unacceptable situation has been initiated.

4 Conclusion

The closed and classified world of defence and security forces makes it difficult to formulate a firm thesis in regard to their internal operations and their legal or organisational framework (especially if there are no relevant acts regulating their existence). However, the presence of the benchmarks that were defined in the thesis can be derived from historical examples and case by case analysis of the defence and security forces actions.

The major benchmark, the duplication of defence and security forces was certainly present in the given examples (Soviet Russia, Nazi Germany and Communist Poland) but is this a characteristic unique to the totalitarian states? What can be said for certain, based on the fact provided in this chapter, is that in a totalitarian state the duplication will always be present, while in a democratic state it is not always the case. The one exception would be the military forces, which should not be duplicated in a democratic state under any circumstances. This statement becomes hazy when reserve or territorial defence forces are taken into account (such as US National

[42] General Security Service Law, 5762-2002.

[43] Hamodia (2020), p. 1.

[44] Security Service Act 1989 Chapter 5.

[45] Intelligence Services Act 1994 Chapter 13.

Guard or Polish Territorial Defence Forces), but with their affiliation to the Ministry/ Department of Defence they should not necessarily be regarded as a competition for the regular armed forces.

As the lack of legal framework for the security agencies had rather negligible effect on the British democracy, it has to be concluded that this factor alone is not sufficient for a claim that such legal void forecasts the coming of a totalitarianism. However, the lack of the provisions for liability of security forces to their own citizens may be regarded as unlawful.

While the lethal force is used by democracies in a legally questionable manner (mostly in the form of targeted killing) it is almost exclusively directed on the foreign subjects. That of course is no excuse for such actions, but it should be considered a flaw rather than a sign of a downfall of the democratic system. Totalitarian states, on the other hand, tend to use terror against their own citizens before exporting it outwards.

Therefore, the thesis was conformed only partially because of two reasons. First, the level of detail of the study is insufficient to present a definitive answer. Second, some of the chosen benchmarks do not apply to all the institutions equally. Based on this, the following conclusion can be drawn:

1. The duplication of forces is a benchmark for a totalitarian regime only in relation to the armed forces, as several security agencies with overarching tasks are usually present in the modern democratic states.
2. The lack of legal framework is only relevant to security forces, as even in totalitarian regimes the military has always had some legal basis. Furthermore, the lack of legal framework for the foreign intelligence may be acceptable, but not for the internal security agencies (counter-intelligence).
3. Lethal force outside the wartime conditions is applied in some democracies to an alarming degree, however, this is partially countered by the accountability of the government. While in a totalitarian state the extent and severity of such actions is much greater, the real benchmark for the dangerous shift in regime occurs when the government focus is changed from external to internal enemies of the states.

As mentioned, the above should be treated as preliminary observation that require a detailed 'case by case' study.

Documents

Act on the national archival resource and archives, "Dziennik Ustaw," No. 38, pos. 173, Dz.U. 1983 nr 38 poz. 173

Decree on the Prison Service, "Dziennik Ustaw," 1954, No. 34, pos. 144, Dz.U. 1954 nr 34 poz. 144

Doucet L (2020), Qasem Soleimani: US kills top Iranian general in Baghdad air strike. https://www.bbc.com/news/world-middle-east-50979463. 1 December 2023

General Security Service Law, 5762-2002. https://knesset.gov.il/review/data/eng/law/kns15_GSS_eng.pdf. Accessed 1 December 2023

Hamodia Staff (2020) High Court Rules Shin Bet Surveillance Needs Legislation. Hamodia, 25 Apr 2020, https://hamodia.com/2020/04/26/high-court-rules-shin-bet-surveillance-needs-legislation/. Accessed 19 Jan 2022

Intelligence Services Act 1994, 1994 C. 13

Mayer J (2009) The Predator War. The New Yorker, 19 Oct 2009, https://www.newyorker.com/magazine/2009/10/26/the-predator-war. Accessed 1 December 20232022

NATO Glossary of terms and definition (English and French), AAP-06, Edition 2019, NATO Standardization Office, Brussels

President Gerald R. Ford's Executive Order 11905: United States Foreign Intelligence Activities, 18 February 1976

Report of the Select Committee on Intelligence, United States Senate, 113th Congress, 1st Session, Report 133-7. https://www.intelligence.senate.gov/publications/report-select-committee-intelligence-covering-period-january-5-2011-january-3-2013. Accessed 1 December 2023

Security Service Act 1989, 1989 C. 5

The Guardian (1933) Enabling Act becomes law in Germany. https://www.theguardian.com/world/2017/mar/24/enabling-act-germany-hitler-nazis-1933. Accessed 1 December 2023

The Treaty of Peace with Germany (Treaty of Versailles), 28 June 1919

References

Abramovitch R (1962) The Soviet Revolution: 1917–1938. International Universities Press, New York

Christie N (1993) Crime control as industry: towards gulags, western style. Routledge, New York

Delarue J (2011) Historia Gestapo. Muza, Warsaw

Gilbert GM (2012) Dziennik norymberski. Świat Książki, Twarda

Hanchett W (2019) Civil War in Russia. University of Iowa. https://doi.org/10.13140/RG.2.2.27297.25444. Accessed 1 Dec 2023

Kozaczuk W (2004) Wehrmacht. Bellona, Warsaw

Larecki J (2007) Wielki leksykon służb specjalnych świata: organizacje wywiadu, kontrwywiadu i policji politycznych świata, terminologia profesjonalna i żargon operacyjny. Książka i Wiedza, Warsaw

Lowe JD (2008) The Comodore. iUniverse, New York

Mac JS (1990) Przesłuchanie supergliny. Fakt, Warsaw

Machiavelli N (1984) Książe. Rozważania nad pierwszym dziesięcioksięgiem historii Rzymu Liwiusza. Państwowy Instytut Wydawniczy, Warsaw

Melzer N (2009) Targeted killing in international law. Oxford University Press, Oxford

Pillar PR (2010) The perils of politicization. In: Johnson LK (ed) The Oxford handbook of national security intelligence. Oxford University Press, New York, pp 472–484

Pytlik B (2011) Forma państwa. In: Oniszczuk J (ed) Współczesne państwo w teorii i praktyce: wybrane elementy. Oficyna Wydawnicza Szkoła Główna Handlowa w Warszawie, Warsaw, pp 97–118

Roszkowski W (2002) Półwiecze - historia polityczna świata po 1945 roku. Wydawnictwo Naukowe PWN, Warsaw

Suworow W (2010a) Akwarium. Dom wydawniczy Rebis, Poznań

Suworow W (2010b) GRU – radziecki wywiad wojskowy. Dom wydawniczy Rebis, Poznań

Suworow W (2011) Wyzwoliciele. Dom wydawniczy Rebis, Poznań

Walsh SM (2009) Leadership and command on the eastern front (1941-1945): the military style of marshal Konstantin Rokossovskiy. Cranfield University, Cranfield

Wheatcroft S (1996) The scale and nature of German and Soviet repression and mass killings, 1930-45. Europe-Asia Stud 48(8):1319–1353

Andrzej F. Piątkowski Obtained PhD in Political Science and MA in Law, both at the University of Warsaw; conducts scientific cooperation with University of Warsaw and Bureau of Research of the Chancellery of the Sejm; specialises in security and defence matters, with focus on position of security and defence institutions within the democratic political and legal system.

Part III
Becoming Second Nature: Constitutional Lessons

The Weimarian Methodological Debate in the Doctrine of Constitutional Law

Max-Emanuel Geis

Abstract This chapter deals with the methodologic dispute in jurisprudence under the Weimar democracy in Germany. The author analyses the philosophical and epistemological environment of the material time and illustrates the topic in the light of the ambivalence of the Weimar Constitution. Finally, he draws parallels to the contemporary doctrine of constitutional law, which focuses on the realisation of fundamental and human rights.

1 Introduction

It is a well-known thesis that the popularity of legal positivism was an important precondition for the formation of the 'Third Reich'. Legal positivism is known for being unable to prevent misuse of power, when the procedure of takeover is performed in legal form.[1] Let me direct your view to the dogmatic and scientific background of the constitutional doctrine during the roaring twenties in Germany, but dating back to the roots of the early 19th century. This controversy was characterised by the famous methodological debate—in German: 'Weimarer Methodenstreit'—between the neo-Kantianist and neo-Hegelian scholars among the professors teaching public law in Germany as well as at several German-speaking universities abroad like Zurich, Basel, Vienna, Graz and Prague.

The topic shall be approached in four steps as follows:

- First step: What exactly was the 'Weimarer Methodenstreit'?
- Second step: The philosophical and epistemological backgrounds

[1] For further lectures regarding the underlying topic of judicial injustice cf. Rüthers et al. (2020), pp. 310, 367; Röhl and Röhl (2008), § 39 Recht und Moral II: Das Hitler-Problem.

M.-E. Geis (✉)
University of Erlangen-Nuremberg, Erlangen, Germany
e-mail: Max-Emanuel.Geis@fau.de

M.-E. Geis et al. (eds.), *Dealing with Totalitarian Regimes and Human Rights*, Interdisciplinary Studies in Human Rights 11,
https://doi.org/10.1007/978-3-031-57338-5_9

- Third step: The main schools of the Weimarian Constitutional law as protagonists
- Fourth step: Consequences for the ongoing debate

2 About the 'Weimarer Methodenstreit'

It can be held that it was the fundamental controversy about the essence of state and law, as well as their relation under the conditions of the new republican and democratic Weimar Constitution. Due to the loss in the First World War and the abolition of the German Wilhelmine Empire together with all other monarchies on German territory, there was a great emptiness concerning the legitimation of power and the rule of law. Simultaneously, a flaming debate arose about the position of jurisprudence among the sciences and their methods altogether.

A prominent example might be Article 1 Sentence 1 of the Weimar Constitution: *'Das Deutsche Reich ist eine Republik'* ('The German Empire is a republic*').

As can be seen here, the Constitution begins with an obvious contradiction concerning the model of legitimation or, at any rate, with the dualism of state and law. The term 'empire', used to make clear the continuity of the Holy Roman Empire of the German nation on the one hand, and the continuation of the Bismarck Empire under international law on the other hand, both connected with the idea of the transcendental or metaphysical legitimation of reign and power founding ultimately on the divine right of kings or 'God's grace' ('Gottesgnadentum'). In sharp contrast, the concept of the republic denies any metaphysical connection: The only reason to legitimise power is the sovereignty of the people. In this sense, Article 1 WRV is the paradigm of the unresolved constructional fault of the 19th century constitutional monarchy: The dualism (or, more accurately: antagonism) of two opposing legitimation models which is not really solved by the Weimar Constitution, where the Reichs-President has partially the function of a 'substitute Emperor'.

Another famous citation originates with Otto Mayer, in the third edition of his leading textbook 'General Administrative law' 1924: 'Verfassungsrecht vergeht, Verwaltungsrecht besteht' ('Constitutional law vanishes, administrative law persists').

This sentence insists that the legitimacy by a constitution is something temporary and volatile, in other words: not really constitutive for the state, whereas the administrative law—outlasts any form of government, any constitutional status. Administrative law so to say embodies an emanation of the idea of the state, an order of reason, pure and objective accuracy.

A full comprehension of this dualism is not possible without a further review in the history of sciences prior to the Age of Enlightenment and the consequences and reactions in the 19th century.

3 Second Step: The Philosophical and Epistemological Background

With natural sciences rising, the segregation of empirical as well as moral and normative sciences (today part of the humanities) took place, too. The main principle of the natural sciences is the provability of facts: the empirism. Only things and facts which can be proven, are in fact existent and form the realm of the 'Sein' (the world of 'being'). It was the Scotsman David Hume who postulated: There is no logical deduction from the 'is' to the 'ought', and vice versa.[2] The 'is'-'ought'-theorem influenced numerous other great philosophers like John Locke, Auguste Comte, and—notably—Immanuel Kant. The doctrines of Kant were developed further, especially by the philosophical schools of Neo-Kantianism at both the University of Marburg and the University of Heidelberg. The Marburg Neo-Kantianism—represented by famous authorities such as Hermann Cohen, Ernst Cassirer and Rudolf Stammler—strictly pronounced the epistemologically grounded dichotomy: empirical nature sciences versus humanities.[3] In reverse, the Heidelberg Neo-Kantianism—practiced by Wilhelm Windelband, Heinrich Rickert and the famous Max Weber complemented the dualism of 'is' and 'ought' with a third category: the realm of values as the epitome of imperative axioms.[4] This was taken over by the philosophical doctrines of phenomenology and ontology, represented by Edmund Husserl, Max Scheler, Nicolai Hartmann and Martin Heidegger. They propagated the intentional feeling of values as an epistemic method.[5]

Contrary to that, the second significant flow in 19th century philosophy followed the tradition of Georg Wilhelm Friedrich Hegel who had emphasised the overcoming of contradictions by his method of dialectic.[6]

However, the neo-Kantianism was neither able to solve the 'is-ought-problem' nor the dualism between the individual and society. Hegel's method concerns the creation of entities in a dialectic operation. In his famous book 'Grundlinien der Philosophie des Rechts' from 1820 he refers to the state as a phenomenon: The state will be the synthesis of the 'Sein' and the 'Sollen', the synthesis of the 'is' and the 'ought'. In a very famous phrasing, Hegel writes in paragraph 257: 'Der Staat ist die Wirklichkeit der sittlichen Idee'[7] (translated: 'The State is the reality of the moral idea'). The State is coincidently real and ideal, as a manifestation of a higher, metaphysical order. In this way, the state gains—in German: Eigenwert—(self-value).

[2] Hume (1739), Book III, Part I, Section I.

[3] Cf. Röhl and Röhl (2008), § 15 Die Dichotomie von Sein und Sollen.

[4] Cf. Röhl and Röhl (2008), § 20 Das Werturteilsproblem.

[5] Hilgendorf and Joerden (2017), p. 162.

[6] Cf. Hilgendorf and Joerden (2017), p. 153; Hassemer et al. (2016), p. 64.

[7] Hegel (1821), § 257.

This conclusion is—admittedly—not easy to understand. Some critics assume that this is only blustering. One of the most famous among them being Karl Raymond Popper.[8] Nevertheless, Hegel's system was undoubtably one of the most influential doctrines in the 19th and early 20th century because of it being an ideal basis of legitimacy for the type of national states characterised by strength and might and by the pronounced subordination of its subjects. Hegel's metaphor of the strong state (in German: 'Der starke Staat') had been adapted by German historians—for instance Heinrich von Treitschke—who were therefore able to explain the legitimate existence of the Bismarck Empire which had been founded after a victory in three wars.[9]

The Hegelian heritage conglomerates finally with another doctrine at the end of the 19th century, called the cultural philosophy. Its main protagonists are Eduard Spranger, Georg Simmel, Wilhelm Dilthey and Theodor Litt. They created the specific method of humanities (in German: 'geisteswissenschaftliche Methode'): Items can only be understood with regard to the historical connotations and the sense that stands behind the simple wording.[10]

Right here, we shall stop and ask ourselves: Why undertake an excursion in philosophical subtleties? The answer is based on a specific German circumstance: Both, jurisprudence and the theory of public law, when discussing the questions of the role of law—as mentioned in the beginning—borrowed and adapted from philosophical doctrines and social sciences in a remarkable way.

Thus, it is fair to say that during the Bismarck Empire the mainstream movement in public law was explicitly influenced by neo-Kantianism. This is surely conditioned by the circumstances following the foundation of the Second Empire in 1871: having delivered the German state, the wish to criticise or even question its legitimacy was not significant. The cognisance of the successful German unification should not be tarnished by academic and theoretic games. We observe this in some famous publications, such as the 'Staatsrecht des Deutschen Reiches' by Paul Laband (1838–1918) or the 'Allgemeine Staatslehre' by Georg Jellinek (1851–1911). They performed the 'juristic method', which pursued the interpretation of legal rules in a formal-logical way. The intention of a particular rule, whether it seems fair and reasonable, will generally be excluded.[11] Still, in the neo-Kantianist tradition, Jellinek distinguished the empiric or ontologic description of the 'Staatslehre' from the purely systematic understanding of the 'Staatsrecht': Two different realms evolved—Staatslehre and Staatsrecht—which would never find together![12]

---

[8] Popper (1992), pp. 35 ff.

[9] Cf. regarding the importance of Hegel, Hilgendorf and Joerden (2017), pp. 153 f.; Geis (1989), pp. 91, 92.

[10] Cf. Geis (1989), pp. 91, 94f; Friedrich (1977), pp. 161, 191f.

[11] Wieacker (1967), p. 431; Friedrich (1986), pp. 197, 206.

[12] Geis (1989), pp. 91, 92; Friedrich (1977), pp. 161, 163, 165.

4 Third Step: The Schools of the Weimarian Constitutional Law

The ultimate point of the conception of Paul Laband and Georg Jellinek is the so-called legal positivism, the next generation of legal positivism and its climax. In Germany, it was represented by Georg Anschütz, Richard Thoma and Eugen Ehrlich, all of them professors of public law, as well as Gustav Radbruch who applied legal positivism to criminal law. The round will be completed—of course—by the eminent Hans Kelsen in Vienna—who reduced the law to a system of rules, the only condition being—rather simplified—to be entirely consistent and without any contradictions.[13] The only reason for the legitimacy of rules was that these had to be adopted by means of a correct procedure, especially in a formal and strict procedure in accordance with the respective constitution.[14]

Contrary to this mainstream in the Weimarian doctrine, more and more voices demanded a shift away from the idea of a blind, relative law. They claimed it should be necessary to recognise historic and cultural contexts and abstract values behind said rules. In contrast to the 'Juristische Methode', this approach was called the 'Geisteswissenschaftliche Methode'[15]—which is not easy to translate; perhaps it is best described as: 'The comprehensive method in state law'. Therefore, it is not astonishing that counter to the legal positivism with its founder Immanuel Kant, the 'Geisteswissenschaftliche Methode' was first correlated with his antipode Hegel, by no means in a uniform understanding, but in a great variance.[16] There are authors who take over most of Hegelian key elements, for example Josef Kohler, Julius Binder, Ernst Rudolf Huber, and Karl Larenz.

A little excursus seems appropriate here: Karl Larenz is mostly known as a doyen of the private law and as the author of the renowned book: 'Legal methodology'. However, most do not know that he started his career in the 1920s as an ambitious private lecturer of public law. He was a member of the 'Kieler Schule', which proclaimed the uncompromising adaption of national-socialist ideology to the public and criminal law. One of his most famous and also notorious sentences was:

> Rechtsgenosse ist nur, wer Volksgenosse ist; Volksgenosse ist, wer deutschen Blutes ist. (...) Wer außerhalb der Volksgemeinschaft steht, steht auch nicht im Recht.[17]

Although being compromised to having been a strong follower of the Nazi-regime, he nevertheless changed to the politically unsuspicious civil law and the even less suspicious basic subject after the war and succeeded starting a second

---

[13] Kelsen (1960).

[14] For Kelsens 'Pure Theory of Law' cf. Hilgendorf and Joerden (2017), p. 163.

[15] Geis (1989), pp. 91, 92; Friedrich (1977), pp. 161, 163, 165.

[16] Geis (1989), pp. 91, 93.

[17] Larenz (1935), p. 241. 'Only he who is a member of the people is a member of the law; a member of the people is whoever is of German blood. (...) Anyone who is outside the national community is also not within the law' (translated by author).

career in Kiel and Munich. Until the last decade. his academic oeuvre had remained with high reputation (negotiating his NS-past).

But back to Weimar: Other proponents of the comprehensive method reduced their collection of Hegelianism to singular elements, especially the idea of the state as a higher being, or—more psychologically—as a super-ego: Hans Freyer, Othmar Spann, Hans Otto Ziegler, Edgar Tatarin-Tarnheyden and several others are to be mentioned in this context. It might not be surprising that most of them made great efforts to tender themselves to the brown potentates, hoping to profit in their careers.

The probably most well-known exponent of the comprehensive method is Rudolf Smend, who was undoubtedly conservative, but never changed to Nazism. In his famous book 'Verfassung und Verfassungsrecht' (published in 1928), Smend tries to construct the legitimacy of the abstract state as an overall experience of all his citizens which transforms them from a multitude of individuals to a unity. Smend himself follows less Hegelianism or neo-Hegelianism but rather the cultural philosophy of Theodor Litt. Litt proclaimed that a collective and social consciousness will arise through integration of common cultural values. Smend transfers the thought of integration on to the state: There are three modi of integration:[18] the personal integration that refers to the charisma of a leading person (which is ambivalent: compare Adolf Hitler to Nelson Mandela); furthermore, the so-called functional integration, which has a more formal characteristic: Considering predetermined procedures, whether in the genesis of rules—think about the several readings of a draft law, or the right to introduce amendments, the rights of the opposition and so on. Functional integration is characterised by its uniformity; it might not be as exciting, but it ought to give the feeling of both legal certainty and protection of trust. That is the difference to the purely formal perspective of the procedure, as is the approach of the legal positivism.

The third way of integration—and perhaps the most extensive one—is the so-called 'sachliche Integration', which may be translated as 'integration by content'. It refers to the existence of commonly practised values, such as language, symbols (particularly religious symbols or political emblems) but also abstract content like human rights and respective basic rights. The 'integration by content' might raise problems since there always is the inherent possibility of causing disintegration—intentionally or not. Think of the recent controversies about the Christian cross in schools, courts and public authorities or the quarrel about wearing Muslim headscarves, burqas or niqabs. There are 'harmless' symbols like the eagles of Poland and Germany,[19] but also 'harmful' symbols like the swastika or the emblem of the 'Islamic State of Iraq and Syria (ISIS)', at least for the—stated in quotation marks—'correct thinking' majority.

Smend, of course, had solely good intentions. In his eyes, the 'Integrationstheorie' was a way to appreciate the catalogue of basic rights by embedding them into the consciousness of the people: 'From consciousness to

[18]Cf. Bickenbach (2005), p. 588; Hennis (1999), p. 485.

[19]Concerning the eagle as one of the eldest symbols for statehood cf. Geis (2004), pp. 439 ff.

commitment'.[20] In this way, the law gains its legitimacy by its ability to integrate the individuals into a or 'the' people.

The influence of Smend's 'Theory of integration' was in fact very strong. Surprisingly, after the Second World War, it connected with the construction of the dogmatic system of the basic rights.[21] Remember the famous 'Lüth' decision of the Federal Constitutional Court (published in the 7th volume of the official collection, page 198—an essential 'must know' among German law students).[22] In this decision, the Court interprets the purpose of basic rights not only as a defence against the state (the so-called subjective defence function), but also as an epitome of all values the young Federal Republic had opted for; therefore it might be necessary to take the basic rights into account whenever courts or authorities have to apply or interpret any rules in criminal, civil, or public law. This phenomenon is known as the dogma of the 'mittelbare Drittwirkung', which can be translated as 'indirect third-party-effect'. Nonetheless, this figure which is absolutely dominant in contemporary dogmatic system is 'the very spirit' of Smend.

Once more: back again to Weimar in the concluding step. There is one person who was not yet named, and that is Carl Schmitt.[23] Schmitt cannot be associated with any particular school of thought because he switched opinions several times. In his early time—as a 'Privatdozent' (private lecturer)—he had been a proponent of neo-Hegelianism and value philosophy . In the middle of the 1920s, he performed a radical pivot and claims for the legitimating effort of the decision: It is the right only of the stronger or the strongest which is crucial. In his own words: 'Souverän ist, wer über den Ausnahmezustand entscheidet' ('Sovereign is who decides about the state of emergency').[24] That is the fundament of his theory of a mighty state, and—of course—this theory will be very useful for the at that time steadily increasing National Socialism. After the takeover of power by the Nazis, he changed his theory once more and creates the 'thinking in concrete orders'.[25] That constitutes an instrument which allows to interpret legal terms entirely in the sense of ideology which culminates in the Nuremberg Laws: Matrimonium is only possible between Arians, other than Arians are subhuman, Jewish property is no longer protected by law and so on. Those were the ultimate consequences of this doctrine.

The Weimarian methodological debate cannot be fully comprehended without mentioning its forum, the highly regarded Vereinigung der Deutschen Staatsrechtslehrer -VDStRL (Association of German Constitutional Law Professors). This association has been established in Berlin in the year 1922 for the purpose of constructing a new system of constitutional and public law under the legal

[20] Smend (1928).

[21] Bickenbach (2005), pp. 588, 591; Hennis (1999), pp. 485, 486.

[22] BVerfGE 7, 198 – Lüth.

[23] For further readings regarding Carl Schmitt cf. Bendersky (1983); Noack (1993); Mehring (2009).

[24] Schmitt (1934a), p. 13; cf. Hofmann (2005), pp. 171–186; Oberreuter (2008).

[25] Rüthers et al. (2020), pp. 358 ff.; Schmitt (1934b).

conditions of transformation from a monarchy to a republic and the real conditions in the troubled times after the loss in the First World War. Discussions and exchange of views beyond borders should stabilise the interpretation and application of the law. The 'founding father' was the professor of public law Heinrich Triepel from Berlin; among the other founding members of the first hour were Gerhard Anschütz, Richard Thoma, Fritz Stier-Somló, Rudolf Smend, Carl Schmitt, Günter Holstein. One can say that all proponents of the methodological debate were members of the association, too. And nearly all of them tried to base and protect their system by deepening philosophical roots. The political sciences had not been developed in a sufficient scope yet. Therefore, the debates were quite predominantly practised within this forum. The Weimar State Court (Article 108 WRV) had only exclusive, limited competences and was not a suitable partner for a legal dialogue between science and jurisdiction, compared to the current Federal Constitutional Court.

5 Fourth Step: Consequences for the Current Debate

After the Second World War, there was a short renaissance of the *Methodenstreit* and a transfer to several legal scholars as its successors. Hence, some legal 'schools', such as the 'Smend-Schule' or the 'Schmitt-Schule' continued.[26] Considering the origin of the Grundgesetz, one can say that the proponents of the 'Geisteswissenschaftliche Methode' have slightly won the battle: The Grundgesetz contains numerous of elements which shall guarantee the protection of itself against erosion and undermining by anti-constitutional powers. Nevertheless, the initial force of the Weimarian methodological debate has never been revived. The actual Staatsrechtslehre does not really ground on a philosophical and epistemological systems anymore. It has been replaced by the dialogue with the political sciences, more and more influenced by the harmonisation with the laws of the EU and the European Convention on Human Rights, including the jurisdiction of the ECJ and the ECtHR.

References

Bendersky JW (1983) Carl Schmitt – Theorist for the Reich. Princeton University Press, Princeton, N.J.

Bickenbach C (2005) Rudolf Smend (15.1.1882 bis 5.7.1975) - Grundzüge der Integrationslehre. Juristische Schulung 2005:588–591

Friedrich M (1977) Der Methoden- und Richtungsstreit – Zur Grundlagendiskussion der Weimarer Staatsrechtslehre. Archiv des öffentlichen Rechts 102(1977):161–209

[26] For a comprehensive example of the conflicts between both schools, cf. Hwang (2013), pp. 219–244; Kaufmann (1991).

Friedrich M (1986) Paul Laband und die Staatsrechtswissenschaft seiner Zeit. Archiv des öffentlichen Rechts 111(1986):197–218
Geis ME (1989) Der Methoden- und Richtungsstreit in der Weimarer Staatslehre. Juristische Schulung 1989:91–96
Geis ME (2004) Symbole im Recht. In: Schlögl R, Giesen B, Osterhammel J (eds) Die Wirklichkeit der Symbole – Grundlagen der Kommunikation in historischen und gegenwärtigen Gesellschaften. UVK, Constance, pp 439–460
Hassemer W, Neumann U, Saliger F (eds) (2016) Einführung in die Rechtsphilosophie und Rechtstheorie der Gegenwart, 9th edn. C.F. Müller, Heidelberg
Hegel GWF (1821) Grundlinien der Philosophie des Rechts. Nicolai, Berlin
Hennis W (1999) Integration durch Verfassung? – Rudolf Smend und die Zugänge zum Verfassungsproblem nach 50 Jahren unter dem Grundgesetz. Juristenzeitung 1999:485–495
Hilgendorf E, Joerden JC (eds) (2017) Handbuch Rechtsphilosophie, 1st edn. J.B. Metzler Verlag, Stuttgart
Hofmann H (2005) Souverän ist, wer über den Ausnahmezustand entscheidet. Der Staat 44:171–186
Hume D (1739) A treatise of human nature – being an attempt to introduce the experimental method of reasoning into moral subjects. London
Hwang SP (2013) Materialisierung durch Entmaterialisierung – Zur Kritik der Schmitt-Schule am wertorientierten Grundrechtsverständnis unter dem GG. Der Staat 52:219–244
Kaufmann A (1991) Die Naturrechtsrenaissance der ersten Nachkriegsjahre - und was daraus geworden ist. In: Stolleis M (ed) Die Bedeutung der Wörter – Studien zur europäischen Rechtsgeschichte – Festschrift für Sten Gagnér zum 70. Geburtstag. Beck, Munich, pp 105–132
Kelsen H (1960) Reine Rechtslehre – mit einem Anhang: das Problem der Gerechtigkeit, 2nd edn. Deuticke, Vienna
Larenz K (1935) Rechtsperson und subjektives Recht – Zur Wandlung der Rechtsgrundbegriffe. In: Dahm G, Michaelis K, Schaffstein F, Siebert W (eds) Grundfragen der neuen Rechtswissenschaft. Junker und Dünnhaupt, Berlin, pp 225–230
Mehring R (2009) Carl Schmitt – Aufstieg und Fall. Beck, Munich
Noack P (1993) Carl Schmitt – eine Biographie. Propyläen, Berlin
Oberreuter H (2008) "Souverän ist, wer über den Ausnahmezustand entscheidet" – Carl Schmitt in der Agonie der Weimarer Republik. In: Hildebrand K (ed) Geschichtswissenschaft und Zeiterkenntnis – von der Aufklärung bis zur Gegenwart – Festschrift zum 65. Geburtstag von Horst Möller. Oldenbourg, Munich, pp 163–176
Popper KR (1992) Die offene Gesellschaft und ihre Feinde, Vol 2: Falsche Propheten – Hegel, Marx und die Folgen, 7th edn. Mohr, Tübingen
Röhl KF, Röhl HC (2008) Allgemeine Rechtslehre – ein Lehrbuch, 3rd edn. Heymanns, Cologne
Rüthers B, Fischer C, Birk A (2020) Rechtstheorie und Juristische Methodenlehre, 11th edn. C.H. Beck, Munich
Schmitt C (1934a) Politische Theologie – vier Kapitel zur Lehre von der Souveränität, 2nd edn. Duncker & Humblot, Munich
Schmitt C (1934b) Über die drei Arten des rechtswissenschaftlichen Denkens. Hanseatische Verl.-Anst., Hamburg
Smend R (1928) Verfassung und Verfassungsrecht. Duncker & Humblot, Munich
Wieacker F (1967) Privatrechtsgeschichte der Neuzeit – unter besonderer Berücksichtigung der deutschen Entwicklung, 2nd edn. Vandenhoeck & Ruprecht, Göttingen

Max-Emanuel Geis is a professor of German and Bavarian public and administrative law at the Friedrich-Alexander-University Erlangen-Nuremberg. Furthermore, he is a Justice at the Bavarian Constitutional Court. He is also a member of the evaluation committee of the German Council of Science.

The Development of the 'Fortified Democracy' Concept

Max-Emanuel Geis

Abstract This chapter is dedicated to the phenomenon that the Nazis seized power in 1933 in a way that conformed to the constitution. The most important disputes in the abolition of the rule of law shall be presented, followed by reflections on how a democracy can protect itself against its enemies. Under the keyword 'fortified democracy', the Basic Law has provided for various protective mechanisms to defend the free democratic basic order against attacks from within. This also includes the possibility of banning anti-constitutional parties or organisations. However, these options will still have to be proven in the future to see whether they are able to protect the constitution from radicalisation.

1 Reaction to Weimar

The issue of 'Fortified Democracy' as a key component of the Basic Law will only be comprehended in comparison with the counter-foil of the Weimarer Reichsverfassung of 1919. It can be said, indeed, it is one of the great tragedies in German history that the Nazi take-over in 1933, followed by the elimination of the fundamental principles of a free, democratic community under the rule of law had been not really an usurpation, neither a revolution, nor a *coup d'état*; rather, this process was performed in accordance with the applicable constitutional law, in other words: the take-over was considered completely legal at the material time.[1] The democratic state was not able to safeguard itself against self-destruction. How could this have happened?

[1] Gusy (2019), p. 567; Dürig and Klein (2019), MN 7; details on the process: Holste (2009), pp. 359 ff; Thrun (2019), pp. 65 ff; Bickenbach (2008), pp. 199 ff.

M.-E. Geis (✉)
University of Erlangen-Nuremberg, Erlangen, Germany
e-mail: Max-Emanuel.Geis@fau.de

M.-E. Geis et al. (eds.), *Dealing with Totalitarian Regimes and Human Rights*, Interdisciplinary Studies in Human Rights 11,
https://doi.org/10.1007/978-3-031-57338-5_10

1.1 The Development of Legal Positivism

The main reason for the hostile take-over may have been the so-called legal positivism as the leading theory in German *Staatsphilosophie* in the first decades of the 20th century.[2] Much more than today, the system and construction of the constitutional law at that time were rooted in philosophical thinking. I shall elaborate on this in greater detail in my previous chapter 'The Weimarian Methodological Debate in the Doctrine of Constitutional Law' in this publication.

Within the 19th century, the sciences influenced by epistemology differentiated themselves in empirical and normative sciences; the dualism of sciences and humanities evolved at this time. The theoretical base of this philosophical thought had been the dichotomy of what 'is' and what 'ought' to be. Already, the Scottish philosopher David Hume had postulated that the conclusion from the world of 'being' to the domain of normativity is logically impossible (the famous 'Is-ought-problem' or Hume's Law).[3] Passed down by the legal philosophy of Immanuel Kant who was strongly influenced by Hume, this thinking became a main premise in the context of neo-Kantianism especially practised at the universities of Marburg and Heidelberg in the 19th century.[4] From this starting point, jurisprudence was influenced by a strict separation of the normative law of the state on the one side, and the descriptive and empiric state theory together with the political sciences on the other. As prestigious representatives, at the end of the 19th century can be named Paul Laband and Georg Jellinek.[5] During the Weimar period, the legal positivism applied Hume's Law to the question to the legitimacy of legal rules: A legal rule gains its validity solely by being adopted in an orderly procedure, in particular by being approved by the parliamentary majority: In this case, the rule is 'positivised', that is, 'set' (from Latin '*ponere, posui, positum*' = to set). 'Positive' in this context does not mean 'good' or 'justified'. Whether the rule pursues a good or a bad target, whether it conforms to or contradicts human rights, whether the rule proclaims central principles or probes them, whether it thwarts them or even abolishes them, that is all without significance.[6] As the main proponents and, so to speak, opinion leaders in the Weimarian constitutional law theory can be seen as Gerhard Anschütz and Hans Thoma, both authors of the leading commentary on the Weimarer Reichsverfassung.[7] Concerning

[2] Schöbener and Knauff (2018), MN 149. Other well-known representatives. Karl Binding (1841–1920), Ernst Rudolf Bierling (1843–1919), Karl Bergbohm (1849–1927), Felix Somlo (1873–1920).

[3] Hume (1739), 1. Pt. 1, Sec. 1.

[4] Hilgendorf (2017), p. 160.

[5] On Jellinek: Kersten (2015), pp. 76 ff.; on Laband: Mußgnug (2015), pp. 20 ff.

[6] On the neutrality of the Weimarian system: Dürig and Klein (2019), MN 6 ff.; Bickenbach (2008), p. 202.

[7] Anschütz (1933); Anschütz and Thoma (1930).

penal law, Gustav Radbruch represents legal positivism. After the collapse of the 'Third Reich', he realised the problematic role of legal positivism and coined the famous 'Radbruchsche Formel'.[8] A somewhat more uncompromising stance can be found in the main work of Hans Kelsen: 'Reine Rechtslehre'.[9]

1.2 Consequences of Legal Positivism

The catastrophic consequences of legal positivism are that the most serious threats to the principles of the rule of law and federalism are vested as a legal process. In 1933, these were:

First, the suspension or, strictly speaking, the abolition of the most important basic rights, especially in the field of corporal freedom and communication, triggered by the 'Reichstagsbrandverordnung' of February 1933[10] pursuant to Article 48 Subsection 2 of the Weimar Constitution ('Emergency Decree on the Protection of the Nation and the People') without participation of parliament.

Second, the abolition of the separation of powers, triggered by the Enabling Act from March 1933 ('Ermächtigungsgesetz').[11] Strictly speaking, the Enabling Act allowed the government to legislate beside the parliament. It thus merged the legislative and the executive power. It is to be kept in mind that parliament did not lose its powers immediately, but in political reality, the parliament lost its sovereignty step by step, even more as the members of parliament were only recruited among politically reliable persons.

Third, the destruction of federalism by the so-called 'Gleichschaltung der Länder', that is the abolition of territorial sovereignty hand in hand with the integration of the former autonomous administration structures of the states in a unified administration.[12]

As an interim conclusion, we can thus establish: The state had nothing to oppose the destruction from within. The Weimar Republic disestablished itself.

[8] In short: In cases of unbearable contradictions between justice and legal certainty, justice needs to be granted priority in exceptional situations Radbruch (1946), pp. 105 ff.

[9] Kelsen (1960), pp. 201ff.

[10] RGBl. 1933 I S. 83.

[11] RGBl. 1933 I, S. 141.

[12] RGBl 1933 I, S. 153.

2 Elements of the 'Wehrhafte Demokratie'

2.1 Article 20 Section 3 GG (German Basic Law) and the 'Radbruch Formula'

From the year 1949, the German Basic Law from opposed this defencelessness, the model of a fortified democracy intending to be capable of active defence against threats to the stability of the system.[13]

Generally, Article 20 Subsection 3 GG provides that all branches of government are bound to statutes and law. This formulation is intended; it states clearly that besides the fixed 'positive' statute there exists an unwritten law that may be legalised.[14] Immediately after the end of the Second World War and in view of the devastations caused by a criminal regime with an inhuman ideology, there idea of the validity of nature law grew,[15] either based on religious foundations or based on reason—in the sense of the Virginia Declaration of Rights from 1776 or the American Declaration of Independence from the same year both mentioning the 'certain unalienable Rights'.[16] Another manifestation would be the thought of customary rights.[17] I have already mentioned the 'Radbruch Formel'; according to this formula, positive law is illegitimate, when its content extraordinarily contradicts human rights, especially by denying the fundamental right of equality to a specific group of human beings. It may be of interest to point out that this formula experienced a renaissance after the German reunification regarding the question of how to judge the so-called 'Mauerschützenfälle',[18] that means: the targeted killing of refugees trying to cross the inner-German border, which was formally legitimated by a military order of the chief of the border guards.

2.2 The Protection of the 'Free Democratic Basic Order'

Designing the Basic Law as a constitution for the democratic Federal Republic of Germany, it was an important goal for the Parlamentarische Rat, to establish a security system in order to prevent attacks by radical forces on the so-called 'free democratic basic order', in German: freiheitlich-demokratische Grundordnung[19]

---

[13]Voßkuhle and Kaiser (2019), pp. 1154ff.; Dürig and Klein (2019), MN 10.; Hopfauf (2018), MN 240.

[14]Schulze-Fielitz (2015), MN 94; Hofmann (2018), MN 90.

[15]Möllers (2019), MN 109 ff.

[16]Specific in the Grundgesetz Art. 79 III GG.

[17]Sachs (2018), MN 106 f.; Hofmann (2018), MN 90.

[18]BVerfGE 95, 96 (133); Kaufmann (1995), p. 83.

[19]Von Coelln (2020) MN 2; Wittreck (2013), MN 44.

(abbreviated: fdGO). The Federal Constitutional Court of Germany had ranked this democratic basic order among these elements:[20]

- The respect for human rights, as they can be found in the Universal Declaration of Human Rights of 1948;
- The separation of powers (in German: 'Gewaltenteilung'), in memory of the systematic destruction of this main element of the modern constitutional state since John Locke and Charles de Montesquieu by Nazis;
- The responsibility of the Government towards Parliament as the representative of the people, in consideration of the detachment of the executive branch from the disempowered Reichstag;
- The principle of the Rule of Law and the principle of legality of all administrative activity;
- The strict independence of the judiciary, considering the influence of the Nazi-leaders on courts, especially on the so-called 'Volksgerichtshof', whose function was merely to hand down death sentences for declared enemies of the people, which were decided before the beginning of the trial;
- The principle of a multi-party-system, considering not only the one-party-system of the 'Third Reich' (NSDAP) but also the one-party-system in the communist countries (KPdSU, SED) as a typical feature of totalitarianism;
- Equal opportunities for parties both in election campaigns and the parliamentary process;
- The fundamental right to found and exercise political opposition, in consideration that a great number of members of the former opposition in the Weimar Republic had been persecuted by the Nazis and sent to prison or concentration camps.

2.3 Components of the 'Fortified Democracy'

In consideration of the many efforts of the Nazi-Regime to eliminate the most important essentials of a free democratic basic order, there was a common opinion among the fathers and the mothers of the newly created constitution about the necessity of safeguard precautions to avoid an undermining of the constitutional system again. Therefore, the state should be given the power to react rapidly and powerfully to anti-constitutional activities by individuals, associations, and parties. For this reason, there is a considerable number of regulations, which embody the principle of what we call 'fortified democracy'. As their components are commonly being considered:[21]

[20] BVerfGE 2, 1 (15 ff.) – SRP-Verbot; BVerfGE 5, 85 (111 ff.) – KPD-Verbot, BVerfGE 144, 20, 3. Leitsatz – 2. NPD-Urteil.

[21] Short overview: Jaschke (2006).

- The legal bond of the general freedom of action to the constitutional order in Article 2 Subsection 1 GG;[22]
- The loyalty of scientists and researchers to the constitution, Article 5 Subsection 3 Sentence 2 GG;[23]
- The legal authority to ban associations who intend the elimination of the free democratic basic order or damaging it, Article 9 Subsection 2 GG;[24]
- Restrictions upon the privacy of correspondence and the postal secrecy in the case of anti-constitutional efforts, Article 10 Subsection 2 GG;[25]
- Restrictions upon the free movement of a person in the case of constitution-hostile endeavours, pursuant to Article 11 Subsection 2 GG);[26]
- The competence to nationalise the means of production in the case of abuse by the owners, Article 15 GG;[27]
- The forfeiture of basic rights in the case of abuse to fight against the liberally democratic order, Article 18 GG. However, concerning the prominent protection of these rights, the forfeiture can only be sentenced by the German Federal Constitutional Court;[28]
- The power to ban a political party that is recognised to pursue constitutional-hostile goals. Because of the outstanding role which is attributed to political parties, this issue demands a special, complex proceeding before the Federal Constitutional Court pursuant to Article 21 GG;[29]
- The enhanced duty of loyalty of all officials to the state as a part of the so-called traditional principles of the professional civil service (settled in Art. 33 sub-section 5 GG);[30]

Finally, the right of resistance of everyone against any person and any organisation enforcing hostile attacks to the constitutional system. Though the constitution was only amended in this regard in 1968 by the first grand coalition in the light of the massive student protests and riots the same year which were world-wide provoked by the Vietnam War, the assassination of Martin Luther King and—in particular in Germany—the default of the opposition in Parliament answered by an increasing and more a more militant extra-parliamentary opposition.[31]

---

[22] Di Fabio (2019), MN 5f.

[23] Gärditz (2019), MN 9 ff; von der Decken (2018), MN 50; Wendt (2021), MN 114.

[24] Wolff (2016), MN 10; Bauer (2013), MN 55.

[25] Gusy (2018), MN 98; Durner (2019), MN 168.

[26] Ipsen (2021), § 14, MN 618; Wollenschläger (2013), MN 8.

[27] Depenheuer and Froese (2018), MN 3; Bryde (2021) MN 1.

[28] Pagenkopf (2018), MN 4 ff.; Jarass (2018), MN 1.

[29] Morlok (2015), MN 144; Pieroth (2018), MN 44.

[30] Battis (2018), MN 32 ff.; Pieper (2018), MN 151 ff.

[31] Wittreck (2015), MN 14; Hofmann (2018), MN 97 ff.

2.4 *Examples of the 'Wehrhafte Demokratie'*

In reality, the instruments of the fortified democracy were used rather sporadically and, in a quite different quantity, especially when connected to special procedures. The forfeiture of Basic Rights for example was attempted only four times[32] in the early period of the Federal Republic, but no case ended with a condemnation.

2.4.1 The Ban of Constitution-Hostile Parties

The strongest counter-mechanism: the ban of constitution-hostile parties by the Federal Constitutional Court has a history of its own. In the 1950s, there were two dramatic procedures. As a replacement for the NSDAP which had been officially forbidden by the allies, the SRP (Sozialistische Reichspartei) was founded. This party claimed to be the true heir of the Nazi-Party and a new platform to collect former party members with the aim of resurrecting the Nazi-ideology. In this first proceeding, the Federal Constitutional Court defined the components of fortified democracy, as was described above, and banned the SRP.[33] Only a few years later, the procedure was initiated concerning the KPD, a spin-off (in modern speech) of the Soviet KPdSU. This trial resulted in a ban, too, and with similar arguments.[34]

In the following decades, there was no need seen by the established parties to pursue further procedures, maybe because they preferred to fight against them in the politic arena rather than forcing these parties to go underground, although, in the meantime, the NPD had been founded as an extreme right-wing party, and the DKP as a new communist party heavily supported by the SED in the GDR. Especially, the NPD was regarded as a largely harmless club of hardliners. Mostly because during that time recurrently right-wing parties were founded—as the German People Union or the Republicans—which entered the parliaments but disappeared after one election period only.

However, nearly half a century after the ban of both the SRP and the KPD, and after the first decade following German Unity, the opinion was growing that the NPD sympathised more and more with new generations of Neonazi-Groups which fuelled hate against several groups of people, especially from abroad. Having monitored this party for a long time, finally, a new procedure was initiated before the Federal Constitutional Court, calling for a party-ban. Unfortunately, to prove the constitutional-hostile character of the party, the prosecution authorities and even the German Secret Service had placed so-called 'agents provocateurs' in several party circles to provoke the members to act criminal and hostile.[35] Thus, it was not surprising that the Federal Constitutional Court decided in 2003 that it might not be

[32] BVerfGE 11, 282, BVerfGE 38, 23, BVerfG Beschl. v. 18.7.1997 – 2 BvA 1/92, 2 BvA 2/92.

[33] BVerfGE 2, (1 ff.).

[34] BVerfGE 5, 85 ff. – KPD-Verbot.

[35] Voßkuhle and Kaiser (2019), p. 1155; Ipsen (2002), p. 868.

correct to prove an anti-constitutional behaviour by an anti-constitutional behaviour and closed the proceedings.[36] This was quite a shock for the applicants. And so it lasted for over ten years until the next attempt for a constitutional proceeding to ban the NPD. But also this trial which was executed accurately, ended with a great surprise: The Federal Constitutional Court, which can ban an anti-constitutional party but is not obliged to do so, decided that the NPD is pursuing anti-constitutional aims, but meanwhile, its influence is so insignificant that a ban is unnecessary.[37] The crucial point, however, is a completely different but most effective: Whenever a party is declared anti-constitutional, the party's financing can be shut down.[38] Meanwhile, this path has been taken.

2.4.2 The 'Radikalen-Erlass' (1972)

In the 1960s and 70s, Germany was facing what was seen as a new struggle: The rise of left-wing student groups and the terroristic acts led by the criminal 'Baader-Meinhof-Gang', from which the developed terroristic organisation 'Rote-Armee-Fraktion (RAF)' emerged. Confronting the fear of the undermining of the constitution from within, especially from the political left, in 1972 the German federal and state (Länder) governments issued a decree regarding the membership of public officials in extremist organisations.[39]

This decree emphasised the background checking of loyalty to the constitution among public officials based in the constitution itself as a traditional principle of professional civil servants in Article 33 Subsection 5 GG, performed by the Federal Office for the Protection of the Constitution (Verfassungsschutz). To keep the public service free of constitutional enemies, the goal of this so called 'Radikalen-Erlass' was to remove the enemies of the constitution or members of organisations which were against the fdGO and deny applicants to enter the civil service based on their evaluation regarding this loyalty.

The main premise in this process was that every applicant's mentality has to be characterised by loyalty to the fdGO, so that they would actively stand up for its values and fully identify with them.[40] In the so-called 'Radikalen-Urteil', the Federal Constitutional Court decided that just the membership in an organisation associated with constitution-hostile goals can be relevant to the negative evaluation of the applicant, whether the organisation has been banned or not.[41]

[36] BVerfGE 107, 339; Volkmann (2003), pp. 593ff.; Knauff (2003), pp. 318ff.

[37] BVerfGE 144, 20 – 367; Ebert and Karaosmanoğlu (2017), pp. 374ff.; Hillgruber (2017), pp. 398ff.; Sachs (2017), p. 377.

[38] Voßkuhle and Kaiser (2019), p. 1155; Art. 21 III GG.

[39] On the history of the Radikalen-Erlass: Hattenhauer (1993), pp. 536 ff.

[40] Brosius-Gersdorf (2015), MN 104.

[41] BVerfGE 39, 334 ff.; Zentgraf (2016).

These general background checks came to an end in 1991, an enquiry to the Verfassungsschutz is nowadays connected to certain doubts about the applicant's loyalty in most of the Länder, a general check-up is not performed anymore.[42] This enhanced duty of loyalty to the constitution builds a counterpoint to the above-mentioned destruction from within that took place in Weimar.

2.4.3 Ban of Associations

More often, the ban on constitution-hostile associations and societies has been practised by the ministries of the interior (in total since 1990: 57 associations and 106 sub- or substitute associations),[43] above all against violent (rocker) gangs (33 bans, most famously the rocker gang Hell's Angels), followed by extreme right organisations which invoke to the body of inhuman Nazi-Thought (20 bans) and against militant religious communities, such as Salafi organisations[44] (14 bans). Regarding other fields, there were 93 bans on foreign extremism (mostly sub- or substitute groups of foreign associations), two bans on unspecified cases and one on an extreme left organisation. In such a case, it is imperative to confiscate the association's funds (Section 3 Subesction I Sentence 2 Nr. 1 VereinsG).

3 Conclusion

Evaluating the impact of the elements of the 'fortified democracy', we can see: The quality of using them has not been very large in the past. Nevertheless, their existence influenced the political opinion for a half-century and appealed on right-wing or left-wing associations in a moderating way by hanging up a visible sword of Damocles. Whether this constant threat will be effective in the future, too—in view of a general trend of diminishing centre parties—is a development we have to observe very carefully.

---

[42] Mühldorfer (2014).

[43] Bundesministerium des Inneren, für Bau und Heimat (Federal Ministry of the Interior) Vereinsverbote. https://www.bmi.bund.de/DE/themen/sicherheit/extremismus/vereinsverbote/vereinsverbote-node.html;jsessionid=49697E930033301DBBA924A03D5E5373.1_cid373 (last accessed 1 December 2023).

[44] Groh (2012) (last accessed 14 January 2024), MN 14 ff.; Sailer and Marx (2018), MN 37; BVerfGE 149, 160 ff.

References

Anschütz G (ed) (1933) Die Verfassung des Deutschen Reichs vom 11. August 1919. Georg Stilke, Berlin

Anschütz G, Thoma R (eds) (1930) Handbuch des Deutschen Staatsrechts, vol 1. Mohr Siebeck, Tübingen

Battis U (2018) Art. 33. In: Sachs M (ed) Grundgesetz Kommentar. C. H. Beck, Munich

Bauer H (2013) Art. 9. In: Dreier H (ed) Grundgesetz-Kommentar, vol 1. Mohr Siebeck, Tübingen

Bickenbach C (2008) Vor 75 Jahren: Die Entmächtigung der Weimarer Reichsverfassung durch das Ermächtigungsgesetz. Juristische Schulung 2008:199–203

Brosius-Gersdorf F (2015) Art. 33. In: Dreier H (ed) Grundgesetz-Kommentar, vol 2. Mohr Siebeck, Tübingen

Bryde B-O (2021) Art. 15. In: Kunig P (ed) Grundgesetz Kommentar, vol 1. C. H. Beck, Munich

Depenheuer O, Froese J (2018) Art. 15. In: Huber PM, Voßkuhle A (eds) Grundgesetz, vol 1. C. H. Beck, Munich

Di Fabio U (2019) Art. 2 Abs. 1. In: Herzog R, Scholz R, Herdegen M, Klein HH (eds) Grundgesetz, vol I. C. H. Beck, Munich

Dürig G, Klein HH (2019) Art. 18. In: Herzog R, Scholz R, Herdegen M, Klein HH (eds) Grundgesetz, vol II. C. H. Beck, Munich

Durner W (2019) Art. 10. In: Herzog R, Scholz R, Herdegen M, Klein HH (eds) Grundgesetz, vol I. C. H. Beck, Munich

Ebert B, Karaosmanoğlu C (2017) Kein Verbot der NPD. Deutsches Verwaltungsblatt 2017:374–378

Gärditz KF (2019) Art. 5 Abs. 3. In: Herzog R, Scholz R, Herdegen M, Klein HH (eds) Grundgesetz, vol I. C. H. Beck, Munich

Groh K (2012) Vereinsgesetz. Nomos. https://beck-online.beck.de/?vpath=bibdata/komm/GroKoVereinsG_1/cont/GroKoVereinsG%2Ehtm. Accessed 1 Dec 2023

Gusy C (2018) Art. 10. In: Huber PM, Voßkuhle A (eds) Grundgesetz, vol 1. C. H. Beck, Munich

Gusy C (2019) “Das Deutsche Reich ist eine Republik” – Die Weimarer Reichsverfassung nach 100 Jahren. Juristische Arbeitsblätter 2019:561–568

Hattenhauer H (1993) Geschichte des deutschen Beamtentums. In: Wiese W (ed) Handbuch des Öffentlichen Dienstes, vol 1. Heymann, Cologne, Berlin, Bonn, Munich

Hilgendorf E (2017) Rechtsphilosophie zwischen 1860 und 1960. In: Hilgendorf E, Joerden JC (eds) Handbuch Rechtsphilosophie. J.B. Metzler, Stuttgart

Hillgruber C (2017) NPD – verfassungsfeindlich, aber nicht verfassungswidrig. Juristische Arbeitsblätter 2017:398–400

Hofmann H (2018) Art. 20. In: Hofmann H, Henneke H-G (eds) Kommentar zum Grundgesetz. Carl Heymanns, Cologne

Holste H (2009) Die Zerstörung des Rechtsstaates durch den Nationalsozialismus. Juristische Ausbildung 2009:359–366

Hopfauf A (2018) Einleitung. In: Hofmann H, Henneke H-G (eds) Kommentar zum Grundgesetz. Carl Heymanns, Cologne

Hume D (1739) A treatise of human nature, Book III: of morals

Ipsen J (2002) Rechtsfragen des NPD-Verbots. Neue Juristische Wochenschrift 2002:866–868

Ipsen J (2021) Staatsrecht II Grundrechte. Verlag Franz Vahlen, Munich

Jarass HD (2018) Art. 18. In: Jarass HD, Pieroth B (eds) Grundgesetz für die Bundesrepublik Deutschland. C. H. Beck, Munich

Jaschke H-G (2006) Streitbare Demokratie. www.bpb.de/politik/extremismus/rechtsextremismus/41891/streitbare-demokratie. Accessed 14 Jan 2024

Kaufmann A (1995) Die Radbruchsche Formel vom gesetzlichen Unrecht und vom übergesetzlichen Recht in der Diskussion um das im Namen der DDR begangene Unrecht. Neue Juristische Wochenschrift 1995:81–86

Kelsen H (1960) Reine Rechtslehre: Einleitung in die rechtswissenschaftliche Problematik. Deuticke, Wien
Kersten J (2015) Georg Jellinek (1851–1911). In: Häberle P, Kilian M, Wolff HA (eds) Staatsrechtlehrer des 20. Jahrhunderts: Deutschland – Österreich – Schweiz. De Gruyter, Berlin, Boston
Knauff M (2003) Einstellung des NPD-Verbotsverfahrens. VR 2003:318–322
Möllers TMJ (2019) Juristische Methodenlehre. C. H. Beck, Munich
Morlok M (2015) Art. 21. In: Dreier H (ed) Grundgesetz-Kommentar, vol 2. Mohr Siebeck, Tübingen
Mühldorfer F (2014) Radikalenerlass. In: Historisches Lexikon Bayerns. https://www.historisches-lexikon-bayerns.de/Lexikon/Radikalenerlass. Accessed 14 Jan 2024
Mußgnug R (2015) Paul Laband (1838–1918). In: Häberle P, Kilian M, Wolff HA (eds) Staatsrechtlehrer des 20. Jahrhunderts: Deutschland – Österreich – Schweiz. De Gruyter, Berlin, Boston
Pagenkopf M (2018) Art. 18. In: Sachs M (ed) Grundgesetz Kommentar. C. H. Beck, Munich
Pieper SU (2018) Art. 33. In: Hofmann H, Henneke H-G (eds) Kommentar zum Grundgesetz. Carl Heymanns, Cologne
Pieroth B (2018) Art. 21. In: Jarass HD, Pieroth B (eds) Grundgesetz für die Bundesrepublik Deutschland. C. H. Beck, Munich
Radbruch G (1946) Gesetzliches Unrecht und übergesetzliches Recht. Süddeutsche Juristenzeitung 1946:105–108
Sachs M (2017) Staatsorganisationsrecht: Parteiverbotsverfahren, Kein Verbot der NPD trotz Verfassungsfeindlichkeit mangels jeglicher Erfolgsaussichten ihrer Bestrebungen. Juristische Schulung 2017:377–380
Sachs M (2018) Art. 20. In: Sachs M (ed) Grundgesetz Kommentar. C. H. Beck, Munich
Sailer W, Marx R (2018) Teil VII öffentliches Vereinsrecht. In: Bäcker M, Denninger E, Graulich K (eds) Handbuch des Polizeirechts. C. H. Beck, Munich
Schöbener B, Knauff M (2018) § 5. Der moderne Verfassungsstaat – Grundprinzipien der Staatsgrundordnung. In: Schöbener B, Knauff M (eds) Allgemeine Staatslehre. C. H. Beck, Munich
Schulze-Fielitz H (2015) Art. 20. In: Dreier H (ed) Grundgesetz-Kommentar, vol 2. Mohr Siebeck, Tübingen
Thrun F (2019) Worum kämpft die wehrhafte Verfassung? Die Öffentliche Verwaltung 2019:65–72
Volkmann U (2003) Einstellung des NPD-Verbotsverfahrens. Deutsches Verwaltungsblatt 2003: 593–609
Von Coelln C (2020) § 39. In: Maunz T et al (eds) Bundesverfassungsgerichtsgesetz. C. H. Beck, Munich
Von der Decken K (2018) Art. 5. In: Hofmann H, Henneke H-G (eds) Kommentar zum Grundgesetz. Carl Heymanns, Cologne
Voßkuhle A, Kaiser A-B (2019) Grundwissen – Öffentliches Recht: Wehrhafte Demokratie. Juristische Schulung 2019:1154–1157
Wendt R (2021) Art. 5. In: Kunig P (ed) Grundgesetz Kommentar, vol 1. C. H. Beck, Munich
Wittreck F (2013) Art. 18. In: Dreier H (ed) Grundgesetz-Kommentar, vol 1. Mohr Siebeck, Tübingen
Wittreck F (2015) Art. 20 IV. In: Dreier H (ed) Grundgesetz-Kommentar, vol 2. Mohr Siebeck, Tübingen
Wolff HA (2016) Art. 9. In: Hömig D, Wolff HA (eds) Grundgesetz für die Bundesrepublik Deutschland. Nomos, Baden-Baden
Wollenschläger F (2013) Art. 11. In: Dreier H (ed) Grundgesetz-Kommentar, vol 1. Mohr Siebeck, Tübingen
Zentgraf R (2016) Bu-C 17, § 7 3. In: Metzler-Müller K, Rieger R, Seeck E, Zentgraf R (eds) Beamtenstatusgesetz: Kommentar. Kommunal- und Schul-Verlag, Wiesbaden

Max-Emanuel Geis is a professor of German and Bavarian public and administrative law at the Friedrich-Alexander-University Erlangen-Nuremberg. Furthermore, he is a Justice at the Bavarian Constitutional Court. He is also a member of the evaluation committee of the German Council of Science.

Dealing with the National Socialist Past in Germany

Hilde Farthofer

Abstract The end of the Second World War was the beginning of the legal reappraisal of the mass atrocities committed by the Nazi regime in Germany. The first steps were taken by the Allied powers by establishing the International Military Tribunal at Nuremberg and its subsequent trials. The national efforts started with the implementation of the denazification law No. 104. The efficiency of the national efforts was different and faced various problems.

1 Introduction

After the Second World War, Germany faced different problems. Besides the challenges resulting from the destruction of infrastructure, the allied occupation, and the lack of a legitimate functioning government, the horrendous crimes committed against the Jewish population in Europe, the Sinti, and Roma[1] and other minorities and against the opponents of the Nazi regime had to be dealt with.[2]

The real extent of the mass atrocities committed became apparent only after the fall of the National Socialist regime. When crimes are committed on a massive scale, a critical reappraisal of the events is always a very challenging task for a new government. Therefore, in order to advance the process, in many cases, international help or interference is required for its success.[3]

The chapter is focused on the steps taken by Germany to cope with its past. At first, the international steps will be outlined that were taken to bring to justice the

[1] Fings and Steinbacher (2021); Heuß and Roßberg (2015).

[2] For a detailed presentation of the initial situation in Germany Farthofer (2019), pp. 22–33.

[3] For the different measures and theories on Transitional Justice and an overview of the steps taken by different states, Mihr et al. (2018).

H. Farthofer (✉)
Friedrich-Alexander University of Erlangen-Nuremberg, Erlangen, Germany
e-mail: hilde.farthofer@fau.de

M.-E. Geis et al. (eds.), *Dealing with Totalitarian Regimes and Human Rights*, Interdisciplinary Studies in Human Rights 11,
https://doi.org/10.1007/978-3-031-57338-5_11

perpetrators of the large-scale atrocities committed by the Nazi regime. Thereafter, the German national efforts will be illustrated.

2 The Postwar Period

In the case of Germany, after the takeover, the allied military government temporarily closed down all national courts due to Proclamation No. 1 Art. III, dated March 1945.[4] For the reopening of the courts, a written permission from the Allied powers was necessary. Allied Control Council Law No. 4 reorganized the court system. The reshaping of the judicial system included the permanent closure of the Imperial Court of Justice (Reichsgericht) and the People's Court (Volksgerichtshof).[5]

2.1 The International Steps

Therefore, it is hardly surprising that the first legal steps to deal with the crimes committed were taken not by national courts but rather by the occupying powers. On October 18, 1945, the indictment against 24 major war criminals was presented at the Grand Conference Room of the Allied Control Authority Building in Berlin. The trial started on November 20, 1945, in Nuremberg.[6]

Already in October 1943, the Allies had emphasized in the Moscow Declaration their willingness to pursue the perpetrators after the end of the war.[7] The legal basis for the trial was established by the London Charter on August 8, 1945, and was restricted to the punishment of the major war criminals of the European Axis countries.[8] The charges were based on four crimes, i.e., conspiracy, crimes against peace, war crimes, and crimes against humanity. War crimes and crimes against humanity were only punishable if the link between the war and the commission of the crime could be established. On October 1, 1946, the International Military Tribunal announced its judgment. The sentences included death penalties, terms of

[4] Eisenhower (1945), p. 49.

[5] Allied Control Authority Germany, Office of Military Government for Germany (US) (1945), pp. 173–175.

[6] Taylor (1992), p. 139 ff.

[7] Joint Four-Nations Declarations (1943) The Moscow Conference, October 1943. https://avalon.law.yale.edu/wwii/moscow.asp (last accessed 1 December 2023).

[8] United Nations (8 August 1945) (ed) Agreement for the prosecution and punishment of the major war criminals of the European Axis ("London Agreement"). In: United Nations Treaty Collection 82, pp. 279 ff. https://www.un.org/en/genocideprevention/documents/atrocity-crimes/Doc.2_Charter%20of%20IMT%201945.pdf (last accessed 1 December 2023).

imprisonment, as well as acquittals.[9] Further international trials were planned but could not be realized because of the growing tensions between the Allies.[10]

2.2 *National and International Justice Efforts*

In the following years, efforts were taken by both sides, the Allied powers and the German authorities, to bring the most responsible to justice and denazify public life. The occupying powers created military and national courts in three of the four occupation zones, which were competent to prosecute war crimes and crimes against humanity according to the Allied Control Council Act No. 10.[11]

2.2.1 The Courts of the Occupying Powers

In the British zone, a national High Court for the British Zone was established, which functioned as an appellate court in cases of war crimes and crimes against humanity.[12] The tribunal issued remarkable judgments, i.e., on participation in crimes.[13] However, the most well-known 12 trials are the ones conducted against the German elite in the American zone. The subsequent Nuremberg trials were focused on particular professional groups, which played an important role in the implementation of the National Socialist ideology, such as the Doctor's trial, the Judge's trial, and the trial against diplomats, the so-called Wilhelmsstraße trial.[14]

In the judges' trial, one of the accused was Ernst Lautz. He was the chief prosecutor at the People's Court from 1938 until the end of the war and, i.e., represented the prosecution in the cases against the participants of the attempted assassination of Adolf Hitler on July 20, 1944.[15]

---

9 International Military Tribunal (1947).

10 Heller (2011), pp. 17 ff.; Etzel (1992), pp. 203 ff.

11 Control Council Law No. 10, Berlin, 20 December 1945. https://www.legal-tools.org/doc/ffda62/pdf/ (last accessed 1 December 2023); Heller (2011), pp. 12 ff. and Appendix C.

12 Ohlenroth (2020), pp. 25 ff.

13 Schubert (2010), pp. 1 ff.

14 Kempner and Haensel (1950); Young (2006), pp. 295 ff.; for a further analysis of the National Socialism history of the Federal Foreign Office, Conze et al. (2010).

15 More detailed to the proceedings against the members of the resistance, von zur Mühlen and von Klewitz (2001).

2.2.2 Denazification Law No. 104

In 1946, the governments of Greater Hesse, Bavaria, and Wuerttemberg-Baden passed Law No. 104 on the Liberation from National Socialism and Militarism, the so-called Liberation Law.[16] It was the legal basis for determining the degree of liability in the western zones. It included five categories, ranging from group V, the exonerated, to group I, the major offenders. According to this law, e.g., a major offender was a person, who among others committed crimes against victims or opponents of the Nazi regime for political reasons or who breached international law through his or her conduct toward civilians of occupied territories or prisoners of war.[17]

The positions, that automatically led to a classification in group I or II, could be found in a separate ranking and organization list. Those who fell into one of these groups were automatically classified as major offenders (I) or offenders (II) until proven otherwise. Unlike in normal criminal proceedings, the burden of proof was shifted to the accused; i.e., the accused had to produce exonerating evidence.[18]

Regional commissions were assigned to categorize the individual applying for the confirmation of denazification. Each commission comprised three independent members, who did not have to be trained judges. Different connecting factors were applied to determine the locally competent commission. This approach took into account both the large number of internally displaced persons and the fact that many of the crimes were committed extraterritorially.[19] The local jurisdiction could arise from the place of residence, the place of action during the Nazi period, and also from the place where the person concerned possessed property.[20]

The expectations from all sides set into the implementation of Law No. 104 were very high. This was highlighted in the preface with the words "the success or failure of the implementation of this law decides over the fate of the German people and their children."[21]

In order to develop consistent case law, an unattainable goal, instructions were issued, for example, on how to handle the status as a National Socialist Party aspirant.[22]

---

[16] Ministerium für Sonderaufgaben (1946); more detailed to the preparation of the law, Ehard (1946), pp. 23 ff.

[17] Gesetz Nr. 104 zur Befreiung von Nationalsozialismus und Militarismus, 5. March 1946. www.verfassungen.de/bw/wuerttemberg-baden/befreiungsgesetz46.htm (last accessed 1 December 2023).

[18] Ministerium für Sonderaufgaben (1947).

[19] Eichmüller (2008), pp. 621–640.

[20] Schmitt (1946), pp. 12 ff.

[21] Höltermann (1946).

[22] Remains of Thomas Dehler, Befreiungsgesetz, AdL N1-337, pp. 74 ff., Weisung der Ständigen Rechtskollegiums zur einheitlichen Auslegung und Anwendung des Befreiungsgesetzes in der US-Zone.

3 A "Bad" Example: The Biography of Franz Schlüter

Franz Schlüter was employed in the Ministry of Justice regardless of his position during the National Socialist regime. This example shows that the cases were handled differently and not all persons of categories I and II, according to Law No. 104, were excluded from public services.[23]

3.1 The Time During the National Socialist Regime

From 1931 to 1937, he was delegated from the head of section Ernst Schäfer to the Reich Ministry of Justice to handle special tasks.[24] In 1938, after working for a few months at the district court Hannover, he returned to the Reich Ministry of Justice and remained there after the beginning of the war due to a request from Roland Freisler,[25] who in 1933 became state secretary and was the president of the People's Court from 1942 until his death in 1945.[26] In 1941, Schlüter started working as an investigating magistrate at the People's Court.[27] He was assigned to the special operation in Bohemia and Moravia. Among other duties, he was an associate judge at the first bench, which was presided over by Roland Freisler.[28] In 1943, due to the war, all men fit for the military were called to military service, including Schlüter. Roland Freisler intervened and requested his employment at the People's Court,[29] where Schlüter worked until the end of the Second World War. The branch office of the People's Court in Austria was transferred to Linz because of the front-line closing. Schlüter was the representative of the Reich prosecutor. In this function, he ordered the immediate execution of several death penalties, including some nonfinal sentences, just days before the end of the war in Austria.[30]

[23] To the biographies of the other consultants to the State Protection Criminal Law at the Ministry of Justice Farthofer (2019), pp. 67 ff.

[24] I.e. Reich Ministry Justice, Personnel record Reich Ministry of Justice, Vol I, p. 1; Schlüter worked for Section II, penal legislation, with a focus on military criminal procedure and criminal procedure under undersecretary Lehmann, who was one of the accused in the High Command Trial. Lehmann was sentenced to seven years' imprisonment.

[25] Reich Ministry Justice, Personnel record, Schlüter Franz, BMJV Ip=Sch 16, p. 45.

[26] Further details to the person of Roland Freisler, Buchheit (1968).

[27] For a detailed account of the peoples' court, Wagner (2011).

[28] Ministry of Justice, Schlüter, BMJV I p 5 Sch. 103, p. 56.

[29] Ministry of Justice, Schlüter Franz, BMJV I p 5 Sch. 103, p. 66.

[30] National Archive Berlin, B Rep 058 Nr. 7547, p. 5.

3.2 The Denazification Proceeding

After the end of the war, he transferred to Marburg, where the denazification commission of Marburg city was responsible for his case. The presiding member of the commission was Karl Kasperkowitz, a former lawyer from Breslau.[31] Despite the accusations that the communist party put forward against Schlüter,[32] the commission revoked its decision to classify him as a major offender and placed him into group V, the exonerated.[33] One of his reference letters was written by Ernst Lautz, the chief prosecutor at the People's Court, who was convicted at the Judge's trial at Nuremberg.[34]

The different approach the commission had taken becomes clear when compared to the decision on Wilmar Hagen. The latter also had been an investigating magistrate at the People's Court. In contrast to Schlüter, Hagen was placed in group II, the offenders, and was sentenced to a long term in prison.[35]

In 1951, Schlüter started working at the Ministry of Justice due to recommendations from Adolf Arndt,[36] a German Socialist Party member of the Parliament, and Josef Schafheutle,[37] undersecretary at the Ministry of Justice.[38] Before 1945, the latter was a colleague of Schlüter at the Reich Ministry of Justice. Schlüter was assigned as a consultant on state security law because of his experiences in dealing with high treason cases. He had attached a multipage declaration to his application.

> It would be unfair not to employ judicial officers who had to deal with high treason and treason before 1945 because their work was connected with the name of the People's Court. "[. . .] The excesses that made the name of the People's Court notorious, in particular in connection with the events of July 20th, 1944, were essentially due to the person of its President Freisler and the influence of the so-called honorary associate members of leading party circles."[39]

In 1952, the commission in Berlin started an investigation against him due to his work for the People's Court. During the investigation, the state secretary of the Ministry of Justice, Walter Strauss, tried to interfere and prevent the proceedings.[40]

---

[31] Spruchkammer Marburg/Lahn, PA Kasperkowitz, Karl, First chairman of the 2. Trial Chamber Marburg, HHStAW Abt. 501, Nr. 935, p. 132.

[32] Denazification Record, Schlüter, Franz, HHStA Wiesbaden Abt. 520/ML Nr. 53 R. 4904, p. 15.

[33] Denazification Record, Schlüter, Franz, HHStA Wiesbaden Abt. 520/ML Nr. 53 R. 4904, pp. 87–90.

[34] Ministry of Justice, Schlüter, Franz, BMJV Bew. I/410, p. 29.

[35] Denazification Record, Hagen, Wilmar, HHStA Wiesbaden Abt. 520/Us Nr. 482, Vol. 6, p. 57.

[36] For a detailed biography of Adolf Arndt see Gosewinkel (1991).

[37] To the person Josef Schafheutle, Görtemarker and Safferling (2016), pp. 327 ff.

[38] Ministry of Justice, Schlüter Franz, BMJV Bew. I/410, p. 6 and Remains of Josef Schafheutle, Part of the Remain 2, State Archive Koblenz BA-N1608-1.

[39] Ministry of Justice, Schlüter Franz, BMJV Bew. I/410, p. 16 (own translation).

[40] Ministry of Justice, Schlüter Franz, Special Edition Vol. 1, BMJV P51-Sch15, pp. 8 and 93 – 93g.

At first instance, Schlüter was fined 50,000 German marks.[41] A year later, the court of appeal reversed the judgment because it could not be determined that any of the People's Court judgments he was involved in were based on the excessive use of law.[42]

4 National Efforts

Germany made different efforts to deal with its past. These measures included attempts to bring perpetrators to justice, to assist in legal proceedings, and, finally, to shield them from legal liability.

4.1 The Legal Protection Unit (Zentrale Rechtsschutzstelle)

After the end of the Second World War, different organizations took care of German prisoners of war, e.g., the legal protection unit in Stuttgart. This department was responsible for making all efforts to return German prisoners of war and offered help for persons who had to stand trial abroad.[43]

In 1949, the German Parliament decided to establish this department on the federal level, firstly as part of the Ministry of Justice and later on as part of the Ministry of Foreign Affairs. Its work was undertaken in cooperation with the International Red Cross, Protestant Aid, and Caritas. The federal legal protection unit, among others, hired and paid defense lawyers from Germany as well as from abroad and provided the defense with exonerating evidence like testimonies and documents. But besides that, the unit informed persons if there were ongoing investigations from other states against them.[44] The trial against Eichmann in Jerusalem in 1961 was an exception.[45] In this case, the German government feared provoking a scandal and therefore refrained from any support for the defense. The federal legal protection unit was closed in 1970.[46]

[41] Die Zeit (1957).

[42] Ministry of Justice, Schlüter, Franz, Special Edition Vol. 3, BMJV P51-Sch15, pp. 349–398.

[43] Görtemarker and Safferling (2016), pp. 209 f.

[44] Görtemarker and Safferling (2016), pp. 208 ff.; Conze et al. (2010), pp. 679 ff.; Frei (2012), p. 163.

[45] For a further analysis of the Eichmann trial see i.e. Arendt (2006); Baumann and Hauff (2011).

[46] Görtemarker and Safferling (2016), pp. 233 ff.; Große (1995), pp. 135 ff.

4.2 The Ulmer "Einsatzgruppen" Trial

In 1958, a well-known trial, the so-called Ulmer Einsatzgruppen trial, brought back the remembrance of the mass-scale atrocities committed by the Nazi regime on civilians. Ten members of the Geheime Staatspolizei (Gestapo), who were part of the task force Tilsit, were brought to justice for the killing of more than 5500 Jewish people close to the German-Lithuanian border. The lawsuit, on reemployment to the police filed by Bernhard Fischer-Schweder, provoked the investigation of this case. The defendants were convicted for aiding and abetting joint murder and not, as the prosecution urged, for direct murder.[47] As a consequence, the prison terms were relatively lenient, which means imprisonment between 3 and 15 years.[48]

A positive outcome of this trial was the considerably greater willingness to prosecute the main offenders. However, 2 years later, the investigations of the several district prosecutions experienced another problem.

4.3 The Debate on the Statute of Limitation for Murder and Manslaughter

The German Criminal Code from 1871 provided a limitation period of 20 years for murder and 15 for manslaughter.[49] In 1960, 15 years after the end of the war, the German Parliament discussed the problematic issue. The German Socialist Party proposed the extension of the limitation period, but it was not accepted by the other members of the Parliament. Therefore, the limitation period for manslaughter was upheld, and the criminal proceedings were restricted to cases of murder and participation in murder.[50]

In 1965, at the end of the limitation period for murder, the debate on this issue came up again. In consequence, the members of the Parliament agreed on the shift of the beginning of the limitation period to December 31, 1949. The ongoing investigations had a positive impact on the decision of the German Parliament.[51]

In 1968, however, the German Administrative Offences Act was amended by the Introductory Law of the German Administrative Offences Act. Some of its rules resulted in the expiry of the limitation period for participation in murder. Following the amendment, the accomplice ought to be punished with a lower sentence than the

[47] For a further analysis of the legal assessment of the different forms of participation, Nehmer (2015), pp. 49 ff.

[48] von Miquel (2004), pp. 150 ff.; Werle and Wandres (1995), pp. 23 ff.; the judgment can be found in Sagel-Grande I, Fuchs HH, Rüter CF (1976) LG Ulm, August 29th, 1958, Ks 2/57 and Federal Supreme Court, February 23rd, 1960, 1 StR 648/59.

[49] § 67 Reich Criminal Code 1871, National Gazette (Reichsgesetzblatt) 1871, No. 24, pp. 127–205.

[50] Deutscher Bundestag (1960), pp. 6679 ff.; Werle and Wandres (1995), pp. 24 f.

[51] Deutscher Bundestag (1965), pp. 8516 ff.

direct perpetrator. The reduction of the range of sentences, along with the shortening of the limitation period for participants, led to the termination of several investigations.[52]

Finally, in 1969, a new debate on this issue came up, and the German Parliament decided to extend the limitation period for murder from 20 to 30 years.[53]

4.4 Central Office of the State Justice Administrations for the Investigation of National Socialist Crimes

In 1958, the Central Office of the State Justice Administrations for the Investigation of National Socialist Crimes was created in Ludwigsburg.[54] In the beginning, it was only responsible for the investigation into National Socialist crimes committed abroad, with a link to the war. In 1964 and 1966, its responsibilities were expanded. Subsequently, the amendment also included the possibility to carry out investigations into the crimes committed in Western Germany. The Central Office is still operating. It carries out preliminary investigations, which leads to several trials before district courts in the last years.[55]

Its responsibility focus lies on the preliminary investigations of National Socialist crimes. In case the determination of a specific perpetrator is possible, the Central Office of the State Justice Administrations for the Investigation of National Socialist Crimes hands over the outcome to the competent district office of public prosecution, which carries out single cases.[56]

The investigations turned out to be very difficult because of the problems related to international legal assistance. Particularly, the contact and transfer of documents from the eastern zone were officially prohibited in the 1950s and 1960s. In many cases, the prosecution bypassed the official channels to receive documents and other information from the archives in the Soviet-occupied zone.[57] These problems caused delays, which at the same time produced difficulties in complying with the limitation period.

---

[52] Werle and Wandres (1995), pp. 25 f.; for a detailed examination regarding the implementation of the introductory law to the German Administrative Offence Act and its negative impacts Görtemarker and Safferling (2016), pp. 399 ff.

[53] Deutscher Bundestag (1969), pp. 13554 ff.; Taube (2010), pp. 29 ff.

[54] Pauli (2001), pp. 45, 46 ff.

[55] Weinke (2009).

[56] Cases of the last years, LG München I vom 11.08.2009, 1 Ks 115 Js 10394/07; LG Aachen vom 23.03.2010, 52 Ks 45 Js 18/83; LG Hagen vom 08.01.2014, 31 Ks-45 Js 7/78-11/12; for further informations Taube (2010), pp. 36ff.

[57] The prosecutors had to travel as private persons to Auschwitz to carry out the research at the Archive of the Museum of Auschwitz, Dobrawa (2013); Eichmüller (2012).

4.5 The Auschwitz Trial

The second remarkable step in the history of Germany was the Frankfurt Auschwitz trials.[58] The Central Office in Ludwigsburg conducted the preliminary investigations. The concentration of the proceedings at Frankfurt could only be realized by the interference of the attorney general, Fritz Bauer.[59]

In April 1963, the prosecution filed indictments against 23 members of the Schutzstaffel (SS) and one operative prisoner. Not only victims testified at the proceeding but also former SS officers. The latter avoided incriminating the accused but could give a better insight into the conditions in the camp. An essential piece of evidence was the records of the camp commander Rudolf Höß, which he wrote during his time in custody in Poland.[60] To verify witness testimonies, a delegation of the court traveled to Auschwitz. The sentences were passed in August 1965 and comprised life sentences, prison terms between 3.5 and 14 years, and acquittals. Two additional trials followed after the Auschwitz trial.[61]

4.6 The Attempts of Berlin to Bring Judges and Prosecutors of the People's Court to Justice

In 1980, the association of persecuted persons of the National Socialist regime filed a criminal complaint on suspicion of murder against all still living judges, honorary judges, and state attorneys of the People's Court.[62] One of the suspects was Franz Schlüter.[63]

In a memorandum, the responsible prosecutor established the conditions for the criminal liability of judges and prosecutors for murder. The basis for each case was the existence of an unlawful judgment. The unlawfulness could lie in the incorrect application of law or its discrepancy to settled case law.[64]

The one responsible for the case of Schlüter concluded that all available judgments rendered with his participation were unlawful.[65] The prosecution had relied in

[58] I.e. Pendas (2013); Wittmann (2005).

[59] Steinke (2020); Wojak (2009).

[60] Höß (1958), p. 87 ff.

[61] Werle and Wandres (1995); Dobrawa (2013).

[62] A detailed analysis of the investigations of the prosecution of the district court Berlin against former judges and prosecutors of the peoples' court, Jahntz and Kähne (1992), pp. 38 ff.

[63] Prosecution Report, Investigation file, Schlüter Franz, National Archive Berlin, B Rep 058 Nr. 6802.

[64] Prosecution Report, Investigation file, Schlüter Franz, National Archive Berlin, B Rep 058 Nr. 6802, pp. 75 ff.

[65] Prosecution Report, Investigation file, Schlüter Franz, National Archive Berlin, B Rep 058 Nr. 6802, pp. 35 f.

all cases on the punishable preparation of high treason. The crimes were aimed at the forcible separation of parts or the entire territory of Czechoslovakia to rebuild Czechoslovakia. In these cases, § 80 para. 1 Reich Penal Code was not applicable since the conduct was directed at an occupied territory and not the territory of the German Reich. This interpretation of the law by the People's Court was not in conformity with international law.[66]

In 1982, Schlüter was informed of the investigation against him and the prosecutors' intention to interrogate him as a suspect. Schlüter wrote back:

> If you allege even the possibility that a civil servant or a judge, who has demonstrated his professional ethos and sense of duty for more than 40 years, would have carried out his duties on base motives or would have intentionally participated to the base motives of others, I find this very painful.[67]

In 1984, the public health officer of Munich determined that Schlüter was incapable of standing trial. As a consequence, the case against him was terminated. Schlüter died in 1992.[68] As it becomes very clear, the networks, which worked before 1945, also functioned after the war.

5 Conclusion

In Germany, the reappraisal of the National Socialist history continues, as the example of the still operating Central Office of the State Justice Administrations for the Investigation of National Socialist Crimes in Ludwigsburg shows. It is unlikely that the society of Germany would have taken any effective measures to bring perpetrators to justice without the initial international efforts. Dealing with mass atrocities committed by one's own government is a challenging task for all affected states, in particular, because the citizens do not want to be confronted with their own responsibility. In addition, some of the efforts taken by Germany could not be implemented in an effective manner, in particular, because of the large number of persons who had to be examined with regard to their potential participation in crimes committed during the National Socialist regime. This problem clearly led to the misuse of the system by persons like the abovementioned Franz Schlüter. To sum up, it is quite clear that the reasons for the failure of some measures can be related not only to the unwillingness of the government but rather to several external factors, in particular by the beginning of the Cold War period and the resulting shift of interest on the side of the occupied powers.

---

[66] Prosecution Report, Investigation file, Schlüter Franz, National Archive Berlin, B Rep 058 Nr. 6802, pp. 174 ff.

[67] Prosecution Report, Investigation file, Schlüter Franz, National Archive Berlin, B Rep 058 Nr. 6802, pp. 92 f. (own translation).

[68] Registration register information from March 24th, 2015, City of Munich, Schlüter Franz.

Documents

Control Council Law No. 10, Berlin, 20 December 1945. https://www.legal-tools.org/doc/ffda62/pdf/. Accessed 25 March 2024.

Die Zeit (1957) Und wieder heißt er Schlüter. Die Zeit no. 27/1957.

Gesetz Nr. 104 zur Befreiung von Nationalsozialismus und Militarismus, 5. March 1946. www.verfassungen.de/bw/wuerttemberg-baden/befreiungsgesetz46.htm. Accessed 25 March 2024.

International Military Tribunal (1947) Trial of the Major War Criminals, 14 November 1945 – 1 October 1946, Vol. I.

LG Ulm, August 29th, 1958, Ks 2/57 and Federal Supreme Court, February, 23th 1960, 1 StR 648/59. In: Sagel-Grande I, Fuchs HH, Rüter CF (1976) Justiz und NS-Verbrechen. University Press Amsterdam, Amsterdam

Ministerium für Sonderaufgaben (ed) (1946) Gesetz zur Befreiung von Nationalsozialismus und Militarismus: vom 5. März 1946; mit den Ausführungsvorschriften, Formblättern, der Anweisung für die Auswerter der Meldebogen und der Rangliste in mehrfarbiger Wiedergabe, München.

Ministerium für Sonderaufgaben (ed) (1947) Rang- und Organisationsliste der NSDAP mit Gliederungen, angeschlossenen Verbänden und betreuten Organisationen unter Beschreibung weiterer Verbände, Einrichtungen, Dienststellen und Personengruppen: mit Angaben der Klassifizierung nach der Anlage zum Gesetz zur Befreiung von Nationalsozialismus und Militarismus vom 5. März 1946, Stuttgart.

National Archive Berlin, B Rep 058 Nr. 7547, p. 5.

Remains of Thomas Dehler, Befreiungsgesetz, AdL N1-337, pp. 74 ff., Weisung der Ständigen Rechtskollegiums zur einheitlichen Auslegung und Anwendung des Befreiungsgesetzes in der US-Zone.

Secretariat of the United Nations (1951) (ed) Agreement for the prosecution and punishment of the major war criminals of the European Axis. Signed at London, on 8 August 1945. In: Treaty Series Volume 82, pp. 279 ff. https://www.un.org/en/genocideprevention/documents/atrocity-crimes/Doc.2_Charter%20of%20IMT%201945.pdf (accessed 25 March 2024).

Spruchkammer Marburg/Lahn, PA Kasperkowitz, Karl, First chairman of the 2. Trial Chamber Marburg, HHStAW Abt. 501, Nr. 935, p. 132.

§ 67 Reich Criminal Code 1871, National Gazette (Reichsgesetzblatt) 1871, No. 24, pp. 127–205.

Personnel File

Denazification Record, Hagen, Wilmar, HHStA Wiesbaden Abt. 520/Us Nr. 482, Vol. 6, p. 57.

Denazification Record, Schlüter, Franz, HHStA Wiesbaden Abt. 520/ML Nr. 53 R. 4904, p. 15.

Ministry of Justice, Schlüter Franz, BMJV Bew. I/410, p. 16 (own translation).
Ministry of Justice, Schlüter Franz, BMJV Bew. I/410, p. 6.
Ministry of Justice, Schlüter Franz, BMJV I p 5 Sch. 103, p. 66.
Ministry of Justice, Schlüter Franz, Special Edition Vol. 1, BMJV P51-Sch15, pp. 8 and 93 – 93g.
Ministry of Justice, Schlüter, BMJV I p 5 Sch. 103, p. 56.
Ministry of Justice, Schlüter, Franz, BMJV Bew. I/410, p. 29.
Ministry of Justice, Schlüter, Franz, Special Edition Vol. 3, BMJV P51-Sch15, pp. 349–398.
Prosecution Report, Investigation file, Schlüter Franz, National Archive Berlin, B Rep 058 Nr. 6802.
Prosecution Report, Investigation file, Schlüter Franz, National Archive Berlin, B Rep 058 Nr. 6802, pp. 75 ff.
Prosecution Report, Investigation file, Schlüter Franz, National Archive Berlin, B Rep 058 Nr. 6802, pp. 35 f.
Prosecution Report, Investigation file, Schlüter Franz, National Archive Berlin, B Rep 058 Nr. 6802, pp. 174 ff.
Prosecution Report, Investigation file, Schlüter Franz, National Archive Berlin, B Rep 058 Nr. 6802, pp. 92 f. (own translation).
Registration register information from March 24th, 2015, City of Munich, Schlüter Franz.
Reich Ministry Justice, Personnel record Reich Ministry of Justice, Vol I, p. 1.
Reich Ministry Justice, Personnel record, Schlüter Franz, BMJV Ip=Sch 16, p. 45.
Remains of Josef Schafheutle, Part of the Remain 2, State Archive Koblenz BA-N1608-1.

References

Allied Control Authority Germany, Office of Military Government for Germany (US) (1945) Enactments and Approved Papers of the Control Council and Coordinating Committee, Volume I. Office of Military Government for Germany
Arendt H (2006) Eichmann in Jerusalem. Piper, Munich
Baumann U, Hauff L (eds) (2011) Der Prozess – Adolf Eichmann vor Gericht. Gedenk-und Bildungsstätte Haus der Wannsee-Konferenz et al., Berlin
Buchheit G (1968) Richter in roter Robe: Freisler, Präsident des Volksgerichtshofs. List, Munich
Conze E, Frei N, Hayes P, Zimmermann M (2010) Das Amt und die Vergangenheit. Karl Blessing Verlag, Munich
Deutscher Bundestag (1960) Protokoll der 117. Sitzung des 3. Deutschen Bundestages, 24. Mai 1960. Bonn
Deutscher Bundestag (1965) Protokoll der 170. Sitzung des 4. Deutschen Bundestages, 10. März 1965. Bonn
Deutscher Bundestag (1969) Protokoll der 243. Sitzung des 5. Deutschen Bundestages, 26. Juni 1969. Bonn
Dobrawa R (2013) Der Auschwitz Prozess. Das Neue Berlin. Berlin

Ehard H (1946) Referat des Staatssekretärs Dr. Hans Ehard vor dem Beratenden Landesausschuss am 9. April 1946. In: Ehard H, Schmitt H (eds) Grundlegende Reden zum Gesetz zur Befreiung vom Nationalsozialismus und Militarismus. Reinhardt, Frankfurt am Main

Eichmüller A (2008) Die Strafverfolgung von NS-Verbrechen durch westdeutsche Justizbehörden seit 1945. Eine Zahlenbilanz. Vierteljahrshefte für Zeitgeschichte 4:621–640

Eichmüller A (2012) Keine Generalamnestie: Die Strafverfolgung von NS-Verbrechen in der frühen Bundesrepublik. Oldenbourg Wissenschaftsverlag, Munich

Eisenhower DD (1945) Proclamation No. 1. In: Verlag v. Friedr. Vieweg & Sohn (eds) Laws and Orders of Military Government/Gesetze und Verordnungen der Militärregierung. Vieweg +Teubner Verlag, Wiesbaden, p 49

Etzel M (1992) Die Aufhebung von nationalsozialistischen Gesetzen durch den Alliierten Kontrollrat (1945-1948). Mohr, Tübingen

Farthofer H (2019) Neuausrichtung des Staatsschutzes nach 1945? : die Beispiele Bundesrepublik Deutschland, Italien und Österreich. Vandenhoeck & Ruprecht, Göttingen

Fings K, Steinbacher S (eds) (2021) Sinti und Roma: der nationalsozialistische Völkermord in historischer und gesellschaftspolitischer Perspektive. Wallstein Verlag, Göttingen

Frei N (2012) Vergangenheitspolitik. C. H. Beck, Munich

Görtemarker M, Safferling C (2016) Die Akte Rosenburg. C. H. Beck, Munich

Gosewinkel D (1991) Adolf Arndt. Dietz, Bonn

Große C (1995) Der Eichmann-Prozeß zwischen Recht und Politik. Lang, Frankfurt am Main

Heller KJ (2011) The Nuremberg Military Tribunals and the Origins of International Criminal Law. Oxford Univ. Press, Oxford

Heuß H, Roßberg A (eds) (2015) Schonung für die Mörder?: die justizielle Behandlung der NS-Völkermordverbrechen und ihre Bedeutung für die Gesellschaft und die Rechtskultur in Deutschland: das Beispiel der Sinti und Roma ; Dokumentation einer Tagung in der Evangelischen Akademie Bad Boll am 20./21. Mai 1992. Zentralrat Deutscher Sinti und Roma, Heidelberg

Höltermann A (1946) Vorwort. In: Ehard H, Schmitt H (eds) Grundlegende Reden zum Gesetz zur Befreiung vom Nationalsozialismus und Militarismus. Reinhardt, Frankfurt am Main

Höß R (1958) Kommandant in Auschwitz. Dt. Verl.-Anst., Stuttgart

Jahntz B, Kähne V (1992) Der Volksgerichtshof. Senatsverwaltung für Justiz, Berlin

Joint Four-Nations Declarations (1943) The Moscow Conference, October 1943. https://avalon.law.yale.edu/wwii/moscow.asp. Accessed 25 Mar 2024

Kempner RMW, Haensel C (eds) (1950) Das Urteil im Wilhelmstrassen-Prozess. Bürger, Schwäbisch Gmünd

Mihr A, Pickel G, Pickel S (eds) (2018) Handbuch Transitional Justice. Springer Fachmedien, Wiesbaden

Nehmer B (2015) Das Problem der Ahndung von Einsatzgruppenverbrechen durch die bundesdeutsche Justiz. Peter Lang GmbH, Internationaler Verlag der Wissenschaften, Frankfurt am Main

Ohlenroth J (2020) Der Oberste Gerichtshof für die Britische Zone und die Aufarbeitung von NS-Unrecht. In: Duve T, Haferkamp H-P, Rückert J, Schönberger C (eds) Beiträge zur Rechtsgeschichte des 20. Jahrhunderts, 112. Mohr Siebeck, Tübingen

Pauli G (2001) Die Zentral Stelle der Landesjustizverwaltung zur Verfolgung nationalsozialistischer Gewaltverbrechen in Ludwigsburg – Entstehung und frühe Praxis. In: Juristische Zeitgeschichte Nordrhein-Westfalen Vol. 9, Justizministerium des Landes NRW, Die Zentralstellen zur Verfolgung Nationalsozialistischer Gewaltverbrechen – Versuch einer Bilanz. Justizministerium des Landes NRW, Düsseldorf, pp 45–62

Pendas DO (2013) Der Auschwitz-Prozess – Völkermord vor Gericht. Siedler, Munich

Schmitt H (1946) Rede des Staatsministers Schmitt vor dem vorläufigen Landesausschuss am 9. April 1946. In: Ehard H, Schmitt H (eds) Grundlegende Reden zum Gesetz zur Befreiung vom Nationalsozialismus und Militarismus. Reinhardt, Frankfurt am Main

Schubert W (2010) Oberster Gerichtshof für die Britische Zone (1948-1950), Nachschlagewerk Strafsachen – Nachschlagewerk Zivilsachen- Präjudizienbuch der Zivilsenate. Peter Lang GmbH, Internationaler Verlag der Wissenschaften, Frankfurt am Main

Steinke R (2020) Fritz Bauer, The Jewish Prosecutor who brought Eichmann and Auschwitz to Trial. Indiana University Press, Bloomington

Taube A (2010) Die Ahndung nationalsozialistischer Gewaltverbrechen. SDV, Dresden

Taylor T (1992) The anatomy of the Nuremberg trials: a personal memoir. Knopf, New York

Von Miquel M (2004) Ahnden und amnestieren? Wallstein, Göttingen

Von zur Mühlen B, von Klewitz A (eds) (2001) Die Angeklagten des 20. Juli vor dem Volksgerichtshof. Chronos, Berlin-Kleinmachnow

Wagner W (2011) Der Volksgerichtshof im nationalsozialistischen Staat. Oldenbourg Verlag, Munich

Weinke A (2009) Eine Gesellschaft ermittelt gegen sich selbst: Die Geschichte der Zentralen Stelle in Ludwigsburg 1958-2008. Wiss. Buchges., Darmstadt

Werle G, Wandres T (1995) Auschwitz vor Gericht. C. H. Beck, Munich

Wittmann R (2005) Beyond Justice – the Auschwitz trial. Harvard University Press, Cambridge, Massachusetts and London, England

Wojak I (2009) Fritz Bauer 1903-1968: eine Biographie. C. H. Beck, Munich

Young W (2006) German Diplomatic Relations 1871-1945, The Wilhelmstrasse and the Formulation of Foreign Policy. iUniverse, Lincoln

Hilde Farthofer is an associate professor at the institute for criminal law and criminal justice at the University of Erlangen-Nuremberg. She worked as an interim professor at the University of Frankfurt, Bonn, Münster, Tübingen, and Munich. In January 2019, she was habilitated at the Friedrich-Alexander-University of Erlangen-Nuremberg. She graduated in Law at the University of Salzburg, Austria. Her primary research area includes national and international criminal procedure, contemporary legal history, and procedural problems deriving from transnational crime, in particular regarding the law of evidence.

Reconciliation, Transformation, Historical Policy. Legal Aspects of Settlements with Totalitarian Systems Toward Poland Since 1989

Adam Bosiacki

Abstract The chapter outlines the issues of three basic public institutions in Poland in recent years, concerning the so-called settlements with the totalitarian system imposed on Poland. Paradoxically, despite the beginning of changes in the Soviet bloc countries, lustration, decommunisation and a discussion about the often-false images of Poland in relation to the past were not fully implemented despite the condemnation of communist and Nazi crimes and many aspects of the communist system that existed against the will of society. This also applies to Poland's bad relations with neighbouring and other countries, with whom many issues have not been regulated so far, not only legally but above all socially. The conclusion is the need to develop international agreements in this area and more broadly a consistent policy of the state in matters such as compensation for the losses of Poland and Polish citizens in the Second World War (from other countries but, in the case of Jewish claims, also from Poland).

1 Historical Background of the Extraordinary Phenomena of Polish History

Although each country has a specific history, Poland is a country with unique phenomenon in its history. The Polish-Lithuanian Commonwealth (having a union with the Grand Duchy of Lithuania), existing since the Renaissance, developed the concept of noble democracy, incomparable with any other country in Europe until the end of the eighteenth century. Such a concept led to the state's collapse, although attempts at reforms resulted in for example, the adoption of the first modern European Constitution, providing for the separation of powers (3 May 1791). After the fall of the First Republic in 1795, the state did not have statehood for 123 years. The survival of the nation and the rebirth of Poland was another great

A. Bosiacki (✉)
University of Warsaw, Warsaw, Poland
e-mail: abosiacki@wpia.uw.edu.pl

M.-E. Geis et al. (eds.), *Dealing with Totalitarian Regimes and Human Rights*, Interdisciplinary Studies in Human Rights 11,
https://doi.org/10.1007/978-3-031-57338-5_12

phenomenon. The Second Republic, however, did not have good relations with many of its neighbours. Bad relations with national minorities were also a problem. After the hecatomb of the war, losing 1/3 of its territory and almost a quarter of its population for 45 years, Poland found itself under the communist yoke with all the negative consequences of this system (including the repression system). After regaining sovereignty in 1989, despite enormous transformations, some civil society institutions such as the health service or a stable system of political parties still remain to be built. Despite the positive development, relations with some neighbours need improvement, as well as issues that have not been settled since the end of the Second World War.

The presented chapter will attempt to indicate and analyse the stages of settling accounts in the past in Poland after 1989 and a short presentation of the most important social institutions in Poland today, including the legal institutions of such settlements. Thirty years after the fall of communism, it is a good turning point for asking about such achievements. Indisputably, the transformation process has not been completed. The dominant issue affecting the changes is of course the scale of changes in many areas, but sooner or later, there is also a question about the scope of settlements with the communist system. It is not possible to answer this question fully in a social sense. However, the presented chapter will try to indicate important political and legal aspects in this respect.

The chapter will also deal with the so-called historical policy, Poland's relations with its neighbours and its international position. Such a policy has been present in Polish public discussion mainly in recent years. In this context, the doctrine of the ruling camp often raises the question of the need to answer or react to the accusations against Poles during the last World War.

2 Tensions in International Relations Between Poland and Its Neighbours

Relations between Poland and other countries after regaining independence did not go well. Until 1939, Poland had formally correct relations only through inter-state treaties with Latvia, Romania and Hungary (Poland obtained the border with the last state after the Munich Treaty or, more precisely, the subordination of Czechoslovakia by the German Reich[1]). Formal non-aggression treaties concluded with the USSR in 1932 and with the German Reich in 1934 did not relieve concerns for the security of the country. They did not protect the country, not only against aggression

[1] In March 1939, troops of the Polish army entered the so-called Zaolzie (west of the Olza River), taking the territories seized without a plebiscite by Czechoslovakia during the Bolshevik offensive against Warsaw in July 1920. However, the re-joining of Zaolzie to Poland was used as an argument for cooperation with the German Reich in the partition of Czechoslovakia, communist propaganda, Czechoslovakia after the Second World War (the worst relations with Poland in 1945–1948), and still now in some political journalism in the Czech Republic.

but also, *contra legem*, from the Polish nation almost being brought on the verge of biological existence. During the Second World War, 6,028,000 Polish citizens (mainly of Polish nationality) died, i.e. 22.2% of the population of the Republic of Poland in 1939.[2] It was a hecatomb, rarely experienced before in modern times (starting from the time of the mass terror of the Jacobins), which before 1945 in Europe was exceeded only by the number of victims of the First World War and communism in Russia after 1917 (civil war and the so-called war communism of 1918–1921, collectivisation of agriculture, the Great Purge of 1937–1938).

After the Second World War, to some extent, the reborn Polish (communist) state[3] still had bad, though suppressed, relations with its neighbours. Friendship with the USSR and other socialist states (the so-called people's democracies) was officially declared, including the German Democratic Republic and the Czechoslovak Socialist Republic. Polish-Jewish relations in Poland and beyond also remained tense. They included mutual accusations from before the war, as well as accusations of blackmailing Jews and handing them over to the Nazi occupation authorities during the war. This was done by the so-called szmalcownicy (from the word "szmalec" or "szmal", meaning money in thieves' dialect). Such acts were punished by the Polish Underground State with the death penalty. Despite this, due to the number of Jews in the lands of the General Government (a small part of Poland under German occupation, not formally incorporated into the Reich), such a phenomenon was so numerous that the Polish Underground State and the Polish government in exile (in Paris and then in London) reacted to it.

Apart from the activities of blackmailers during the occupation of Polish territories in 1939–1945, Jews were said to be sometimes murdered by some people of Polish nationality on the basis of robbery also in local relations. The case of the so-called pogrom in the small town of Jedwabne in north-eastern Poland, where, after the Germans occupied the town in July 1941, 300–1500 Jews were supposedly murdered by the local population by burning them alive in a barn. Despite the fact that the circumstances and motives of the murder are not clear to this day (many Polish authors believe that the actions took place with the leading participation of the Germans) and many perpetrators of the murder were sentenced to death in communist Poland, the example of Jedwabne echoed in recent years in Polish-Jewish relations.

After the war, out of the 3,500,000 Jews who had lived in Poland until 1939, about 500,000 survived. In some communities, relations remained tense, which was reflected in new stereotypes, such as the cooperation of some Jews with the communist system during and after the war. On 4 July 1946, the largest pogrom of Jews (38–42 victims) took place in Kielce, when a child testified at a militia station that they had been held "by Jews" in the basement of a building, and the crowd then attacked the Jewish residents of the building, who were refugees from the

[2] Madajczyk (1970), p. 371.

[3] As I wrote in the previous article, in the current constitution, the formally Polish state as the Third Republic is a continuation of the First Republic, which existed until 1795, and the Second Republic, which existed in the interwar period (1918–1939).

territories of the USSR. The militia, soldiers, and officers of the communist Internal Security Corps (*Korpus Bezpieczeństwa Wewnętrznego*) participated in the murder. According to Polish research on the subject, the events caused by the communists almost certainly lasted all day and were long in the awareness of some Polish and Jewish circles of mutual antagonism.

The apogee of supported anti-Semitism came in March 1968, when the communist authorities first accused students of an undefined attempt to restore Stalinism based on demonstrations for freedom of speech. Children of former functionaries of the party apparatus from before 1956 were selected as an example and then accused of agitating students at universities.[4] As a result, several thousand Jews and people of Jewish origin, including communists, were forced to emigrate.

Regardless of the indicated cases of supporting antagonism towards Jews by the communist authorities, as can be seen from the above-mentioned examples, anti-Semitism in Poland found fertile ground. Before the war, however, it was not of a state character, and in the times of the sovereign Second Polish Republic, it was usually exterminated.[5] The above-mentioned phenomena, unfortunately, took the form of implications in Polish-Jewish relations after 1989. Despite recent incidents, where accusations of Polish complicity in the extermination of Jews during the Second World War returned, relations at the inter-state level should be considered good. According to at least some circles in Israel, the issue of compensation for property lost by the heirs of Jews murdered during the war or displaced in 1968–1969, remains to be settled. In discussions on Polish-Jewish relations during and after the war, however, one should not forget about the great help of Poles to Jews during the Second World War and the non-existence of state and social anti-Semitism among Poles in many circles—unlike many other countries, including Poland's neighbours.

The main problem in relations with neighbours after the Second World War was the issue of relations with Germany. Władysław Gomułka, the leader of Polish communists in 1956–1970, was paramount for obtaining the borders on the Oder River and Nysa Łużycka, i.e. the western borders of Poland, as a result of the arrangements of the victorious powers (without the participation of the Polish side) at the conferences in Yalta and Potsdam in 1945 as compensation for the lost lands in the east.[6] Gomułka considered the signing of the treaty with West Germany in December 1970 to be his greatest success. The western border of Poland was also

[4] It seems that Mieczysław Moczar, the Minister of the Interior, seeking to take power and presenting anti-Semitic views, by provoking to some extent student demonstrations, met with the anti-Semitic views of Władysław Gomułka, the communist leader. The political crisis resulted in the decisively anti-Jewish speeches of the latter, which was an unprecedented fact, not only in post-war Poland.

[5] However, it is necessary to mention, for example, the so-called bench ghetto, used by students with the sometimes active support of the authorities, at some Polish universities at the end of the 1930s.

[6] In total, from 388 thousand km^2 in 1939, the territory of today's Poland is 312 thousand km^2.

confirmed in the peace treaty, formally ending the Second World War, which concluded in November 1990.[7]

Obviously, until 1989, relations between the Polish People's Republic (PRL) and the USSR remained unsettled. From today's point of view, in some matters, these relations are still not regulated. This applies in particular to war reparations not discussed at all on the legal level due to the conclusion of relevant agreements between the PRL and the USSR after the Second World War and the failure to explain the entirety of the Katyn massacre committed against nearly 22,000 Polish citizens in the spring of 1940.

3 Reconciliation with the Neighbours Since 1989

The issue of reconciliation in Poland's relations with other nations can be considered a phenomenon that has been occurring since the 1960s. A milestone in the concept of reconciliation in this case was the Letter of Polish bishops to German bishops of 1965, written by leading hierarchs of the Roman Catholic Church in Poland during their stay at the Vatican Council Secundum. The most famous expression of the letter, "We forgive and ask for forgiveness" (for the crimes of the Second World War), which was carefully used by the communist authorities, was badly received in Polish society. First of all, comments were made that Poles had nothing to expect in terms of forgiveness from the Germans for the events of the Second World War or that during the 20 years after the end of the war, the Germans did not ask Poles for forgiveness. In a broader sense, it was also argued that the expression put the behaviour of Poles and Germans on an equal footing and that the German reaction to the letter remained insufficient. It was and is, however, a social conviction because the letter of the Polish bishops was a reaction to the so called Eastern Memorandum, i.e. the appeal of the German Evangelical Church, issued a month earlier.[8] Since then, relations between the two countries have evolved in a positive direction, which has harmoniously led not only to the recognition of post-war borders but also, for example, the payment of compensation for former war victims. In recent years, the Polish side has made an attempt to obtain compensation for war reparations (not less than the amount of 6,200 000 000 euro). Earlier, it was symbolic to sign a joint declaration on efforts to reconcile both countries and nations during the meeting of the Federal Chancellor of Germany, Helmut Kohl, and the first non-communist prime minister of Poland, Tadeusz Mazowiecki, in November 1989 (the so-called reconciliation mass).

Summing up, it should be stated that after 1989, Poland had good relations with Germany, but relations with the Jewish community in the world and with Lithuania, introducing their own originally Polish-speaking surnames, require improvement.

[7]Zięba (2010), pp. 53–54.

[8]Kłaczkow (2006), pp. 165–178.

The relations with the Czech Republic and Slovakia should be considered neutral. The most important relations for Poland with Russia are fraught with tensions. In the latter, as has already been mentioned, there is no discussion about the disclosure of the entire file of the Russian investigation into the Katyn massacre. There is also no discussion about the property left behind by Polish citizens in the former USSR within the present Russia.

4 Black Features of Transformation

The transformation from the communist regime to the civil society system and market economy faced enormous problems that needed to be solved. Post-communism emerged as a result of a peaceful transformation. However, the alternative probably did not exist at the time. In August 1989, in his expose, the first non-communist prime minister, Tadeusz Mazowiecki, used the statement: "We the history of our recent past with a thick line. We will be responsible only for what we have done to help extract Poland from her current predicament, from now on."[9] The prime minister's opponents argued that it also meant a failure to settle accounts with the communist system, which was quickly accepted by the liberal and social circles of Solidarity, as well as post-communist circles. In political and legal aspects, efforts were made to carry out the so-called lustration and decommunisation, including the punishment of communist crimes and mass communist crimes. However, it was only after almost a decade (the Act of December 1998) that it was possible to pass a resolution that communist crimes are not subject to any statute of limitations and attempts at decommunisation began. The intention of the legislator was to treat communist crimes in the same way as Nazi crimes (statutory term). As mentioned above, the argument of the necessity of non-retroaction was also refuted (the principle of retroactive action of the criminal law), which was also reflected in the Constitution. The previously discussed issues of Polish and international property were a separate issue. Therefore, a concept of compensation for Poles was developed but not for foreigners (their heirs). In 2010, the Constitutional Tribunal took the position of *restitutio in integrum* or payment of compensation for lost property. In fact, however, there were few cases of real estate return.

The problem of the so-called "beyond the Bug River" lost property (outside the present eastern Polish borders), i.e. for the eastern territories of Poland, west of the Curzon Line, incorporated into USSR in 1945. Obviously, the act introduced, in this case, only financial compensation or preferences for the purchase of other real estate. However, the proposed conversion amounts were also too small.

The scandal also ended with the false privatisation of Warsaw tenement houses, which, instead of returning the property to the heirs of the rightful owners, made it possible to purchase documents, often falsely certifying ownership and later forming

[9]Mazowiecki (1989), p. 3.

the basis for claims. Its greatest intensity occurred in 2010–2016, and after detecting the scale of abuses, an extraordinary commission was established to revoke the decisions of the local government of the capital city of Warsaw in many similar cases.

5 The Polish Lustration

Similarly to decommunisation, lustration in Poland is one of the social institutions of settlement with the totalitarian system. After the failure of its conduct in 1991–1992 (in the latter year, the disclosure of persons registered as secret collaborators or officials of the communist civilian secret services led to the dismissal of the government at the request of President Lech Wałęsa, accused of secret cooperation with the Security Service of the People's Republic of Poland from December 1970 to June 1976), the Act of 2006 concerns a wide range of persons performing public functions.[10] Its essence, however, is to submit a truthful lustration declaration, whereby in the event of a lustration lie the sanction is a ban on holding public functions for a period of 10 years. The Constitutional Tribunal also questioned several provisions of the Act, such as the lustration of all scientists, journalists, members of management boards and supervisory boards of listed companies and banks, auditors, tax advisers, directors of non-public schools, members of sports unions, recognition of the censorship of the People's Republic of Poland as "security organs of the People's Republic of Poland" (of the Central Office for the Control of Press, Publications and *Performances,* i.e. the communist censorship), and the *Office for Religious Affairs* (as one of the "bad opinion offices" responsible for the fight with the Catholic Church); automatically imposed penalties for failure to submit a lustration declaration and submitting a false declaration, creating at the Institute of National Remembrance a catalogue of secret collaborators and operational contacts of the security authorities of the People's Republic of Poland and publication of this catalogue, of the President of the Institute of National Remembrance of the decision on granting or not granting a scientist or journalist access to the file, without specifying the criteria for the decision. However, lustration took place, and the currently designed counterpart at universities is to be a consequence or complement of it.

[10] Ustawa z dnia 18 października 2006 r. o ujawnianiu informacji o dokumentach organów bezpieczeństwa państwa z lat 1944–1990 oraz treści tych dokumentów (Act of October 18, 2006 on the disclosure of information about documents of state security organs from 1944–1990 and the content of these documents).

6 The Questions of Contemporary Polish Historical Policy

In a short overview of the institutions that are to overcome the communist system in Poland, the most recent institution is the so-called historical policy. Introduced by the current government in 2015, it is to constitute the historical policy, consisting of shaping the good name of Poland abroad and promoting Polish identity in society. According to this concept, Poland and Poles have an unfairly negative reputation abroad. In this case, however, the former (until 2023) government has failed: a historical policy strategy has not yet been developed, and attempts to penalise the behaviour of foreign entities considered to be insulting to Poland (e.g. as an untrue expression of "Polish concentration camps" or accusations of Poland's or Poles' in general in participation in the Holocaust) have been lifted. On the contrary, the Polish state did not manage to work out a formula for the property restitution of former Polish citizens of Jewish origin or Jewish nationality, lost during the Second World War or after its end (also in the years of forced emigration after 1968). The process of departing from the communist system, presented in this article by identifying the problems and the most important institutions in this area, has not, for sure, been completed yet.

Documents

Ustawa z dnia 18 października 2006 r. o ujawnianiu informacji o dokumentach organów bezpieczeństwa państwa z lat 1944–1990 oraz treści tych dokumentów

General Reading

Grabowski J (2004) "Ja tego Żyda znam!" Szantażowanie Żydów w Warszawie 1939–1943. Centrum Badań nad Zagładą Żydów (ed) Wydawnictwo IFiS PAN, Warszawa, p. 12

References

Kłaczkow J (2006) Memorandum Rady Kościoła Ewangelickiego w Niemczech "Sytuacja wypędzonych a stosunek narodu niemieckiego do jego sąsiadów wschodnich – reakcje w Europie i w Polsce w świetle polskiej dokumentacji. Dzieje Najnowsze, r. XXXVIII — 2006, vol 4:165–178

Madajczyk C (1970) Polityka III Rzeszy w okupowanej Polsce, t. 2. Państwowe Wydawnictwo Naukowe, Warszawa

Mazowiecki T (1989) Przeszłość odkreślamy grubą linią Przemówienie Tadeusza Mazowieckiego w Sejmie. Gazeta Wyborcza 1989 no. 78:3

Zięba R (2010) Główne kierunki polityki zagranicznej Polski po zimnej wojnie, wyd. 1. Wydawnictwa Akademickie i Profesjonalne, Warszawa

Adam Bosiacki is a full professor at the University of Warsaw, Faculty of Law and Administration, Chair of the Department of Political and Legal Doctrines. Editor-in-chief of the semi-annual journal Warsaw University Law Review, advocate. Collaboration with some Polish and foreign academic universities (Hoover Institution at Stanford University CA, with his individual web side, University of Zurich, Friedrich-Alexander University Erlangen-Nürnberg, formerly Moscow and St. Petersburg). In his research activity, Bosiacki deals with the history of Russia and the USSR, the history of Central and Eastern European law, the history of administration, including local and corporate self-government, the history of legal thought (especially modern), comparative law (mainly public), and the history of science. Author of several monographs and more than a hundred scientific articles, scientific editor of the publishing series and thematic editor and member of the editorial boards of some scientific journals.

Polish Property Transformations in the Context of Transitional Justice (Since 1988)

Dariusz Mańka

Abstract This chapter aims to analyse Polish property transformations since 1988 in the context of transitional justice. Dealing with the communist past in this field is as much important as dealing with criminal or political crimes of the regime. The chapter addresses the problems of privatisation of state ownership in the 1980s and the 1990s and the restoration of private property acquired in various ways by the communist state, seeking in its beginning a social reconstruction. According to the main conclusion, dealing with the past from the perspective of property issues has not been finished in Poland yet. Despite the 30 years that passed since the political transformation and regime fall, many issues remain unexplained and unregulated, which affects the contemporary socio-political situation, undermining the legitimacy of democracy. Another problem is that the fundamental principle of common good did not apply generally to the Polish property transformations after 1988. Only well-organised social groups managed to take advantage of possibilities opened by the change of social and political system, sometimes through the abuse of law and their rights.

1 Introduction

Property is a central point of reference for communist ideology. Therefore, attempts to its introduction in Poland after the Second World War focused also on a complete, revolutionary transformation of ownership relations. Fifty years later, the collapse of the communist rule opened a completely new chapter in this regard. The democratic state faced a necessity to deal with the past from various perspectives, also from the perspective of the economic system.

The purpose of this chapter is to analyse Polish transformations from communism to democracy in the field of property issues through the prism of transitional justice

D. Mańka (✉)
Faculty of Law and Administration, University of Warsaw, Warsaw, Poland
e-mail: d.manka@wpia.uw.edu.pl

M.-E. Geis et al. (eds.), *Dealing with Totalitarian Regimes and Human Rights*,
Interdisciplinary Studies in Human Rights 11,
https://doi.org/10.1007/978-3-031-57338-5_13

mechanisms. It should be stipulated that due to the wide and complicated nature of this matter, it will be limited to a general outline of its main manifestations. The first part is dedicated to the problems of privatisation of state ownership in the 1980s and the 1990s. The analysis concerns the perception of property from an ideological point of view and its evolution in Poland after 1988, as well as the general shape of the redistribution of public wealth. The second fragment focuses on the restoration of private property acquired in various ways by the communist state. Reflections refer to the legal dealing of contemporary Poland with mass nationalisation and with the impact of the Second World War on private property.

2 Privatisation

2.1 Ideological Perception of Property and Its Evolution After 1988

The transformation from communism to capitalism changed dramatically the ideological perception of property in Polish political and legal discourse. The majority of public opinion rapidly adopted the neoliberalism of Milton Friedman and his "Chicago School", ruling on the West in the 1980s and 1990s, as the one and only way of building a new economic system.[1] Influences of the laissez-faire spirit might be already observed in the Act of 23 December 1988 on business activity, called the "Wilczek Act", after its author Mieczysław Wilczek, the Polish Minister of Industry from 1988 to 1989. It regulated economic activity and is often considered to be the "model of regulations guaranteeing freedom of business activity" and as the "true beginning of the economic revolution" in Poland. This is mainly because of Article 4, which states: "Economic entities may carry out activities and activities that are not prohibited by law as part of their business operations."

After 1989, the neoliberal privatisation programme was advocated, in a quite technocratic manner, as "a fundamentally apolitical exercise", which represented the "best route to the pursuit of greater human freedom and welfare".[2] A radical turn towards the affirmation of broadly understood liberty, quite natural after almost 50 years of communist serfdom, resulted also in a cult of private property. Private was a priori considered better and more efficient than public, which was associated with an inefficient planned economy during the so-called real socialism. In some areas of economy, Privatisation was reduced to a huge, almost uncontrolled redistribution of national wealth. What is more, the famous Plan of Balcerowicz, a normative framework of the Polish economic transformation, was introduced within only 10 days in a "social and informational vacuum".[3] Balcerowicz himself, holding

[1] Izdebski (2017), p. 66.
[2] Rittich (2002), p. 131.
[3] Szkodlarski (2000), p. 540.

the office of deputy prime minister, publicly doubted a need to explain radical changes to the Polish society.[4] Due to the rapid implementation process and the violent nature of the effects of the "Plan", it is customarily referred to as an example of the so-called shock therapy based on the view that economic reforms should be implemented as fast as possible so that it is practically impossible to abandon the changes that were made.[5]

From a purely economic perspective, such an approach turned out to be rather successful in the opinion not only of liberals but quite also of moderate analysts.[6] According to a report published in 2015 by the Civil Development Forum, the foundation of Leszek Balcerowicz, "Poland has achieved great success in the last 25 years. For more than two decades, the country has been developing at a pace exceeding an average of 4% a year, faster than other countries of Central Europe. Per capita income, adjusted for differences in price levels, increased from 29% of income per capita in Germany in 1992 to 55% this year."[7] Considering that the socio-economic situation of Poland on the eve of transition was the worst among other communist countries in Central and Eastern Europe and that the programme of building capitalism was the most radical, the macroeconomic results, including—theoretically—the widespread of private ownership, were the best.[8] Finally, a fundamental aim of privatisation was to break up the socialist state hegemony and facilitate democracy, which is, as contemporary research shows, in deep correlation with the level of private ownership in societies.[9] This, in Poland, seems to be achieved.

On the other hand, the radical reception of neoliberalism brought a lot of issues. Wrongly understood individualism and the cult of private property paradoxically fell on fertile ground in Poland. Communism gave a guarantee—theoretically an obligation—of work and salary regardless of its effects. In addition, "worthless" social property could not be possessed but could be used for individual benefit. The neglect of common ownership reappeared in post-communism, weakening the sense of common good in political and legal practice. Polish philosopher and Catholic priest Józef Tischner wrote in this context about *Homo Sovieticus*, a product of the communist system, who "does not know the difference between his own interest and common good" and could "burn a cathedral to make himself scrambled eggs in fire".[10] This phenomenon eased the cult of private property against the common good.[11] In the contemporary Polish legal system, there are still numerous examples

[4] Dudek (2013), p. 84.
[5] Klein (2007), pp. 175–184.
[6] Zagóra-Jonszta (2017), pp. 209–214.
[7] Balcerowicz and Rzońca (2015), p. 2.
[8] Jarmołowicz and Piątek (2008), pp. 225–227.
[9] Aslund (2001), p. 297.
[10] Tischner (2005), p. 145.
[11] Kaczmarczyk (2006), p. 32.

of such approach, especially in spatial planning, vulnerable to influences of various lobbies.[12]

As a consequence, the idea of common property, of course peculiarly perceived, was the only thing associated with the previous system and radically "condemned" in the 1990s. Paradoxically, to some extent, one may claim that less was done in democratic Poland for the criminal prosecution of communist crimes, lustration and the decommunisation of the public sphere, than for the liquidation of the socialist property system and its symbols. The general assumption to sell an unprofitable industry, which was economically totally justified, often turned into some kind of mass "sell-out" regardless of the market value of particular companies. It is even hard to determine how many state-owned companies were privatised, to whom and even what was the price. A crucial point of the transition plan was a shift from heavy industry to consumer goods production.[13] The shutdown of the Gdańsk Shipyard could be a spectacular example of such "deindustrialisation". Despite the best economic results of all major Polish shipyards, the birthplace of Solidarity was put into liquidation in 1988 by the last communist government of Prime Minister Mieczysław Rakowski, under the pretext of poor economic results. It is not hard to notice that the right reason was not economic but purely political. Often, those most involved in the fight against the previous system, such as industrial workers, became the main victims of the transformation. Among other interesting souvenirs of radical economic transformation in Poland, there is also a private highway, probably one of the most expensive roads in Europe.[14]

Apart from the radical admiration for private property, the Polish early neoliberals strongly believed that capital had no nationality. It is a great paradox that this quote is borrowed from Karl Marx, which they probably did not realise.[15] Countless entities were sold to foreign investors, often in strategic areas such as infrastructure, communication or the financial sector. As a result, currently over 70% of domestic exports are carried out by companies with foreign capital, and as much as 65% of the banking sector is in foreign hands. The insurance sector itself is even more dominated by foreign capital than banking—it has been estimated that the share of the Polish capital in the domestic insurance market reaches only 30%.[16]

As one scholar wrote, "privatisation was supposed to change not only the economy but the entire society. Therefore, it must not be judged merely by the degree of enterprise restructuring, but it must also be related to democracy, other structural reforms, and market structure."[17] The "shock therapy" provoked constant problems with mass unemployment, the rise of corruption, increasing poverty and

[12] Wagner (2016), pp. 396–404.

[13] Klein (2007), p. 180.

[14] The official website of the highway is accessible at https://www.autostrada-a2.pl/ (last accessed on 21 December 2023).

[15] Brustein and Roberts (2015), p. 100.

[16] Kaczyńska (2016), p. 4.

[17] Aslund (2001), p. 295.

inequalities which resulted in areas of social exclusion.[18] Gavin Rae points out that during the Polish transition, social benefits were not universally provided, and large social groups remained ineffectively covered. In turn, some other social groups managed to retain relatively high social benefits, often passed over from the previous system.[19] These economic exclusions and hierarchies, similarly to the Second Polish Republic, seriously weakened the social legitimisation of a young democracy. Jean Jacques Rousseau once noticed in his classical work that when a political community is under construction, "as for equality, the word must not be taken to mean that the degrees of power and wealth should be exactly the same, but [. . .] as regards wealth, that no citizen should be rich enough to be able to buy another, and none so poor that he has to sell himself".[20]

It is obvious that poverty extremely complicates political participation. As is known, the Polish economic transformation opened a long period of populism and political contestation in the public sphere, dividing society into "elites"—new order beneficiaries—and those disappointed or harmed by the changes, who do not identify themselves with the system. Indirect effects may have been observed in Polish politics, having tremendous problems in shaping the idea of the common good.

The negative impact of economic transition, of course, did not pass unnoticed among politicians. Some efforts to mitigate it, more or less efficiently, were undertaken already in the 1990s. On a constitutional level, the doctrine of social market economy was introduced to the Polish legal system with the Constitution of 1997, as a reception of German ordoliberalism.[21] Private ownership, in theory, was to be more "socially oriented", limited with solidarity and dialogue between employers and employees. The most important was, though, as is known, the protection of market competition. Similarly to Rousseau, ordoliberals warned about any kind of ownership monopoly that could result in the concentration of political and economic power, dangerous for individual liberty. This threat relates obviously to both communism and the radical laissez-faire ideology. "Just as private ownership of the means of production is a precondition for competition, so competition is a precondition if the private ownership of the means of production is not to lead to economic and social abuses", wrote Walter Eucken.[22] In social market economy, the property rights, as a legal institution, have to be defined in their forms and functions so that the individual's power and freedom to dispose of one's property are combined with the impossibility of preventing others from using their rights. This definition, to some extent, makes it possible for the pursuit of private interests not to infringe on the general interest.[23] Naturally, the diffusion of ideas and general directives into

[18] Sadowski (2007), p. 771.

[19] Rae (2015), pp. 54–55.

[20] Rousseau (1999), p. 87.

[21] Powałowski (2017), p. 52.

[22] Leipold (2001), p. 338.

[23] Broyer (2001), pp. 111–112.

economic and social life lasts longer than in the normative sphere. Therefore, particular aspects of the social market economy, especially in the approach to private ownership, are still being shaped and developed in Polish reality.

In terms of foreign capital's role in Poland, accession to the European Union implied the following of common market rules and a temporary suspension of discussions on this issue. However, it came back after the experience of the global financial crisis of 2008. At the EU and national levels, several normative solutions were implemented to protect and control strategic state resources, accumulated in commercial companies significant for national security and public order.[24] Recently, there has been a dispute about the idea of the so-called re-polonisation of the financial system and other branches of the market, including even the media sector. Being justified as a way to secure the national economy, such projects raise continuous doubts and controversies from both the legal and economic perspectives.[25]

2.2 *(Un)Just Redistribution*

The most controversial problem of the transformation in Poland is the role of the communist elite in privatisation. Besides, this phenomenon was characteristic for most post-communist countries and was called the "enfranchisement of nomenclature" or the "nomenclature privatisation".[26] The point is that political power was converted into economic capital. Its history is quite longer than the famous Round Table Agreement of 1989. A gradual departure by the communist party from socialist dogmas in economic policy already began in the 1980s, during the extremely difficult economic situation of the Polish People's Republic, with the creation of so-called Polish diaspora companies. However, a large-scale "enfranchisement" started with the reforms of Balcerowicz.

Not all the causes of this process are clear enough. For sure, representatives of the ruling elite were naturally privileged within the framework of the "free competition" system without any systemic state supervision, having political influences and access to information and capital from state entities.[27] Moreover, the very legal construction of the institution of property turned out to be extremely convenient. The ownership system consisted, as one of the researchers indicated, of multiple and overlapping

[24] For instance, Council Directive 2008/114/EC of 8 December 2008 on the identification and designation of European critical infrastructures and the assessment of the need to improve their protection (Text with EEA relevance) or Polish Act of 25 July 2015 on the Protection of Certain Investments (Journal of Laws of 2020 pos. 117).

[25] Pera (2017), p. 301; Charlish A (2019), Polish government to "repolonize" media in next term, article accessible on-line at: https://www.reuters.com/article/us-poland-media/polish-government-to-repolonize-media-in-next-term-deputy-pm-says-idUSKCN1TL1EX (last accessed on 21 December 2023).

[26] Bałtowski (1998), pp. 135–136.

[27] Surdykowska (1997), p. 20.

administrative rights over the "state's unitary fund". The socialist state as a supreme owner granted "rights to administrate" to its hierarchical inferiors, who, in turn, could further grant rights downwards, for instance to sell or to exchange goods. As a result, transmission concerned an administrative right over one product or another, while the state remained in theory the owner of a respective good.[28]

In commercial practice, the boundaries within the unitary state's property system were blurred as objects moved among various people and juridical entities exercising rights on them similar to property rights but not recognised as such.[29] When the privatisation occurred, many of the communist managers were becoming private owners, in a process that this hierarchy of administrative rights over ownership had facilitated.[30] Soon, thanks to subsequent laws and regulations, it was possible to create private companies based on the assets of state-owned enterprises, officially for greater efficiency in its use. Private companies formed in this way, usually established by the management of the same state-owned enterprises, communist party activists or secret service officers, took over the most profitable parts of assets, eventually leading to the removal of assets and the bankruptcy of state entities.[31] Eventually, there is an open question whether it was part of a broader plan. Sometimes communist China is presented as an example of its practical implementation. Such a project would aim at far-reaching liberalisation and partial privatisation of the economy while maintaining an authoritarian system of government, especially under the influence of military and secret service elites. According to this theory, already mentioned Polish diaspora companies would be a kind of testing ground, where activities of market entities were trained and used for covert operations. At the same time, there was a mass phenomenon of fraternisation between company owners and persons belonging to the apparatus of the Polish People's Republic.[32] After 1989, a radical increase in white-collar crimes was observed, with spectacular examples of the FOZZ and "Art.B" scandals. It was also the beginning of Polish organised crime. In all these issues, the involvement of communist apparatus members was proven. What is more, in August 1990, the authorities decided to liquidate the Offices for the Fight Against Economic Crimes of the Polish Police. It did not exist for almost 2 years.[33] Consequently, during the greatest demand for such entities, the justice system was practically helpless. Due to these commonly known facts, there are voices claiming a broader, organised and centrally led transition plan of Wojciech Jaruzelski's regime to control the changes.[34] Nevertheless, one can guess that Poland experienced rather independent

[28] Verdery (2003), pp. 56–58.

[29] Damşa (2016), p. 116.

[30] Verdery (2003), pp. 58–59.

[31] Bałtowski (1998), p. 136.

[32] Dudek (2009).

[33] Pływaczewski (2005), p. 94.

[34] Domański (2010), p. 227.

actions of communist groups aiming to preserve and enforce their influences, especially on the economic level.

The new democratic state did not take any systemic legal action against the nomenclature privatisation. While there were numerous attempts, unfortunately mostly unsuccessful, to judge criminal and political crimes of the communist regime—apart from several trials in 1999 when the Institute of National Remembrance was established—property transformation issues passed rather untouched. Only in the case of the loudest scandals, like FOZZ or Art. B mentioned above, that there have been legal proceedings lasting for years. Such an approach is the most evident example of the famous "thick line" policy of non-punishment, announced by Tadeusz Mazowiecki during his first speech in the Polish Parliament in 1989.[35] Dominant political discourse saw it as a necessary and even beneficial element of building a liberal economic system. There was a belief in some kind of economic "rehabilitation" of communist activists.

One of the post-Solidarity journalists wrote: "It must be an offer for the whole apparatus ... you need to open to these people the opportunity to apply for the ownership of some of the property they manage, if they offer no worse than other guarantees of its use. Certainly, they should be promised at least one year's termination with the real value of earnings, preservation of letting annoying privileges, comprehensive help in starting a new job or independent business activity. Possibility of favourable earlier pensions. And—it is essential—no personal billing for their previous activities."[36] Another one, for the sake of successful political transformation, called: "To make economic reforms deep and irreversible, it is worth getting people of nomenclature involved in business so that they are personally interested in the success and sustainability of reforms."[37]

What is more, similar signals were coming from abroad. Richard Pipes thought that "everything resulting in a disintegration of the [communist] state and conducting the transfer of property from public to private hands even criminal is progressive".[38] In fact, such strategy stabilised market reforms. One of the analysts indicates that, to some extent, not only political connections but also the managerial position of the core nomenclature made the new legal framework of privatisation tolerable for the ruling regime. This is why the steps taken for curbing the most striking forms of nomenclature privatisation did not threaten permanently their aspirations.[39] Some more radical critics of the Polish transition model describe economic transition even as an "intellectual alliance" of communists and liberals.[40]

[35] Szporer (2012), p. 269.

[36] Skalski (1989), pp. 3–4.

[37] Szperkowicz (1989).

[38] Pipes (1994), p. 44.

[39] Tittenbrun (1999), p. 236.

[40] Domański (2010), p. 206.

The nomenclature privatisation was addressed also in the theory of law, trying to conceptualise the transition to democratic principles.[41] The amendment to the Constitution in 1989 introduced to the Polish system the rule of law principle, derived from the German concept of the *Rechtsstaat*, based, as is known, inter alia, on the prohibition of retroactivity of the law and the principle of protection of acquired rights.[42] Therefore, the procedural possibility of taking away legally acquired property—in pure positivist sense—from the communist apparatus was practically closed. The principle of acquired rights was strongly criticised by a few influential representatives of the legal community associated with the radically anti-communist wing of the Solidarity camp as premature and contributing to the "defence of nomenclature systems".[43]

However, it was a minority view. Legal theory and jurisprudence were dominated by "the legalistic philosophy of political changes in Poland"—as one of the influential theorists at the time described it.[44] This legalism seemed to be a kind of quasi-conservatism. The "Legalists" perceived the transition of power to Solidarity as a "revolution" also against the current legal system. It was a clear scepticism towards any settlements with the new regime. Paradoxically, they thought that out of the changes could emerge new "revolutionary legal awareness" as the basis for brutal anti-communism prosecution.[45] Of course, this notion was borrowed from the legal discourse of the Russian Revolution. The representatives of the analysed theory called for prudence in "rash lavishing with revolutionary changes in law" and to be guided in legislation with "rational conservatism and evolution".[46]

Furthermore, it is interesting that the concept of acquired rights quickly appeared in the jurisdiction of the newly established[47] Constitutional Tribunal, which even before the political transition stood strongly for the preservation of this principle. In the sentence issued on 28 May 1986 (U 1/86)—one of its first—the Tribunal argued that "the principle of non-retroactivity, although it was not expressed in the Constitution of the Polish People's Republic, is the basic principle of the legal order. It is based on values such as legal security, legal certainty, and respect for acquired rights. For these reasons, the principle of non-retroactivity should be exceptionally abandoned for very important reasons." In another verdict of that time (30 November 1988, K 1/88), there was a prohibition of "establishing inter-temporal rules that are to determine the content of legal relations arising under the rule of old norms and lasting during the entry into force of newly established norms, if these rules have negative legal (and consequently social) consequences for legal security and respect

[41] Nowacki (1992), pp. 102–103.

[42] Sokolewicz (2005), p. 11; Lubera and Sikorska (2010), pp. 129–130; Jackowski (2008), p. 11.

[43] Olszewski (1991) and Strzembosz (1991).

[44] Zieliński (1992), p. 3.

[45] Ziembiński (1991), p. 5.

[46] Łętowska (1989), pp. 362–363.

[47] The Constitutional Tribunal was introduced into the Constitution of the Polish People's Republic in 1982 and began its judicial activity in 1985.

for acquired rights". These views were fully upheld by the case law of the early 1990s.[48] The Tribunal also recognised that in some cases, a necessity of adapting legal solutions to changing social and economic relations should be considered, which may justify an omission of this rule. However, it should not lead to a breach of the principle of social justice.[49]

Apart from the legal and political controversies concerning nomenclature privatisation, it seems to be especially harmful to the process of building a true democratic political community in Poland, creating instead a system of post-communism. Perhaps no one like John Rawls showed how important is the equality of chances for building a modern liberal, democratic society.[50] However, the Polish redistribution of public property was far away from the ideal of the "veil of ignorance". As a result, a belief in fair, transparent procedures of public authorities and legal safety was seriously disturbed. A conviction that the "first million must be stolen" became a myth of early transformation, appearing sometimes even in public statements of politicians. Therefore, there are still stereotypes assuming that it is impossible to get rich without any clandestine activities. Unfortunately, financial scandals and poverty became constant elements of public life, disturbing official "success-story" narration. One should agree with the thesis, often present in Polish political and legal history, that property structures impact group relations, and when one group owns a disproportionate amount of property, the resulting asymmetries in social status and economic power can leave weaker groups open to various forms of subordination, which can foster deep resentment that undermines social reconstruction.[51]

3 Restoration of Private Property

3.1 Dealing with the Communist "Social (In)Justice"

From a theoretical point of view, concepts of restitution and reparation are essential transitional justice mechanisms.[52] It is equally important in criminal and civil laws of transition from communism. Considering property issues in Poland from this perspective, there is a problem of mass nationalisation after the Second World War to be dealt with. The communists have been taking over actual power over Polish territories successively since 1944. With the support of the Soviet army and on the basis

[48] Filipczyk (2013), pp. 46–47.

[49] Banaszak (2012), p. 5.

[50] Rawls (1999), p. 118.

[51] Atuahene (2010), p. 69.

[52] Damşa (2016), p. 146; Mégret and Vagliano (2017), p. 96; Posner and Vermeule (2004), p. 762; Kaminski et al. (2006), p. 295; Czarnota (2015), p. 18; Snarski (2010), Szczerbiak (2002).

of several normative acts, the constitutional legality of which has been questioned,[53] they wanted to change the ownership structure of the future "People's Poland" in accordance with the socialist ideology. It was definitely the most significant social revolution in Polish history, resulting in many groups of victims. However, there is a constant conflict in this case between the significant values funding the legal system: the need to compensate a harm done by the state to its own nation on the one hand and solidarity and the principle of the common good on the other, which require limiting the size of the restitution so that it does not cause even greater damage than nationalisation.[54] Before going further, there is one more important point to make. Since 1989, Poland adopted the principle of the continuity of the state. All Polish nationalisation laws had been issued by an internationally recognised government of that time. Therefore, all legislation of the 1944–1989 period, including nationalisation laws, is considered valid, unless it was repealed.[55] It seems that post-war nationalisation should be analysed from two perspectives.

Firstly, one ought to perceive communist expropriation as a method of social revolution, symbolised by the so-called agricultural reform introduced with the Decree of Polish Committee of National Liberation (PKWN) of 6 September 1944[56] and with some other detailed acts issued in the 1950s.[57] The reform was officially designed to improve the structure of the country's agricultural industry by parcelling out large areas of agricultural real property (over 100 ha, in some cases 50 ha) for the benefit of small farms. Some of the nationalised areas were moreover reserved for schools, various public facilities (hospitals etc.) and academic facilities for seed production, breeding and the agricultural industry, subject to the central or local government. Within the scope of the reform, there was not only real property but also farm buildings, animals and agricultural tools and machinery. Generally, only the nationalisation of forests was permanent. Land, converted into the property of the state, was then sold to small and medium-sized farmers for a nominal fee. Expropriated owners had no right to compensation.[58]

From an ideological point of view, the agricultural reform aimed at the reduction of the economic independence of the most influential "social powers" in Poland, which would effectively oppose the "people's government": the Catholic Church (traditionally the biggest Polish landowner), other religious communes and the nobility. Considering the nobility, this goal was almost completely achieved. One of the Marxist state theorists wrote after 20 years that "landownership as a social

[53] Krzywoń (2015), p. 10.

[54] Lang (2001), p. 138.

[55] Wyrzykowski (1995), p. 19.

[56] Journal of Laws of 1944, entry 4, position 17.

[57] Among others: the Act of 20 March 1950 on Acquisition of Mortmain Estates by the State, Suretyship of the Possession of Farms to Rectors and the Establishment of the Church Fund (Journal of Laws of 1950, entry 9, position 87); the Decree on Liquidation of Foundations of 24 April 1952 (Journal of Laws of 1953, entry 172).

[58] Stec (2001), pp. 360–361.

class has disappeared as a result of agricultural reform from the surface of economic and social life and lost direct political influence".[59] The Catholic Church, in turn, was expropriated from the majority of its property a few years later, after the communist regime has been stabilised. New authorities argued that the land of the Church institutions was not used for religious purposes but had a "feudal" character and served the political aims of foreign hostile powers.[60] Theoretically, in exchange, the social and economic needs of the clergy were to be satisfied with the Church Fund and small farms belonging to parishes. This idea was generally copied from absolutist Austria, where the emperor, Joseph II, created scientific and religious funds to subordinate the Church and other religious communities to the state.[61] In practice, during the communist rule, funds spent on the clergy were not equivalent to the worth of nationalised lands. Moreover, the largest funding was received by so-called patriot priests, loyal not to the Vatican but to the government. As a result, the Fund became some kind of a material base for the fight against the Church.[62] However, the creation of a special financial entity—no matter how efficient in reality—shows that the clergy had a far more important political position in Poland than the landowners. Thanks to its universal character and the leadership of famous cardinal Stefan Wyszyński, the Catholic Church preserved political influence and became a fundamental symbol of social resistance against the communists in Poland throughout the next decades.

From a purely normative perspective, due to the nihilist character of the communist "rule of law" doctrine,[63] expropriation was carried out often in an obvious violation of law and in an extremely restrictive manner.[64] Limiting reflections only to the essentials, the most evident example of such nihilism was a refusal of compensation for expropriated ownership. According to the PKWN Manifesto of 22 July 1944, the National Council and the Polish Committee of National Liberation were to operate on the basis of the Constitution of 17 March 1921,[65] which would guarantee in its article 99 an adequate compensation for the expropriated persons. As a result, in the absence of compliance with the constitutional condition of abolition or restrictions on ownership with paying compensation, such provisions of the Decree on Agricultural Reform should be considered unconstitutional.[66] Obviously, there are researchers deriving such unconstitutionality from the doubtful legal status

[59] Ryszka (1966), p. 106.

[60] Mazgaj (2010), p. 55.

[61] Borecki (2012), p. 20.

[62] Zawiślak (2009), p. 265.

[63] Bosiacki (2012), p. 367.

[64] Oleszko (1996), p. 32.

[65] As it is known, the last valid constitution, however controversial due to its authoritarian connotations, before 1939 was the April Constitution of Poland passed by the act of the Polish Sejm on 23 April 1935 by the supporters of Józef Piłsudski.

[66] Kiszka (2011), p. 72; Kociubiński (2013), p. 221.

of the PKWN itself.[67] Nevertheless, as Robert Jastrzębski indicates, legal acts issued by the Polish Committee of National Liberation were based on the status quo prevailing in the areas liberated from German occupation by the Red Army and Polish People's Army units. Currently, a return to the *status quo ante* or a repeal of the legal consequences of agricultural reform is impossible due to ownership transformation, the passage of time and enormous sociopolitical costs.[68] In this situation, considering especially the legal continuity of statehood, any contemporary discussions about the constitutionality of agricultural transformations after 1944 seem a bit pointless. A significant number of entities have acquired property in good faith under these laws and are protected by the principle of the protection of acquired rights. Nowadays, depriving them of property and attempting to reverse history would be both unjust and obviously unconstitutional. Another issue is governmental terror,[69] ordinary in the Soviet system and quite common during the nationalisation. For instance, a generally legitimate expropriation of Nazi collaborators, people who participated voluntarily in the so-called *Volksliste* and other types of people legally convicted for treason, was often abused as a tool for fighting with imagined "enemies of the people", which were potentially dangerous for the communist rule.

The current ideological analysis of the agricultural reform omits rather the perspective of the peasantry. As is known, Polish society in the first half of the twentieth century had a mainly agricultural character, with the great majority of people living in the countryside. Due to the long feudal traditions, poverty and "hunger" of land, the need for agricultural reform has been indisputable since the regaining of independence in 1918. Unfortunately, such attempts failed in interwar Poland, mostly because of low economic development, the impact of the Great Depression and, of course, war.[70] Nevertheless, political groups in the country and in exile did not stop working on developing new rules for future reform, which were planned to be carried out after the war in a more or less radical way.[71] It shows that ownership transformation in the rural areas became a key element of legitimisation of any future political power of post-war Poland. Eventually, the communists took advantage of it. For them, however, such reform was to be only an introduction to mass collectivisation according to the Soviet model, which fortunately was not carried out completely. State agricultural farms, as a result of these failed attempts, became one of the symbols of economic ineffectiveness and were liquidated in 1991. Their downfall often caused damage to the structure of the local communities, not adapted to the new situation of economic activity, which made thousands of people unemployed, along with the devastation of public property.[72] On the other hand, the

[67] Osajda (2009), p. 15.

[68] Jastrzębski (2018), pp. 124, 149. See also Katner (2003), p. 22.

[69] Jakubowska (1999), pp. 24–33; Łuczak (2011), pp. 53–58.

[70] Ziętara (2015), pp. 35–37; Noniewicz (2016), p. 79.

[71] Jastrzębski (2018), p. 119.

[72] Niedzielski (2017), p. 129.

reform of 1944 created a quite solid sector of private agriculture in Poland, which, along with the independent Catholic Church—unique in the Soviet bloc—contributed to the mitigation of the regime and, in the long term, to its final breakdown.[73]

Besides controversial issues of land ownership, private industry was another area of nationalisation. It was carried out mainly on the basis of the Act of 3 January 1946 on the Acquisition of Basic Branches of the National Economy[74] and a few other normative acts.[75] That legislation applied to private enterprises employing more than 50 people on one shift and certain other types of companies regardless of their size. Theoretically, dedicated committees were supposed to calculate indemnification for expropriated owners. In fact, they were never compensated.[76] What is more, communist authorities aimed constantly at the practical expropriation of the remaining private businesses, for instance, with exceeded taxation or other public burdens.[77]

The political transformation obviously made room for dealing with communist expropriations described before. However, it is hard to resist the impression that, in this case, injustice was not replaced with justice. Firstly, there is no systemic solution to these issues, which would be inspired by the idea of the common good. Due to political and social reasons, the restitution of property covered, on different rules, only one group of legal entities: churches and other religious associations, especially the Catholic Church.[78] The landowners, in turn, may theoretically pursue their claims individually; nonetheless, *de facto* inconsistent case law limits the protection of their subjective rights.[79] Besides, it is interesting that during their meeting in Warsaw in February 2001, Polish landowners, after a long and heated discussion, resigned from claims for full compensation and approved a partial compensation for their losses after considering the public good, that is, the poor economic situation in Poland.[80] Finally, even though private initiative in business was so much praised in the 1990s, no legal and political actions were taken to restore or even compensate the industry expropriated and haunted a few decades earlier by the communists, who suddenly became businessmen themselves. Perhaps a possibility given to heirs to continue expropriated businesses or, in the case of landowners, to rebuild often ruined palaces would contribute to the development of the private economy and enhance the social acceptance of the transformation.

[73] Kamiński (1992), p. 372.

[74] Journal of Laws of 1946, entry 7.

[75] The decree of 26 April 1949 on the Acquisition and Transfer of Real Estate Necessary for the Implementation of National Economic Plans (Journal of Laws of 1949, number 3, position 1); the Decree of 25 October 1948 on Banking Reform (Journal of Laws of 1948, entry 279); Act of 8 January 1951 on the Acquisition of Pharmacies by the State (Journal of Laws of 1951, entry 1).

[76] Stec (2001), p. 360.

[77] Skąpska (2005), pp. 214–215.

[78] Borecki (2011), p. 61; Stec and Walencik (2011), p. 23.

[79] Tracz (2016), p. 28.

[80] Skąpska (2005), p. 230.

3.2 Dealing with the Impact of World War II on Private Property

The second perspective on post-war expropriations is connected directly to the impact of the Second World War. Border changes—independent of any domestic political power—mass displacements and obviously the death of millions of Polish citizens, also during the Shoah, made restitution after almost 50 years a multidimensional dilemma.[81] Democratic Poland inherited numerous problems created by the communist legislation.

It would seem that the issue of pre-war private property on the "Recovered Territories" attributed to Poland during the Potsdam Conference was the less controversial. Because of the Decree on Agricultural System and Settlement in the Area of the Recovered Territories and the Former Free City of Gdańsk of 6 September 1946[82] and the Decree of 8 March 1946 on Abandoned and Former German Property,[83] the agricultural reform of 1944 was adopted there similarly to the rest of the new Polish territory. These acts were applicable as well to the property of religious associations, including primarily the Jewish communes.[84] However, in the 1990s, in spite of the official recognition of post-war border changes by the Federal Republic of Germany, various entities, including the German Federation of Expellees (*Heimatvertriebene*), submitted their "claims" to property left on former eastern territories of the German Reich. Such obviously illegitimate and unjustified demands[85] have been negatively influencing Polish-German reconciliation and diplomatic relations. In many cases, even the status of "expellee" is questionable from a historical perspective. A good example is Erika Steinbach, a former president of Federation of Expellees. Her family inhabited during the war a flat in Gdynia—the most important industrial harbour of interwar Poland—that had belonged to the Polish officials before the German invasion in September 1939.[86] The European Court of Human Rights in Strasbourg issued several judgements recognising the legality of Polish legislation in this area and rejecting the demands of the "Expellees", who seek an analogy between this displacement or eviction and genocide.[87] Sometimes contemporary owners of real estate who are left at the Polish Recovered Territories face a risk of claims from expropriated German citizens due to the negligence of Polish authorities. A spectacular example was the case of Agnes

[81] Skąpska (2005), p. 212.

[82] Journal of Laws of 1946, number 49, position 279.

[83] Journal of Laws of 1946, number 13, position 8.

[84] Borecki (2011), p. 62.

[85] Apart from the obvious German responsibility for World War II, from a purely legalistic point of view, the German government created a system for compensating persons who had suffered a loss. See, for instance, Yearbook of the European Convention on Human Rights (2013), p. 232.

[86] Szubarczyk and Semków (2004), p. 49; Kwiatkowska-Dróżdż (2010), pp. 45–48.

[87] Preussische Treuhand GmbH & CO. KG A. A. v. Poland, n. 47550/06, 7 October 2008; Krzyżanowska-Mierzewska (2009), p. 45.

Trawny, to whom the court, in a decision, returned a house in Masuria that was inhabited by two families, which were forced to leave it. Paradoxically, the property had been abandoned by Trawny's family in the 1970s when they left for Germany as part of the so-called family reunification actions. The claims of German heirs are based on pre-war land and mortgage registers that were not updated by competent authorities in Poland while issuing decisions on granting ownership after the war. What is more, local people who lost such trials and lived there in good faith, on the basis of a legitimate administrative decision, are being refused compensation by Polish authorities.[88]

A problem of compensation for property, considered also Polish citizens resettled from the so-called Bug River land. The Republican Agreements, the legality of which is questionable and which were concluded in 1944 between PKWN and the USSR, transferred to Poland an obligation to compensate its citizens for the loss of private property.[89] During the so-called People's Poland, the only form of compensation adopted by the legislator for the ownership left outside the eastern borders was the right to offset its value against the price of ownership or perpetual use purchased in Poland. After 1989, representatives of the people who resettled from the Bug River land demanded a systemic solution, arguing that the existing compensation mechanism did not correspond with the value of property they left. The European Court of Human Rights shared their argumentation and imposed on Poland an obligation to create satisfying legal mechanisms of compensation.[90] This was finally adopted in the Act of 8 July 2005 on exercising the right to compensation for leaving real estate outside the current borders of the Republic of Poland.[91] Apart from the existing right of offset, the legislator added a cash benefit of up to 20% of the value of the abandoned immovable property.

Currently, the most controversial issue of re-privatisation is associated with immovable property in Warsaw. The almost complete devastation of the Polish capital city during the war implied a necessity for state involvement in its reconstruction. This is why all land properties within the city borders were nationalised by the Decree on Ownership and Usufruct of Land in the Area of the Capital of Warsaw issued on 26 October 1945, also known as the "Bierut Decree", after Bolesław Bierut, the leader of communist-ruled Poland from 1947 until 1956.[92] Despite numerous controversies, it remains generally recognised that this Act is still in force and that entitled persons or their legal successors may, under certain circumstances, seek the restoration of property or compensation under these provisions.[93] Since the 1990s, when the first cases of Warsaw re-privatisation were examined by the courts, there have been numerous fraudulent practices, such as the so-called trade

[88] Szymowski (2012), p. 63.

[89] Młynarska-Sobaczewska (2010), p. 58.

[90] Broniowski v. Poland, n. 31443/96, 22 June 2004.

[91] Journal of Laws of 2005, number 169, item 1418.

[92] Journal of Laws of 1945, entry 279.

[93] Turower and Janczarska (2018), p. 38.

of claims resulting from the possibility of transferring such claims, false powers of attorney etc. Moreover, in the case of many re-privatisation decisions, it turned out that some lands had been already cleared with bilateral compensation agreements between the so-called People's Poland and other countries. Such agreements were concluded in order to authenticate the communist government on the international scene. An evident manifestation of discrimination on grounds of nationality because Polish citizens were not paid compensation in the same circumstances.[94] The illegal and unethical activities of lawyers and new landlords towards tenants have raised a negative attitude of public opinion. As a consequence, it was decided to adopt the Act of 9 March 2017[95] on Special Rules for Removing Legal Effects of Reprivatisation Decisions Regarding Real Estate of Warsaw Issued in Breach of Law. On the basis of Article 3 of this Act, a special commission, called the "Verification Commission", was established to remove the legal effects of re-privatisation decisions regarding Warsaw real estate that were issued in violation of the law. According to the explanatory memorandum to the Act, the primary goal of this Commission is to verify the correctness of decree decisions issued and to remove the effects of violations of law that have taken place during ongoing proceedings. Nevertheless, the legal status of this entity, similar to that of a judicial authority, remains in terms of separation of powers and the rule of law.

4 Conclusion

One must admit that dealing with the past regarding property issues has not been finished in Poland yet. It does not seem far from the truth that more was achieved in political and criminal settlements. Despite the 30 years that have passed since the political transformation and the communist regime fell, many issues remain unexplained and unregulated, which affect the contemporary sociopolitical situation in the country. As one of the contemporary researchers indicated, it is the awareness of settlement with the past that builds the legitimacy and authority of a state that rejected this past.[96] Consequently, it is still necessary to analyse and address privatisation and re-privatisation in Poland. The feeling of social injustice, whether caused by unemployment or poverty or justified by unsatisfied claims, poses a great risk for democracy, pushing society towards populist currents.

Furthermore, reflection on Polish property transformations leads to the conclusion that it is another sphere of contemporary public life where a notion of the common good practically does not apply. All political forces ruling after 1989, despite a few attempts, did not elaborate systemic solutions to crucial property problems connected with the transition from communism to democracy. As far as

[94] Stec (2001), pp. 361–362.

[95] Journal of Laws of 2017, position 718.

[96] Młynarska-Sobaczewska (2010), p. 69.

the restoration of property is concerned, in Central-Eastern Europe, only Poland has no complex piece of legislation on this matter.[97] Only those that were well organised and had political influences and financial backgrounds managed to take advantage of the possibilities that opened with the change of the social and political system, sometimes through the abuse of law. As a result, citizens who do not have such assets may often feel disappointed with the rule of law that does not meet its basic functions. It should be recalled in this context that the constitutional task of the Polish state is to implement social justice, while, in particular, the issue of property requires taking into account the principle of the common good so that the repair of old damage does not cause new, even greater, ones. Finally, dealing with the past is essential not only for contemporary society but also for the future development of the economy, which is conditioned upon legal certainty.

References

Aslund A (2001) Building capitalism. The transformation of the former Soviet bloc. Cambridge University Press, Cambridge

Atuahene B (2010) Property and transitional justice. UCLA Law Rev Discourse 58:65–93

Balcerowicz L, Rzońca A (2015) Summary of a report "The next 25 years: what reforms we need to implement to catch up with the West?". Civil Development Forum, Warsaw

Bałtowski M (1998) Prywatyzacja przedsiębiorstw państwowych. Przebieg i ocena. PWN, Warsaw

Banaszak B (2012) Konstytucja RP. Komentarz. C. H. Beck, Warsaw

Borecki P (2011) Reprywatyzacja nieruchomości na rzecz gmin wyznaniowych żydowskich. Państwo i Prawo 9:61–73

Borecki P (2012) Dylematy likwidacji Funduszu Kościelnego i komisji regulacyjnych. Przegląd Sądowy 6:19–33

Bosiacki A (2012) Utopia, władza, prawo: doktryna i koncepcje prawne bolszewickiej Rosji 1917-1921, 2nd edn. Liber, Warsaw

Broyer S (2001) German contemporary analyses of economic order: standard Ordnungstheorie, Ordoliberalism and Ordnungsdkonomik in perspective. In: Labrousse A, Weisz J-D (eds) Institutional economics in France and Germany German ordoliberalism versus the French regulation school. Springer, Berlin-Heidelberg, pp 93–128

Brustein W, Roberts L (2015) The socialism of fools? Leftist origins of modern anti-semitism. Cambridge University Press, Cambridge

Czarnota A (2015) Między polityką a prawem, czyli o sprawiedliwości okresu przejściowego. Acta Universitatis Lodziensis 27:13–35

Damşa L (2016) The transformation of property regimes and transitional justice in Central Eastern Europe. In search of a theory. Springer, Heidelberg

Domański (2010) Kwestia własnościowa w transformacji systemowej. Dlaczego tak łatwo upadł komunizm i dlaczego tak trudno znaleźć zgodę społeczną. Economic Studies 2:193–228

Dudek A (2009) Wielki skok. Tygodnik Powszechny of 22 April 2009

Dudek A (2013) Historia polityczna Polski 1989 – 2012. Znak, Krakow

Filipczyk H (2013) Postulat pewności prawa w wykładni operatywnej prawa podatkowego. Wolters Kluwer, Warsaw

[97] Makarzec (2003), p. 101.

Izdebski H (2017) Doktryny polityczno-prawne. Fundamenty współczesnych państw. Wolters Kluwer, Warsaw

Jackowski M (2008) Zasada ochrony praw nabytych w polskim prawie konstytucyjnym. Przegląd Sejmowy 1:11–28

Jakubowska L (1999) Między ideologią i praktyką reformy rolnej: pamięć ziemiaństwa. Polska 1944/45-1989: studia i materiały 4:7–44

Jarmołowicz W, Piątek D (2008) Strategie transformacji a doświadczenia wybranych krajów. Elementy analizy porównawczej. Polskie Towarzystwo Ekonomiczne. Zeszyty Naukowe 6: 205–232

Jastrzębski R (2018) Reforma rolna po drugiej wojnie światowej. Ustawodawstwo państwa polskiego. Czasopismo Prawno-Historyczne 1:111–151

Kaczmarczyk M (2006) Wstęp do socjologicznej teorii własności. Oficyna Naukowa, Krakow

Kaczyńska D (2016) Kapitał ma narodowość. Polscy gracze przechodzą do kontrofensywy. Klub Jagielloński, Warsaw

Kamiński AZ (1992) An institutional theory of communist regimes. Design, function and breakdown. Institute for Contemporary Studies Press, San Francisco

Kaminski M, Nalepa M, O'Neill B (2006) Normative and strategic aspects of transitional justice. J Conflict Resolut 3:295–302

Katner W (2003) Uwarunkowania prawne reprywatyzacji w Polsce. Państwo i Prawo 17:17–32

Kiszka T (2011) Ochrona prawa własności w świetle dekretu PKWN o przeprowadzeniu reformy rolnej z dnia 6 września 1944 roku. Studia Prawnicze KUL 3–4:59–84

Klein N (2007) The shock doctrine: the rise of disaster capitalism. Metropolitan Books, New York

Kociubiński T (2013) Powojenne przekształcenia własnościowe w świetle konstytucji. Wolters Kluwer, Warsaw

Krzywoń A (2015) Podstawowe założenia systemu źródeł prawa PRL a postępowania wywłaszczeniowe. Przegląd Legislacyjny 4:9–24

Krzyżanowska-Mierzewska M (2009) Skarga Powiernictwa Pruskiego - glosa do orzeczenia ETPCz z 7.10.2008 r. w sprawie Preussische Treuhand GmbH & CO. KG A. A. przeciwko Polsce. Europejski Przegląd Sądowy 2:44–47

Kwiatkowska-Dróżdż A (2010) It's not (only) about Erika Steinbach. Three myths in the German discourse on the resettlements. OSW, Warsaw

Lang W (2001) Problem reprywatyzacji w kontekście zasad państwa prawa i aksjologii polskiego systemu prawa. Studia Iuridica Toruniensa 1:131–146

Leipold H (2001) The contribution of neoliberal Ordnungstheorie to transformation policy. In: Labrousse A, Weisz D (eds) Institutional economics in France and Germany. German ordoliberalism versus the French regulation school. Springer, Berlin-Heidelberg, pp 334–349

Łętowska E (1989) Polityczne aspekty prawa intertemporalnego. In: Łętowski J, Sokolewicz W (eds) Państwo, prawo, obywatel: zbiór studiów dla uczczenia 60-lecia urodzin i 40-lecia pracy naukowej profesora Adama Łopatki. Zakład Narodowy imienia Ossolińskich, Wrocław, pp 349–364

Lubera B, Sikorska A (2010) Retroaktywność dekretu o stanie wojennym w świetle Konstytucji z 1952 i 1997 r. Przegląd prawa konstytucyjnego 4:125–142

Łuczak A (2011) Reforma rolna i represje wobec polskiego ziemiaństwa po roku 1944. Biuletyn IPN 3:53–58

Makarzec P (2003) Reprywatyzacja w Polsce i w innych państwach Europy Środkowo-Wschodniej. Studia luridica Lublinensia 2:95–110

Mazgaj M (2010) Church and state in communist Poland. A history, 1944–1989. McFarland & Company, Jefferson-London

Mégret F, Vagliano R (2017) Transitional justice and human rights. In: Lawther C, Moffett L, Jacobs D (eds) Research handbook on transitional justice. Edward Elgar Publishing, Northampton, pp 95–116

Młynarska-Sobaczewska A (2010) Odpowiedzialność państwa polskiego za mienie zabużańskie. Państwo i Prawo 2:57–69

Niedzielski E (2017) Powstanie, funkcjonowanie i likwidacja państwowych gospodarstw rolnych. Roczniki Naukowe Stowarzyszenia Ekonomistów Rolnictwa i Agrobiznesu 1:126–130
Noniewicz C (2016) Istota reformy rolnej w II Rzeczypospolitej. Optimum. Studia Ekonomiczne 6: 76–82
Nowacki J (1992) Sprawozdanie z Posiedzenia Komitetu Nauk Prawnych PAN z 19 XII 1991 r. pt. "Zasada ochrony praw nabytych w okresie przemian ustrojowych". Państwo i Prawo 3:102–103
Oleszko A (1996) Problematyka własnościowa w świetle reformy oraz uporządkowania spraw związanych z reformą rolną i osadnictwem. Rejent 11:28–48
Olszewski J (1991) Państwo przede wszystkim, "Rzeczpospolita" z 1 VII 1991
Osajda K (2009) Nacjonalizacja i reprywatyzacja. Akty prawne. Orzecznictwo. Piśmiennictwo. C.H. Beck, Warsaw
Pera J (2017) Repolonization. Risk factor. Zeszyty Naukowe Politechniki Śląskiej 102:291–302
Pipes R (1994) Pytania o Rosję. Politicus - Biuletyn ISP PAN 2:43–53
Pływaczewski E (2005) Przestępczość zorganizowana. Świadek koronny. Terroryzm. W ujęciu praktycznym, Zakamycze, Krakow
Posner E, Vermeule A (2004) Transitional justice as ordinary justice. Harv Law Rev 117(3): 761–825
Powałowski A (2017) Społeczna gospodarka rynkowa w prawie polskim. Gdańskie Studia Prawnicze 1:51–62
Rae G (2015) Privatising capital. The commodification of Poland's welfare state. Peter Lang, Frankfurt am Main [etc.]
Rawls J (1999) A theory of justice. Harvard University Press, Cambridge
Rittich K (2002) Recharacterizing restructuring: law, distribution, and gender in market reform. Kluwer International, Hague-London-New York
Rousseau JJ (1999) Discourse on political economy and the social contract. Oxford University Press, Oxford
Ryszka F (1966) "Sprawa Polska" i sprawy Polaków. Szkice z lat 1944–1946. Wiedza Powszechna, Warsaw
Sadowski Z (2007) Od sporu o transformację do strategii rozwoju. Ekonomista 6:771–780
Skalski E (1989) Wielki kompromis. Gazeta Wyborcza 60, 31 July 1989, pp 3–4
Skąpska G (2005) Restitutive justice, rule of law, and constitutional dilemmas. In: Czarnota A, Krygier M, Sadurski W (eds) Rethinking the rule of law after communism. Central European University Press, Budapest-New York, pp 211–235
Snarski T (2010) Sprawiedliwość transformacyjna, filozofia prawa i rozliczanie przeszłości przez demokratyczne państwo prawa. Pamięć i Sprawiedliwość: biuletyn Głównej Komisji Badania Zbrodni przeciwko Narodowi Polskiemu Instytutu Pamięci Narodowej 2:211–228
Sokolewicz W (2005) Artykuł 2. In: Garlicki L (ed) Konstytucja, T. 5. Wydawnictwo Sejmowe, Warsaw
Stec P (2001) Reprivatisation of nationalized property in Poland. In: Cooke E (ed) Modern studies in property law, vol 1. Hart Publishing, Portland, pp 357–373
Stec P, Walencik D (2011) Rewindykacja nieruchomości osób prawnych Kościoła katolickiego w postępowaniu przed sądami powszechnymi. Przegląd Prawa Wyznaniowego 3:23–50
Strzembosz A (1991) "Rzeczpospolita Polska państwem prawnym – czy naprawdę? "Rzeczpospolita" z 7 X 1991 r.
Surdykowska S (1997) Prywatyzacja. PWN, Warsaw
Szczerbiak A (2002) Dealing with the communist past or the politics of the present? Lustration in post-communist Poland. Europe-Asia Stud 54(4):553–572
Szkodlarski P (2000) Zarys historii gospodarczej Polski. PWN, Warsaw-Łódź
Szperkowicz J (1989) Uwłaszczać nie żałować. Gazeta Wyborcza, issue of 25 September 1989
Szporer D (2012) Solidarity: the great workers strike of 1980. Lexington Books, Lanham
Szubarczyk P, Semków P (2004) Erika z Rumii. Biuletyn IPN 50:49–53
Szymowski L (2012) Rugi Pruskie. Nieruchomości i Prawo 11–12:62–63
Tischner J (2005) Etyka solidarności oraz Homo sovieticus. Znak, Krakow

Tittenbrun J (1999) Własność i interesy. Prywatyzacja w Polsce w ujęciu socjologii gospodarki. Ruch Prawniczy, Ekonomiczny i Socjologiczny 3–4:233–248

Turower A, Janczarska E (2018) Odszkodowanie za grunty warszawskie utracone na mocy dekretu Bieruta, "Temidium" March 2018

Tracz G (2016) Sytuacja prawna byłych właścicieli nieruchomości ziemskich w III Rzeczypospolitej. Forum Prawnicze 4:3–29

Verdery K (2003) The vanishing hectare: property and value in postsocialist Transylvania. Cornell University Press, New York

Wagner M (2016) Evading spatial planning law - case study of Poland. Land Use Policy 57:396–404

Wyrzykowski M (1995) Selected problems of system transformation in Poland. In: Aregger J, Poczobut J, Wyrzykowski M (eds) Rechtsfragen der Transformation in Polen. Wydawnictwo Baran i Suszczynski, Warsaw, pp 9–26

Yearbook of the European Convention on Human Rights (2013), Vol. I3. Springer, The Hague

Zagóra-Jonszta U (2017) Polscy ekonomiści o przebiegu i skutkach transformacji. Studia Ekonomiczne. Zeszyty Naukowe Uniwersytetu Ekonomicznego w Katowicach, pp 208–219

Zawiślak M (2009) Wydatkowanie środków Funduszu Kościelnego w latach 1950-1989. Studia z Prawa Wyznaniowego 12:241–266

Zieliński T (1992) Ochrona praw nabytych – zasada państwa prawnego. Państwo i Prawo 3:3–11

Ziembiński Z (1991) Lex a ius w okresie przemian. Państwo i Prawo 6:3–14

Ziętara W (2015) Społeczny czy ekonomiczny charakter reform rolnych w Polsce w okresie między i powojennym. Roczniki Naukowe Ekonomii Rolnictwa i Rozwoju Obszarów Wiejskich 1:31–45

Dariusz Mańka is a lawyer, assistant professor (adiunkt) and lecturer at the Faculty of Law and Administration of the University of Warsaw. He specialises in comparative public law, the theory of law and the history of legal thought. His doctoral thesis concerned supranational concepts of sovereignty and critique of the nation-state in French political and legal thought from the Enlightenment to the European Union. He is the author of publications concerning French legal thought and the axiology of contemporary social market economy, especially in the context of the legal framework of public and private property. He participated in research projects on transitional justice, radical ecologism and the axiology of legal systems.

The Legal Status of the Institute of National Remembrance – Commission for the Prosecution of Crimes Against the Polish Nation

Jarosław Kostrubiec

Abstract The aim of this chapter is to identify the legal position of the Institute of National Remembrance – Commission for the Prosecution of Crimes Against the Polish Nation. To this end, the author carried out an analysis of the responsibilities, powers and organisational structure of the institution in question. The chapter consists of four main parts that address the following issues: the origins of the Institute of National Remembrance in Poland, the responsibilities and powers of the Institute, the bodies and its organisational structure and the functioning of the Institute in the light of official data. Within the framework of the Institute's activities, the investigative, archival, research-educational and vetting functions were distinguished. The text also considers the actual operations of the Institute, which is shown based on official statistical data, mainly in the scope of the investigative function. The main point of the chapter is that the effective implementation of statutory tasks by the Institute of National Remembrance must assume regular cooperation between those organisational divisions of the Institute that are responsible for carrying out the investigative, archival, research-educational and vetting functions. The author used mainly the research methods and techniques typical of legal sciences, in particular by applying formal and dogmatic methods.

1 Introduction

This chapter seeks to define the position of the Institute of National Remembrance – Commission for the Prosecution of Crimes Against the Polish Nation within the legal and political system and present its activities. In view of the above, the discussion covers a description of the tasks and responsibilities of the bodies and the organisational structure of the institution in question. The second aspect addressed in the chapter has been to show the actual implementation of tasks by

J. Kostrubiec (✉)
Faculty of Law and Administration, Maria Curie-Skłodowska University, Lublin, Poland
e-mail: jaroslaw.kostrubiec@mail.umcs.pl

M.-E. Geis et al. (eds.), *Dealing with Totalitarian Regimes and Human Rights*, Interdisciplinary Studies in Human Rights 11,
https://doi.org/10.1007/978-3-031-57338-5_14

the Institute of National Remembrance (IPN). These research objectives were achieved, first of all, through the use of legal-science-specific research methods and techniques. The primary method used in the studies was the formal dogmatic method and the use, above all, of the interpretative rules of linguistic interpretation of the law. Consequently, the existing legislation was analysed and evaluated on the basis of the Act of 18 December 1998 on the Institute of National Remembrance – Commission for the Prosecution of Crimes Against the Polish People (consolidated text Journal of Laws of 2019, item 1882) and the statutes of the Institute. The description and systematisation of the existing legislation allowed for the formulation of proposals regarding the law as it stands (*de lege lata*). Moreover, empirical studies were carried out, which allowed assessing the actual activities of the Institute of National Remembrance in Poland. To this end, official data related to the activities of the Institute for the last three years were examined. This generated the opportunity to examine the extent to which the Institute of National Remembrance actually carried out its legally defined tasks.

2 Background of the Establishment of the Institute of National Remembrance in Poland

The reasons behind establishing the Institute of National Remembrance are listed in the preamble of the Act of 18 December 1998 on the Institute of National Remembrance. These include the remembrance of the enormity of the number of victims; the losses and damages suffered by the Polish people during the Second World War and after it ended; the patriotic tradition of the struggle of the Polish people against the occupiers, Nazism and communism; the actions of the citizens for the sake of the independence of the Polish State and in defence of freedom and human dignity; the obligation to prosecute crimes against peace and humanity and war crimes; and the obligation of the state to compensate all those aggrieved by a state that violated human rights. The legislator also stressed that the adoption of the Act on the Institute of National Remembrance is an expression of the belief that no unlawful action by the state against the citizens can be guarded as classified or left to oblivion.

The law of 1998 repealed the provisions of the hitherto applicable Act of 6 April 1984 on the Chief Commission for the Investigation of Nazi Crimes in Poland – the Institute of National Remembrance (Journal of Laws, No. 21, item 98), which had replaced the decree of 10 November 1945 on the Chief Commission and District Commissions for the Investigation of German Crimes in Poland in force for nearly 40 years. In the period of the sociopolitical transformation in Poland, the Act of 1984 was amended, and the Institute was renamed the Chief Commission for the Investigation of Crimes Against the Polish Nation – the Institute of National Remembrance (Journal of Laws of 1991, No. 45, item 195). In the light of the Act of 1984, the responsibility of the Commission covered investigative, archival and scientific research activities in the field of German Nazi crimes, Stalinist crimes and other crimes constituting war crimes or crimes against humanity, if they took place on the territory of the Polish State (Article 2 (1) to (2), the Act of 6 April 1984 on the Chief Commission for the Investigation of Nazi Crimes in Poland – the Institute of National Remembrance). The subjective scope of this Act covered ethnic Poles and Polish citizens of other ethnic identities.

The Chairman of the Chief Commission for the Investigation of Crimes Against the Polish Nation was the Minister of Justice, whose powers included the appointment and dismissal its members. The executive body of the Commission was the director, who organised its activities and represented the Institute externally (Article 8 (1–2) of the Act of 6 April 1984 on the Chief Commission for the Investigation of Nazi Crimes in Poland – the Institute of National Remembrance). The tasks of the Institute of National Remembrance were carried out by its defined organisational units: the Bureau of Investigation, Archives, Scientific and Research Team and the regional commissions. The Commission's consultative and advisory body was the Scientific Council (Article 9 (1) to (2) of the Act of 6 April 1984 on the Chief Commission for the Investigation of Nazi Crimes in Poland – the Institute of National Remembrance).

The drawbacks of the legal solutions under the Act of 1984 included excessively lengthy proceedings, which dragged on for years even in simple cases. This was so since the prosecutor's office had to initiate investigations that had already been the subject of proceedings conducted by the Chief Commission and regional commissions, which did not allow the Institute of National Remembrance to carry out its tasks quickly and efficiently.[1] The Chief Commission for the Investigation of Crimes Against the Polish Nation had no rights of procedural termination of the investigations conducted. In addition, the activities of the Institute of National Remembrance in the light of the Act of 1984, despite its amendment in 1991, were limited to Stalinist crimes, i.e. those committed until 31 December 1956.

The Act did not cover communist crimes committed after 1956. As a result, after many months of debate on the draft of a new legal act defining the legal status of the Institute of National Remembrance, and despite the veto of the President of the Republic of Poland, the Polish Parliament adopted, on 18 December 1998, a new Act on the Institute of National Remembrance.[2] The Act of 1998 remains in force to this day and has been subjected to numerous amendments.

3 Responsibilities and Powers of the Institute of National Remembrance

The tasks of the Institute of National Remembrance include the recording, collecting, storing, processing, securing, making available and publishing the documents of state security authorities, produced and accumulated from 22 July 1944

[1] Zięba-Załucka (2005), p. 31.

[2] Act of 18 December 1998 on the Institute of National Remembrance - Commission for the Prosecution of Crimes against the Polish Nation, Journal of Laws of 2019, item 1882.

until 31 July 1990, as well as the documents of the security authorities of the Third Reich and the Soviet Union (Article 1 (1) of the Act of 18 December 1998 on the Institute of National Remembrance). The scope of the analysed acts refers to Nazi crimes, communist crimes and other crimes against peace or humanity or war crimes perpetrated on persons of Polish nationality or Polish citizens of other nationalities from 8 November 1917 until 31 July 1990.

In view of the foregoing, the responsibilities of the Institute of National Remembrance include also the elaboration and publication of the archival inventory and making it available. As can be noticed, the Polish legislature set the beginning of the time limit of the Act based on the date of the outbreak of the October Revolution. It is, therefore, not possible to relate all the categories of crimes listed in the law to such a broad time frame. It is worth mentioning here that the activities of the Institute of National Remembrance since March 2018, due to the amendment of the Act on the Institute of National Remembrance,[3] also included the crimes of Ukrainian nationalists and members of Ukrainian troops collaborating with the Third Reich.[4] However, this provision was declared unconstitutional by the Polish Constitutional Tribunal.[5]

The Act on the Institute of National Remembrance contains legal definitions of communist crime and crimes against humanity. The Polish legislature did not provide a statutory definition of Nazi crimes. Nevertheless, it can be assumed that Nazi crimes are to be understood as acts constituting crimes against peace or humanity or war crimes committed during the Second World War by officials of the German state in the course of their activities, taking into account the provisions contained in Chapter XVI of the Polish Penal Code (Act of 6 June 1997, Criminal Code, consolidated text Journal of Laws of 2020, item 1444) and the provisions of the Decree of 31 August 1944 on the exercising of punishment for Nazi-Fascist criminals guilty of the murder and torment of the civilian population and prisoners, and for traitors to the Polish Nation (consolidated text, Journal of Laws of 1946, No. 69, item 377).[6] On the other hand, the Act on the Institute of National Remembrance defines the notion of communist crimes unknown to the previous legal regulation. According to Article 2 (1) of the Act, communist crimes are actions performed by officers of the communist state between 8 November 1917 and 31 July 1990 which consisted of applying reprisals or other forms of violations of human rights in relation to individuals or groups of people or which as such constituted crimes according to the Polish penal act in force at the time of their perpetration.

[3] Act of 26 January 2018 amending the Act on the Institute of National Remembrance - Commission for the Prosecution of Crimes against the Polish Nation, the Act on war graves and cemeteries, the Act on museums and the Act on the responsibility of collective entities for acts prohibited under penalty (Journal of Laws of 2018, item 369).

[4] Wyrzykowski (2018), p. 364.

[5] Judgement of the Constitutional Tribunal of 17 January 2019, case ref. no. K1/18, Journal of Laws of 2019, item 131.

[6] Stadnicki (2006), p. 104.

As a result, the Polish legislature also formulated the definition of a communist state officer as a perpetrator of communist crimes. It should be emphasised here that the concept of communist officers is only applicable under the Act on the Institute of National Remembrance and is not binding under other legal regulations.[7] Pursuant to the Act on the Institute of National Remembrance, the communist state officer is a public functionary, as well as a person who was granted equal protection to that of a public functionary and, in particular, a public functionary and a person who performed executive functions within the statutory body of the communist parties. Crimes against humanity are especially considered crimes of genocide as understood by the Convention on the Prevention and Punishment of the Crime of Genocide, adopted on 9 December 1948,[8] as well as other serious persecutions based on the ethnicity of the people and their political, social, racial or religious affiliations, if they were performed by public functionaries or were either inspired or tolerated by them. It should be noted that the Polish legislature introduced penal provisions to the Act. Pursuant to Article 55 of the Act in question, whoever publicly and contrary to the facts denies the crimes referred to above shall be subject to a fine or a penalty of imprisonment of up to 3 years. This provision may be of particular importance in cases of "Holocaust denial".[9]

The Institute of National Remembrance exercises investigative functions regarding the above-mentioned Nazi and communist crimes and other offences that constitute crimes against peace or humanity or war crimes. Investigations in cases of the crimes mentioned shall be commenced and conducted by the prosecutors of branch (departmental) commissions for the prosecution of crimes against the Polish Nation, applying the provisions of the Code of Criminal Procedure.[10] The prosecutors of the Institute of National Remembrance shall have all the prosecuting powers, also in cases subject to the judicial decisions of military courts (Article 45 (1) to (2) of the Act on the Institute of National Remembrance).[11] The purpose of investigations in the case of such crimes shall also be to provide an explanation of the circumstances of the case, in particular to determine who the aggrieved parties are. The prosecutors are entitled to file motions and to stand before courts in matters related to recognising the invalidity of judgements issued with respect to persons repressed for their activities for the independent existence of the Polish State (Article 45b of the Act on the Institute of National Remembrance in conjunction with Article 1 (1) of the Act of 23 February 1991 on recognising invalidity of judgements issued with respect to persons repressed for their activities for the independent existence of the Polish State, consolidated text Journal of Laws of 2018, item 2099).

[7] Kulesza (2006), p. 84.

[8] The Convention on the Prevention and Punishment of the Crime of Genocide, adopted by the United Nations General Assembly on 9 December 1948, Journal of Laws of 1952 No. 2, item 9 as amended.

[9] Janisławski and Konopka (2009), pp. 55–59.

[10] Act of 6 June 1997, Code of Criminal Procedure, Journal of Laws of 2020, item 30.

[11] Mazowiecka (2015), p. 161.

The responsibilities of the Institute of National Remembrance also include the protection of the reputation of the Republic of Poland and the Polish Nation (Article 1 (2a) of the Act of the Institute of National Remembrance). This task was introduced under the amendment to the Act on the Institute of National Remembrance dated 26 January 2018. It was a response by the Polish legislature to expressions, frequently used in the media, such as "Polish death camps" or "Polish concentration camps". In such cases, the Institute of National Remembrance has judicial capacity and may bring a suit for the protection of the good name of the Republic of Poland or the Polish Nation. It is worth noting that the suit in the above matter may also be brought by a non-governmental organisation as part of its statutory tasks. The compensation or damages adjudicated are then awarded to the State Treasury.

An important area of the activity of the Institute is related to its vetting function. The responsibilities of the Institute include the preparation and publishing of catalogues kept by the Vetting Office. These are the catalogues containing the personal data of employees, functionaries and soldiers of state security organs, as well as the personal data of persons in relation to whom there are existing documents which testify that the security organs collected information on them on the basis of deliberately gathered data, including data collected in a confidential way (Article 52a (6) to (7) of the Act on the Institute of National Remembrance). The tasks of the Institute also include the preparation and publication of catalogues containing the personal data of persons who occupied managerial positions in the former Polish Workers' Party and in the former Polish United Workers' Party, as well as in the United People's Party and the Democratic Party, and who were also members of the Council of Ministers, held the posts of secretaries and under-secretaries of the Communist state until 23 August 1989 or were managers or deputy managers of central state administration organs or central state authorities in that period (Article 52a (8) of the Act on the Institute of National Remembrance). The Institute maintains registers of vetting declarations, carries out an analysis of these declarations and prepares vetting proceedings (Article 1 (2b) to (2c) of the Act on the Institute of National Remembrance). These powers are exercised by the Vetting Office of the Institute of National Remembrance.

The Institute of National Remembrance pursues research and educational activities (Article 53 (1) to (7) of the Act of 18 December 1998 on the Institute of National Remembrance).[12] As part of this activity, it shall inform society about the structures and methods of action applied by the institutions within the framework of which the crimes against the Polish Nation were committed and shall inform about the structures, the personnel and the methods applied by state security organs. The Institute conducts academic research about Polish history, as well as grants access to the collected documents to other academic institutions and persons or for purposes of such research. Among the responsibilities of the Institute are providing information about the collected documents and publishing academic and popular academic publications, as well as disseminating within the country and abroad the results of

[12] Koczwańska-Kalita (2015), pp. 287–288.

its work and of the research performed by other institutions. Moreover, the Institute conducts educational activities, holds exhibitions, acts as a publisher and formulates conclusions relating to historical education.

The activities of the institution analysed here also include informing society about the discovered resting places of persons killed in the fight for the independence and unity of the Polish State. The educational function of the Institute of National Remembrance is performed, in particular, by disseminating in the country and abroad opinions concerning the most important historical events for the Polish Nation and popularising the history of Poland as an element of patriotic education. The Institute promotes knowledge about the participation of Poles and Polish military formations in the fights at the fronts and prevents the dissemination of information and publications containing false historical contents that are harmful, detrimental or libellous to the Republic of Poland or the Polish Nation. The Institute of National Remembrance shall also inform about the methods, places, and perpetrators of crimes against the Polish Nation and support social undertakings intended to promote patriotism and to strengthen national identity (Article 53a (1) to (6) of the Act of 18 December 1998 on the Institute of National Remembrance).

An important area of the Institute's activity is looking for the resting places of persons killed in the fight for the independence and unity of the Polish State and conducting activities related to commemorating historic events, places and persons in the history of the struggle and martyrdom of the Polish Nation, as well as the places of struggle and martyrdom of other nations within the territory of the Republic of Poland, in the period between 8 November 1917 and 31 July 1990 (Article 1 (5) to (6), Article 53j, Article 53k of the Act of 18 December 1998 on the Institute of National Remembrance).

4 Bodies and Organisational Structure of the Institute of National Remembrance

The bodies of the Institute of National Remembrance are as follows: the President, the Council of the Institute and the Director of a Branch Office of the Institute of National Remembrance.

The organisation of the Institute of National Remembrance has been defined in the Act and in the statutes conferred on by the President of the Institute.[13] The President directs the Institute of National Remembrance and is independent in his functions from the organs of state authority. The President of the Institute of

[13] Decision No 26/21 of the President of the Institute of National Remembrance - Commission for the Prosecution of Crimes Against the Polish Nation of 6 September 2021 on the statutes of the Institute of National Remembrance - Commission for the Prosecution of Crimes Against the Polish Nation, https://ipn.gov.pl/pl/o-ipn/statut/159562,Statut-Instytutu-Pamieci-Narodowej-Komisji-Scigania-Zbrodni-przeciwko-Narodowi-P.html (last accessed 20 December 2023).

Remembrance is appointed and dismissed by the Parliament (Sejm) of the Republic of Poland at the agreement of the Senate and at the application of the Council of the Institute of Remembrance, which shall present a candidate who is not its member (Article 9 and Article 10 (1) of the Act of 18 December 1998 on the Institute of National Remembrance).

No sooner than 6 months and no later than 3 months before the termination of the tenure of the President of the Institute of Remembrance, the Chairman of the Council of the Institute of Remembrance shall announce a public competition for this post. The interviews with the candidates for the post of President of the Institute of Remembrance shall be public (Article 10 (2) and (3) of the Act of 18 December 1998 on the Institute of National Remembrance). The position of the President of the Institute of National Remembrance can be held by a person who is a Polish citizen, has not been sentenced with a valid sentence for an intentional criminal offence prosecuted ex officio, is distinguished by a strong moral character and the knowledge necessary to perform the tasks of the Institute and holds the following Polish scientific titles: PhD, post-PhD degree (doctor habilitatus) or professor. The President of the Institute cannot belong to any political party or trade union nor carry out a political activity that is incompatible with the dignity of the office.

The function of the President of the Institute cannot be combined with the mandate of a member of Parliament or a senator (Article 11 (1) points 1 to 4, Article 11 (3) and (5) of the Act of 18 December 1998 on the Institute of National Remembrance). The President of the Institute of National Remembrance enjoys criminal procedural immunity.[14] The President of the Institute cannot, without the prior consent of the Sejm of the Republic of Poland, be prosecuted or imprisoned and be detained or arrested unless he is detained in the act of committing a crime and his detention is indispensable to ensure the correct course of the proceedings (Article 14 (1) and (4) of the Act of 18 December 1998 on the Institute of National Remembrance).

The consultancy and advisory function for the President is exercised by the Council of the Institute, whose term of office is 7 years. The Council of the Institute of National Remembrance is composed of nine members, including two members appointed by the President of the Republic of Poland, five members appointed by the Sejm of the Republic of Poland and two members appointed by the Senate (Article 15 (2) and (3) points 1 to 3, Act of 18 December 1998 on the Institute of National Remembrance).

In order to perform the tasks of the Institute of National Remembrance in places that are seats of appellate courts, there are branch offices headed by the directors. In other cities, there are delegations of the Institute of National Remembrance managed by the heads of the delegation (Article 17 (1) to (2) of the Act of 18 December 1998 on the Institute of National Remembrance).

The organisation and operation of the Institute of National Remembrance are the responsibilities of the Director General within authorisations granted by the

[14] Janusz-Pohl (2011), p. 112.

President. The organisational structure of the Institute is made up of headquarters and branch offices with subordinate delegations.

The head office of the Institute of National Remembrance is composed of organisational units that, as a rule, are subordinated directly to the President. The organisational units dealing with the implementation of the statutory tasks of the Institute of National Remembrance include the following: the Chief Commission for the Prosecution of Crimes Against the Polish Nation, the Vetting Office, the Archive of the Institute of National Remembrance, the Office for Commemorating the Struggle and Martyrdom, the Office of Search and Identification, the National Education Office, the Historical Research Office (Section 11 (1), item 1, of the Statutes of the Institute of National Remembrance). The Director General of the Institute supervises organisational units of an administrative nature, such as the Administration and Maintenance Office and the Legal Office.

The Institute of National Remembrance currently has 11 branch offices with delegations in the following cities: Branch Office in Białystok (Delegation in Olsztyn), Branch Office in Gdańsk (Delegation in Bydgoszcz), Branch Office in Katowice, Branch Office in Kraków (Delegation in Kielce), Branch Office in Lublin (Delegation in Radom), Branch Office in Łódź, Branch Office in Poznań, Branch Office in Rzeszów, Branch Office in Warszawa, Branch Office in Wrocław (Delegation in Opole) and Branch Office in Szczecin (Delegations in Gorzów Wielkopolski and Koszalin) (Sections 27 (1) and 31 (1), items 1 to 6, of the Statutes of the Institute of National Remembrance).

The branch offices of the Institute of National Remembrance include organisational units of a substantive nature, such as a branch commission for the prosecution of crimes against the Polish Nation, a branch vetting office, branch archives of the Institute of National Remembrance, a branch office for commemorating the struggle and martyrdom, a branch office of national education and a branch office for historical research (Section 27 (2), items 1–5, of the Statutes of the Institute of National Remembrance).

The territorial jurisdiction of the delegations of the Institute of National Remembrance is determined by the President of the Institute in consultation with the branch office's Director. Archival departments and investigative units are established in the Delegations.

5 Activity of the Institute of National Remembrance in View of Official Data

The President of the Institute of National Remembrance is required to submit once a year a report to the Sejm and Senate on the activities of the Institute. The President of the Institute presents to the Council of the Institute the report on the activities of the Institute for a given calendar year no later than 31 March of the next year (Article

24 and Article 24a of the Act of 18 December 1998 on the Institute of National Remembrance).

This chapter presents official data on the implementation by the Institute of National Remembrance of the investigative and vetting functions that are the most typical of the Institute's areas of activity.

In 2019, prosecutors from the Institute of National Remembrance's branch commissions carried out a total of 1603 criminal proceedings, with 560 investigations still pending in 2018. During 2019, a total of 1043 new proceedings were registered, of which 704 cases concerned communist crimes, 288 cases concerned Nazi crimes and 51 cases concerned other crimes constituting crimes against peace or humanity or war crimes. In 2019, 1105 cases were completed, of which 749 cases concerned communist crimes, 305 cases concerned Nazi crimes, 51 concerned cases of other crimes constituting crimes against peace or humanity or war crimes. For the purposes of pre-trial proceedings, 4216 people were heard as witnesses. Out of 1105 proceedings completed, only 11 cases were brought before the courts with indictments against 15 people, while 940 cases were dismissed at the pre-trial stage, in particular because the perpetrators of the crime had not been identified or the perpetrators had died during the investigations.[15]

Regarding the vetting function, 31,362 vetting declarations were registered and included in the IPN resource in 2019. There are currently 458,108 vetting statements registered with the Vetting Office of the Institute of National Remembrance. For 3471 vetting declarations, those who completed them stated that they had worked with, served in or cooperated with the security authorities of the Polish People's Republic.[16] Such a large number of vetting declarations submitted in the year covered by the report were related to local elections in Poland held in that year.

In 2018, the prosecutors of the branch commissions of the Institute of National Remembrance conducted 562 proceedings, including 407 cases concerning communist crimes, 130 involving Nazi crimes, 25 proceedings related to cases of other offences constituting crimes against peace or humanity or war crimes. In 2018, a total of 1140 new proceedings were registered, of which 768 concerned communist crimes, 280 related to Nazi crimes and 92 were other offences constituting crimes against peace or humanity or war crimes. In 2018, the prosecutors concluded 1142 cases, of which 759 concerned communist crimes, 285 related to Nazi crimes and 98 cases were other crimes against peace or humanity or war crimes. Investigations were discontinued in 930 cases. In 2018, indictments were brought in seven cases involving nine people.[17] As regards the vetting function, it should be noted that a

[15] Instytut Pamięci Narodowej – Komisja Ścigania Zbrodni przeciwko Narodowi Polskiemu. Informacja o działalności 1 stycznia 2019 – 31 grudnia 2019, (2020), pp. 272–273.

[16] Instytut Pamięci Narodowej – Komisja Ścigania Zbrodni przeciwko Narodowi Polskiemu. Informacja o działalności 1 stycznia 2019 – 31 grudnia 2019, (2020), p. 308.

[17] Instytut Pamięci Narodowej – Komisja Ścigania Zbrodni przeciwko Narodowi Polskiemu. Informacja o działalności 1 stycznia 2018 – 31 grudnia 2018, (2019), pp. 284–286.

total of 9955 vetting statements were included in the resources of the Institute of National Remembrance in 2018.[18]

In 2017, 1053 new cases were registered, of which 748 cases concerned communist crimes, 260 cases involved Nazi crimes and 45 cases related to other offences constituting crimes against peace or humanity or war crimes. Regardless of the above, there were 605 cases that were not completed in 2016. The prosecutors acting as part of the work of the Institute in 2017 concluded 1096 proceedings in total. As regards closed cases, 164 decisions were issued on the refusal to initiate an investigation, while 885 proceedings were discontinued. Indictments were filed in 11 cases, covering 11 defendants. In 2017, a total of 4150 witnesses were heard in connection with the cases conducted.[19] Exercising the vetting function, the Institute of National Remembrance received 34,984 vetting declarations.[20]

6 Conclusion

To define the legal status of the Institute of National Remembrance – the Commission for the Prosecution of Crimes Against the Polish Nation, this chapter presents the responsibilities, powers and organisational structure of the Institute. The analysis of the above issues made it possible to distinguish the main areas of its activity. The most important functions of the Institute, in the light of the responsibilities defined by the legislature, include investigative, vetting, archival and research and educational activities. The analysis of the reports on the operation of the Institute of National Remembrance demonstrates its importance and its activity in the field of investigative function. The prosecutors of the Institute of National Remembrance conduct approximately 1500 criminal proceedings per one calendar year. Most part of the investigative activity concerns communist crimes, which constitute approximately 70% of all criminal proceedings. In the recent 3 years, Nazi crimes have accounted for approximately 25% of all the proceedings initiated. It should be noted that only in approximately 1% of the cases in which pre-trial proceedings were conducted was it possible to file indictments with the courts. In most cases, there was discontinuation at the pre-trial stage due to the failure to identify the perpetrators of the crime or because of their death, which, however, does not mean that the activities of the Institute of National Remembrance are unnecessary. The number of proceedings pending proves something completely different. Moreover, attention should be paid to other particularly important areas of its activity, such as the

[18] Instytut Pamięci Narodowej – Komisja Ścigania Zbrodni przeciwko Narodowi Polskiemu. Informacja o działalności 1 stycznia 2018 – 31 grudnia 2018, (2019), p. 323.

[19] Instytut Pamięci Narodowej – Komisja Ścigania Zbrodni przeciwko Narodowi Polskiemu. Informacja o działalności 1 stycznia 2017 – 31 grudnia 2017, (2018), pp. 242–244.

[20] Instytut Pamięci Narodowej – Komisja Ścigania Zbrodni przeciwko Narodowi Polskiemu. Informacja o działalności 1 stycznia 2017 – 31 grudnia 2017, (2018), p. 276.

implementation of the research and educational function. Quoting the words of Janusz Kurtyka, the President of the Institute of National Remembrance in 2005–2010, "One of the roles of the Institute of National Remembrance is to make the hermetic knowledge public, so that it becomes a public good".[21] On the other hand, the correct operation of the research department would be not possible without the Institute's archival activity. To sum up, it can be stated that the effective implementation of statutory tasks by the Institute of National Remembrance must assume, in particular, the cooperation of those organisational structures of the Institute that are responsible for the implementation of the investigative, archival, research-educational and vetting functions. They form a kind of a system of interconnected vessels that allow the Institute of National Remembrance to effectively fulfil its tasks.

References

Janisławski A, Konopka P (2009) Zagadnienie penalizacji "kłamstwa oświęcimskiego". Palestra 1–2:50–63

Janusz-Pohl B (2011) Ustrój organów ochrony prawnokarnej. Zarys wykładu. Ars Boni et Aequi, Poznań

Koczwańska-Kalita D (2015) (Nie)chciane dziecko III RP. Instytut Pamięci Narodowej 2000-2010. Geneza, funkcjonowanie, kontekst społeczny i polityczny. Wydawnictwo Arcana, CraCow

Kulesza J (2006) Funkcjonariusz państwa komunistycznego jako podmiot zbrodni komunistycznych. Palestra 9–10:84–95

Kuta C, Tęsiorowski J (2019) Obudzić naród do wielkości. Wystąpienia Janusza Kurtyki przed Parlamentem RP 2005-2010. Instytut Pamięci Narodowej, Warsaw

Mazowiecka L (2015) Prokuratura w Polsce (1918-2014). Wolters Kluwer, Warsaw

Stadnicki T (2006) Funkcja śledcza Instytutu Pamięci Narodowej - Komisji Ścigania Zbrodni przeciwko Narodowi Polskiemu. Prokuratura i Prawo 9:102–107

Wyrzykowski M (2018) Ustawa o Instytucie Pamięci Narodowej przed Trybunałem Konstytucyjnym. Gdańskie Studia Prawnicze 2:355–370

Zięba-Załucka H (2005) Status prawny Instytutu Pamięci Narodowej. Przegląd Sejmowy 5:31–56

Jarosław Kostrubiec is a professor at the Maria Curie-Sklodowska University (Poland), Ph.D., Habilitated Doctor of Law; the vice dean of the Faculty of Law and Administration of the Maria Curie-Sklodowska University (Poland); and an expert of the Polish Accreditation Committee (discipline: law). He is the managing editor of such journals as "Studia Iuridica Lublinensia" (Scopus) and "Lex Localis – Journal of Local Self-Government' (Scopus, Web of Science), the latter being an international journal for the study of local policy, administration and the management of local affairs, and a member of the editorial board of "Juridical Tribune – Tribuna Juridica" (Scopus, Web of Science). Between 2005 and 2006, he worked as a researcher at the Department of Public Law, Philosophy of Law and General Science of State at the Faculty of Law of the University

[21] Kuta and Tęsiorowski (2019), p. 48.

of Heidelberg under a scholarship of Deutscher Akademischer Austausch Dienst (DAAD). In 2005 and 2006, he held research stays at the Max Planck Institute in Frankfurt am Main. His scientific interests focus on the history of public administration and administrative thought, administrative law as well as the theory of state. He is an author or editor of about 150 academic publications (monographs, academic textbooks, legal commentaries, articles and book reviews).

SPRINGER NATURE

GPSR Compliance

The European Union's (EU) General Product Safety Regulation (GPSR) is a set of rules that requires consumer products to be safe and our obligations to ensure this.

If you have any concerns about our products, you can contact us on ProductSafety@springernature.com

In case Publisher is established outside the EU, the EU authorized representative is:

Springer Nature Customer Service Center GmbH
Europaplatz 3
69115 Heidelberg, Germany

The manufacturer's authorised representative in the EU is Springer Nature Customer Service Centre GmbH, Europaplatz 3, 69115 Heidelberg, Germany. If you have any concerns regarding our products, please contact ProductSafety@springernature.com

Printed and bound by CPI Group (UK) Ltd, Croydon, CR0 4YY
30/09/2026
02225558-0011